D1322982

Series Editors: B. Guy Peters, Jon Pierre and Gerry Stoker

Political science today is a dynamic discipline. Its substance, theory and methods have all changed radically in recent decades. It is much expanded in range and scope and in the variety of new perspectives — and new variants of old ones — that it encompasses. The sheer volume of work being published, and the increasing degree of its specialization, however, make it difficult for political scientists to maintain a clear grasp of the state of debate beyond their own particular subdisciplines.

The *Political Analysis* series is intended to provide a channel for different parts of the discipline to talk to one another and to new generations of students. Our aim is to publish books that provide introductions to, and exemplars of, the best work in various areas of the discipline. Written in an accessible style, they provide a 'launching–pad' for students and others seeking a clear grasp of the key methodological, theoretical and empirical issues, and the main areas of debate, in the complex and fragmented world of political science.

A particular priority is to facilitate intellectual exchange between academic communities in different parts of the world. Although frequently addressing the same intellectual issues, research agendas and literatures in North America, Europe and elsewhere have often tended to develop in relative isolation from one another. We intend this series to provide a framework for dialogue and debate which, rather than advocating one regional approach or another, is the key to progress.

The series reflects our view that the successful development of political science should be both coherent and located in the wider international context. It is not likely to be matched by carefully constructed and exhaustive empirical investigation. The key challenge is to ensure quality and integrity in what is produced rather than to constrain diversity in methods and approaches. The series is intended as a showcase for the best of political science in all its variety, and demonstrate how nurturing that variety can further improve the discipline.

Political Analysis Series
Series Standing Order
ISBN 0–333–78694–7 hardback
ISBN 0–333–94506–9 paperback
(outside North America only)

You can receive future titles in this series as they are published by placing a standing order. Please contact your bookseller or, in the case of difficulty, write to us at the address below with your name and address, the title of the series and the ISBN quoted above.

Customer Services Department, Macmillan Distribution Ltd
Houndmills, Basingstoke, Hampshire RG21 6XS, England

POLITICAL
ANALYSIS

Series Editors: B. Guy Peters, Jon Pierre and Gerry Stoker

Political Analysis

Colin Hay

palgrave
macmillan

First published 2002 by
PALGRAVE
Houndmills, Basingstoke, Hampshire RG21 6XS and
175 Fifth Avenue, New York, N.Y. 10010
Companies and representatives throughout the world

PALGRAVE is the new global academic imprint of
St. Martin's Press LLC Scholarly and Reference Division and
Palgrave Publishers Ltd (formerly Macmillan Press Ltd).

ISBN-10: 0–333–75002–0 hardback
ISBN-13: 978-0–333–75002–5 hardback
ISBN-10: 0–333–75003–9 paperback
ISBN-13: 978-0–333–75003–2 paperback

This book is printed on paper suitable for recycling and
made from fully managed and sustained forest sources.
Logging, pulping and manufacturing processes are expected
to conform to the environmental regulations of the country
of origin.

A catalogue record for this book is available
from the British Library.

Library of Congress Cataloging-in-Publication Data

Hay, Colin, 1968–
    Political analysis : a critical introduction / Colin Hay.
        p.   cm. – (Political analysis)
    Includes bibliographical references and index.
    ISBN 0-333-75002-0 (cloth) – ISBN 0-333-75003-9 (paper)
    1. Political science.   I. Title.   II. Political analysis (Palgrave)

JA71 .H348 2002
320 – dc21   2002020889

10   9
11 10 09 08

Printed and bound in China

To Elspeth, without whom it would not have been possible

Contents

List of Figures, Tables and Boxes

Figures

Tables

Boxes

Preface and Acknowledgements

As was perhaps always likely to be the case, this book has taken rather longer to complete than I had originally hoped and anticipated. Nonetheless, it is, I think somewhat better for that. One of the reasons for this is the support, encouragement and advice that I have received from innumerable colleagues and other friends.

Given the rather lengthy gestation of my thoughts on political analysis, I have incurred an unusually extensive array of debts, both personal and intellectual. A large number of people have commented at various stages upon the ideas which have found their way in some form or another into this text. Still others have badgered me into clarifying, amplifying and developing the position I here seek to defend. Among those that spring immediately to mind are (alphabetically): Mark Blyth, David Coates, Mick Cox, Catherine Fieschi, Andrew Gamble, Peter Hall, Jonathan Hopkin, Chris Howell, Jeremy Jennings, Bob Jessop, Peter Kerr, Dave Marsh, Ben Rosamond, Paul Pierson, Vivien Schmidt, Steve Smith, Roger Tooze, Helen Wallace, Matthew Watson, Richard Weiner and Daniel Wincott. I must also thank my colleagues in the Department of Political Science and International Studies at the University of Birmingham for creating a unique intellectual environment in which to develop the argument I here present. Guy Peters, Jon Pierre and Gerry Stoker provided invaluable feedback and detailed comments on an earlier draft of the entire manuscript. Whatever its remaining weaknesses, the book has benefited immeasurably from their wonderfully sage advice. At a late stage Keith Dowding also provided a range of characteristically incisive comments, giving me the opportunity to address a number of potential hostages to fortune. For this I am extremely grateful. I must also thank Steven Kennedy at Palgrave for being such an exemplary and, above all, patient editor. It was he who put the idea into my head to write such a book and he has, from its inception, offered a wonderful combination of sensitive advice and enthusiastic encouragement.

Finally, I must again thank Elspeth without whom this book would have proved impossible to write. It is, appropriately enough, dedicated to her.

COLIN HAY

Chapter 1

Analytical Perspectives, Analytical Controversies

While the issues with which this volume is principally concerned have, arguably, always divided political analysts, it is only in recent years that they have started to receive the sustained theoretical reflection their importance warrants. Political analysts have always been able to choose from a wide diversity of analytical strategies and have, as a consequence, been divided by such strategies as much as by anything else. Yet, the systematic reflection on the means by which one might adjudicate between contending analytical perspectives has tended to be something of a marginal concern. Moreover, where attention has been paid to the choice of analytical strategies in political science and international relations (for instance, King, Keohane and Verba 1994), the range of strategies considered has tended to be limited to those considered consistent with the dominant positivist assumptions of the discipline's core. Accordingly, the appreciation of alternative analytical strategies and, indeed, the appreciation that there may be more than one way to explore the political world is less widespread than it might be. This is changing – and that is no bad thing.

In this context, the aim of the present volume is two-fold. First, it seeks both to highlight the significance of, and to provide a critical introduction to, a series of issues of contemporary controversy in political analysis. Second, and arguably more significantly, it seeks to contribute to the growing reflexive turn in political science and, perhaps more notably, international relations. In so far as this book can be regarded as a manifesto for anything in particular, it is manifesto for a political analysis more conscious and explicit about the underlying assumptions upon which its choice of analytical strategies is premised and more sensitive to the trade-offs necessarily entailed in any choice of foundational premises. The chapters which follow are, of course, not entirely neutral with respect to such choices. But what they seek to do is to uncover and render explicit the assumptions which make those choices possible. My hope in so doing is to contribute to a political analysis whose internal dialogues, controversies and disputes are char-

1

acterised by mutual understanding and respect for the analytical choices which lead analysts in often divergent directions.

In this context, the aim of the present chapter is relatively modest. It is to provide the necessary background for the task of later chapters. In it, I consider (briefly) the nature of political analysis itself, before introducing, in a necessarily stylised manner, the core theoretical perspectives which have come to define mainstream debate in political science and international relations today. In the final sections of the chapter, I pare this diversity of perspectives down to three distinct analytical traditions – rationalism, behaviouralism and institutionalism/constructivism. I consider the positions adopted by each with respect to the issues which form the key themes of the volume.

The scope and limits of political analysis

The term 'political analysis' is by no means unambiguous. From the outset, then, it is important to be clear what I mean, and what I do not mean, by it in this context. For many, political analysis is synonymous with analytical politics, which is, in turn, synonymous with rational choice theory (see, for instance, Hinich and Munger 1997). That is most definitely *not* the sense of the term invoked here. While I will have much to say about rational choice theory and rationalism more generally, this is not a book about analytical politics. Indeed, it would be to forejudge the issues of this volume to assume from the outset that political analysis can, or should, be circumscribed by rationalist analytical strategies. This book, in keeping with the spirit of the series of which it forms a part, is about the *diversity* of analytical strategies available to those engaged in the analysis of 'the political'. Though rationalism is one such strategy, and a highly distinctive, influential and important one at that, it is but one strategy among many. It has no privileged or exclusive claim on the analysis of the political or the label political analysis.

To talk of political analysis is not, then, in itself to advance a particular perspective. The term, at least in the sense in which it is deployed here, is neutral with respect to analytical strategies and traditions. This particular conception of political analysis is inclusive. Yet the notion of political analysis that I will seek to advance and defend in this and consecutive chapters is inclusive in another sense too.

Here we move from the descriptive to the prescriptive. For while my concern is to explore the full range of analytical strategies that might inform political inquiry, it is not my intention to hide my preference for certain analytical strategies and perspectives over others. Thus, while I hope to reveal an inclusive conception of the field of political analysis, the political analysis I will seek to defend is inclusive in another sense – its specification of 'the political'. While acknowledging that many approaches to political analysis confine themselves to the narrowly political analysis of narrowly political variables, I will call for a conception of the political and of political analysis that is very different. It is explored in far greater detail in Chapter 2. In brief, it is encompassing in two senses.

First, the political should be defined in such a way as to encompass the entire sphere of the social. The implication of this is that events, processes and practices should not be labelled 'non-political' or 'extra-political' simply by virtue of the specific setting or context in which they occur. All events, processes and practices which occur within the social sphere have the potential to be political and, hence, to be amenable to political analysis. The realm of government is no more innately political, by this definition, that that of culture, law or the domestic sphere. Consequently, the division of domestic labour is no less political – and no less appropriate a subject for political analysis – than the regulation of the domestic division of labour by the state. Indeed, one might well argue that any adequate analysis of the politics of the regulation of the domestic division of labour itself entails a *political* analysis of the domestic division of labour. Yet this raises an obvious question. What makes political analysis *political*? In other words, what distinguishes political analysis from cultural or sociological analyses which might also claim to encompass the entire sphere of the social? What is here required is a definition of the political itself. What makes a political analysis political is the emphasis it places on the political aspect of social relations. In the same way, what makes a cultural analysis cultural is the emphasis it places on the cultural aspects of social relations. A variety of definitions of the political might be offered and are discussed further in the following chapter. The specific definition that I advance, however, is of politics and the political as concerned with the distribution, exercise and consequences of power. A political analysis is, then, one which draws attention to the power relations implicated in social relations. In this sense, politics is not defined by the *locus* of its operation but by its nature as a *process*.

This has interesting implications. For it suggests that the terrain of political analysis, and hence the span of this volume, should include all perspectives, whether consciously political or not, which might have something to say about the distribution and exercise of power. In this sense, the sphere of political analysis is broad indeed, ranging from the narrowly political analysis of narrowly political variables to the sociology of structural inequality within contemporary societies.

This brings us to the second key feature of the political analysis I will seek to defend in this volume. It concerns the role of extra-political variables. Though the definition of the political that I advance in this volume is inclusive, this is not to say that all aspects of the social can be captured in political terms, nor that the political is indistinguishable, say, from the economic or the cultural. Economic and cultural processes may be inherently political – in so far as they concern relations of power they more certainly are – but this does not mean that they are exhausted by this description. This raises the thorny question of the role political analysts should accord to extra-political variables. Again, my approach is inclusive. Political analysts simply cannot afford to leave the analysis of economics to economists, history to historians and so forth. In so far as there are economic and/or cultural conditions of existence of political dynamics, these need to be acknowledged and interrogated by political analysts. Disciplinary boundaries have always been rather arbitrarily drawn and, in an age in which the degree of interdependence between cultural, political and economic processes is increasingly acknowledged those boundaries surely threaten the quality of the analysis we are capable of generating. For, in a world of (acknowledged) interdependence, rigidly disciplinary approaches to social, political and economic analysis will tend to find themselves reliant upon assumptions generated by other disciplinary specialisms whose validity they are either incapable or unwilling to adjudicate. The clear danger is that the conclusions of our analyses may increasingly come to depend upon externally generated assumptions whose empirical content we do not regard ourselves worthy to judge. This is a now all too familiar experience and is nowhere more clear than in the literature on the political economic imperatives globalisation supposedly summons for social democratic regimes. Here the debate circles endlessly around the nature and degree of negotiability of the constraints that economic integration is seen to imply. Opinions vary – wildly (compare Garrett 1998; Gray 1997; C. Pierson 2001; Wickham-Jones 2000). Yet what is almost entirely absent from such discussions is any attempt to describe empirically, let alone to evaluate, the precise nature of social democratic regimes' external economic relations – with respect to trade, finance and foreign direct investment (FDI). Indeed, in the vast majority of accounts a crude, simplistic and never more than anecdotally empirical business school globalisation orthodoxy is simply internalised and assumed to reflect the limits of our knowledge on such matters, with scant regard to the now substantial empirical evidence. That evidence, for what it is worth, shows if anything a consistent de-globalisation of European economies over the last forty years associated with the process, almost wholly absent from the existing debate, of European economic integration (Hay 2002).

The debate on the constraints implied by globalisation (real or imagined) is but one example. What it, and others like it, suggest is that, as political analysts we simply cannot afford, if ever we could, to get by without a rather more thorough grasp of the cognate disciplines on whose assumptions we have increasingly come to rely. That implies a political analysis which refuses to restrict its analytical attentions to obviously political variables and processes; in one sense it implies, too, an interdisciplinary political analysis.

Issues of interdependence and international economic integration raise a final issue, crucial to the practice of contemporary political analysis and integral to the concerns of this volume. That is the relationship between the domestic and the international and, hence, between political science (as traditionally conceived) and international relations. Here, again, I am an advocate of integration and the need to dispense with an arbitrary and increasingly problematic division of labour within political analysis (see also Coates and Hay 2001). It is worth briefly explaining why. It is tempting to argue, as many have, that the world we inhabit is more complex, interdependent and interconnected than ever before. Yet what is important here is not whether contemporary levels of interdependence are unprecedented historically, but that we inhabit an interdependent world which much be analysed as such. The point is that conventional approaches to the social sciences, based on rigid disciplinary and sub-disciplinary fault lines and demarcations, do not prepare us well for a world of interdependence.

In a world in which the domestic and international, the political and the economic were indeed *independent* this would not present a problem – though whether such a world can ever have been said to exist is another matter altogether. Arguably, though patterns of spatial interdependence have changed, the interdependence of political and economic processes at a variety of spatial scales is nothing new. Furthermore, the distinction between, say, political and economic variables – and hence between political science and economics as disciplines – was always arbitrary, the boundary between the two necessarily characterised by interdependencies which have remained poorly understood as a consequence of the often sectarian policing of disciplinary boundaries. These are important points in their own right. Yet the key point for now is that if we accept that we live in an interdependent world which does not respect spatial and sectoral divisions of analytical labour (if ever it did), such divisions of labour will no longer suffice. This entails a political analysis which refuses to accept a resolute internal division of labour between political science and international relations just as it refuses to accept that it can leave the analysis of economic variables to economists.

Analytical perspectives, analytical choices, analytical controversies

The approach to political analysis that I seek to adopt in this book is one in which contending analytical perspectives are adjudicated, as much as possible, in their own terms, rather than those imposed upon them from outside. It is also one which seeks to foreground discussion of such matters by focusing on the *issues* which divide political analysts, rather than the *camps* into which they divide themselves as a consequence. As such this is a book about contemporary controversies in political analysis much more than it is a book about the analytical perspectives themselves. It is less a book about labels and badges of analytical self-identification than it is about the analytical choices which all approaches to political analysis necessarily face. This is reflected in Chapters 2–6, each of which focuses specifically upon a key contemporary controversy – the boundaries of the 'political'; the relationship between structure and agency; the strategies appropriate to the analysis of political change; the conceptualisation of power; and the relationship between the realm of political practice and the real of political discourse, respectively. Moreover, while Chapter 7 does focus attention on an increasingly influential perspective to political analysis, namely postmodernism, it does so by exploring the challenges this most self-conscious mode of reflection poses to all other approaches to political analysis, rather than by treating it as a perspective in its own right.

This is perhaps a rather unconventional strategy to adopt, but there are good reasons for it. First, to concentrate attention principally on the analytical choices, strategies and rationales of well-established traditions of political analysis may serve merely to reinforce the dominance of those traditions. This, in turn, may have the effect of diverting attention from original and potentially significant interventions which are not easily reconciled with a conventional mapping of the fault-lines of contemporary debate. It may also serve, in so doing, to discourage innovative and heterodox approaches to issues of ongoing controversy. In short, focusing on the lie of the land at any particular moment in time may blind us to the processes already under way serving to reconfigure that landscape.

Second, as a number of recent commentators have noted, it is more difficult than once it was to delineate clearly the boundaries of contemporary analytical approaches. Many important recent contributions (such as rational choice institutionalism in political science and constructivism in international relations theory) have served to explore and thereby transcend the boundaries between perspectives previously considered distinct and incommensurate (see, for instance, Wæver 1996; S. Smith 2001; von Beyme 1996: 523–5).

Third, if the conventional approach to mapping the discipline's principal divisions is more problematic today than once it was, then this should not lead us to overlook the limitations of such a strategy at each and every stage in the discipline's history. Paradigmatic perspectives have certainly always existed within political science and international relations, but they have rarely been as insular, self-contained, internally consistent and unyielding in their engagement with contending approaches as their invariably clichéd textbook depiction. Accordingly, if political analysis is to be presented as an essentially contested and dynamic field, it is important that we resist the temptation to present it as comprised of a series of timeless, closed and almost entirely self-referential traditions.

The conventional 'textbook' presentation of the discipline's principal fault-lines has never been much more than a crude and distorted cliché – a one-dimensional depiction of a multi-dimensional reality. It is a presentation, as far as possible, that I have sought to resist. In the chapters that follow, then, my aim has been both to respect and to reflect as accurately as possible the positions held by genuine (named) protagonists in the controversies which characterise contemporary political analysis. As far as possible, I have resisted the temptation to fall back on the parsimony and anonymity of the standard 'textbook' formulations of approaches such as behaviouralism, neo-realism and rational choice theory. Nonetheless, it is important for what follows that we establish from the outset the range and diversity of strategies in political analysis. In so doing there is some utility in adopting a perspectival approach, if only as a point of departure for what is to follow. In this sense, the present chapter is something of an exception to the general rule. For in the following section I seek briefly to map the contemporary field of political analysis by examining the key themes, assumptions and contributions of the main perspectives in political science and international relations. These are summarised schematically in Tables 1.1–1.8, designed to provide a point of reference for the chapters which follow.

Mapping the political science mainstream

It is conventional to see the political science mainstream today as characterised by three distinctive perspectives: rational choice theory; behaviouralism; and the new institutionalism. Each adopts a very different approach to political analysis.

Table 1.1   *Rational choice theory*

Aim/ contribution	• To import the rigour and predictive power of neo-classical economics into political science
	• To produce a deductive science of the political on the basis of a series of simplifying assumptions
	• To model (mathematically) the implications of human rationality for political conduct
Key assumptions	• Individual actors are the basic units of analysis
	• They are rational, efficient and instrumental utility-maximisers who seek to maximise personal utility net of cost alone
	• They have a clear and 'transitive' hierarchy of preferences such that in any given context there is only one optimal course of action available to them
Key themes	• The aggregation of individually rational behaviour frequently produces collectively irrational outcomes
	• Social welfare is often compromised by collective action problems and 'free-riding'
	• The narrow pursuit of self-interest ensures that public officials cannot be trusted to deliver collective welfare (public choice theory)
	• The behaviour of political parties in liberal democracies is predictable given the structure of the electoral system and the distribution of voter preferences
	• Even where actors share a common collective interest, 'free-riding' is likely to militate against collective action in the absence of other incentives
	• Where such collective action dilemmas can be overcome powerful interest groups will deploy 'rent-seeking' behaviour, lobbying for monopoly powers and subsidies that are inefficient *cont. opposite*

Rational choice theory is, in essence, what you get if you seek to model political behaviour on the simplifying assumption that political actors are instrumental, self-serving utility-maximisers (Table 1.1). In other words, it seeks to construct stylised (and often mathematical) models of political conduct by assuming that individuals are rational and behave *as if* they engage in a cost-benefit analysis of each and every choice available to them before plumping for the option most likely to maximise their material self-interest. They behave rationally, maximising personal utility net of cost while giving little or no consideration to the consequences, for others, of their behaviour.[1]

The purpose of rational choice theory is to produce a deductive and

Table 1.1   *Continued*

Key concepts	• Rationality • Collective action problems • 'Free-riding' • 'Rent-seeking'
Silences and limitations	• Limited attention given to preference formation • Limited attention given to the institutional contexts in which rationality is exercised • Relies upon a series of implausible theoretical assumptions • Though ostensibly predictive, tends to confine itself to post hoc rationalisation • Limited conception of the human subject • Deals poorly with contexts in which altruism and collectively rational behaviour is displayed • Deals poorly with processes of change (though note the contribution of evolutionary game theory)
Seminal works	• Anthony Downs' *Economic Theory of Democracy* (1957) • Mancur Olson's *The Logic of Collective Action* (1978) • William A. Niskanen's *Bureaucracy and Representative Government* (1971) • James Buchanen and Gordon Tullock's *The Calculus of Consent* (1962)

predictive science of the political, modelled on precisely the same assumptions that have proved so influential in neo-classical economics. Its contribution to political science has been considerable, drawing attention to the often perverse and collectively irrational effects of individually rational action. It points, in particular to the problem of 'free-riding'. Here, despite a situation in which cooperation will secure mutual advantage, actors have a perverse incentive not to participate in such collective action. This sounds paradoxical, but the logic, if we assume rationality, is impeccable. For, in situations where collective action is required to achieve a given end, a rational actor knows that her individual behaviour will not influence significantly the overall outcome. Moreover, if others cooperate she will reap the benefits of their cooperation regardless of her participation. So why incur personal costs by taking unilateral action? In such scenarios, the dependence of a favourable outcome upon coordinated or collective action is sufficient to create (perverse) incentives for actors to free ride on the conduct of others. Tragically, if all individuals behave rationally, no cooperation arises and an outcome which is both collectively and individually sub-optimal ensues.

A now classic example is the so-called 'tragedy of the commons', first identified by Garrett Hardin (1968; for an excellent discussion of the strengths and limitations of this perspective see Pepper 1996: 56–9). It provides an intuitively plausible and all too compelling model of the seemingly intractable problem of environmental degradation in con-temporary societies. The systematic exploitation and pollution of the environment, it is argued, is set to continue since individual corpora-tions and states, despite a clear collective interest, choose not to impose upon themselves the costs of unilateral environmental action. Their logic is entirely rational. They know that environmental regulation is costly and, in an open international economy, a burden on competitiveness. Accordingly, in the absence of an international agency capable of enforc-ing the compliance of all states and all corporations, the anticipation of free-riding is sufficient to ensure that corporations and states do not burden themselves with additional costs and taxes. The long-term effects for the environment are all too obvious. Once again, individual ratio-nality translates into collective irrationality.

Though *behaviouralism*, too, would claim to advance a predictive science of the political, it proceeds very differently, basing its approach to political analysis not on the deduction of testable hypotheses from simplifying (and ultimately untestable) assumptions about human nature, but upon extrapolation and generalisation from observed empiri-cal regularities (Table 1.2). In the primacy it gives to evidence and to the search for evidence, behaviouralism might be thought neutral with respect to subject matter. As a consequence it is not, like rational choice theory or the new institutionalism, a distinctive theoretical approach associated with a series of key substantive claims so much as a set of analytical techniques and methodologies. These might be applied – in principle – to any area of political analytic inquiry. That having been said, the tendency to emphasise the observable and those variables which might more easily be quantified, has tended to result in certain distinctive features of behaviouralism. These include a focus on power as decision-making and a tendency to assume that an analysis of the inputs into the political system, such as the pressure exerted by interest groups upon the state, is sufficient to account adequately for political outcomes.

Of the three perspectives which serve to define the mainstream in con-temporary political science, the *new institutionalism* is the new pretender (Table 1.3). It has emerged since the early 1980s as a conscious response both to the 'behavioural revolution' of the 1960s and to the growing ascendancy of rational choice theory in subsequent decades (see

Figure 1.1   *The evolution of mainstream political science*

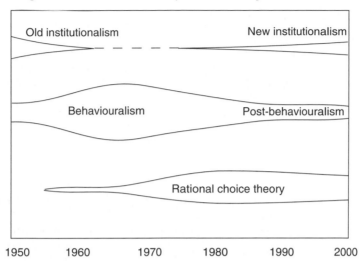

Figure 1.1).[2] It marks a return, albeit rather more consciously theorised, to an older tradition of institutional analysis. This had dominated political science in the early decades of the twentieth century. By the 1960s, however, despite the influence it continued to exert on public administration in Europe, it had long since relinquished any ascendancy is had once enjoyed over the discipline as a whole (Peters 1999; Rhodes 1995; W. R. Scott 1995). This was particularly so in the USA, where the legacy of the old institutionalism was negligible.

The new institutionalism departs from the mainstream of the 1980s in two key respects. First, it rejects the simplifying assumptions which make possible rational choice theory's modelling of political behaviour. Second, it challenges the assumed regularity in human behaviour on which rests behaviouralism's reliance on a logic of extrapolation and generalisation (or induction). In their place, new institutionalists propose more complex and plausible assumptions which seek to capture and reflect the complexity and open-endedness of processes of social and political change.

Unremarkably, perhaps, new institutionalism emphasises the mediating role of the *institutional* contexts in which events occur, rejecting what it sees as the input-weighted political analysis of behaviouralism and rational choice theory. In so doing, it draws attention to the significance of history, timing and sequence in explaining political dynamics. It points, in particular, to the 'path dependent' qualities of institutional, and hence political, development, as large and frequently irreversible

Table 1.2   *Behaviouralism*

Aim/ contribution	• To use rigorous statistical techniques in the analysis of political data • To develop an inductive science of the political capable of generating predictive hypotheses on the basis of the quantitative analysis of human behaviour at an aggregate level
Key assumptions	• The logic of induction is sound – general 'covering laws' can be inferred from specific empirical observations • Political behaviour exhibits regularities over time which allow law-like statements to be generated inductively • The neutral and dispassionate analysis of raw political data is possible • There is no separation of appearance and reality
Key themes	• No *a priori* theoretical assumptions should be allowed to inform political analysis • All theoretical propositions and assumptions must be exposed to rigorous and systematic empirical testing before they are deployed deductively • Ethical judgements must not be allowed to inform, distort or interfere with the systematic collation, recording and analysis of empirical evidence • Theoretical hypotheses take the form of probabilistic predictions based on the assumption that exhibited regularities in the data analysed are generalisable beyond the immediate context and time period in which the data was collected *cont. opposite*

consequences may follow from seemingly minor or contingent events. This places clear limits on a predictive science of the political (P. Pierson 2000). Institutions, they suggest, tend to become embedded in routine and convention and are, consequently, difficult to transform. Accordingly, political time tends to be characterised by periods of relative tranquillity punctuated, periodically, by phases of rapid and intense institutional change.

From relatively humble origins in the movement to 'bring the state back into' the more input-weighted or society-centred political analysis of the times (Evans, Rueschemeyer and Skocpol 1985), the new institutionalism has grown significantly, with a number of influential converts from rational choice theory (Knight 1992, 2001; North 1990) and, even, behaviouralism (for a discussion of which see Dunleavy 1996). The result has been a series of hybrid positions and a proliferation of inter-paradigm debates within contemporary political science. The most influ-

Table 1.2   *Continued*

	• Political power is synonymous with decision-making and may, as a consequence, be operationalised quantitatively • Political outcomes can largely be derived from an analysis of political inputs
Key concepts	• Causation and correlation • Statistical significance • Decision-making
Silences and limitations	• Problem of differentiating causation and correlation • Tends to restrict itself to 'visible' variables and to those which can readily be quantified • Assumptions about regularity problematise the extent to which behaviouralism can inform an analysis of social and political change • The dependence of inductive inference on the assumption of regularity renders behaviouralism problematic in periods of social and political change • Lacks a conception of agency • Suffers from a narrow conception of politics and power
Seminal works	• Robert A. Dahl's *Who Governs?* (1961) • Ted Gurr's *Why Men Rebel* (1970) • Gary King, Robert O. Keohane and Sidney Verba's *Designing Social Inquiry* (1994)

ential of such hybrids is undoubtedly rational choice institutionalism which examines the extent to which institutions might provide solutions to collective action problems and, more generally, the (institutional) context-dependence of rationality. Some so-called sociological institutionalists have also sought to apply (neo-)behaviouralist techniques and methods to an institutionalist research agenda (Tolbert and Zucker 1983; Tuma and Hannan 1984).

Mapping the mainstream in international relations

The international relations mainstream is somewhat more complex and contested. It is, partly as a consequence, rather more difficult to specify. Its core is in fact relatively undisputed and comprises classical realism, structural or neo-realism and a position variously referred to as pluralism, liberalism, liberal institutionalism, liberal intergovernmentalism, interdependence theory and, as here, neo-liberalism (compare Baldwin 1993; Baylis and Smith 2001; Hollis and Smith 1990b; Jackson and

Table 1.3   *New institutionalism*

Aim/ contribution	• To restore the link between theoretical assumptions and the reality they purport to represent • To acknowledge the crucial mediating role of institutions in shaping political conduct and translating political inputs into political outcomes • To acknowledge the complexity and contingency of political systems
Key assumptions	• 'Institutions matter' – political conduct is shaped profoundly by the institutional context in which it occurs and acquires significance • 'History matters' – the legacy the past bequeaths to the present is considerable • Political systems are complex and inherently unpredictable • Actors do not always behave instrumentally in pursuit of material self-interest
Key themes	• Rationalism and behaviouralism tend to concentrate too heavily on political inputs in explaining political outcomes, ignoring the key mediating role of political institutions • Institutions become embedded in routine and convention and are, consequently, difficult to reform, transform or replace • The timing and sequence of events matters since history is 'path dependent' – large consequences may follow from small or contingent events • Actors are socialised within institutional settings which define informal rules and procedures • Accordingly, logics of appropriateness may better explain political behaviour than those which assume instrumental self-interest *cont. opposite*

Sørensen 1999; M. Nicholson 1998; Steans and Pettiford 2001; Wæver 1996).

Altogether more contentious is the inclusion of constructivism and postmodernism within the mainstream. For there are many who would suggest that constructivism still has much to prove – not least its scientific status and its substantive contribution to the understanding of world politics (Keohane 1989; Moravcsik 2001) – before it can be welcomed into the court of international relations (IR) theory. And if this is said of constructivism, it need hardly be stated that few, if any, of those who regard themselves as defenders of the mainstream would be prepared to

Table 1.3 *Continued*

	• The rigidity of institutions means that political time tends to be characterised by periods of relative stability, punctuated periodically by phases of intense institutional change
Key concepts	• Institutions • Path dependence • Timing/sequence/history • Punctuated equilibrium
Silences and limitations	• Despite its sensitivity to history, it is poor at accounting for institutional change, tending merely to invoke (untheorised) exogenous shock • Tends to exhibit a rather structuralist logic in which actors are prisoners of institutional contexts and the logics of appropriateness they define • In pointing to the mediating role of institutions and the high degree of variation between institutional contexts, institutionalism tends towards rich description • It is, as a consequence, perhaps overly reticent of bold theories and hypotheses • In its emphasis upon path dependence and historical legacies it is rather better at explaining stability than change
Seminal works	• Douglass C. North's *Institutions, Institutional Change and Economic Performance* (1990) • Sven Steinmo, Kathleen Thelen and Frank Longstreth's *Structuring Politics* (1992) • James G. March and Johan P. Olsen's *Rediscovering Institutions* (1989) • Paul Pierson's *Dismantling the Welfare State?* (1994) • Theda Skocpol's *States and Social Revolutions* (1979)

credit postmodernism with a seat at the table. Moreover, and perhaps more to the point, few postmodernists would themselves be happy with such an invitation, seeing any inclusion within the mainstream as an alarming portent of assimilation and capitulation.

So why then insist on discussing constructivism and postmodernism in the context of the mainstream? My reasons are, in fact, relatively simple. The first of these is the seemingly inexorable rise of constructivism in recent years. This might be gauged in a variety of ways, from the large number of converts to its position since the 1990s, its impressive hold over a younger generation of international relations scholars,

Figure 1.2 *The evolution of international relations theory*

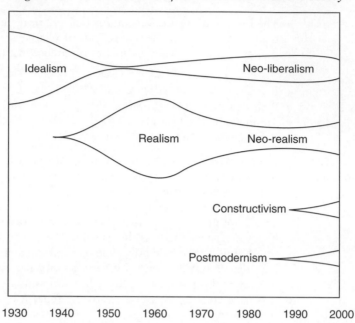

Idealism

Neo-liberalism

Realism

Neo-realism

Constructivism

Postmodernism

1930   1940   1950   1960   1970   1980   1990   2000

the extent to which its contribution has been acknowledged, taken seriously and responded to by the mainstream, or just the reception that a seminal constructivist work, such as Alexander Wendt's *Social Theory of International Politics* (1999) has received from neo-realists and neo-liberals alike. If there are still those who would be uncomfortable with constructivism's inclusion within the mainstream, then it is surely only a matter of time before they will be forced to concede that, whether they like it or not, it is already treated as such.

The position of postmodernism is obviously more controversial and there are, I think, good reasons for seeing it less as a (potentially) mainstream perspective than as a challenge to the very notion of a mainstream (see also S. Smith 2001: 241). I include it here for two reasons: (i) because the challenge it poses to the mainstream is, if ultimately problematic, fundamental and worthy of a response; and (ii) because constructivism defines itself, at least in part, in and through its opposition to neo-realism/neo-liberalism on the one hand and postmodernism on the other (Figure 1.2).

In many respects, the key point of departure for *all* contemporary contenders for mainstream status in international relations theory is *realism* (Table 1.4). It was fashioned as a direct response to the naïve or 'utopian idealism' of the period immediately following the Great War (Carr

1939). Such idealism, horrified by the brutality of total war, had sought to build an institutional architecture of international mediation and mutual cooperation that might serve to guarantee perpetual peace. Realism rose to dominance out of the ashes of that optimism in the late 1930s and throughout the 1940s. It prided itself upon its sanguine view of world politics, premised on a realist(ic) if depressing view of human nature. Rather like rational choice theory, it effectively derived the instrumental rationality of the state and the anarchical character of a world system in which the state was sovereign from essentially Hobbesian assumptions about human nature. Life was nasty, brutish and, in the context of the late 1930s and early 1940s, all too short. For realists the study of international relations is the study of the interaction between sovereign states whose principal, indeed essentially sole, motivation for action is self-preservation (security) and, in pursuit of that end, the acquisition of power. Realism is, in short, rational choice theory applied at the level of the state system, with states cast in the image of utility-maximising rational actors. The result, a product to a considerable extent of its times, is a most depressing view of human affairs in which conflict is the norm and cooperation a rare and, above all, fragile product not of cooperative intent but of a temporary balancing of strategies of narrow self-interest and mutual distrust.

Neo-realism emerged in the 1970s as an attempt to produce a more refined, rigorous and structural account of world politics – though one still couched very much in realist terms (Table 1.5). It sought to emulate the mathematical rigour (as it saw it) of rational choice theory and, indeed, neo-classical economics through the careful choice of simplifying assumptions on which the rational behaviour of states within the international system might be modelled. Yet rather than proceed from ultimately universal, metaphysical and essentialist assumptions about human nature, as had its realist forebears, it assumed only that states (as unified actors) were rational in the pursuit of relative (rather than absolute) gains. Consequently, given the structure of the international system (anarchy), their behaviour was entirely predictable. For neo-realists, then, the conflictual and competitive nature of inter-state relations was the product not of any innately belligerent or aggressive qualities of states, but merely of the pursuit of national interest under conditions of anarchy.

Neo-liberalism, too, might be seen to share much with realism, though it arose first as a response to realism and was later shaped by its ongoing engagement with neo-realism (Baldwin 1993). (Table 1.6) Moreover, and despite any such similarities, its origins lie in precisely the 'utopian idealism' so categorically rejected by realists like E. H. Carr in the late 1930s, an idealism still reflected in its rather more positive and flexible

Table 1.4   *Realism*

Aim/ contribution	• In the context of the 1930s, to re-inject a healthy does of realism into the discussion of international relations following the delusions of idealism • To be sanguine and realistic about the frailty of human nature and to trace the implications for the conduct of international relations • To render international relations a rigorous and dispassionate science of world politics
Key assumptions	• The realm of international relations is governed by objective laws which have their origins in human nature • The pursuit of power by individuals and states is ubiquitous and unavoidable – consequently, conflict and competition is endemic • The state is sovereign and the natural unit of analysis in international relations since states recognise no authority above themselves and are autonomous of non-state actors and structures • States are unified actors, motivated exclusively by considerations of national interest • National interests are objective • The principal national interest is that of survival/security • There is a total separation of domestic and international politics with the former subordinated to the latter
Key themes	• The study of international relations is the study of the interaction between sovereign states • The self-interested behaviour of states in the absence of any overarching authority on a global scale produces a condition of anarchy *cont. opposite*

view of human nature than that of realism. All this having said, neo-liberals like neo-realists and realists before them are, at heart, rationalists, committed to a notion of the human subject as a rational actor carefully weighing up the respective merits and demerits of various courses of action in an attempt to maximise his or her personal utility. Yet here they part company, with neo-liberals drawing rather different conclusions. In particular, and in marked contrast to neo-realism, they emphasise the capacity of human agents to shape their environment and hence their destiny and, in marked contrast to classic realism, their capacity to achieve cooperation for mutual advantage. Characteristically, and as evidence for both, they cite the building of a global capitalist economy regulated by a series of interconnected international institutions. Such achievements, they suggest, demonstrate the conditions under which

Table 1.4 *Continued*

	• In so far as conflict is avoided, this is not because of the pacific intentions of states, but precisely because of the balance produced by the aggressive pursuit of power and security by states • It is naïve to assume that cooperation rather than conflict is the natural condition of world politics • The evolution of world politics is cyclical, characterised by timeless laws rooted in human nature
Key concepts	• Security • Sovereignty • National interest • Power politics
Silences and limitations	• Limited attention to the role of non-state actors • Little or no consideration to economic processes • Relies on an impoverished conception of human nature and implausible assumptions • Narrowly state-centric • Less an accurate theory of world politics than the image in and through which world politics was made – hence, 'nothing but a rationalisation of Cold War politics' (Hoffman 1977: 48)
Seminal works	• E. H. Carr's *The Twenty Years' Crisis* (1939) • Hans Morgenthau's *Politics Among Nations* (1948)

cooperation may arise and in which states can pursue absolute rather than relative gains.

Though there are clear differences in emphasis between neo-realists and neo-liberals, successive rounds of the so-called 'inter-paradigm debate' have drawn the two perspectives ever closer together such that it is now often difficult to position clearly once prominent neo-realists or neo-liberals (Wæver 1996). This has led to the identification of a 'neo-neo-synthesis' which some would see as having come to circumscribe the parameters of theoretical debate in mainstream international relations (Kegley 1995; Lamy 2001; S. Smith 2001).

It is this cosy synthesis that constructivism and, in rather more radical terms, postmodernism, challenge. Like the new institutionalism in political science, *constructivism* rejects the rationalism on which the neo-neo-synthesis is premised, seeking to render its analytical assumptions more complex and realistic (Table 1.7). It is also characterised, again like the new institutionalism in political science, by its broadening of the field of political analysis to encompass not just interests but the means by which

Table 1.5   *Neo-realism*

Aim/ contribution	• To produce a more systematic, rigorous and *structural* account of international relations in the realist tradition • To liberate realism from essentialist and universal assumptions about human nature • To produce a deductive science of world politics on the basis of parsimonious assumptions about the international system
Key assumptions	• World politics can be analysed as if states were unitary rational actors seeking to maximise their expected utility • The context in which states find themselves – a condition of anarchy – determines the content of the rationality they exhibit • The behaviour of states can be explained exclusively in terms of the structure of the international system itself, since states are rational and in any given setting there is only one optimal course of action open to them • The state is again sovereign and the natural unit of analysis in international relations • However, the role of international institutions in the governance of international relations (both political and economic) cannot be overlooked • States are, again, unified actors, motivated solely by considerations of national interest • States seek relative rather than absolute gains
Key themes	• The anarchical structure of the international system compels states to act as they do • Accordingly, conflict is a consequence not of state belligerence but of the pursuit of national interest under conditions of anarchy *cont. opposite*

interests are identified and constructed in the first place and the institutional context in which such interests are expressed, acted upon and revised. This is a more dynamic and open-ended approach to world politics which refuses to accept the primacy of material over ideational factors, thereby opening up for empirical analysis the whole area of social construction which realism, neo-realism and neo-liberalism had closed off. The overriding theme of constructivist work is the problematic nature of the concept of interests. Material interests are by no means transparent and uncontested. Moreover, it is *perceptions* of interests rather than material interests *per se* on which states act. Consequently, if we wish to understand world politics we need to explore the means and mechanisms by which states come to identify, act upon and

Table 1.5 *Continued*

	• Though states are inherently conflictual and competitive, actual conflict can be averted in situations in which there is a balance of power • Though there is always a tendency to instability in the international system, this can be attenuated if a dominant state assumes a leadership (or hegemonic) role • Under such conditions of hegemonic stability international institutions can serve to provide a secure basis for cooperation between nations, such as is evidenced in the international economic system which developed in the post-war period
Key concepts	• Balance of power • Relative (as opposed to absolute) gains • Hegemonic stability
Silences and limitations	• Lacks clarity about the conditions of cooperation and the conditions of conflict in the international system • Incapable either of predicting or of explaining the end of the Cold War despite its focus on the balance of power within the international system • State-centric • Displays a very limited and impoverished conception of state agency • Relies on a series of implausible assumptions about the unity and rationality of the state
Seminal works	• Robert Gilpin's *War and Change in World Politics* (1981) • Charles Kindleberger's *The World in Depression, 1929–1939* (1973) • Kenneth Waltz's *Theory of International Politics* (1979)

revise their perception of both their interests and, in the process, their identity – who they are and what they stand for. A favoured example concerns the issue of security itself. States act in response to perceived security threats, not to the (material) volume of armoury which a state might (potentially) direct against them. As Alexander Wendt notes, '500 British nuclear weapons are less threatening to the US than five North Korean nuclear weapons, because the British are friends of the US and the North Koreans are not, and amity and enmity is a function of shared understandings' (1995: 73). The neo-neo-synthesis has little or no way of dealing with this, appealing, as it does, to a notion of material interests as objective, uncontested and transparent. For constructivists, by contrast, crucial to understanding the conduct of states

Table 1.6 *Neo-liberalism*

Aim/ contribution	• To counter the state-centrism of realism and neo-realism and to reinsert economic dynamics into international relations • To explore the possibilities for cooperation within the international system • To explore the implications of a more flexible and positive view of human nature
Key assumptions	• Individuals and states, though rational, have the capacity to solve problems through collective action • International cooperation for mutual advantage is both desirable and possible • Actors other than states – multi-national corporations, religious and nationalist movements – play a central role in international events • States cannot be conceptualised as unified actors but are themselves multi-centric and subject to a variety of competing domestic and international pressures • Power, within the international system, is diffuse and fluid • Liberal democratic states do not wage war upon one another (the doctrine of the democratic peace) • Military force is by no means the only, or the most effective, instrument of foreign policy • States seek absolute rather than relative gains
Key themes	• An advanced international division of labour within the world economy encourages relations of interdependence and cooperation between nations which are mutually advantageous • The condition of complex interdependence which characterises the international system renders national economies ever more sensitive and vulnerable to events in other countries *cont. opposite*

are the shared or inter-subjective understandings they fashion. In the end, then, if anarchy is indeed the condition of the international system it is important to acknowledge that 'anarchy is what states make of it' (Wendt 1992).

If the challenge posed by constructivism to the mainstream is considerable, despite attempts by Wendt and others to convince realists in particular that they have little to fear from taking constructivism seriously (1999, 2000), then that posed by *postmodernism* is altogether more fundamental (Table 1.8). Indeed, arguably it calls into question the whole enterprise of international relations, as it does political analysis

Table 1.6   *Continued*

	• This entails a significant loss of state capacity and autonomy • There is a complex relationship between domestic and international politics with no clear or consistent hierarchy • International institutions and organisations, though in some sense themselves the product of state action, may come to assume an independent identity and display agency in their own right
Key concepts	• Interdependence/complex interdependence • Absolute (as opposed to relative) gains • Cooperation • International regimes
Silences and limitations	• Like realism, it lacks clarity about the conditions under which we should expect cooperation and those under which we should expect conflict • For realists and neo-realists, liberals adopt a naïve and utopian conception of both human nature and the possibilities for international cooperation • Tends to exaggerate the role of international institutions, the extent of globalisation and the limited capacity of the state • Tends to legitimate the status quo • The empirical evidence does not seem to confirm the democratic peace thesis – democratic states can be quite belligerent
Seminal works	• Robert O. Keohane and Joseph S. Nye's *Power and Interdependence* (1977) • Joseph S. Nye's *Understanding International Conflicts* (1993) • James N. Rosenau's *Turbulence in World Politics* (1990)

and social science more generally. While it might have some sympathy for the idea that the interests of states are constructions rather than objective properties, postmodernism, quite simply, rejects all of the above. Though it has given rise to a series of substantive contributions to international relations scholarship (see, for instance, Ashley 1987; Campbell 1992; Walker 1993; C. Weber 1995), its principal contribution is to challenge the stated and, above all, unstated assumptions of conventional international relations theory (realist, idealist or constructivist). It problematises and ultimately rejects the notion of a neutral or

Table 1.7   *Constructivism*

Aim/ contribution	• To open up a 'middle way' (Adler) between rationalism (neo-realism and neo-liberalism) and postmodernism • To explore the implications of acknowledging that political realities are socially constructed and of according ideas an independent role in the analysis of international relations • To explore the implications of replacing rationalism's logic of instrumental rationality with a more sociological conception of agency • To explore the implications of treating interests and preferences as social constructions rather than as objectively given
Key assumptions	• Our beliefs play a crucial role in the construction of our reality • The social and political world is not a given but an inherently intersubjective domain – a product of social construction • There is no objective social or political reality independent of our understanding of it – there is no social realm independent of human activity • Ideational factors should be accorded as significant a role in international relations as material factors • For most constructivists, positivism cannot be reconciled with an emphasis upon the significance of intersubjective understanding
Key themes	• 'Anarchy is what states make of it' (Wendt) – the structure of the international system does not dictate state behaviour; it is the interaction and intersubjective understandings of states which gives rise to the condition of anarchy *cont. opposite*

dispassionate science of international relations, pointing, like constructivism, to the role of theory in the constitution of the objects of its analytical attentions. Yet it takes this line of argument far further, charting the complicity of international relations theory in the reproduction of existing power relations and in the production – invariably in the name of progress, liberty or emancipation – of new power relations while emphasising what it would see as the inherently partisan and political subject-positions from which such theory is written. It suggests, in short, that though students of world politics are loath to admit it, all theories are conceived and formulated to reflect a particular vantage-point or

Table 1.7 *Continued*

	• Assesses the transformative impact of novel social constructions (such as the European Union) on the state system • Emphasises the impact of national norms on international politics and international norms on national politics • Emphasises the importance of discursive construction and naming in the identification and response, say, to security 'threats' – threats are perceptions and it is perceptions rather than realities that are responded to
Key concepts	• Social construction • Intersubjectivity • Identity
Silences and limitations	• Unified more by what they distance themselves from than by what they share • For rationalists, much of what they claim theoretically, though plausible, remains either untestable to untested • May be seeking to reconcile the irreconcilable – the choice between rationalism and postmodernism may be starker than constructivists assume • Despite its ostensible aim to define and inhabit a middle ground between rationalism and postmodernism, many of its proponents seem to gravitate towards one or other pole • Despite its theoretical appeal its promise is, as yet, largely unrealised
Seminal works	• Friedrich Kratochwil's *Rules, Norms and Decisions* (1989) • Nicholas Onuf's *A World of Our Making* (1989) • Alexander Wendt's *Social Theory of International Politics* (1999)

subject-position in a world characterised by near infinite profusion of potential subject-positions. Consequently, all theories, despite any pretensions they may make to universality, neutrality or scientific status, are partial and partisan. They are, as a consequence, either complicit in the reproduction of the status quo and the power relations it serves to institutionalise or calls for the transformation of the existing state of affairs couched in the name of a progress. The latter can only serve to replace one system of domination and oppression with another.

Table 1.8 *Postmodernism*

Aim/ contribution	• To cast doubt on modernist assumptions about the ability to generate objective knowledge of the social and political world • To draw attention to the conceptual prisms in and through which supposedly dispassionate and neutral theories are formulated • To expose the silences, implicit assumptions and universal pretensions of such theories and to reveal the power relations in whose reproduction they are complicit • To explore the implications of an international relations which does not rely on universal claims, privileged access to knowledge or the possibility of liberation or emancipation from power
Key assumptions	• There is no neutral vantage-point from which the world can be described and analysed objectively • All knowledge is partial, partisan and power-serving • Knowledge claims are never neutral with respect to power relations which are, as a consequence, ubiquitous and diffuse • There are no facts about the social and political world, only interpretations advanced from a particular vantage-point • The social and political world is characterised not by sameness and identity but by difference, diversity and 'otherness'
Key themes	• The identification and exploration of the way power operates in the discourses and practices of world politics • The celebration of difference, diversity and plurality

cont. opposite

Postmodernism raises a series of crucial and troubling issues which deserve a sustained and systematic discussion. This will be the principal concern of Chapter 7. Suffice it for now to note that *if* the postmodernist challenge cannot be rebuffed it has very serious implications for the conduct of political analysis and the claims we might legitimately make in its name. It is conventional, both in international relations and political science, to dismiss such issues and to suggest that until such time as postmodernism has something 'better' to put in its place, its critique of the mainstream does not deserve to be taken seriously. Though certainly convenient, given the implications of the issues the postmodernist challenge raises, this is wholly inadequate and, in fact, profoundly

Table 1.8   *Continued*

	• A challenge to the notion of history as 'progress' • The attempt to establish universal conditions for human emancipation can only serve, in practice, to replace one set of relations of domination with another – there is no escape from tyranny • The universal pretensions of general theories and emancipatory projects (metanarratives) is mythical • Power relations often function through the construction, in language, of hierarchical distinctions of identity/difference, sameness/otherness
Key concepts	• (Incredulity towards) 'metanarratives' • Deconstruction • Difference/otherness
Silences and limitations	• Tendency towards nihilism, fatalism and passivity – an abstention from judgement • Is not postmodernism's normative respect for 'difference' in the end self-defeating – precluding the taking of action to protect that difference? • Are its implications not profoundly conservative – deconstruction without the possibility of the reconstruction of an alternative? • Internal contradictions – is not postmodernism itself the metanarrative to end all metanarratives and hence a contradiction in terms? • Tends towards pure descriptive narrative as opposed to political analysis
Seminal works	• David Campbell's *Writing Security* (1992) • R. J. Walker's *Inside/Outside* (1993) • Cynthia Weber's *Simulating Sovereignty* (1995)

irresponsible. Moreover, if the postmodernists are right then there is nothing 'better' to put in place of the mainstream, for the enterprise itself is profoundly flawed. Though this is a view that I will ultimately reject, it is one that needs to be examined very closely.

Analytical strategies in contemporary political science and international relations

As the above paragraphs serve to demonstrate, there are certain resemblances between many of the perspectives which have come to characterise the mainstream in political science and their counterparts in international relations. Nonetheless, the degree of dialogue between the two sub-disciplines has been somewhat limited. As I have sought already to suggest, rational choice theory, realism, neo-realism and neo-liberalism are all, essentially, rationalist. Moreover, constructivism in international relations theory and the new institutionalism in political science would seem to perform very similar roles within their respective sub-disciplines, valuing similar things and drawing attention to the role of institutions and ideas in the understanding of complex political change. Finally, behaviouralism, though rather more influential within political science than international relations, might be applied – and, indeed, has been applied – to world politics (see, for instance, Deutsch 1953, 1963; Guertzkow 1950; Kaplan 1957; Singer 1968). There are certainly perspectives, such as liberal intergovernmentalism and rational choice institutionalism, which are more difficult to position and seem to inhabit hybrid-locations between rationalism and institutionalism, but this merely reveals the limits of any fixed analytical schema. Within those limits, however, it is plausible to suggest the existence of three distinctive analytical traditions in political analysis which span international relations and political science: *rationalism*, *behaviouralism* and *constructivism/new institutionalism*.[3] In what follows, and in keeping with my desire to resist as far as is possible the artificial and polarising distinction between international relations and political science, I will refer not to the sub-discipline-specific perspectives outlined in the preceding section but to the three distinctive analytical strategies on which they rest.

In the remaining sections of this chapter my aim is to introduce the key themes of the volume by examining the stance adopted with respect to a series of key analytical issues by these three analytical paradigms. Their distinctive features are summarised, albeit in a rather stylised fashion, in Table 1.9.

Yet my aim is not to present a commentary on each paradigm in turn. Rather, I introduce the distinctiveness and diversity of analytical strategies adopted in political science and international relations by considering some of the principal analytical issues and choices which divide them. Three issues in particular will prove particularly significant in the chapters which follow. They are: (1) the parsimony versus complexity trade-off; (2) the role of theory within political analysis; and (3) the relationship between political conduct and the context within which it occurs and acquires significance (the thorny perennial of structure and agency). Each warrants a brief introduction at this point.

Table 1.9   *Analytical paradigms in contemporary political science*

	Rationalism	*New institutionalism and Constructivism*	*Behaviouralism*
Role of theory	To simplify the world – as a means to generate testable hypotheses	To inform and sensitise analysis to the complexity of the process of change	No analytical role for theory; theory as a language for recording exhibited regularities
Theoretical assumptions	Simple	Complex	None required (evidential)
Analytical approach	Deductive (hypotheses derived from theoretical assumptions)	Sensitising and informative (guides analysis)	Inductive
Method	(Mathematical) modelling; 'predictive'	Theoretically informed; comparative and historical	Empirical; statistical
Values	Parsimony; predictive capacity	Sophistication; complexity; realism of assumptions	Evidence; methodological rigour; neutrality

The parsimony versus complexity trade-off

Though rarely discussed in any sustained or systematic manner (for an important exception see Sober 1988), the choice – perhaps better seen as a *trade-off* – between parsimony and complexity is central to the selection of analytical strategies in political science and international relations. Yet, as King, Keohane and Verba observe, 'the word has been used in so many ways in casual conversation and scholarly writings that the principle has become obscured' (1994: 20).

Before proceeding further, then, it is important that we are clear about what the term implies. Here it is instructive to differentiate clearly between two rather different logics of political inquiry – the *inductive* and the *deductive*. As we shall see, the trade-off between parsimony and complexity has rather different implications for inductive and deductive approaches to political analysis.

Deductive and inductive logics in political analysis

Inductive approaches to political analysis take as their starting point the (supposedly) neutral and dispassionate assessment of empirical evidence. They begin, in short, with specific observations from which they seek to generate (though inductive generalisation and inference) more general or even universal theoretical propositions (Hempel 1966: 11; Wolfe 1924: 450). As Norman Blaikie suggests, induction 'corresponds to a popular conception of the activities of scientists [as] persons who make careful observations, conduct experiments, rigorously analyse the data obtained, and hence produce new discoveries or theories' (1993: 133). Theory, in such a strategy, logically follows observation and generalisation and is little more than the statement of generalisable 'covering laws' consistent with an existing set of empirical observations (Hempel 1994). This inductive logic is depicted schematically in Figure 1.3.

Induction in the social sciences is associated with *empiricism*, the privileging of evidence and observation over theory, reason or intuition. It proceeds from relatively direct, simple and specific observations ('in 1992 corporation X left country A for country B with a lower rate of corporate taxation' or '*this* swan is white') to more general, even universal, covering laws ('in an era of globalisation capital will leave high-taxation regimes for low-taxation regimes' or '*all* swans are white').

Deductive approaches to political analysis are essentially a mirror image of such a strategy (see Figure 1.3). Rather than commencing with, and thereby privileging, observation they seek to derive (or deduce) testable propositions or hypotheses from pre-established facts or initial theoretical assumptions. The predictive hypotheses thereby formulated are subsequently exposed to rigorous empirical scrutiny; the hypothesis either confirmed or rejected. The logic is, in Karl Popper's memorable terms, one of 'conjecture and refutation' (1969).

A good example of such a deductive logic is that exhibited in Anthony Downs' influential *An Economic Theory of Democracy* (1957); see also Black (1958); Hotelling (1929). Downs starts with a series of simplifying theoretical assumptions which establish the parameters of the model (that parties in democratic polities are analogous to firms in a profit-seeking economy, that both voters and political parties are rational in pursuit of their preferences, that opposition parties seek only election, governments re-election and that parties have complete information as to the distribution of preferences of the electorate, to name but a few).

Figure 1.3   *Deductive and inductive logics in political analysis*

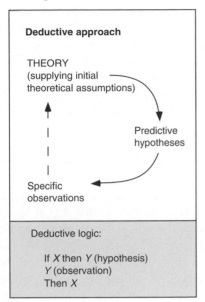
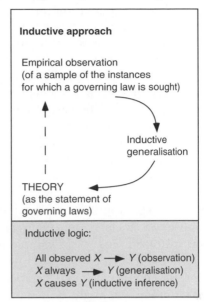

Through a process of logical theoretical deduction, Downs generates the prediction (or hypothesis), that in a first-past-the-post, two-party electoral system in which voters' preferences are normally distributed, the political parties will gravitate towards the preferences of the median voter. In other words, opposition and government will converge on the political centre-ground. Such a prediction was seemingly confirmed by the bipartisan centrism of the US Democrats and Republicans of the time and, indeed, has been resuscitated to account for similarly bipartisan convergence in countries such as Australia, Britain, Ireland and New Zealand in recent years (for a critical assessment of this literature see Hay 1999e: Ch. 3).[4]

Having established the distinctiveness of inductive and deductive rationales in political research, we can now return to the trade-off between parsimony and complexity.

Parsimony, complexity and induction

In inductive approaches to social and political analysis the aim, essentially, is to fit a theoretical model to a set of empirical data. Here parsimony is most simply understood as getting value for one's variables. A parsimonious explanation or model is one which includes as few variables as possible yet which explains (or offers the potential to explain) as much as possible (see also Jeffreys 1961: 47; Zellner 1984). In some sense, a better explanation (certainly a more complete one) is one which includes more variables. But here we run the risk of sacrificing a simple and elegant account for a complex and sophisticated yet cumbersome and inelegant alternative. In more technical (in fact, classically behaviouralist) terms, we run the risk of 'saturating' our model with additional variables each of which account for progressively less of the overall 'variance'. The casualty in such a strategy is the analytical and explanatory precision of a more *parsimonious* account.

This makes parsimony sound like a very attractive proposition and something to aspire to in one's theoretical models. Who, after all, could possibly prefer a cumbersome and inelegant account saturated with variables of only marginal (if any) significance when presented with a simple, neat and elegant alternative in which each variable's contribution to the causal chain is clear and unambiguous? Yet this is to present a somewhat distorted view. An example might serve to indicate why. Say we are interested in formulating a general theory of electoral success and failure in advanced liberal democratic polities. Impressed by the allure of parsimony, we might be tempted to suggest that the key factor predisposing political parties to electoral success at a given election is their success at the previous election.[5] This is a highly parsimonious model, yet one which is wholly inadequate. While it might well be the case that incumbent administrations are marginally more likely to be re-elected than they are to be expelled from office at any given election, a model of democratic electoral competition incapable of predicting anything other than the perpetuation of a one-party state is at best somewhat anomalous. Clearly parsimony can be taken too far. Our overly simplistic model might be rendered more complex and sophisticated (in other words, less parsimonious) by the incorporation of a series of additional variables – the length of the incumbent administration's tenure in office, the perceived relative economic competence of the principal parties, and so forth. The question is, of course, how far to go. At what point are the merits of greater complexity more than outweighed by the loss of parsimony their incorporation in the model would entail?

In seeking to draw causal inferences from the observed pattern of correlations between a given set of variables, this is precisely the sort of choice behaviouralist political scientists face on a routine basis. For them, by and large, parsimony is a good thing; a plausible parsimonious explanation is to be preferred to a similarly plausible yet more involved alternative. In the end, however, the choice of how many variables to incorporate – in other words, where precisely to position one's model on the parsimony–complexity axis – is a subjective judgement, though one influenced significantly by the data under consideration. Some relationships (and the data sets in and through which behaviouralists investigate such relationships) avail themselves of more parsimonious explanatory models than others.

Parsimony, complexity and the nature of political reality

It is at this point that the discussion of parsimony, to the extent that it occurs at all, usually terminates (see, for instance Miller 1995: 172; Ragin 1994: 214; Ragin, Berg-Schlosser and de Meur 1996: 760–2). Yet it is here, I would suggest, that it should really begin. For if we acknowledge that the extent to which parsimony might be deemed desirable depends upon the object of our analytical attentions, then we can usefully ask under what conditions the world avails itself of parsimonious explanation.

This brings us to a crucial point and one of relevance not only to inductive logics of political inquiry. As King, Keohane and Verba perceptively note, for parsimony to be adopted as a guiding principle of good political analysis implies 'a judgement, *or even assumption*, about the nature of the world: it is *assumed* to be simple'. Moreover, as they go on to suggest, 'the principle of choosing theories that imply a simple world is a rule that clearly applies in situations where there is a *high degree of certainty* that the world is indeed simple'. Consequently, 'we should never insist on parsimony as a general principle of designing theories, but it is useful in those situations where *we have some knowledge of the simplicity of the world we are studying*' (1994: 20, emphasis mine). This interesting and important passage contains a subtle and highly significant slippage: the progressive blurring (in the emphasised passages) of judgements, assumptions and knowledge of the simplicity of the world we inhabit. What are merely judgements or assertions in the first sentence have acquired the status of knowledge by the second. This raises a series of key questions. Do we have to make (presumably subjective and untestable) *assumptions* about the degree of simplicity or complexity of the world in which we find ourselves, or can we acquire (objective) *knowledge* of such things? What does it mean to have 'knowledge of the simplicity of the world we are studying'? How would we ever test such a proposition? No clear answers are provided to such disarming questions. However, what is clear is that, in the absence of unambiguous means to assess the degree of complexity of the world we inhabit, the choice between parsimonious and more complex models of political reality appears altogether more arbitrary and subjective than King, Keohane and Verba seem to imply. Here it is instructive to note that, among political scientists, it tends to be behaviouralists who make some of the simplest assumptions about the world in which they find themselves.[6] It is perhaps not then surprising that they consistently prize parsimony.

This brings us for the first time to a recurrent theme of this volume. Generally untestable assumptions about the nature of the social and political world affect, fundamentally, the manner in which political analysis is conducted and the status of the knowledge claims we feel we may legitimately make as political analysts.

Parsimony, complexity and deduction

The force of this remark becomes clear if we move from *inductive* logics of political analysis (such as characterise behaviouralism) in which the theoretical generalisations are inferred from the evidence to *deductive* logics (such as characterise rational choice theory and neo-realism) in which testable theoretical hypotheses are derived from initial theoretical assumptions. Here parsimony has rather different implications and is generally taken to refer to the theoretical assumptions upon which the process of theoretical deduction is premised. Opinions and styles of political analysis vary. Certain traditions in political science and international relations – notably rational choice theory and neo-realism – prize themselves on the parsimony of their theoretical assumptions. Others, notably new institutionalism in political science and constructivism in international relations theory, might be seen as reactions to what they perceive to be the dangers of *overly* parsimonious theoretical assumptions (for a particularly lucid explanation, see P. Pierson 2000). They prize themselves not on the parsimony but the realism of their analytical premises.

A brief consideration of Downs' *An Economic Theory of Democracy* is again instructive. Downs is a rational choice theorist whose model of bipartisan convergence rests, essentially, on the theoretical assumptions out of which it is constructed. Those assumptions are undoubtedly parsimonious, but frankly implausible. Voters are not simply self-serving egoists motivated only by economic self-interest, parties are not blessed with perfect information of the distribution of voter preferences, nor are they motivated solely by the pursuit of office at any cost. Interestingly, Downs himself is prepared to concede the point, clearly stating from the outset that his assumptions are chosen not for their accuracy or sophistication but for their simplicity. As he remarks, 'theoretical models should be tested primarily for the accuracy of their predictions rather than for the reality of their assumptions' (1957: 21).[7] Though refreshingly sanguine, this might seem like a somewhat strange concession to make. After all, what confidence can we have in a theory based on premises whose implausibility is freely acknowledged by its most prominent exponents? Yet, there is another way of looking at this. For were

Downs to render more complex the theoretical assumptions on which the model is based, it would almost certainly preclude the sort of modelling in which he engages. If there is utility in Downs' *An Economic Theory of Democracy* – probably the single most influential work of political science in the post-war period (Goodin and Klingemann 1996: 32) – then it is largely despite, not because of, the parsimony of its assumptions. Nonetheless, it would have been unthinkable in the absence of such simplifying assumptions.

For increasing numbers of political scientists and international relations theorists, however, this is no excuse. For new institutionalists and constructivists in particular, theoretical assumptions must certainly be plausible and, arguably, as accurate as possible. If, in a complex and interdependent world, this makes political analysis difficult and the sort of mathematical modelling beloved of rational choice theorists and some neo-realists impossible, then so be it. For them, parsimony is a dubious virtue indeed – a synonym for the irrelevance that invariably accompanies high theoretical abstraction. It is, in short, an excuse for indulgent exercises in the production of models with little or no genuine reference to the real world.

What this suggests is that parsimony, at least in deductive approaches to political analysis, is achieved at some price in terms of the realism of theoretical assumptions (a point acknowledged by many rationalists, see Hinich and Munger 1997: 4). This clearly matters. For, notwithstanding the suggestion that it is only the predictive accuracy of analytical models that really counts, the extent to which one can legitimately claim to have explained political outcomes in terms of such models surely depends on the use of credible assumptions.

Yet if parsimony should not be regarded as an unambiguous good, we should perhaps be equally wary of viewing it as an unequivocal evil. For no less problematic is the refusal, often associated with postmodernism, to make theoretical assumptions at all (on the grounds that assumptions distort the complexity of reality). Equally debilitating is the attempt, characteristic of some institutionalists and constructivists, to render our analytical assumptions so complex and sophisticated as to preclude any generalisation between cases. Pure description, at one end of the spectrum, explains nothing yet is true to the complexity of reality. At the other end of the spectrum, abstract theoretical reflection and modelling based on simplifying assumptions (as in rational choice theory) offers the potential to explain much. But it does so only by virtue of the violence it inflicts on the nuance and complexity of the reality it purports to explain. Abstraction and simplification makes prediction possible; but the greater the degree of abstraction and simplification the less useful that prediction is likely to prove. There is, in short a trade-off: parsimony and predictive capacity (the power of explanation) on the one

Figure 1.4   *The parsimony–complexity trade-off*

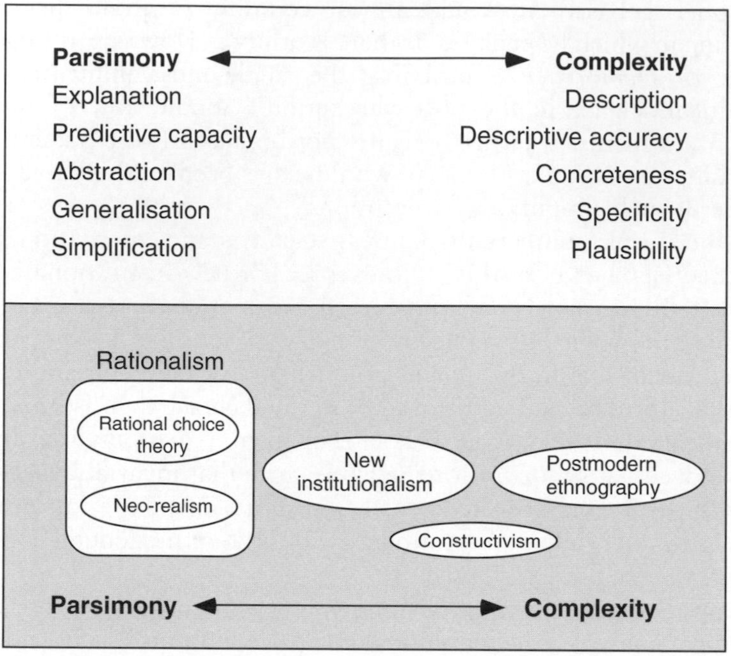

Parsimony ◄————————► **Complexity**

Explanation   Description

Predictive capacity   Descriptive accuracy

Abstraction   Concreteness

Generalisation   Specificity

Simplification   Plausibility

Rationalism

Rational choice
theory

New
institutionalism

Postmodern
ethnography

Neo-realism

Constructivism

Parsimony ◄————————► **Complexity**

hand versus accuracy of assumptions (or, in the case of pure description, the absence of assumptions) and the ability to reflect the complexity and indeterminacy of political processes on the other.

The trade-off is captured schematically in Figure 1.4. It provides a particularly useful way of highlighting the range and diversity of rationales underpinning strategies of political analysis.

At the parsimonious end of the spectrum, rationalist perspectives value the predictive capacity that comes with the choice of simplifying theoretical assumptions. Some way towards the opposite end of the spectrum we find the new institutionalists and constructivists who insist on more precisely specified and contextually specific assumptions, scaling down their ambitions for the construction of generalisable and predictive theory as a consequence. Finally, and still further along this axis, we find postmodernists, happy to sacrifice any such lingering (modernist) ambitions. As we shall see in Chapter 7, these authors argue that all theoretical abstractions and generalisations necessarily distort, and thereby do violence to, the distinctiveness of each and every context. Such contexts, they suggest, deserve to be respected for what they are and analysed in their own terms rather than those imposed upon them by political analysts writing, invariably, from altogether different vantage-points. Postmodernists thus shun generalisation, theoretical abstraction and prediction, preferring instead analyses conducted in terms familiar to the participants in the political behaviour being considered. For them, parsimony is little more than a signal of the universalising, totalising and colonising pretensions of mainstream political science.

The role for and nature of theory in political analysis

This brings us fairly directly to the nature of and role for theory in political science and international relations. It is tempting to assume that theory serves but one purpose in political analysis, a purpose that is essentially the same regardless of the analytical tradition within which that purpose is to be realised. Yet as the above discussion already serves to indicate, this is far from being the case. For positivists, keen to model the analysis of the political upon the natural sciences, a theory is not a theory unless it is capable of generating testable (preferably falsifiable) hypotheses (King, Keohane and Verba 1994: 100–5; Nagel 1961). While this perhaps remains the dominant understanding of theory within political analysis, such a restrictive conception is sectarian in dismissing (as atheoretical) those whose philosophical worldview tells them that the political world is so complex and indeterminate that it is not amenable to prediction. It is yet another instance of the imposition of a universal standard which happens to conform to one (of many) strands of political analysis. What it fails to appreciate is that the role for and nature of theory in political analysis is itself variable, reflective of different assumptions about the nature of the political reality being investigated, the extent of the knowledge we can hope to acquire of it, and the strategies appropriate to its analysis. It also fails to acknowledge the theoretical content of precisely such assumptions.

As the previous sections have already made clear, a variety of competing tendencies can be identified in contemporary political science and international relations, pulling in different directions. Three in particular have proved influential in setting the terms of contemporary controversy within the discipline. Each has a rather different conception of the role of theory.

Rationalism and formal theory

First, and perhaps still the dominant strand at least in US political science and international relations, is *rationalism*. This broad school of thought encompasses both rational choice theory in political science and neo-realism in international relations theory. As we have seen, rationalists, often in the face of mounting criticism from neo-institutionalists and constructivists, continue to value parsimony, predictive power and the scientific assuredness both make possible.

Rationalists are positivists, committed not only to a unity of method between the natural and social sciences (*naturalism*), but to the idea that the natural sciences provide a model of good practice to which the social sciences should aspire. In short, they seek to model political analysis upon the natural sciences. However, as we shall see in more detail in the following chapter, there is more than one way to do this. Rationalists, rather like theoretical physicists, tend to privilege deduction over induction, proceeding on the basis of extremely pared-down and parsimonious theoretical assumptions (invariably relating to the narrow instrumental rationality of political actors or states cast in the image of unified political actors) to derive testable propositions. As in neo-classical economics, on whose assumptions rationalism tends to draw, the preferred mode of analysis is (mathematical) modelling (on rationalism's debt to neo-classical economics see Buchanen and Tullock 1962; Moe 1984; Tullock 1976). This certainly gives the impression of analytical rigour, as a quick glance at the pages of algebraic notation in any issue of the *American Political Science Review* or *International Studies Quarterly* will surely testify. Whether, in the end, pages of algebraic notation tell us anything that words cannot better convey, is an interesting – and understandably contentious – issue.[8] Whatever one's view, it is important to acknowledge that despite methodological and computational innovations, such modelling entails a significant simplification of the complexity of political life. It is manifestly impossible, computational advances notwithstanding, to render mathematically anything even vaguely approximating the rich complexity of social and political interaction. However impressive and seemingly complex the maths, then, rationalism must assume a world far more simple and predictable than our experiences would suggest.

Paul Pierson makes the point with characteristic clarity:

Since the rise of behaviouralism, many political scientists have had lofty aspirations about developing a science of politics, rooted in parsimony and generalisation and capable of great predictive power. Despite modest achievements over four decades, these aspirations remain. Setbacks are shrugged off with calls for more time or more sustained application of the proper methods, but the inability to generate powerful generalisations that facilitate prediction remains a puzzle. (2000: 266; see also Crick 1962)

In seeking to account for this troubling disparity between ambition and realisation, political scientists have been looking in the wrong place. Rather than focusing quizzically on their various attempts to put positivism into practice in political analysis, they would have been better advised to come to terms with the inherent complexity of political reality. The problem, as Pierson explains, 'lies in the character of the political world itself' (2000: 266). In short, 'reality' does not avail itself of the sort of parsimony on which rationalism is premised.

As the above discussion indicates, the role of theory for rationalists is the simplification of an external reality as a condition of the generation of predictive hypotheses. These are, at least in principle, capable of falsification. That having been said, the emphasis in rational choice theory and more formal variants of neo-realism tends to be on the deduction and derivation from initial assumptions of stylised models of political behaviour, rather than on the testing of the formal models thereby generated. As Melvin J. Hinich and Michael C. Munger explain in an influential text, 'formal theories help social scientists explore "what if?" questions by deducing the implications of a set of premises ... the particular "what if" implications derived from abstract theory may have little to do with the world of directly observable phenomena' (1997: 1, 4).

This is an important statement, for it suggests something of a tension, characteristic of much rational choice theory, between the practice of rationalism on the one hand and the positivism its exponents invariably espouse on the other. The tension becomes somewhat clearer if we compare the above extract with the following passage, a little later in the same volume:

> the external application, or 'testing', of formal theory is by *analogy*: the theory is tested by measuring relationships among observable phenomena, in the hope that the observable phenomena are 'like' the relationships the model focuses on. (1997: 5, emphasis in the original)

Well, which is it to be? Are rationalism's assumptions genuinely chosen for interest's sake as means to the end of conducting hypothetical thought experiments (along the lines, 'what if the world were like this?'). Or are they intended to provide approximations, however rough, of an external reality against which they might be evaluated? In the former case, the plausibility or implausibility of the assumptions is of no great consequence. For the purpose of the process of theoretical deduction is, presumably, to reveal the consequences of a world (unlike our own) in which the hypothecated assumptions *were* true. While this might make rationalism sound like a rather fanciful and indulgent pursuit, the value of such hypothetical reasoning should not be so easily dismissed. The positing of 'what if' questions can be extremely useful, having the potential to provide, for instance, timely and powerful warnings about the likely consequences of existing political trajectories. If it appears as though political parties increasingly appeal to the electorate in much the same way as corporations appeal to consumers, then it might be useful to model formally the consequences, say, within a two-party, first-past-the-post electoral system, of such a dynamic. The point, of course, would not be to seek to *explain* the conduct of the parties exhibiting such a logic, but rather to point to the positive and/or negative consequences of such a dynamic in the hope that it might either be encouraged or resisted. Such reflection might also draw attention to the conditions under which political parties come to exhibit this particular 'rationality'.[9]

Similarly, were we concerned about the seemingly growing power of capital with respect to the state under conditions of regional and/or global economic integration, we might usefully construct a formal model of an open and global economy in which capital is freely mobile. Though hypothetical, this might allow us to examine the potential implications of further doses of capital liberalisation. Again, the assumptions would be chosen not for their correspondence to the existing state of affairs but as a means of exploring potential futures. The purpose would be not so much to produce predictive hypotheses so much as *conditional predictions*. As in the case of the free mobility of capital, these might take the form of precautionary political warnings of the potential consequences of the untempered unfolding of existing dynamics, made at a point at which such logics might still be checked.

Sadly, however, little work in the rationalist tradition adopts this kind of rationale. Instead, speculative and implausible ('what if') assumptions are used as the basis from which to construct formal models of the polity or economy. Such models are then presented, and frequently accepted by policy-makers, as accurate representations of the systems they purport to reflect. The hypothetical nature of the initial assumptions is now forgotten, as open economy macroeconomic models are used to derive optimal taxation regimes (Tanzi and Schuknecht 1997; Tanzi and Zee 1997), as central banks are given independence on the basis of, frankly, fanciful assumptions about the 'rational expectations' of market actors (Lucas 1973; Kydland and Prescott 1977; Sargent 1986; Sargent and Wallace 1975), and as public bureaucracies are retrenched or marketised on the basis of equally implausible assumptions about the narrow self-interest of public bureaucrats (Buchanen 1977; Niskanen 1971, 1975; Tullock 1965).[10] While these remain the principal contributions of rationalism to the social sciences, its full potential has yet to be realised.

Behaviouralism and inductive theory

The basic principle of behaviouralism is succinctly captured by Steve Smith in the following maxim: 'let the facts, with some help and a receptive audience, speak for themselves' (1995: 7). If rationalism places its emphasis upon the elucidation and deduction from initial theoretical assumptions of hypotheses that are, in principle, testable, then behaviouralism adopts an altogether different logic, proceeding from observation through inductive generalisation to theory. Where rationalism places its emphasis upon the process of logical theoretical deduction, giving little or no sustained attention to the means by which theoretical propositions might be tested empirically, behaviouralism tends to take for granted the means by which theoretical propositions might be inferred from empirical evidence, while focusing considerable attention on the means by which reliable empirical evidence might be gathered in the first place. In short, what rationalism treats as intuitive and unproblematic – namely, the gathering of empirical evidence – behaviouralism problematises; what behaviouralism treats as intuitive and unproblematic – namely, the relationship between theory, inference and deduction – rationalism problematises. Accordingly, while behaviouralists tend to rely upon a simple logic of induction that many rationalists would regard as deeply suspect in its attempt to draw generalisable conclusions from specific observations, rationalists tend to rely upon a similarly simplistic, intuitive and often anecdotal appeal to empirical evidence which many behaviouralists would certainly see as no less problematic.

Shunning theory, certainly as a guide to the investigation of political reality, behaviouralism proceeds from the empirical evidence itself. The (acknowledged) role for theory in pure behaviouralism is, then, strictly limited. Empirical observations, though potentially capable of adjudicating between contending theoretical accounts, are, or at least should be, conducted in a matter that is entirely neutral with respect to such theories. Indeed, ideally, the analysts should be oblivious to all contending theoretical approaches at the point of observation. For the genuinely dispassionate assessment of empirical evidence relies upon, as it implies, the absence of *a priori* assumptions. Thus, as Martin Hollis and Steve Smith suggest,

> For behaviouralists, the path to theory started with what was observable, and strict behaviouralists held that there should be no nonobservable elements in the theory at all. The guiding light in the search for theory was the methods of the natural sciences (usually equated with physics), construed in strictly observational terms. The social sciences were conceived as a realm of enquiry to which the transfer of these methods was essentially unproblematic. Embarrassment at the

lack of results was brushed off by pointing out that the social sciences were new, and therefore could not be expected to achieve the theoretical power of the natural sciences straight away. (1990: 29b)

Two points might here be made. First, the analogy with physics, as we have already seen, is a poor one, with many theoretical physicists adopting a largely formal and deductive approach considerably at odds with behaviouralism's empiricism. If anything, it is the rather more empirical natural sciences, such as biology or genetics, that classic behaviouralism resembles. That having been said, an older tradition of experimental physics, epitomised by Newtonian mechanics, did exhibit a more inductive approach. Yet this perhaps only serves to draw attention to a second and more general point: the rather dated nature of pure behaviouralism. That the above extract is expressed in the past tense is by no means accidental. That was then, this is now. However influential it might have been in the 1950s and 1960s, especially in the USA, few pure behaviouralists remain today. Indeed, it is surely testimony to the severity of the critique that behaviouralism endured in the late 1960s and throughout the 1970s that those adopting an essentially inductive approach to political analysis today now invariably refer to themselves not even as 'neo-behaviouralists' but as 'post-behaviouralists' (see, for instance, Easton 1997; Sanders 1995: 64, 74–5). Nonetheless, as David Easton has recently remarked, contemporary political science is characterised by an increasing neo/post-behavioural content (1997). The same might also be said of international relations (for an excellent review see Vasquez 1996).

However qualified in recent years, behaviouralism's core assumptions are simply stated (Crick 1959; Dahl 1961a; Easton 1967: 16–17, 1979: 7, 1997: 14; Hayward 1999: 23; Sanders 1995; S. Smith 1996):

1. Social and political reality can be said to exist 'out there' and is directly accessible to scientific inquiry unencumbered by pre-existing beliefs
2. Political behaviour exhibits discoverable regularities and uniformities, such as might be captured in general 'covering' laws
3. The validity of any such covering laws can be established only by testing them by reference to the relevant political behaviour – all theoretical propositions must be testable
4. The means for acquiring and interpreting data poses a series of methodological challenges and cannot be taken for granted
5. Accuracy and precision in the recording of empirical evidence entails measurement and quantification

6. Ethical judgements and theoretical assumptions must not be allowed to inform, distort, or otherwise interfere with the systematic collation and recording of empirical evidence
7. Data collection, interpretation and explanation logically proceed, and should not be influenced by, concerns relating to the utilisation of the knowledge thereby acquired.

Many of these assumptions (especially 5–7) have been softened considerably since the high point of the 'behavioural revolution' in the 1960s. Indeed, most self-proclaimed post-behaviouralists would openly acknowledge the following qualifications:

8. Key variables may be difficult or impossible to quantify or gauge precisely
9. Normative agendas and theoretical assumptions inevitably play a part in influencing the choice of data to be analysed
10. In an age of restricted research funding the anticipated utility and application of research findings can and should inform the choice of research strategy (Easton 1997: 15–20; Sanders 1995: 64–8).

As a consequence, today's heirs to the behaviouralist inheritance would tend to see the quantitative methods with which they are principally associated not as a necessary condition of a science of the political so much as a potentially useful set of analytical techniques, among others, in the service of such a science. They are thus far more prepared than once they were to accept an academic division of labour within political analysis, rejecting, in so doing, the totalising vision of an integrated behavioural social science in favour of methodological pluralism.

Nonetheless, the basic behaviouralist rationale, as encapsulated in assumptions 1–4 above, remains essentially intact. Post-behaviouralists thus still retain a highly distinctive conception of theory in political analysis and one which is not so very different from that of their behaviouralist forebears. As much as possible, theory should not be allowed to interfere with or, worst still, *inform* empirical observation (as in constructivism and the new institutionalism). Rather, it is best seen as following naturally from empirical observation. Theory, for behaviouralists, is in a sense little more than a language for registering statistical correlations between observed variables – a repository, in short, of empirical generalisations. Theory provides a set of abstracted re-descriptions (couched in the form of empirically testable hypotheses) of the patterns exhibited in observed political data. As David Sanders usefully suggests, it acts as something of a short-hand, 'distancing the analyst from the potentially overwhelming detail of what can be directly

observed, so that abstract deductions can be made about the connec-
tions between different phenomena' (1995: 74).

In this way, as James C. Charlesworth notes, behaviouralists are

> at once modest and immodest . . . [T]hey do not pretend to know the
> origin and destiny of man [*sic*], but conclude that the only way to
> understand him is to observe him and record what he does in the
> courtroom, in the legislative hall, in the hustings. If enough records
> are kept we can predict after a while (on an actuarial basis) what he
> will do in the presence of recognised stimuli. Thus we can objectively
> and inductively discover *what* and *where* and *how* and *when*,
> although not *why*. (1967: 3, emphasis in the original)

This is an important point and brings us to the limitations of behaviouralism, about which we will have more to say presently and in later
chapters. Those limitations tend to derive from the fundamental (meta-
theoretical) assumptions which make behaviouralism possible, and
which behaviouralists tend not to acknowledge as theoretical (or meta-
theoretical) assumptions in the first place. Arguably this already problematises their central conviction that the analysis and interpretation of
empirical evidence should be conducted in a theoretical vacuum. As soon
as one acknowledges, as many post-behaviouralists now would, that to
presume a world in which appearance and reality are one and the same
(assumption 1) or in which social relations exhibit discoverable regularities and uniformities over time (assumption 2) is itself to make
(untestable) theoretical assumptions, behaviouralism's pristine empiricism is quickly tarnished.

While the first of these assumptions is, in the end, a matter of belief
(either reality presents itself to us as really it is, or it does not), the second
is arguably more of a matter of convenience. For while human behaviour does, undoubtedly, exhibit regularities over time, such regularities
are far from universal, varying both historically and culturally. Few
would now accept that what might be inferred inductively about political behaviour, say, from an analysis of voting behaviour in Britain before
the passing of the 1832 Reform Act would have much to say about
voting behaviour in the Czech Republic today. What allows behaviouralists to draw predictive inferences from the empirical evidence they
analyse is the convenient assumption that any regularities thereby
observed will continue to hold in the future – or, indeed, in other cultural contexts or institutional domains. Under certain conditions, that
may well be an appropriate assumption to make, but it effectively
silences behaviouralism's contribution to the analysis of political change.

Less fundamental, perhaps, but arguably no less significant in matters
of substantive political analysis, is behaviouralism's 'tendency to empha-

sise what can be easily measured rather than what might be theoretically important' (Sanders 1995: 65). We have already encountered a similar limitation of rationalism – namely the tendency to emphasise that which might easily be incorporated within a formal model, at the expense of that which might be more causally significant. Largely as a consequence of these mutually reinforcing tendencies in rationalism and behaviouralism a series of crucial issues, such as the role of ideas in processes of political causation (discussed in Chapter 6), have remained systematically unexplored. As a consequence, behaviouralists (and, indeed, rationalists) invariably overlook the significance of subjective and/or cultural factors in political processes. Often, as Walter Berns has persuasively argued, the most significant aspects of political 'reality' are invisible to the analyst only concerned to describe and catalogue or, worst still, to model an unfolding sequence of events. As he suggests in a revealing example, racial segregation

> is only seen by the observer because he [*sic*] can see the injustice of the practice . . . Through the 'eye of the mind' we are enabled to see the injustice and hence the political; with the eye alone we would see only men of dark skin sitting in the balconies of theatres marked 'coloured', or *not* sitting at Woolworth lunch counters. Out of the millions of so-called factual events that pass within the range of our vision, we could not single out these events except as they are seen by the eye of a mind that is not blinded by prejudice or a fallacious theoretical commitment. It is this commitment that accounts for political science books devoid of political content. (Cited in Sibley 1967: 55)

No less troubling, as Sanders again notes, is behaviouralism's 'tendency to concentrate on readily observed phenomena – such as voting – rather than the more subtle, and perhaps deeper, structural forces that promote stability and change in social and political systems' (1995: 66). Ironically, this leaves behaviouralists incapable of accounting for precisely the stability and regularity of the political world which they assume and on which their appeal to induction rests. The combination of such limiting factors serves perhaps to indicate why rationalism and behaviouralism have so frequently provided the point of departure for alternative approaches to political analysis. It is to two of these, the new institutionalism and constructivism, that we now turn.

New institutionalism, constructivism and theory as a heuristic device

While rationalism is relatively easily characterised in terms of its deductive and formal theory and behaviouralism in terms of its empiricist appeal to the logic of induction, the new institutionalism in political science and constructivism in international relations are rather more disparate schools of thought. In terms of their understanding of the nature of and role for theory they are characterised more by what they reject than what they embrace (Christiansen, Jørgensen and Wiener 2001: 4; Hall and Taylor 1996: 936; Hay and Wincott 1998; Peters 1999: 15–7; W. R. Scott 1995: 26). As such, they are united, more than anything else, by their opposition to behaviouralism and, if in a rather more uneven and somewhat lesser extent, rationalism.[11] While it is probably something of an exaggeration, then, there is surely some substance to Grant Jordon's suggestion that the new institutionalism has attracted the attention it has largely because the label signalled 'a disposition to oppose the political science mainstream' (1990: 482).[12] With a similar caveat the same might also be said of constructivism's opposition to the so-called 'neo-neo-synthesis' in international relations theory (Baldwin 1993; Kegley 1995; Lamy 2001; S. Smith 2001; Wæver 1996).

What is clear, however, is that proponents of the new institutionalism and constructivism are united in their resistance to purely deductive and purely inductive logics in political analysis. At the same time, both are broad churches in such matters, with so-called rational choice institutionalists and 'thin' constructivists like Wendt himself close to one end of the spectrum and historical and sociological institutionalists and more radical constructivists close to the other (for a perhaps overly stylised depiction see Figure 1.5).

When compared with more formal and purist variants of rationalism, rational choice institutionalism certainly tends to be more cautious in its specification of initial assumptions, seeking to capture theoretically something of the detail of the specific institutional contexts within which actors' 'rationality' is exercised.[13] This often precludes the sort of formal modelling otherwise characteristic of rationalism while encouraging a rather closer appeal to the empirical evidence. Thus, though by no means inductive in approach, rational choice institutionalism exhibits a *qualified* deductive logic. Similarly, though from the other end of spectrum, while historical and sociological institutionalists and radical constructivists tend to shun what they regard as the overly theoreticist abstraction of purely deductive models in favour of richer descriptive narratives (see, for instance Thelen and Steinmo 1992: 12), such narratives are invariably informed by abstract theoretical reflections and are thus far from purely inductive (see, especially, Skocpol 1979: 33–40, 1994: 322–3; cf. Burawoy 1989; Kiser and Hechter 1991).

Accordingly, historical institutionalists and constructivists in particular tend to view theory in rather different terms to behaviouralists and rationalists. Yes, theory is about simplifying a complex external reality,

Figure 1.5 *Inductive and deductive logics in the new
institutionalism and constructivism*

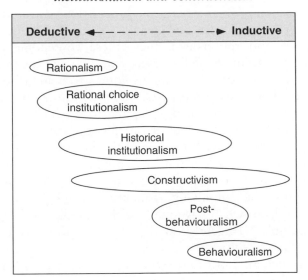

but not as a means of modelling it, nor of drawing predictive inferences
on the basis of observed regularities. Rather, theory is a guide to empirical exploration, a means of reflecting more or less abstractly upon
complex processes of institutional evolution and transformation in order
to highlight key periods or phases of change which warrant closer empirical scrutiny. Theory sensitises the analyst to the causal processes being
elucidated, selecting from the rich complexity of events the underlying
mechanisms and processes of change.

In this way, institutionalist and constructivist political analysis proceeds by way of a *dialogue* between theory and evidence as the analyst,
often painstakingly, pieces together a rich and *theoretically informed*
historical narrative. In preference to the more abstract and generic
explanations offered by rationalists and behaviouralists, such historical
narratives seeks to preserve and capture the complexity and specificity
of the process of change under consideration, examining the interplay
of actors, ideas and institutions and establishing the conditions of existence of the mechanisms of evolution and transformation described.
Institutionalists and contructivists thus resolutely refuse to foreclose or
prejudge discussion of the temporality of change by fitting to it a more
general covering law or model. Instead they pay particularly close attention to the specificity of sequence and timing in the precise context under
consideration (see, for instance, Campbell and Pedersen 2001b, 2001c;
Hay 2001b; P. Pierson 2000; Skowronek 1993, 1995).

The emphasis of such work tends to be upon the identification and tracing of causal processes over time and the theoretical elucidation of such processes – on *process-tracing* and *process-elucidation* (Katzenstein 1978; Krasner 1984; Thelen and Steinmo 1992: 21–2). In contrast to behaviouralism and rationalism, then, these contending approaches tend to value the accuracy and specificity of assumptions in a world of acknowledged complexity. They are also quick to emphasise the limitations of political analysis as a *predictive* science of the political (domestic, comparative or international), pointing to the inherent complexity and contingency (or open-endedness) of processes of change in which human subjects are involved. For them, the intrinsically unpredictable character of human behaviour renders a predictive science of the political impossible. Institutionalists and constructivists thus tend to target and problematise the simplifying assumptions employed in rationalism and behaviouralism which have made such a predictive science *appear* possible (see Table 1.10). Accordingly, they come to focus, theoretically and more substantively, on those areas of political analysis and inquiry closed off by such attempts to preserve a pristine and predictive science of the political.

Where behaviouralists simply assume a political universe characterised by the regularities which might render possible a predictive (albeit probabilistic) science of the political, institutionalists and constructivists prefer (ironically, perhaps) a more empirical approach which refuses to foreclose the issue theoretically. Thus, rather than take regularity as a given, they explore the conditions of existence of both regularities and of irregularities in political behaviour. As such they treat the issue of change and temporality (discussed further in Chapter 4) as an open empirical matter rather than one to be resolved on the basis of analytical convenience. Similarly, where rationalists assume the rationality of political actors blessed with perfect information in the pursuit of egoistic self-interest alone, institutionalists and constructivists adopt a more flexible and, again, empirical approach, acknowledging the open-ended nature of the process of strategic deliberation and the role of ideas is shaping the range of strategic options considered by actors. As Kathleen Thelen and Sven Steinmo explain,

> By taking the goals, strategies and preferences as something to be explained, historical institutionalists show that, unless something is known about the context, broad assumptions about 'self-interested behaviour' are empty . . . [H]istorical institutionalists would not have trouble with the . . . idea that political actors are acting strategically to achieve their ends. But clearly it is not very useful simply to leave it at that. We need a historically based analysis to tell us what they

Table 1.10 *Beyond rationalism and behaviouralism*

	Parsimonious assumptions of rationalism and behaviouralism	*New institutionalism and constructivism*	
		Theoretical stance	*Substantive concerns*
Regularity	Political world characterised by regularities	The question of regularity/irregularity is empirical and context-dependent	Elucidation of the mechanisms and temporality of institutional and behavioural change
Rationality	Rationality is universal – time and context-invariant	Rationality is culture-, context- and time-dependent; the relationship between rationality and exhibited behaviour is empirical	Elucidation of the process of strategic deliberation
Closure/ openness of political systems	Political systems are closed and predictable	Political systems are open and contingent	Analysis of the evolution and transformation of social and political systems
Causal role for ideas in political analysis?	Materialism: ideas have no independent causal efficacy	Ideas (knowledge, norms, convictions) influence political behaviour; they are irreducible to material factors	Elucidation of the mechanisms and temporality of ideational change and the role of ideas in institutional change

are trying to maximise and why they emphasise certain goals over others. (1992: 9)

Again, where both behaviouralists and rationalists assume that political systems are, like those examined in the natural sciences, closed and predictable, institutionalists and constructivists make no such assumption, acknowledging the contingency injected into political systems by political actors themselves. For them the limitations of a predictive science of politics reside not so much in the limitations of political scientists and scholars of international relations, but in the inherently contingent and indeterminant nature of our subject matter. In the search for a predictive science of politics we are bound to be disappointed because there is no predictive science of the political to be had.

Context and conduct: dealing with the 'problem' of agency

This brings us fairly directly to a quite fundamental issue which lies at the heart of this volume and which is explored at some length in the following chapters. It is what might here be termed the 'problem' of human agency. Arguably what renders the social sciences qualitatively different from the physical sciences is that the former must deal with conscious and reflective subjects, capable of acting differently under the same stimuli, whereas the units which comprise the latter can be assumed inanimate, unreflexive and hence entirely predictable in response to external stimuli. Agency injects an inherent indeterminacy and contingency into human affairs for which there is simply no analogy in the physical sciences (see also Bernstein *et al.* 2000).

In itself, there is probably nothing terribly contentious about this claim. Yet it has important implications, particularly for those keen to model the science of the political upon the natural sciences. For, if actors' behaviour is not given by the context in which they find themselves (in the same way that a particle's kinetic energy is given by the gravitational field within which it is situated) – indeed, if actors may refashion the context in which they find themselves and hence any regularities it may previously have given rise to – then what hope is there for a predictive science of the political? It is for precisely this reason that agency does indeed pose a 'problem' for aspiring political *scientists*.

The central contention of what is to follow, and a logical correlate of the above argument, is simply stated. If one is prepared to acknowledge that human agency does inject an inherent indeterminacy and contingency into all social systems, then this poses a fundamental and largely insurmountable problem for a predictive science of the political modelled upon the natural sciences.[14] If agency, and the indeterminacy that its acknowledgement implies, poses a fundamental problem for positivists (committed not only to a unity of method between the natural and social sciences but to the idea that the natural sciences provide that method), then it is interesting to note that it is a problem handled very differently by behaviouralists and rationalists. Consider each in turn.

Behaviouralism: aggregation as a 'solution' to the 'problem' of agency

In so far as behaviouralism deals with the problem of agency at all, it does so in the same way as whole animal biology (which also has to cope with, certainly, animate and, arguably, reflexive subjects). It does so by (statistical) *aggregation*. The logic here is relatively simple. While the behaviour of any single individual (fruit fly, gazelle or human) is likely to prove unpredictable, even in response to a common stimulus, analysis of a *population* of individuals will invariably throw up patterns of behaviour which can be detailed, described and catalogued. Thus, for instance, while the preferences of voters will vary from one to another, the distribution of voter preferences may well exhibit a consistent pattern which might be exposed to empirical analysis. Strictly speaking, then, for behaviouralists it is such exhibited regularities in the behaviour of political populations rather than political behaviour itself that forms the subject matter of political analysis. If one assumes, as behaviouralists invariably do, that such exhibited regularities are generalisable beyond the immediate context and time-frame within which they were observed, a probabilistic and predictive science of political behaviour is possible, after a fashion. The logic of such probabilistic prediction runs something like this:

1. Empirical observations in a particular context over a particular time-frame (or, more likely, at a particular instant) reveal a series of (statistically significant) correlations between the observed variables
2. Let us assume that such correlations are indeed generalisable beyond the context in which, and the time period over which, they were generated
3. On the basis of this assumption, we can infer that in another context over another period in time the same relationship between these variables will pertain
4. If the relationship holds, then we can predict the following . . .

What is clear from the above is that this is a science of the political in which there is no recognition of the role of agents as anything other than the carriers of behaviours which aggregate to form a particular pattern. It is, moreover, a mode of political analysis which, in its concern to map the relationship between variables often sampled at the same moment in time, finds it very difficult to differentiate between mere *correlation* and genuine *causation* (C. Marsh 1982: Chs 2, 4; Miller 1995: 168–79). Finally, while this type of probabilistic predictive inference may be valid under conditions of social and political stability, it is almost wholly incapable of dealing with periods of social and political upheaval and transformation. For in these, arguably the most interesting periods of political time, the assumption of regularity on which its inductive logic is premised is shattered, as agents depart from the 'rules' which had previously governed their behaviour and 'make history' (cf. Callinicos 1989).

Rationalism: taking the choice out of rational choice

If behaviouralism is characterised by the attempt to by-pass the question of agency through statistical aggregation, then rationalism responds to the challenge of agency in a very different and rather more direct fashion. As I shall argue at greater length and in more detail in the Chapter 3, rationalism is characteristically ingenious in its attempts to negotiate the indeterminacy that would otherwise be injected into its stylised modelling of rational choice by agency.

In this respect, above all, rational choice theory is not all that it might first appear. What, after all, could be better placed to deal with the 'problem' of agency than a perspective which emphasises the rationality exhibited by (presumably) conscious and reflective actors in the process of making choices? Is it any wonder that an author of the stature of David Easton should describe rational choice theory as the predominant post-behavioural response to 'behaviouralism's neglect of the actor' (1997: 20)? In one sense, he is right to do so, for rationalism probably does owe its ascendancy in those quarters of the discipline in which it is ascendant to its perceived ability to offer a solution to the problem of agency that behaviouralism left unresolved. Yet that solution, as I will argue, is almost entirely illusory and it is here that Easton surely gets it wrong.[15] The rational actor model, he suggests,

> gained sway because it inadvertently fit into the voluntarist tendencies of the countercultural sentiments of the time ... The image of the individual was subtly changed by rational modelling. He or she was not just a subject reacting to external circumstances but was proactive – choosing, selecting, rejecting in terms of his or her own preferences or utility-maximising behaviour. The focus shifted decisively from the structure or constraints surrounding behaviour ... to the actor and his or her strategies of choice in pursuit of individual volitions. (1997: 21–2)

The extent to which voluntarism (the view that individuals are essentially masters of their own destiny) chimed with the 'countercultural sentiments of the time' need not concern us here. The point is that, all appearances to the contrary and such sentiments notwithstanding, rationalism is in fact about as far from voluntarism as one can get. For, within any rationalist model, we know one thing above all: that the actor will behave rationally, maximising his or her personal utility. Moreover, we know that there is, by definition, only one optimal course of action by which the actor's personal utility might be maximised. It follows, logically, that *a rational actor in a given context will always choose precisely the same course of action.* So much for voluntarism. What this implies is that the agent's 'choice' (in fact the absence of choice) is rendered entirely predictable given the context. Accordingly, for rationalist models, context determines conduct, structure determines agency. While actors are free to choose, they will always choose the optimal strategy; consequently, their behaviour is entirely predictable. This is most clearly seen in neo- or *structural* realism (Waltz 1979), in which the rational conduct of states is considered derivable from the anarchic character of the international system.

It is in this way that rationalism deals with the problem of the contingency otherwise injected into social systems by agency. It does so simply by denying that agents exercise any meaningful choice at the moment of strategic deliberation. They have, if you like, a nominal choice between rationality and irrationality but, as rational actors, always opt for the former. This is an extremely ingenious and convenient, if perhaps rather disingenuous, solution to the problem of agency and one which does salvage a (natural) science of the political. Yet it does so only on the basis of denying the inherent indeterminacy of individual choice. It relies, in short and in the name of parsimony once again, on a convenient assumption that we know to be false: that individuals in a given context will always choose the same (rational) option. In so doing it translates what would otherwise be a moment of contingency and indeterminism (at least from the political analyst's point of view) into one of complete and absolute determinism.

Dealing with structure and agency: post-positivism

Behaviouralism and rationalism go to considerable pains to avoid having to acknowledge what, to the uninitiated, might appear entirely obvious: the ability of actors to transform both the environment and the laws governing the environment in which they find themselves. This may seem, at best, somewhat bizarre, at worst, wilfully perverse. However, as I have sought to demonstrate, for positivists in particular, there is much at stake in these issues. If they concede, or are forced to concede, the capacity of actors to influence the course of social and political change and hence the contingency of social and political systems, then they may also have to abandon any pretensions for a science of the political capable of generating testable (i.e. predictive) hypotheses. The best that might be hoped for is a more *retrospective* science of the political, capable of adjudicating between contending accounts of events that have already occurred. The limits of such a political science are wonderfully encapsulated in Jack Hayward's disarming aphorism, 'political scientists have the capacity to offer some hindsight, a little insight and almost no foresight' (1999: 34). This may indeed be all that we can legitimately aspire to as political analysts, a view now silently endorsed by many; but it is far less than rationalists and behaviouralists have traditionally projected for the discipline.

For self-professed post-positivists, however, it is not agency *per se* that poses the problem, but the relationship between structure and agency, conduct and context. For behaviouralists and rationalists, of course, the relationship between structure and agency is quite simple. As I have argued, behaviouralists are interested principally in the (structural) regularities exhibited in political behaviour; and for rationalists, agency is essentially reducible to the (structural) context in which it is exercised. For institutionalists, constructivists, critical theorists and other avowed post-positivists, however, things are more complex and involved. Indeed, arguably the central controversy of contemporary political analysis concerns the dynamic relationship between conduct and context, agents and structure. It is to a detailed examination of that relationship that we turn in Chapter 3.

The structure of the book

My aim in this chapter has been to introduce the theoretical perspectives which tend to characterise the mainstream within political science and international relations, pointing to the analytical choices, trade-offs and strategies on which they are premised.

In Chapter 2, we turn to two of the most frequently asked questions of political analysis – *should political analysis be scientific?* and *what does it mean to claim that it should?* – and two of the most infrequently asked questions – *should political analysis be political?* and *what is the nature of the 'political' that forms the subject matter of political analysis?* These questions, as we shall see, lie at the heart of the contemporary controversies that divide those engaged in the analysis of the political. It is important to deal with these issues first since we can say little about the techniques and strategies of political analysis and the claims that one might make for them, without first giving due attention to the nature of the 'political' and to the implications of according 'scientific' status to its analysis. My aim is to demonstrate the essentially contested nature both of the boundaries of 'politics' and the 'political' on the one hand, and the nature of 'scientific' enquiry on the other.

In Chapter 3 we turn to another crucial question that has consistently plagued political analysis and divided political analysts: that of the relationship between political actors and political institutions, between political conduct and political context, between structure and agency. Questions of structure and agency, however implicit, are implicated in all attempts to fashion notions of social and political causality. Accordingly, we can benefit greatly from seeking to render explicit the conceptions of structure and agency that we necessarily appeal to, thereby interrogating the notions of causality we formulate. The argument of this chapter also proceeds in two parts.

In the first, I demonstrate the pathologies of both *structuralism* (the tendency to reduce social and political outcomes to the operation of institutional or structural beyond the control of actors) and *intentionalism* (the tendency to account for observable effects in purely agential terms), before considering, in the second, a series of recent attempts to move beyond the unhelpful and polarising dualism of structure and agency. I demonstrate how such perspectives *might*, and indeed *have been*, used to inform discussions of social and political causality and complex institutional change.

This theme is developed further in Chapter 4. Despite Régis Debray's enticing comment that 'time is to politics what space is to geometry' (1973: 103), contemporary political analysis exhibits considerable difficulties in accounting for continuity and discontinuity and in reflecting theoretically the uneven temporality of political change. I argue that there are two principle reasons for this. First, the complexity and uneven temporality of political change can only be grasped if structuralist and intentionalist tendencies are first rejected and a more complex view of the relationship between structure and agency is set in their place. Second, positivist tendencies within political science prize predictive capacity, parsimony and the simplifying assumptions that this entails. The result has been to privilege simple, general and 'elegant' theoretical models that cannot deal adequately with complex political dynamics. For the simplifying assumptions upon which they draw, and by which their parsimony is achieved, tend to involve an understanding of context as static and unchanging. In the attempt to move beyond these limitations, I examine those contemporary developments in political analysis (associated, in particular, with the new institutionalism) that offer the potential for a more adequate understanding of political change, continuity and discontinuity.

In Chapter 5 I turn my attention to the highly contested concept of power, focusing on the Anglo-American discussion of the concept arising out of classical pluralism in the post-war period and the contrasting discussion of the term in continental Europe which follows the work of Michel Foucault. That political analysts remain divided by the common language of power is perhaps testimony to the centrality of the concept to political inquiry. For power is probably the most universal and fundamental concept of political analysis. It has been, and continues to be, the subject of extended and heated debate. I review the highly influential 'faces of power' controversy, examining the extent to which its various protagonists succeed in transcending the residues of behaviouralism that they inherit from classic pluralism. I advance a definition of power as 'context-shaping' and demonstrate how this helps us to disentangle the notions of power, responsibility and culpability that the faces of power debate conflates. In so doing, I suggest that we differentiate clearly between analytical questions concerning the identification of power within social and political contexts, and normative questions concerning the critique of the distribution and exercise of power thus identified.

In the final section of the chapter, I consider the challenge posed to orthodox accounts of power and to mainstream conceptions of political analysis more generally by the work of Michel Foucault. I examine critically his conception of power as ubiquitous and as manifest in a constant succession of 'power–knowledge regimes'. His argument, if accepted, has important implications for the practice of political inquiry, especially that which would claim to inform an emancipatory politics of resistance to relations of power and domination. Foucault's disarming and provocative perspective rejects the notion of a neutral vantage-point from which the relative merits of different power–knowledge regimes might be adjudicated, paving the way in so doing to the postmodernist position considered in Chapter 7.

In Chapter 6, attention switches from a concern with structure, agency and power to a consideration of the increasingly controversial question of the relationship between the material realm and the realm of ideas. In recent years this has emerged as an issue of crucial significance and much controversy in debates on the appropriate analytical techniques and strategies of political analysis. Like the question of structure and agency, however, there has been a certain tendency for political analysts to choose between one of two rather polarised positions on this question. These might be referred to as *materialism* and *idealism*. Materialists refuse to accord much significance to the role of ideas, insisting that notions of causality must be couched in material (normally institutional, political or economic) terms. Idealists, by contrast, argue that in so far as one can posit a notion of reality, that reality is itself the product of 'discursive construction'. Quite simply, there is no external or pre-discursive reality outside of our constructions and imaginings of it.

If we are to move beyond this stark opposition, constructivism and the new institutionalism have much to offer. Drawing on both perspectives, I argue that political actors inhabit complex and densely structured institutional environments that favour or privilege certain strategies over others. Yet such actors do not appropriate these contexts directly, blessed with a perfect knowledge of the contours of the terrain. Rather their ability and capacity to act strategically is mediated and filtered though perceptions (and indeed mis-perceptions) of the context they inhabit. These may either facilitate or militate against their ability to realise their intentions through strategic action. This basic schema allows a sophisticated analysis of institutional change over time that is sensitive both to the uneven temporality of political change (referred to in Chapter 4) and to the independent role of ideas in the mediation of political dynamics.

In Chapter 7 the focus turns eventually to the rather shadowy notion of postmodernism. My aim is to demonstrate that postmodernism represents perhaps the greatest single challenge to the strategies and techniques of political analysis (classical and contemporary, positivist and interpretivist alike). I present a guide to its key theorists and to its key claims – its incredulity towards 'metanarratives', its epistemological scepticism, its disavowal of critical theory, and its tendency towards relativism. I argue that despite its obvious and increasing appeal, postmodernism is but one way of answering the key questions dealt with in this volume that currently trouble and divide political analysts. Although it may provide an important corrective to the characteristic tendency of political analysts to assume a privileged vantage-point from which to accord their insights a scientific status, the relativism and political fatalism with which it is so often associated are not warranted. Political analysis after postmodernism is still possible.

In the Conclusion, I aim to draw together the disparate strands of the argument presented in the proceeding chapters, in presenting one interpretation of what political analysis after postmodernism might look like. Contemporary political analysis, it is argued, can no longer afford to privilege the political in explanations of political phenomenon; must be sensitive to the perils of structuralism and intentionalism, materialism and idealism; must give far greater consideration to the uneven temporality of political change and the importance of political ideas therein; and must take seriously the challenge presented by postmodernist critics, above all by acknowledging the value-laden and normative content of many of its assumptions. These ideas are illustrated with respect to a particularly significant, contentious and potent example: that of globalisation. I conclude then by demonstrating how the ideas discussed in previous chapters can be brought to bear on the question of the limits of the political (and of political autonomy in particular) in an era of much-vaunted globalisation.

Chapter 2

What's 'Political' About Political Science?

A *reflexive revolution* seems recently to have engulfed the discourse and discipline of political science on both sides of the Atlantic.[1] For the first time in a long time, political scientists and those no longer quite so happy to embrace the 'science' designation, debate the very nature of their subject matter and the claims they might legitimately make about it.

This debate is both descriptive and prescriptive. For, it refers not only to the practices and habits of political science as a discipline but also to the revisions to such disciplinary conventions that a sustained reflection on the nature of the 'political' and on the claims we might legitimately make about it suggests. In Europe, where this debate has perhaps been rather more explicit and long-running, controversy has tended to focus around the very definition of the legitimate terrain of political inquiry (see for instance Leftwich 1984a) and, more recently, the challenge posed to the political science and international relations mainstream by the distinctly post-positivist agendas of constructivism, critical realism, post-structuralism and postmodernism (for a flavour see Booth and Smith 1995; Hollis and Smith 1990b; Marsh and Stoker 1995). In recent years, however, the debate has been joined by the North American core of the discipline (see, for instance Almond 1990; Der Derian 1995; George 1994; Green and Shapiro 1994; Lapid and Kratochwil 1995; Wendt 1999).[2] Thus, American political scientists, just as much as their European counterparts, are currently embroiled in a host of fundamental debates, disputes and controversies over the discipline's legitimate concerns and what might be taken to constitute '"minimal professional competence" within the discipline' (Goodin and Klingemann 1996: 6).

This return to fundamentals has invariably been occasioned by one of three tendencies: (i) the rejection of the 'malestream' mainstream by feminist scholars (see, for instance, Hirschmann and Di Stefano 1996a); (ii) the challenge posed to the ascendancy of rational choice theory and behaviouralism in political science by neo-statist and neo-institutionalist perspectives (Evans, Rueschemeyer and Skocpol 1985; March and Olsen 1984, 1989; Skocpol 1979; Steinmo, Thekn and Longstreth 1992;

for a review see Hall and Taylor 1996); and (iii) that posed to neo-realism and neo-liberalism in international relations theory by both constructivism and more radically 'reflectivist' or postmodernist positions (see, for instance, Adler 1997; Ashley 1984; Campbell 1992; Kratochwil 1989; Onuf 1989; Ruggie 1998; S. Smith 2001; Tickner 1993; Walker 1993; Wendt 1992, 1999). This contestation of the mainstream has served to problematise a series of quite basic and fundamental issues on which the principal protagonists remain, and are likely to remain, divided and with which this volume is principally concerned. These include: (i) the nature of political power and the techniques appropriate to its analysis; (ii) the relationship between political conduct and political context (more conventionally, structure and agency); (iii) the respective significance of behavioural, institutional and ideational factors in political explanation; (iv) the relationship between the political world and the ideas held by political actors about that political world (more conventionally, the relationship between the material and the discursive); and (v) the nature of political time and the understanding of social and political change.

It is with two yet more fundamental issues, however, that I am principally concerned in this chapter. They relate to the nature of the 'political' that forms the focus of our analytical attentions (the 'political' question) and the status of the claims we might make about such a subject matter (the 'science' question). The former involves us in posing some quite basic questions about the nature of the political world itself – its essence (if it might be said to possess one), its boundaries and the constituent units out of which it is comprised. The latter is certainly no less significant, raising the question of what we have the potential to know about the (political) objects of our enquiry and the means by which we might come to realise that potential.

These are, arguably, the most two most basic questions of all for political analysts. For, what kind of discipline, we might ask, lacks a clear sense of its terrain of enquiry and the means appropriate to adjudicate contending accounts of what occurs within that domain? Yet, to point to the logical primacy of such issues is, of course, not to suggest that they have always been accorded the attention such a fundamental nature might warrant. Nor is it to suggest that they have been accorded equal attention.

Despite the paltry interest it has attracted over the years, of the two, the question of the nature and scope of the political is logically prior. For the degree of confidence that we might have in the knowledge we acquire of our subject matter (our answer to the 'science' question) depends, crucially, on what we choose that subject matter to be (our answer to the 'political' question). In short, the claims we might make of our subject matter are conditional upon the nature of that subject matter. It is, then, with the concept of the 'political' that we must begin.

Yet, before doing so, it is important to introduce the terminology in which such debates tend to be conducted.

Ontology and epistemology: the 'political question' and the 'science question'

From the outset it is important to puncture the veil of impenetrability which invariably accompanies the philosophy of the social sciences, the language of ontology, epistemology and methodology in particular. In the philosophy of the social sciences, what we have thus far termed the political question is referred to as an *ontological* issue; what we have thus far termed the science question is referred to as an *epistemological* issue. Both, as we shall see, have *methodological* implications.

It is in many respects unfortunate that what are, in fact, simple and intuitive ideas should be referred to in a language which is far from immediately transparent and accessible. Nonetheless, this is the language in which much political analytical debate is now conducted and it is important that we familiarise ourselves with it before we proceed.

Ontology, is, literally, the science or philosophy of being.[3] As a first step in the process of clarification, this may not seem like progress. Rather more illuminating is Norman Blaikie's definition. Ontology, he suggests, 'refers to the claims or assumptions that a particular approach to social [or, by extension, political] enquiry makes about the nature of social [or political] reality – claims about what exists, what it looks like, what units make it up and how these units interact with one another' (1993: 6). Ontology relates to *being*, to what *is*, to what *exists*. One's ontological position is, then, one's answer to the question: what is the nature of the social and political reality to be investigated? Alternatively, what exists that we might acquire knowledge of? However put, this is a rather significant question and one whose answer may determine, to a considerable extent, the content of the political analysis we are likely to engage in and, indeed, what we regard as an (adequate) political explanation. Thus, for 'ontological atomists', convinced in Hobbesian terms that 'basic human needs, capacities and motivations arise in each individual without regard to any specific feature of social groups or social interactions' (Fay 1996: 31), there can be no appeal in political explanation to social interactions, processes or structures. For 'ontological structuralists', by contrast, it is the appeal to human needs and capacities that is ruled inadmissible in the court of political analysis. Similarly, for those convinced of a separation of appearance and reality

– such that we cannot 'trust' our senses to reveal to us that which is real as distinct from that which merely presents itself to us *as if* it were real – political analysis is likely to be a more complex process than for those prepared to accept that reality presents itself to us in a direct and unmediated fashion.

A great variety of ontological questions can be posited. Adapting Uskali Mäki's thoughtful (and pioneering) reflections on economic ontology (2001: 3) to the political realm, we might suggest that all of the following are ontological questions:

> What is the polity made of? What are its constituents and how do they hang together? What kinds of general principles govern its functioning, and its change? Are they causal principles and, if so, what is the nature of political causation? What drives political actors and what mental capacities do they possess? Do individual preferences and social institutions exist, and in what sense? Are (and of) these things historically and culturally invariant universals, or are they relative to context?

Yet the ontological questions with which we will principally be concerned are the following:

- The relationship between structure and agency (the focus of Chapter 2)
- The extent of the causal and/or constitutive role of ideas in the determination of political outcomes (the focus of Chapter 6)
- The extent to which social and political systems exhibit organic (as opposed to atomistic) qualities (in which the product of social interaction is greater than the sum of its component parts)

and, most fundamentally of all;

- The extent (if any) of the separation of appearance and reality – the extent to which the social and political world presents itself to us as really it is such that what is real is observable.

The crucial point to note about each of these issues is that they cannot be resolved empirically. Ultimately, no amount of empirical evidence can refute the (ontological) claims of the ontological atomist or the ontological structuralist; neither can it confirm or reject the assumption that there is no separation of appearance and reality.[4]

Epistemology, again defined literally, is the science or philosophy of knowledge.[5] In Blaikie's terms, it refers 'to the claims or assumptions made about the ways in which it is possible to gain knowledge of reality' (1993: 6–7). In short, if the ontologist asks 'what exists to be known?', then the epistemologist asks 'what are the conditions of acquiring knowledge of that which exists?'. Epistemology concerns itself with such issues as the degree of certainty we might legitimately claim for the conclusions we are tempted to draw from our analyses, the extent to which specific knowledge claims might be generalised beyond the immediate context in which our observations were made and, in general terms, how we might adjudicate and defend a preference between contending political explanations.

Methodology relates to the choice of analytical strategy and research design which underpins substantive research. As Blaikie again helpfully explains, 'methodology is the analysis of how research should or does proceed' (1993: 7). Thus, although methodology establishes the principles which might guide the choice of method, it should not be confused with the methods and techniques of research themselves. Indeed, methodologists frequently draw the distinction between the two, emphasising the extent of the gulf between what they regard as established methodological principles and perhaps equally well-established methodological practices. For our purposes methodology is best understood as the means by which we reflect upon the methods appropriate to realise fully our potential to acquire knowledge of that which exists.

What this brief discussion hopefully serves to demonstrate is that ontology, epistemology and methodology, though closely related, are irreducible. Moreover, their relationship is directional in the sense that ontology logically precedes epistemology which logically precedes methodology.

To summarise, *ontology relates to the nature of the social and political world, epistemology to what we can know about it and methodology to how we might go about acquiring that knowledge.* The directional dependence of this relationship is summarised schematically in Figure 2.1.

To suggest that ontological consideration are both irreducible and logically prior to those of epistemology is not, however, to suggest that they are unrelated. The degree of confidence that we might have for the claims we make about political phenomena, for instance, is likely to be vary significantly depending on our view of the relationship between the ideas we formulate on the one hand and the political referents of those ideas on the other (the focus of Chapter 6). In this way, our ontology may shape our epistemology. If we are happy to conceive of ourselves as disinterested and dispassionate observers of an external (political) reality existing independently of our conceptions of it then we are likely to be rather more confident epistemologically than if we are prepared to concede that: (i) we are, at best, partisan participant observers; (ii) that there is no neutral vantage-point from which the political can be viewed

Figure 2.1   *Ontology, epistemology and methodology: a directional dependence*

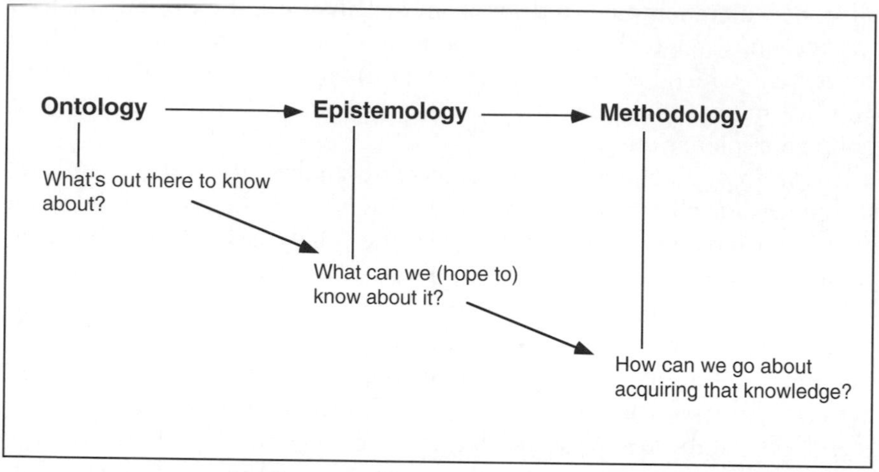

objectively; and that (iii) the ideas we fashion of the political context we inhabit influence our behaviour and hence the unfolding dynamic of that political context.[6] These are issues to which we return.

Second, the significance of ontological and epistemological questions for the practice and, indeed, the status of political science can scarcely be overstated. Chief among the ontological and epistemological concerns of this chapter are the nature of the political and the possibility of a science of the political. As their shorthand designation as the 'political question' and the 'science question' might imply, a political science without a ready answer to both – and hence without a clear sense of what there is to know and what might be known about it – scarcely warrants the label political science.

Moreover, if we put these two questions together we get the question of political science itself: *what is the nature and purpose of political science?* Posed in such a direct and stark a manner, this may well be a rather uncomfortable question to ask. For such a simple and obvious question surely demands an equally obvious and simple answer. In the absence of an intuitively appealing, instantaneous and collective response from the discipline, we might well be advised not to raise such issues, at least in public. But burying our heads in the sand is not a realistic option either, as we are increasingly called upon to justify our practices publicly. As Gerry Stoker notes, 'the case for setting out explicitly the core features of political science . . . has become increasingly compelling as the outside world increasingly demands evaluations of both its teaching and research' (1995: 1; cf. Goodin and Klingemann 1996). Whether that task is as simple as Stoker's disarming remark seems to imply is an interesting question, and one which will concern us presently. Suffice it for now to note that while we may well be able to agree on the questions that divide us, the 'core features of political science' remain as contested as ever. Indeed, arguably, they have become if anything rather more contested as an array of authors have felt the need to respond in recent years to the challenge here summarised by Stoker. In so far as the 'core' of the discipline might be identified, it remains remarkably elusive and hardly lends itself towards the type of unequivocal and unambiguous statement that Stoker's challenge would seem to require. While such a state of affairs persists, the best we can perhaps do is to acknowledge, with the appropriate twinge of embarrassment, that it is far easier to identify (and thereby justify) the purpose of a particular piece of political analysis than it is to make the more general case for political analysis which is not so much a distinct mode of enquiry as a collection of often mutually incompatible analytical strategies. For many, this is a deeply worrying and depressing state of affairs; for just as many others, however, it is a sign of theoretical vibrancy and intellectual pluralism (cf. Rule 1997).

Nonetheless, while generalised answers to such discomforting questions may be difficult to reach at least in any consensual fashion and while, for many, attempts to establish standards of 'minimal professional competence' within the 'discipline' are part of the problem and not the solution, there is much that can be gained from thinking aloud about such issues. Indeed, if the community of political scientists and political analysts is to establish in its own procedures the type of informed and democratic dialogue that it so frequently espouses for others (Dryzek 1990; Giddens 1994; cf. Cohen and Rogers 1995; Habermas 1993, 1996), it is precisely to such fundamental foundational and procedural questions that it must attend. While we will no doubt continue to be divided by our answers, it is important that we consider what we can and should legitimately expect of political analysts. Can we aspire to 'science' and, if so, what precisely does that aspiration entail? Is there a radical separation between the subject matter of the natural and the social 'sciences' which might qualify the extent to which social and political analysts can make 'scientific' claims? Are there costs of modelling the analysis of the political upon the natural sciences? And, if so, do they more than outweigh the benefits? Are the questions that *can* be answered objectively or scientifically the most interesting and compelling ones? These are the themes of this chapter. They serve as points of departure for the argument to follow.

Specifying and respecifying the political

Quite clearly, and despite the various claims made about the disciplinary nature of political science, there are no definitive nor for that matter even commonly accepted answers to such questions. The nature of political analysis is, like the focus of its attentions, profoundly value-laden, profoundly contested and above all profoundly political. It is, then, not that surprising that with few rare exceptions, political analysts have tended to shy away from the question of the nature of politics or of the political itself (for notable exceptions see, for instance, Arendt 1958; Crick 1962; Duverger 1964/6; Goodin and Klingemann 1996: 7–9; Lasswell 1936/50; Leftwich 1984a; Morgenthau 1948).[7] Thus, rather than justify, defend or even render explicit the conception of the political appealed to within political analysis, the tendency has been to proceed on the basis of an implicit and unquestioned conception of the legitimate terrain of political inquiry.

Where the concept of 'politics' or, more usefully perhaps, the 'political' has been rendered explicit this has remained very much on the margins of the discipline. It has usually taken the form of a challenge to the parochialism and formalism held to characterise a political science 'mainstream', in particular by feminist scholars (Benhabib 1996; Hirschmann and Di Stefano 1996a; see also Leftwich 1984a). Through a rather protracted and attritional process, such criticism has in recent years begun to scratch the surface of a previously tightly guarded and policed disciplinary core, facilitating the emergence of a more inter-disciplinary, even post-disciplinary analysis of the political – an integral part of a more integrated social science.

If the conception of the 'political' within political science has still to attract significant attention, the same is certainly not true of 'science'. It is no exaggeration to suggest that hundreds of books and thousands of articles have been written on the (more or less) scientific status of knowledge claims made within the social 'sciences', the imperative to be 'scientific' and, indeed, the very nature of 'science' itself.[8]

That the 'political' has given rise to a paltry smattering of interest while the 'scientific' has generated a remarkable profusion of literature, at least among more reflexive political analysts, might suggest that the two questions are in fact rather unrelated. Yet further reflection would suggest otherwise. For, by and large, those with the most narrow, re-strictive and formal conceptions of politics are the most attached to the label 'science' and most likely to acknowledge no qualitative differ-ence between the subject matters of the natural and social sciences (see Figure 2.2).

This suggests, again, a directional dependence between the epistemo-

Figure 2.2 *Alternative conceptions of the political in political analysis*

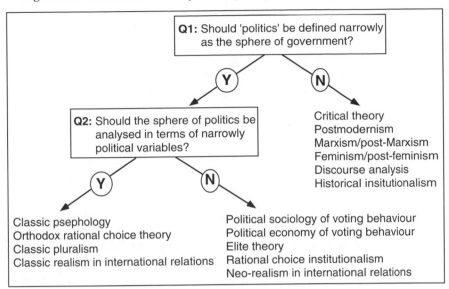

logical and the ontological. Yet we need to proceed with some caution here. Directional dependence there certainly is; but that directional dependence is not determinant. Ultimately one's epistemology is not reducible to one's ontology. What this means, in more practical terms, is that we should resist the temptation to jump too swiftly to the conclusion that whether one can conceive of the practice of political analysis as scientific or not is in turn ultimately dependent upon the conception of the political – a narrow conception of the political sustaining a claim to a scientific epistemology that a more inclusive conception might not. Nor, indeed, should we uncritically accept the converse – that a belief in the unity of method between the natural and social sciences (naturalism) necessitates a narrow specification of the political. There are at least two good reasons for this.

First, the consequences of so doing are to create a powerful temptation to sacrifice a more integral and inclusive conception of the political (such as that proposed by feminist critics of the mainstream) on the altar of the scientific imperative. Moreover, as we shall see, there may be good reasons for rejecting both *naturalism* (in Bhaskar's terms 'the thesis that there are or can be an essential unity of method between the natural and social sciences' (1989: 67)) and *positivism* (the view that the methods of the latter should be modelled on the former since the natural sciences provide a privileged, indeed the *only* access to neutrality and objectivity – in short, 'truth'). Accordingly, there is no reason to suggest that a more restrictive specification of the political will liberate us from the 'limits of naturalism' (Bhaskar 1979).

Whatever the reasons, then, for the characteristic affinity between a restrictive view of the political and a positivistic view of scientific method, they are not based on logical correspondence. More plausible, perhaps, is that they are bound up with a certain professionalisation of 'knowledge' (and the pursuit of knowledge) within the 'discipline' and the academy more generally. Here we might note the vested interest bound up in rigidly policing disciplinary boundaries and the rhetorical authority conjured in the 'scientific' claims that positivism might sustain. When we note, further, that a rigidly specified disciplinary core almost necessarily entails a narrow conception of the discipline's subject matter and that claims to positivism are only likely to be taken seriously if accompanied by the confident proclamation of naturalism, then the relationship between professionalisation and a narrowly political and rigidly scientific conception of the discipline would appear somewhat more than merely contingent. There may be obvious reasons for this. Put simply, if one wishes to preserve and defend a disciplinary core and to see that continuing resources are available for the analysis of its content, it is likely to prove instrumental to specify narrowly one's subject matter and to claim for its analysis scientific status.

In this context, it is surely telling to note that outside of the political science mainstream (or, as some would have it, the political science 'malestream'), the concept of the political is rarely held synonymous with the realm of formal government. Indeed, one might go so far as to suggest that it is *only* within the political science mainstream (and even here only in certain quarters) that such a narrow specification of the political retains many enthusiasts.

The tarnished authority of science?

In assessing the reasons for the contemporary reappraisal of the content and status of political analysis, one final factor is also relevant. Interestingly, and as a growing number of commentators have noted, 'science' is not quite all that it once was; its rhetorical authority tarnished somewhat in a society characterised, for many, by a proliferation of 'high-consequence risks' with which scientific 'progress' itself appears directly implicated.[9] Consequently, the softening of naturalist and positivist claims in recent years and the corresponding broadening of the concept of the political may reflect, as some have suggested, a certain re-evaluation of the utility to be gained by constructing political science in the image of its previously more esteemed big brother.[10] As an explanation for the re-evaluation of the scientific content of political analysis this would certainly appear more plausible than any more profound change of heart on the part of a discipline that has always been characterised, as much as by anything else, by its pragmatism.[11] What is clear is that, for the first time in a long time, the question of political science has become admissible again in the court of political analysis.

The nature of politics, the nature of the political

Although they can agree on little else, there is at least some unanimity within the discipline that political analysis is concerned essentially with the analysis of the processes and practices of politics.[12] Yet, as we shall soon see, this covers a multitude of differing perspectives, and a wide diversity of often mutually incompatible approaches to the political. Definitions of the legitimate terrain of political analysis range broadly, from 'politics is what the government does' at one end of the spectrum to 'the personal is the political' at the other. Thus political analysts differ widely over the relevance of extra-political factors (the economic, the social, the cultural) in political analysis. Some, for instance, insist that a political science worthy of the name must resolutely privilege the political (constructing political explanations of political phenomena) while others favour a more avowedly multi-dimensional approach (compare, for instance, Easton 1979; Keohane 1986; Moravcsik 1997, 1998; Morgenthau 1948; Waltz 1979; with Grofman 1997: 77–8; D. Marsh 1995; Vasquez 1998; Wendt 1999). And this, it should be noted, is to put to one side their equally diverging views on the nature of the political itself.[13]

In turning our attention to the scope and range of the political we can usefully distinguish between a series of closely related (if not quite interchangeable) conceptual dualisms often associated with the delimiting of the political (see also Hay and Marsh 1999a). These are summarised in Table 2.1.

For those who wish to delineate strictly the sphere of political inquiry, the focus of political analysis is generally specified by the first term of

Table 2.1 *Delimiting the Political*

Political	Extra-political
Public	Private
Governmental	Extra-governmental
State	Society

each conceptual pairing. Politics (big 'P') is concerned with the public sphere, the state and the sphere of governmental activity because politics (little 'p') occurs only in such arenas. From such a perspective, the personal is certainly not political – *by definition*. Moreover, with respect to all but the first dualism, the processes by which, say, trade unions select their leadership and formulate strategy are again not political – *by definition*. Such a focus, narrow as it is, has a certain obvious appeal in specifying precisely a subject matter.[14] Nonetheless, such a definition has serious and potentially rather disturbing consequences. To be fair, few authors have sought to defend such a rigidly formalistic understanding of the limits of the political. Nonetheless, analyses which confine themselves in practice to the narrowly political analysis of narrowly political variables abound.[15]

To begin with, it is important to note the deeply normative (and, in any lay sense of the term, 'political') content of this boundary question. This suggests an interesting comparison with other arenas in which the boundaries of the 'political' are contested. The call to restrict the realm of the political has become extremely familiar in recent years, occurring with increasing regularity in the rhetoric and practice of public policy reform since the 1980s. This raises an interesting question: is the populist cry to 'take the political out of' . . . sport, the economy, the domestic sphere, and so forth, so very different from the theoretical attempt to delimit tightly the political realm? Suffice it to note that party political attempts to circumscribe the scope of the political have in recent years tended to be associated with the neoliberal and libertarian right. They have been expressed in terms of the desire to restrict, or further restrict, the realm of government from the overbearing influence of a Leviathan, and in so doing to remove from public scrutiny and accountability an area of social regulation. It is no huge leap to suggest that there may be similar consequences of a restrictive *conceptual* definition of the political. For, if we are to conceive of political analysis as one means (albeit, one means among many) of exposing political practice to public scrutiny, then to restrict one's definition of the political to the juridico-political (that most narrowly and formally constitutive of the state) is to disavow the democratic privilege afforded political analysts.

Two points might here be made. First, to restrict the analysis of the political to that conventionally held to lie within the sphere of formal politics (that associated with the state, the Government and the process of government narrowly conceived) at a particular context at a particular moment in time is to exclude a consideration of the mechanisms, processes and, above all, struggles and conflicts by which the 'political' comes to be thus understood. It is, in short, to treat as immutable, given and *apolitical* our fluid and contested conceptions of the legitimate scope, scale and penetration of government and the state within the private sphere, civil society and the economy. It is to deprive the political analyst of the conceptual armoury to interrogate the processes by which the realm of the political is both specified and respecified. A political analysis that restricts its field of vision to that formally (and legally) codified as such is, in this respect, complicit in the exclusions which such a formal politics sustains. It is perhaps not merely a science *of* the state, but a science *for* the state. This, as we shall see in Chapter 5, is an argument frequently made of pluralist and neo-pluralist perspectives.

Beyond 'malestream' political analysis: the feminist challenge

This suggests a second parallel line of critique, associated in particular with contemporary feminist scholarship. Stated most simply, to insist that the political is synonymous with the public sphere is to exclude from political analysis the private arena within which much of women's oppression, subordination and, indeed, *resistance* occurs. It is, moreover, to dismiss as apolitical (or perhaps even *pre*-political)[16] all struggles, whether self-consciously political or not, on the part of women which do not manage to traverse the public–private divide. For it is only in so doing that they can thereby register themselves as 'political'. More fundamentally still, it is to exclude from consideration the processes by which the historical and contemporary confinement of women to a predominantly 'private' existence centred upon the family and domestic 'duty' have been sustained, reproduced and, increasingly, challenged (Elshtain 1981; Pateman 1989; Young 1987; for a useful review see Ackelsberg and Shanley 1996). It is, in the most profound way, to deny the possibility of a feminist political analysis.

Feminism, in its concern to interrogate the politics of women's subordination in all the contexts in which it occurs, thus constitutes a profound challenge to the traditional and conservative conception of the political that has tended to dominate malestream political science. Similarly, malestream political science constitutes a fundamental rejection of the very space from which a feminist political analysis might be constructed. In this context it is surely telling to note the response of some liberal political theorists to such attempts by feminists to reclaim for critical social inquiry more generally the concept of the political. This has been to misrepresent fundamentally feminists' call for a broadening of the definition of the political, by presenting it as an invitation for the state to encroach still further into the pristine and pre-political arena of privacy that they identify *beyond* 'the political'. In so doing they betray their own inability to think beyond their own narrow and formal conception of politics. For, to see politics beyond the realm of the public sphere, as feminists do, is not to invite a colonisation of the latter by the state. As Nancy Hirshmann and Christine Di Stefano note, 'feminism offers a radical challenge to the notion of politics itself and has instigated a redefinition of politics to include things that 'mainstream' theory considers completely non-political, such as the body and sexuality, the family and interpersonal relationships' (1996b: 6). This in no way constitutes an invitation to the state to engage in the formal political regulation of the body, sexuality, the family and interpersonal relationships. Such a reading is made all the more ridiculous when the characteristic antipathy of feminist theorists towards a *patriarchal* state, intimately associated with the subordination of women, is considered (for a variety of views on which, see Allen 1990; Brown 1992; M. Daly 1978; MacKinnon 1985; Pateman 1989).

Revisioning the political: from politics as arena to politics as process

It is one thing to dismiss the parochial, conservative and perhaps malestream definitions of the political that have tended to characterise traditional and contemporary mainstream political science alike; it is quite another to advance an alternative formulation of politics and the political. Yet feminist scholars, at least in recent years, have not shied away from this task of 'revisioning the political' (Hirschmann and Di Stefano 1996a). Nonetheless, in considering alternative and more inclusive conceptions of the political it would be wrong to give the impression that it is only feminists who have seen the need to reject a rigid legal/institutional definition of politics. As Iris Marion Young notes, it is not only women who are relegated to the realm of the private sphere (1990: 100–1). Consequently, it is not only feminists who sought to acknowledge the politics of the private sphere.

As Adrian Leftwich is surely right to note, 'the single most important factor involved in influencing the way people implicitly or explicitly conceive of politics is whether they define it primarily in terms of a *process*, or whether they define it in terms of the place or places where it happens, that is in terms of an *arena* or institutional forum' (1984b: 10, emphasis in the original). It is clear that for those who would restrict the realm of political inquiry to that of the state, the public sphere or government, politics (a term they prefer to the political) is an arena. Politics is the process of governing, an activity or a range of activities made meaningful, significant and worthy of investigation by virtue of the (formal) context in which it occurs. The same processes displaced, mirrored or reproduced in other institutional environments are not, by definitional fiat, political. As such, they remain the preserve of other disciplines. The feminist's concern with the patriarchal character of the institution of the nuclear family, for instance, whatever the merits of such a focus, simply lies beyond the realm of political inquiry thus conceived and has no place within such a political science.[17] This, by and large, is the approach adopted by the behaviouralist and rationalist core of the discipline.

By contrast, those for whom the political (a term they tend to prefer to politics) is ubiquitous, occurring (or at least having the potential to occur) in all social contexts in all societies at all points in their history, must clearly reject such a narrow definition of politics as an arena. Political inquiry, within such an alternative framework, is concerned with *process*; more specifically, with the (uneven) distribution of power, wealth and resources. As such it may occur in any institutional and social environment, however mundane, however parochial. As Leftwich again notes, politics thus conceived 'is at the heart of all collective social activity, formal and informal, public and private'. It may occur, 'in all human groups, institutions and societies' (1984c: 63).

Yet if this captures the spirit of the contemporary challenge to an institutionally rigid specification of the terrain of political inquiry, then it still leaves largely unanswered the question with which we began – *what is politics*? By now it should come as no great surprise that opinions vary as to its defining essence. Some emphasise violence, though not necessarily *physical* force, concentrating for instance on mechanisms of coercion, persuasion and what the French sociologist Pierre Bourdieu terms 'symbolic violence' by which the deployment of physical force is deferred.[18] Others emphasise distributional conflict over scarce resources (though one might argue that in the advanced capitalist North the issue is less one of scarce resources *per se* than of distribution so unequal as to render plentiful resources scarce in certain social locations). Still others emphasise the claim to legitimate authority or the conflict arising from the paucity of human judgement (Moodie 1984).

Yet the conception of the political which captures most fully the challenge posed by contemporary feminism and critical theory, and arguably the most inclusive, is that which conceives of politics as power and political inquiry as the identification and interrogation of the distribution, exercise and consequences of power. This position is well expressed by David Held and Adrian Leftwich,

> politics is about power; about the forces which influence and reflect its distribution and use; and about the effect of this on resource use

and distribution; it is about the 'transformatory capacity' of social agents, agencies and institutions; it is not about Government or government alone. (1984: 144)

Yet arguably even this merely displaces the problem. For politics is defined in terms of power; and power itself remains unspecified. Suffice it to say that there is no more contested concept in political analysis than that of power. As I shall argue in Chapter 5, political science is divided by a common language – that of power. Clearly, however, only certain conceptions of power are compatible with the spirit of Held and Leftwich's remarks. Indeed they allude to a specific conception of power in their tangential reference to Anthony Giddens' notion of power as 'transformatory capacity' (1981: Ch. 2). Such a conception might be further specified in the following terms.

> Power ... is about context-shaping, about the capacity of actors to redefine the parameters of what is socially, politically and economically possible for others. More formally we can define power ... as the ability of actors (whether individual or collective) to 'have an effect' upon the context which defines the range of possibilities of others. (Hay 1997a: 50)

Yet there is at least one obvious objection to such an integral and universal conception of politics. This is well articulated by Andrew Heywood, 'one danger of expanding "the political" to include all social institutions ... is that it comes close to defining everything as politics, thus rendering the term itself almost meaningless' (1994: 25–6). Though superficially attractive, this is, I think, to confuse and conflate a conception of *politics as an arena* on the one hand and *politics as a process* on the other. Were one to advance a conception of politics as a locus, site or institutional arena and then suggest that this arena were universal, Heywood's comments would be entirely appropriate. We would merely have emptied the term 'politics' of all content, effectively dispensing with the distinction between the political and the extra-political. Yet to suggest that politics *as process* has the potential to exist in all *social* locations, since all social relations can be characterised as relations of power (making them potential subjects of political inquiry), is neither to insist that we must see politics everywhere, nor that such social relations are exhausted by their description and analysis in political terms. It is to suggest that political analysis avails us of the opportunity to interrogate power relations in any social context without either suggesting that we could or should reduce our analysis to that. Nor is it to suggest that viewing specific social relations in terms of political categories (of power and domination, etc.) will necessarily further our inquiries. To suggest that all social relations have political dimensions is to open to scrutiny the power relations that pervade social institutions, without in any sense denying the economic and cultural processes with which they are articulated. Though all social relations may also be political relations, this does not imply that they are *only* political relations, nor that they can adequately be understood in such terms. It is useful – indeed, I would suggest essential – to be able to consider relations of domestic violence for instance as political relations. To suggest that they are exhausted by their description in such terms, however, would be to present an analysis that is both grossly distorting and wholly inadequate. The political is perhaps then best seen as an aspect or moment of the social, articulated with other moments (such as the economic or the cultural). Though politics may be everywhere, nothing is exhaustively political.

Science, politics and ethics

If there is much at stake in political scientists' attempts to specify the terrain of legitimate political inquiry, then there is certainly no less at stake in adjudicating the claims that political analysts might make of this subject matter. Yet, as noted above, while the former has prompted comparatively little explicit attention, the 'science question' has provoked almost incessant and intense controversy. Opinions again range widely. In so far as these can be arrayed along a spectrum – and it is to distort somewhat the complexity of the issues at hand to suggest that they can – this ranges from (i) those who would like to construct political science in the image of the 'hard' and value-neutral physical sciences, via (ii) those who deny the neutrality of the latter and wish to 'reclaim' a conception of 'science' liberated from the conceptual shackles of positivism and feigned value-neutrality, to (iii) those happy to leave the fundamentally tarnished concept of science to such natural scientists as would wish to embrace it while openly acknowledging the essentially normative and value-laden nature of social and political analysis and the ethical responsibilities this places upon the analyst. A number of issues are involved here which it is useful to unpack in terms of a series of key questions:

Q1 What does it mean to claim that a statement or theory is scientific? What is science?

Q2 Are scientific claims theory- and/or value-neutral?

Q3 Can there be an essential unity of method between the natural sciences and social/political inquiry (the basis of *naturalism*)?

Q4   Should social/political inquiry be modelled on the natural sciences (the basis of *positivism*, of which naturalism is a necessary but not in itself sufficient condition)?

Q5   Can social/political analysts afford to dispense with the rhetorically significant claim to scientific knowledge?

Q6   Are there privileged vantage points from which knowledge of the social and political world can be generated?

When cast in such terms, what is revealed is a complex, voluminous and multi-faceted debate (for excellent introductions to which see Benton and Craib 2001; Blaikie 1993; Bohman 1991; Delanty 1997; Fay 1996; Hollis 1994; Kincaid 1996; Kukla 2000; May and Williams 1998; M. Williams 2000). The following remarks may, as a consequence, only serve to scratch the service of that debate. My aim is not to provide an exhaustive survey but to indicate the nature of the issues at stake in such discussions.

Cartesianism and the Enlightenment

Let us begin, as it were, at the beginning with Descartes and the birth of the modern sciences in seventeenth-century Europe. The distinctiveness of Descartes' approach was its rigorous attempt, an attempt that would later come to characterise the Enlightenment more generally, to liberate reason and knowledge from the clutches of traditional clerical authority. From its inception, then, modern science was deeply associated with the secularisation of knowledge. As Martin Hollis notes, 'by removing the imprimatur of Reason from all traditional authorities and [by] giving it to every reflective individual with an open mind, Descartes laid the ground for a secular science, which would be neutral on questions of meaning and value' (1994: 16). That, at least, was his aim. There is no little irony in the fact that contemporary debate in the philosophy of science (whether natural or social) seems to have come full circle, returning to the question of whether there is any qualitative difference between the knowledge claims made in the name of science and those made in the name of religion (Feyerabend 1987; for commentaries see Chalmers 1986; Couvalis 1988, 1989, 1997: 111–39).

If knowledge and reason were to be prised from the clutches of a clerical elite, some basis from which to generate and ground alternatively premised knowledge claims had first to be established. The basis from which to construct such secular knowledge claims was sought in innate human characteristics. As Alan Chalmers explains,

Since it is human beings who produce and appraise knowledge in general and scientific knowledge in particular, to understand the ways in which knowledge can be appropriately acquired and appraised we must consider the nature of the individual humans who acquire and appraise it. (1990: 12)

He goes on to suggest that, for seventeenth-century philosophers of science, those relevant characteristics were 'the capacity of humans to reason and the capacity of humans to observe the world by way of the senses' (1990: 12).

This was to give rise to two rival traditions of scientific inquiry with *rationalists* emphasising reason and deduction, whilst *empiricists* placed their confidence in the dispassionate observation of an external reality.

Rationalism

Descartes was a rationalist, arguing for an approach premised on the development – through reflection, 'intellectual intuition' and, as he put it, the 'natural light of reason' – of general axioms from which might be derived an understanding of the underlying and unobservable structures which he believed constituted the 'reality' of the natural order. In so doing he appealed to the (ontological) distinction between appearance and reality, arguing that it was only by deploying the innate human capacities of reason and intuition that one could transcend the ephemeral world of surface appearance to reveal the structured reality beneath. This argument clearly mirrors that now frequently made by philosophical realists (for instance, Archer 1995; Bhaskar 1975, 1979, 1989; Delanty 1997: Ch. 6; Harré 1970; Harré and Madden 1975; Sayer 1992). The spirit of Descartes' rationalism is beautifully depicted in Bernard de Fontenelle's allegorical introduction to the new astronomy, *The Plurality of Worlds*, published in 1686. In this remarkable volume, the author sought to explain to an elite yet lay audience the operation of nature as revealed by (Cartesian) science and philosophy:

> Upon this I fancy to myself that Nature very much resembleth an Opera, where you stand, you do not see the stage as really it is; but it is plac'd with advantage, and all the Wheels and Movements are hid, to make the Representation the more agreeable. Nor do you trouble yourself how, or by what means the Machines are moved, though certainly an Engineer in the Pit is affected with what doth not touch you; he is pleas'd with the motion, and is demonstrating to himself on what it depends, and how it comes to pass. This Engineer then is like a Philosopher, though the difficulty is greater on the Philosopher's part, the Machines of the Theatre being nothing so curious as those of Nature, which disposeth her Wheels and Springs

so out of sight, that we have been long a-guessing at the movement of the Universe. (1686/1929, cited in Hollis 1994: 27)

There are problems with such a schema, enticing and elegant though it certainly is. For our access to reality (a reality, recall, not accessible from surface experience) comes only through logical deduction from axioms that we can never test and must simply assume as valid. These axioms are in turn the product of inspiration, one might even suggest divine inspiration. Is this so very different from seeking a religious sanction for knowledge claims?[19] The arbitrariness of so doing is clear, and surely flies in the face of Descartes' attempt to generate a secular foundation for objective knowledge.

Empiricism and the principle of induction

If rationalism placed its faith, so to speak, in the mind and the realm of reason, then empiricism came to privilege experience, assuming (conveniently) that there is no appearance–reality dichotomy and that the world presents itself to us in a direct, 'real' and unmediated way through our senses. In this way empiricism's deductive logic can be replaced with an inductive approach, proceeding from particular observations through inductive generalisation to general axioms or covering laws. These tend to take the form of observable correlations rather perhaps than explanations *per se*. This, as should now be clear, is the classical antecedent of modern-day behaviouralism. Behaviouralism is to seventeenth-century empiricism what rational choice theory is to Cartesian rationalism.

Yet such an approach is scarcely less arbitrary than its Cartesian counterpart, relying on two at best questionable and untestable assumptions: (i) that reality does indeed present itself to us in a direct and unmediated way (the very antithesis of the rationalists' starting point, it should be noted); and (ii) that what has been found true in known cases to date will also hold true in other cases where the same conditions pertain (the principle of induction). Accordingly, once the behaviour of a single apple falling from a tree has been observed and analysed so as to reveal the details of its motion and hence the 'laws' governing its descent, we can expect similar objects to behave in a manner consistent with those laws. This, at any rate, is the assumption which makes empiricism possible. Though not strictly untestable, this assumption is unverifiable. For how, other than observing each and every instance for which a covering law is formulated, does one verify the proposition that the covering law is correct?

Moreover, however plausible and intuitive such an assumption might seem in the realm of the physical sciences, it is far more problematic in a world populated by active, conscious and reflexive social subjects. We are back to the 'problem' of agency introduced in Chapter 1. For, once identified as general laws governing social behaviour, social scientific propositions enter public discourse. Once in this public domain they may lead actors to modify their behaviour, effectively changing the rules of the game. Thus, even something as mundane as identifying an inner-city area as a high crime zone may initiate a fresh and complex series of causal processes with important, if initially unpredictable, implications for the subsequent rate of crime in the area. Such effects may be entirely unintended. However, in many cases propositions in the social sciences are formulated with the explicit intention of disrupting the regularities on which they are based.

In this way, social and political analysts may come to play an active role in the reproduction and transformation of the very conduct that forms the focus of their attentions. There is simply no analogy in the natural sciences. Intentionality and reflexivity are complications which the natural sciences do not have to deal with; molecules do not modify their behaviour in the light of the claims scientists may make about it. This is an issue to which we will return in much greater detail in Chapters 6.

A further problem, alluded to in Chapter 1 and again above, might usefully be introduced at this point. It concerns the question of causality. At best, it seems, empiricism can establish observable correlations between events. Yet this is hardly sufficient to establish causation, on which any adequate conception of explanation must surely be founded (de Vaus 1991: 5; May 1997: 104). Ultimately, pure empiricism can establish no basis for adjudicating between relations of cause and effect on the one hand and mere coincidence on the other, save except for:

1. an appeal to other cases in which a similar sequence can be observed (a probabilistic approach), and
2. an appeal to arguments about the specific temporality of that sequence (causal factors must be chronologically prior to those they might explain).

As Martin Hollis notes, within an empiricist epistemology 'a cause is simply an instance of a regularity and a causal law or law of nature simply a regularity made up of instances . . . The cause of an event is thus a regular sequence which we have come to expect to hold' (1994: 48–9).

If accepted, this has important implications. For while an inductive and empiricist approach might supply us with potentially useful sets of correlations, an inherently interpretative and creative act of translation is still required to produce something recognisable as a causal explanation from such correlations.

The logic of positivist social inquiry

Despite such more or less fundamental problems, and the existence of a substantial literature charting them in infinitesimal detail, empiricism continues to dominate the natural sciences and certain sections of the social sciences. Within political science its clearest exponents are the behaviouralists who deny the existence of underlying mechanisms and structures not apparent to the immediate participants in social and political conduct, concentrate on the analysis of observable behaviour and insist that all explanation be subject to empirical testing (for an admirable summary, see Sanders 1995; see also Carmines and Huckfeldt 1996; King, Keohane and Verba 1994).

As argued in Chapter 1, however, modern-day behaviouralists tend to soften the rigid empiricism and purist logic of induction this would imply. Contemporary empiricism thus proceeds in the following manner. A confidence in the principle of induction allows general theoretical statements or law-like generalisations to be derived inductively from empirical regularities between observed phenomena. Yet in a departure from classic empiricism, suggesting a certain rapprochement with rationalism, the resulting body of theory may be used to generate, deductively, a series of hypotheses and predictions. These, in clear violation of the strictures of narrow empiricism, are inevitably theory-laden (Easton 1997; Sanders 1995). Such propositions and predictions are subsequently exposed to empirical testing, leading either to (partial) verification of the thesis (and the theory on which it is premised) or rejection and the consequent revision or replacement of the existing theory (this is depicted schematically in Figure 2.3).

This positivist approach to social inquiry has been exposed to a range of rather different critiques. These range from (i) those who would wish to tighten its purchase on the 'reality' it claims to reveal, to (ii) those who seek to demonstrate its fundamental and irredeemable contradictions, to (iii) those pointing to the 'limits of naturalism' who would merely wish to challenge the appropriateness of such a framework for the analysis of social phenomena, to (iv) those who would reject the very scientific label it seeks to systematise. It is to the challenge to positivism, both historical and contemporary, and the implications for the scientific content of political analysis that we now turn.

Figure 2.3 *The logic of positivist social and political analysis*

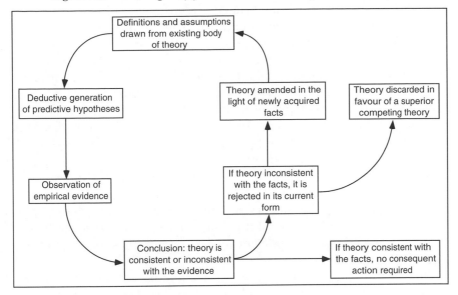

The retreat from positivism

Popper's positivist revisionism

When it comes to the epistemology of science, the influence of Karl Popper can hardly be overstated. Despite launching what amounts to a profound critique of the practice of traditional positivism, his contribution should certainly be seen as a *revision* rather than a rejection of positivism. As a devout believer in *naturalism* he has come to be championed by advocates of an empirical approach to both the natural and social sciences as the saviour of (an albeit qualified) positivism from its own internal contradictions and its many detractors.[20]

Popper's target is the principle of induction, conventionally held to distinguish science from pseudo-science and metaphysics. The scientific method, for classic positivists, is characterised by induction – the movement from observation and experiment to scientific law. It is this, its defenders suggest, that differentiates science from pseudo-science, science from speculation; and it is this that Popper rejects. There is, he suggests, no logical way of deducing general (far less universal) theories from particular statements. If there were, as classic positivists attest, then the weight of confirming empirical evidence would indeed provide an indication of the veracity (or truth-content) of a theoretical system. The consequence, that the theories of Marx, Adler and Freud (for which, he conceded, there was much confirming evidence) should be regarded as scientific, was so unpalatable to him that it led him to seek alternative and rather more discriminating means of differentiating science from pseudo-science. Popper's disdain for Marxism in particular, and the irritation it so obviously caused him that such a theory might be accorded the label 'scientific', is well captured in his comment that 'a Marxist could not open a newspaper without finding on every page confirming evidence for his [*sic*] interpretation of history' (Popper 1969: 35). This observation, and others like it for Freud, Adler and the like, led Popper to the conclusion that 'the criterion of the scientific status of a theory is its falsifiability, or refutability, or testability' (37). Marxism was not scientific since whatever was observed (be it *A*, the absence of *A*, or the opposite of *A*) could be adequately accounted for within the body of the theory after the fact.[21] In short, Marxism was pseudo-scientific not because it lacked confirming evidence but because it simply could not be refuted.

The basis of the argument is worth examining in just a little more detail. The principle of induction states that the more *A*s are found to be like *B*, the better confirmed is the hypothesis that *A*s are *B*s. Thus, if a hypothesis (*H*) implies an observation (*O*), and this anticipated observation is confirmed, then the hypothesis is verified (Box 2.1).

Box 2.1   The principle of induction

(1) $H \rightarrow O$
(2) O
∴ (3) H

Popper rejects this as an invalid inference. In its place, he proposes a logic of falsifiability (Box 2.2).

Box 2.2   The principle of falsification

(1) $H \rightarrow O$
(2) not O
∴ (3) not H

The process of empirical testing, Popper argues, should not proceed on the basis of seeking to establish verification for a hypothesis, since no amount of confirming evidence can warrant the claim that the hypothesis is correct. Rather, it should seek to eliminate false hypotheses, since a falsification is final. A statement can never be verified, but it can be exposed to rigorous and incessant testing. For Popper, then, scientific theory, at best, is composed of a set of provisional truth claims constantly in the process of being refuted. Truth is never absolute though falsification is. The genuine scientist is thus animated by what might at first appear a rather perverse and perplexing drive to falsify any plausible theoretical proposition she generates. For it is only by so doing that she can improve the state of our knowledge of the natural and social environment.

Popper's 'falsificationism' has proved phenomenally influential. It is probably fair to suggest that the majority of social and political scientists who regard themselves as positivists profess some variant of falsificationism (whether strictly Popperian or in its qualified, Lakatosian, guise).[22] Nonetheless, there are three obvious objections to the account Popper presents, a significant advance on classic positivism though it undoubtedly is.

The first is largely semantic and can be dealt with fairly swiftly. It constitutes a direct attack on Popper's claimed asymmetry between confirming and falsifying statements – the notion that we can never have enough confirming evidence to verify a thesis, but that one piece of evidence inconsistent with the thesis is terminal. The critics point out that this asymmetry is purely semantic. For, in Roberta Corvi's admirably succinct summary, 'whenever we falsify a statement we automatically verify its negation' (1997: 23). This may sound devastating for falsificationism, but an example quickly reveals that this elegant (if pedantic) criticism is somewhat less devastating than it might at first appear. Consider Popper's own illustration, the statement 'all swans are white'. If we falsify this statement by observing a black creature that we are prepared to concede is a swan, we are indeed verifying the statement's negation, the statement 'not all swans are white'.[23] The point is, however, that this latter statement cannot, in Popper's terms, be falsified, whereas it can be verified – the observation of one black swan will suffice. The asymmetry persists, even if our labelling of the statements which comprise it has to be reversed. The logic of Popper's argument, if not the precise terminology within which it is couched, remains essentially intact.

A second and ultimately far more fundamental criticism concerns the extent to which we can be certain about a statement or proposition's falsification. For Popper, let us recall, the moment of falsification is perhaps the only moment in the scientific process in which there is an unmistakable and decisive moment of clarity and revelation, the moment in which 'truth' speaks to science. Yet, as Martin Hollis explains, there cannot possibly be such a decisive moment unless we are sure that the same would always occur if the test were repeated. But that depends on an inductive inference from the present occasion to the next ... Deny the soundness of induction [as Popper does], and we have no reason to eliminate a theory just because its predictions have not been upheld on particular occasions. If Popper has indeed shown that induction is a myth, we cannot rest content with the logic of falsification. (1994: 76)

Popper, it seems, has been hoisted by his own petard. His response, that this may be true but that it does not invalidate the claimed asymmetry between basic and universal statements and the ability of the former – *if* true – to refute the latter, does not seem altogether adequate and concedes much ground (1985: 185). For it is to acknowledge, at pain of self-contradiction, that all claims, whether verifications or falsification, are provisional and probabilistic. It is, in short, to relativise the notion of scientific progress that Popper had sought to defend. For if, as Popper seems to concede, not even falsification may provide adequate grounds for adjudicating knowledge claims and knowledge claims are regularly adjudicated within both the natural and social sciences then science may well be a far more arbitrary, or at least norm-driven, mode of conduct than most positivists would be happy to acknowledge. For some then, far from rescuing positivism, Popper may well have buried it.[24]

A final objection, which merely shuffles further soil over the coffin of Popperian falsificationism and empiricism alike, concerns Popper's assumption that theories can be tested in the singular on which, arguably, the edifice of positivism hangs. The philosopher Quine in a remarkable essay, 'Two Dogmas of Empiricism', convincingly demonstrates that it is impossible to test single hypotheses in isolation from others (1953). As Harold Kincaid neatly puts it, 'hypotheses do not confront experience or evidence one by one' (1996: 20). Consider an example. When we observe evidence from an electron microscope inconsistent, say, with a widely accepted theory of the molecular composition of a given material, do we revise our theory of the way in which the electron microscope operates, our theory of the way in which the image in front of us is produced, or the theory of the molecular composition of the substance itself? Should we question the purity of the sample, the dedication of the technician who prepared it, or the physics and chemistry of the processes used in that preparation – or, indeed, should we put in a requisition for a new electron microscope? The truism that no scientific proposition can ever be tested in isolation from others presents considerable difficulties for the scientist diligently following Popper's prescriptions since she can never hope to identify and isolate precisely the guilty false theoretical proposition that her observations refute. Still further space is opened for the role of scientific norm and convention in dictating the course of scientific development, forcing a concession many would see as bringing Popper perilously close to abandoning any claim for science's privileged access to reality, truth and knowledge.

The limits of naturalism

Thus far our discussion has tended to assume that there is no sharp distinction to be drawn between the natural and social sciences and that common methodological standards can and should be brought to bear in each domain of scientific inquiry. This is the basic premise of naturalism, a position often associated with positivism, though by no means reducible to it. It does not, however, take much thought to reveal that the subject matter of the social and political sciences is in certain crucial respects qualitatively different from that of the natural sciences, for reasons already touched upon. In making this claim I follow Roy Bhaskar in arguing that 'it is the nature of the object that determines the form of its science . . . to investigate the limits of naturalism is *ipso facto* to investigate the conditions which make social science, whether or not it is actualised in practice, possible' (1989: 67–8).

Bhaskar, though ultimately a defender of a highly qualified and distinctly non-positivist naturalism, is nonetheless acutely aware that 'ontological, epistemological and relational considerations reveal differences that place limits on the possibility of naturalism, or rather qualify the form it must take in the social sciences' (1989: 67). In particular, he identifies three clear qualitative differences between the subject matter of the social and natural sciences which places limits on the possibility of methodological affinities between their respective 'sciences':

1. social structures, unlike natural structures, do not exist independently of the activities they govern
2. social structures, unlike natural structures, do not exist independently of the agents' conceptions of what they are doing in their activity
3. social structures, unlike natural structures, may be only relatively enduring (so that the tendencies they ground may not be universal in the sense of space–time-invariant) (Bhaskar 1989: 79).

Though Bhaskar suggests that even given these fundamental differences in subject matter, a qualified naturalism is still possible (and, as such, desirable), it is clear that such a naturalism simply cannot be grounded in positivism (however modified its inductivist logic).

   The limitations of positivism within the social sciences are revealed if we consider the evolution and transformation of a complex social system such as the global political economy. For it is in such systems, characterised as they are by incessant change that the (simplifying) assumptions used by positivists to generate scientific models, propositions and testable hypotheses about the social and political environment are rendered most problematic. The most basic assumption of the natural sciences – arguably the assumption that makes most if not all natural science possible (and a very good assumption at that) – is that the rules of the game do not change with time. The laws of physics, for instance, can be assumed to pertain in all situations – past, present or future. Each time an apple falls, its motion can be accounted for adequately (given a few starting conditions) by the application of Newtonian physics. Moreover, that just such an apple fell in just such a way to land on Newton's head can be assumed not to have changed the 'natural' and trans-historical laws of physics; but only our understanding of them.[25] Consequently, natural scientists never have to deal with the effects of their understandings on the very rules of the game that form the subject matter of those understandings.

   Sadly for those who study them (and thankfully for those who participate in them), neither assumption is valid for social and political systems. In so far as they can be identified, the rules of social and political life are themselves subject to constant reproduction, renewal and transformation. They are, one might suggest, culturally, spatially and historically specific. This is simply not the case for the laws of gravity,[26] or even, say, for Heisenberg's Uncertainty Principle which can both be assumed universal. Furthermore, in what Anthony Giddens rather cryptically refers to as the 'double hermeneutic' (1984: 374), the ideas that we all hold about the social and political world – whether as theorists, commentators or merely as social subjects – *are part of that world* and may profoundly shape it.[27] Thus, whereas 'theories in the natural sciences which have been replaced by others which do the job better are of no interest to the current practice of science . . . this cannot be the case [as in the social sciences] where those theories have helped to constitute what they interpret or explicate' (1984: xxxv).

   The nature of the 'economic' and the 'political' is different after Keynes and Marx in a way that the 'physical' and the 'natural' is not after Newton or Einstein.[28]

Conclusion: the limits of political science and the ethics of political analysis

The above remarks raise two crucial issues which many would see as compromising fundamentally the basis for a *science* of the social or political altogether – if, by science, we mean the ability to generate neutral, dispassionate and objective knowledge claims.

The first concerns the unavoidable location of the social or political analyst within the social and political environment that forms the subject of his or her analytical attentions. This, it is suggested, compromises the notion of the disinterested, dispassionate and above all *external* gaze of the analyst so central to the claim that science provides a privileged vantage-point and a direct access to knowledge of an external reality. The analyst, commentator, theorist, lay participant and scientist alike are all socially and politically embedded within a complex and densely structured institutional and cultural landscape which they cannot simply escape by climbing the ivory tower of academe to look down with scientific dispassion and disinterest on all they survey. On what basis then can the scientist claim a more privileged access to knowledge? On what basis should we adjudicate between the variety of mutually incompatible accounts generated by a variety of differentially located social participants (some of them claiming scientific licence for their propositions, others none)? Moreover, if the analyst can indeed legitimately claim no privileged access to reality, truth and knowledge, what implications does this have for the claims that the analyst does make about the social and political environment?

If an acknowledgement of the social embeddedness of the social or political analyst raises certain epistemological issues about the claims to knowledge that such a subject might make, then this should not allow us to overlook the ethical dilemmas that this recognition also throws up. Social and political commentators sensitive to the epistemological issues discussed above may choose not to claim a privileged vantage-point from which to adjudicate knowledge claims, but they do nonetheless inhabit a peculiarly privileged position in the potential shaping of (ideas about) the social and political context in which they write. For, as in the case of Keynes or Marx discussed above, social and political analysts (whether they claim a scientific pedigree for their ideas or not) may come to redefine perceptions of the politically desirable, the politically possible and the politically necessary, thereby altering – in some cases quite profoundly – the realm of the possible, the feasible and the desirable.

This brings us eventually to the crucial question of ethics and above all the ethical responsibilities of social and political analysts, a consideration of which the discourse of science tends to displace. There are perhaps three distinct ways of dealing with the closely related ethical and epistemological concerns dealt with in the proceeding paragraphs. The first and perhaps the easiest is simply to ignore them as, arguably, positivists have done for decades, hiding behind the comforting rhetoric of science, objectivity, neutrality and truth. Quite simply, if one refuses to acknowledge the normative content of social and political analysis then the question of ethical responsibility does not arise, save except for the ethical imperative to seek out and reveal 'the truth'. A second, and perhaps increasingly widespread response (associated in particular with relativism, post-structuralism, postmodernism and deconstruction) has been to acknowledge and indeed openly embrace the value- and theory-laden nature of all social and political inquiry. Such authors take extremely seriously the ethical responsibilities that this brings (particularly for those 'others' repeatedly marginalised, silenced and subjugated by the privileged voice of science). Their response is to deny both the possibility of generating social scientific knowledge and of grounding a critical theory capable of thinking that things might be different and of seeking to influence conceptions of the possible, the feasible and the desirable.

There is, however, a possible third way which avoids both the parochialism and self-assuredness of positivism's blindness to ethical considerations and the nihilism and fatalism frequently engendered by relativism (see Chapter 7). This is to insist that, like its subject matter, the analysis of social and political processes is itself inherently, irre-deemably and essentially political. Thus, as soon as we move from the realm of mere description to that of explanation we move from the realm of science to that of interpretation. In this realm there are no privileged vantage-points, merely the conflict between alternative and competing narratives premised on different ontological, ethical and normative assumptions. To take seriously the ethical responsibility that comes with an acknowledgement that epistemology cannot adjudicate political claims is then to insist on three things: (i) that political analysis remains essentially political and refuses to abandon its ability to think of a world different from our own simply because such claims cannot be adjudi-cated with ultimate certainty; (ii) that it seeks to acknowledge its neces-sarily normative content; and (iii) that it strives to render as explicit as possible the normative and ethical assumptions on which it is premised. It is perhaps only in the context of discussions within political analysis that to insist on this would be to insist on very much at all. Such an insistence, however, maps out the terrain of the critical political analy-sis I seek to defend in this volume.

Chapter 3

Beyond Structure versus Agency, Context versus Conduct

In Chapter 2 we dealt with what might be regarded as the two most fundamental questions of political analysis – how we define the 'political' and how we might adjudicate between contending accounts of what occurs within that domain. In this chapter we descend one rung on the ladder of conceptual abstraction to deal with a scarcely less significant issue – that of structure and agency (or context and conduct). Essentially, what we are concerned with here is the relationship between the political actors we identify (having decided upon our specification of the sphere of the political) and the environment in which they find themselves; in short, with the extent to which political conduct shapes and is shaped by political context. Clearly on such a fundamental issue as this we are likely to find a considerable variety of opinions. Some authors (notably pluralists and elite theorists) place their emphasis upon the capacity of decision-makers to shape the course of events. By contrast, other more structuralist authors (notably many institutionalists and neo-Marxists) emphasise instead the limited autonomy of the state's personnel and the extent to which they are constrained by the form, function and structure of the state itself.

Historically, such abstract issues as the relationship between actors and their environment have been thought the exclusive preserve of sociologists and philosophers. Yet, although for a long time silent on such questions, in recent years political scientists and, in particular, international relations theorists have felt the need to return to, to render explicit and to interrogate their own assumptions about structure and agency.[1] In so doing they have increasingly sought to acknowledge, problematise and revise the implicit sociologies and social theories underpinning conventional approaches to their respective spheres of inquiry. This move is nowhere more clearly stated that in the title of Alexander Wendt's seminal *Social Theory of International Politics* (1999). Even five years before its publication the idea that international relations needed, far less was necessarily premised upon, a social theory would have been unthinkable.

What is – and what is not – at stake in the structure–agency debate?

Given the sheer volume of literature devoted in recent years to the question of structure and agency in political science and international relations, it might be tempting to assume that the need for a series of reflections on this question is relatively undisputed. The reality, however, it somewhat different. For even in sociology, perhaps the natural home of the structure–agency question, there are dissenting voices. If we are, then, to make the case for the centrality of the relationship between structure and agency to political analysis it is perhaps appropriate that we first deal with the potential objections. Among the most vociferous of critics of the 'structure–agency craze', as he terms it, has been Steve Fuller. His central argument is simply stated:

> Given the supposedly abortive attempts at solving the structure–agency problem, one is tempted to conclude that sociologists are not smart enough to solve the problem or that the problem itself is spurious. (Fuller 1998: 104)

The case is certainly well made. If sociologists have spent 200 years on the issue and have got no further than Marx's truism that men make history, but not in circumstances of their own choosing, then either the question wasn't a very good one in the first place or sociologists have revealed themselves singularly incompetent in their attempts to answer it. Either way the reflections stimulated by pondering this great imponderable have hardly proved very constructive. Consequently, there would seem to be little to be gained by international relations theorists and political analysts in following their sociological forebears into this cul-de-sac of obfuscation and meaningless abstraction.

However tempting it may be to concur and to terminate the discussion at this point, Fuller's remarks are not quite as devastating as they might at first appear. For, in certain crucial respects, they reveal a systematic, if widespread, misinterpretation of the nature of the structure–agency debate itself. In this regard they prove quite useful in helping us establish what is – and what is not – at stake in the structure–agency debate (cf. Dessler 1989). Put most simply, the question of structure and agency is not a 'problem' to which there is, or can be, a definitive solution. Accordingly, the issue cannot be reduced to one of whether sociologists, political scientists or international relations theorists are smart enough to solve it.

Yet at this point it must be noted that if the very language of 'problem' and 'solution' is itself problematic, then it is precisely the language in which much of the debate is couched (see, for instance, Doty 1997;

Wendt 1987; Wight 1999). Let's consider why it is so problematic. To appeal to the issue of structure and agency as a 'problem' with a potential 'solution' or, indeed, 'solutions' – such that one could speak, in Fuller's terms, of progress towards a solution over time – is effectively to claim that the issue is an empirical one that can be resolved definitively. Yet, claims as to the relative significance of structural and agential factors are founded on ontological assumptions as to the nature of a social and political reality. To insist that such claims can be resolved by appeal to the evidence (as Fuller seems to suggest) is, then, to conflate the empirical and the ontological. To put this in more practical and prosaic terms, any given and agreed set of empirical observations can be accounted for in more or less agential, more or less structural terms. We might, for instance, agree on the precise chain of events leading up to the French Revolution of 1789 while disagreeing vehemently over the relative significance of structural and agential factors in the explanation of the event itself. As such, the relationship between structure and agency is not one that can be adjudicated empirically. It is, presumably, this which frustrates Fuller's desire for a solution after two hundred years of reflection and debate. *Structure–agency is not so much a problem as a language by which ontological differences between contending accounts might be registered.*

The language of structure and agency provides a convenient means of recording such ontological differences in a systematic and coherent manner. It should not be taken to imply an empirical schema for adjudicating contending ontological claims.

Two important implications follow directly from the above discussion. First, if the relative significance of structural and agential factors cannot be established empirically, then we must seek to avoid all claims which suggest that it might. Sadly, such claims are commonplace. Even Wendt himself, doyen of the 'structure–agency problematique' in international relations, is not above such conceptual confusions. Consider the following passage from an otherwise exemplary chapter co-written with Ian Shapiro:

> The differences among . . . 'realist' models of agency and structure – and among them and their individualist and holist rivals – are differences about where the important causal mechanisms lie in social life. As such, *we can settle them only by wrestling with the empirical merits of their claims about human agency and social structure . . . These are in substantial part empirical questions.* (Wendt and Shapiro 1997: 181, emphasis mine)

Wendt and Shapiro are surely right to note that ontological differences such as those between, say, more agency-centred and more structure-centred accounts, tend to resolve themselves into differences about where to look for and, indeed, what counts as, important causal mechanisms in the first place. This implies that ontology proceeds epistemology. Such a view is entirely consistent with the argument of Chapter 2 – we must decide what exists out there to know about (ontology) before we can consider how we might go about acquiring knowledge of it (epistemology). Yet having noted this, Wendt and Shapiro almost immediately abandon the logic it implies, suggesting that we might choose between contending ontologies on the basis of what we observe empirically. Surely this now implies that epistemology proceeds ontology. If our ontology informs where we look for causal mechanisms and what we see in the first place (as they contend), then how can we rely upon what we observe to adjudicate between contending ontologies?

Wendt and Shapiro's confusion is further compounded in the passage which immediately follows, in which a Popperian logic of falisifiability is invoked:

> The advocates of individualism, structuralism and structuration theory have all done a poor job of specifying the conditions under which their claims about the relationship of agency and social structure would be falsified. (Wendt and Shapiro 1997: 181)

Putting to one side the problems of Popperian falsificationalism dealt with in Chapter 2, here again we see direct appeal to the possibility of an epistemological refutation of ontological propositions. A similar conflation underpins Wendt's prescriptive suggestion that 'ontology talk is necessary, but we should also be looking for ways to translate it into propositions that might be adjudicated empirically' (1999: 37). If only this were possible. When, as Wendt himself notes, ontological sensitivities inform what is 'seen' in the first place and, for realists, provide the key to peering through the mists of the ephemeral and the superficial to the structured reality beneath, the idea that ontological claims as to what exists can be adjudicated empirically is rendered deeply suspect. Quite simply, perspectives on the question of structure and agency cannot be falsified – for they make no necessary empirical claim. It is for precisely this reason that logical positivists (like many Popper lans) reject as meaningless ontological claims such as those upon which realism and structuration theory are premised.

The danger of assuming an ultimate empirical court within which ontological claims might be adjudicated is revealed if we consider the ultra-structuralist theory of predestination. There is perhaps no more extreme position on the structure–agency spectrum than the theory of predestination – the view that all events, however mundane and ephemeral, represent the unfolding of a preordained, inexorable and immutable historical path. The point is that there is no empirical evidence capable of refuting such a theory. True, a proponent of predestination might falsely predict a particular political outcome, yet this would constitute not so much a refutation of predestination *per se* as of the theorist's access to its particular path. Similar points might be made of social ontologies usually considered more plausible, including Wendt's own 'thin' constructivism.

It is important, then, that we avoid claiming empirical licence for ontological claims and assumptions. Yet arguably more important still is that we resist the temptation to present positions on the structure–agency question as universal solutions for all social scientific dilemmas – whether ontological, epistemological or methodological. In particular, social ontologies cannot be brought in to resolve substantive empirical disputes. Giddens' structuration theory can no more tell me who will win the next US Presidential Election than the theory of predestination can tell me whether my train will be on time tomorrow. The latter might be able to tell me that the movements of trains is etched into the archaeology of historical time itself, just as the structuration theorist might tell me that the next US Presidential Election will be won and lost in the interaction between political actors and the context in which they find themselves. Neither is likely to be of much practical use to me, nor is it likely to provide much consolation if my train is late and my preferred candidate loses. It is important, then, that we do not expect too much from 'solutions' to the 'problem' of structure and agency.

Conceptualising structure and agency

Having established that while much is at stake in the agent–structure debate, not everything is at stake, we are now in a position to review more dispassionately the terms 'structure' and 'agency' themselves.

It is no exaggeration to suggest that the question of structure and agency has troubled, concerned and occupied the attentions of very many social scientists over the years. Yet, as noted above, it is only relatively recently that it has been taken up by political scientists and international relations scholars, as both disciplines have gone through more or less intensive processes of soul searching and have begun again to ask the big questions. Structure and agency is one of the biggest.

Put most simply, the question of structure and agency is about the explanation of social and political phenomena. It is about what is deemed to constitute a valid or adequate explanation of a political effect or outcome; about what adequate political explanation entails.

If we look at how political phenomena have traditionally been explained, we can differentiate relatively easily between two types of explanation: (i) those which appeal predominantly to what might be called *structural factors* on the one hand, and (ii) those which appeal principally to *agency* (or *agential*) *factors* on the other. If we are to do so, however, we must first define our terms.

Structure basically means context and refers to the setting within which social, political and economic events occur and acquire meaning. Yet by appealing to a notion of structure to describe context or setting, political scientists are implying something more. In particular, they are referring to the ordered nature of social and political relations – to the fact that political institutions, practices, routines and conventions appear to exhibit some regularity or *structure* over time. To appeal to the notion of structure to refer to political context may, then, not be to assume very much; but it is to assume that political behaviour tends to be ordered.

At this point it is important to note that to refer to political behaviour as ordered is not necessarily to imply that such behaviour is, consequently, predictable. Nonetheless, as we shall see, the greater the influence of structure, the more predictable political behaviour is assumed to be.

Here the analogy with the natural sciences is again informative. As suggested in Chapter 2, the most fundamental premise of the latter is that the physical world is ordered in such a way as to render outcomes predictable given a few initial conditions and knowledge of the structuring principles of the universe. The purpose of the natural sciences is to elucidate such universal and trans-historical governing axioms. Given knowledge of these and a set of initial conditions (for instance, the theory of gravity and the position and mass of an object to be dropped), the outcome is (assumed to be) predictable.[2] This is seldom the case – and seldom assumed to be the case (theories of predestination notwithstanding) – in the social sciences.[3] For although the social and political context is structured, it is not structured in this ultimately determinant sense. The reason for this, quite simply, is agency – a term which has no obvious analogue in the natural sciences.[4]

Agency refers to action, in our case to political *conduct*. It can de defined, simply, as the ability or capacity of an actor to act consciously and, in so doing, to attempt to realise his or her intentions. In the same way that the notion of structure is not an entirely neutral synonym for context, however, the notion of agency implies more than mere political action or conduct. In particular, it implies a sense of free will, choice or autonomy – that the actor could have behaved differently and that this choice between potential courses of action was, or at least could have been, subject to the actor's conscious deliberation.[5] In this sense, the term agency tends to be associated with a range of other concepts, notably reflexivity (the ability of the actor to monitor consciously and to reflect upon the consequences of previous action), rationality (the capacity of the actor to select modes of conduct best likely to realise a given set of preferences) and motivation (the desire and passion with which an actor approaches the attempt to realise a particular intention or preference).

Set up in this way, the concepts of structure and agency tend to be thought of as oppositional – the extent to which we appeal to agential factors in a particular explanation is the extent to which we regard structural factors as incidental and vice versa. As we shall see, however, this need not necessarily be the case. For now, however, it is important that we distinguish clearly between structural and agential explanations. An example might here prove instructive.

Consider the long-running controversy over the most effective means to reduce (or, more realistically, to stabilise) the rate of crime in contemporary societies. The controversy invariably crystallises itself into a dispute between, on the one hand, those advocating deterrent or retributive forms of punishment and those, on the other, advocating broadly redistributive or re-educative programmes and policies designed to alleviate social deprivation and/or to resocialise the criminal into society. In recent years, in countries as different in their political cultures as Britain and South Africa, the debate has tended to focus around the popular, if perhaps rather unhelpful, slogan 'tough on crime, tough on the causes of crime'.[6] Equally significant, however, was the comment, associated in Britain with John Major, that when it comes to crime, we should understand a little less and condemn a little more. Implicit within both of these aphorisms is the notion that those who choose to 'understand' crime by offering causes for it tend to attribute it to socio-economic factors which, in some sense, the individual bears subconsciously. This, it is suggested, implies a 'softness' on crime itself. By contrast, those who choose to 'understand rather less', preferring a more immediate and intuitive notion of causation, focus instead upon the direct responsibility and culpability of the criminal, thereby resisting the ('sociological') temptation to 'explain away' or dissolve notions of moral deviancy and individual guilt. For present purposes, suffice it to note that the former places the emphasis upon structural factors, the latter upon agential factors.

In sum, in most contexts a series of structural and agential factors can be identified. Structural factors emphasise the context within which political events, outcomes and effects occur – factors beyond the immediate control of the actors directly involved; whereas agential factors emphasise the conduct of the actors directly involved – implying that it is their behaviour, their conduct, their agency that is responsible for the effects and outcomes we observe and are interested in explaining. The specific blend of factors we choose to appeal to will reflect the analytical questions we pose of the contexts which interest us. But those questions should not be considered theoretically neutral. Those predisposed to structural explanations will tend to pose questions which lend themselves to the appeal to structural factors, just as those predisposed to more agential explanations will tend to frame their inquiries in such a way as to select for more agency-centred accounts.

Operationalising structure and agency: the rise of fascism in Germany in the 1930s

Having examined the terms 'structure' and 'agency' in some detail, it is instructive to turn, for a more detailed exposition, to a specific illustration.

Consider the rise of fascism in Germany in the 1930s. In this particular case, the contrast between structural and agential factors and associated explanations is stark. Consider first the structural or contextual factors appealed to in accounts of the rise of fascism in Germany in the 1930s (summarised in Table 3.1).

These fall, fairly clearly, into three categories, though they are by no means mutually exclusive. First, a number of accounts place considerable emphasise upon the immediate social and economic context, arguing that it was only under conditions such as those that Germany experienced in the 1930s that fascism could arise, and that this explains to a significant extent the appeal of Nazism at the time. Such explanations tend to appeal to the internal economic, social and political tensions and contradictions of the Weimar regime. Over time these condensed to precipitate a widespread sense of a state, economic and governmental crisis. This, in turn, predisposed the German population to a decisive rejection of the seemingly crisis-prone ruling ideas of the time and, in particular, to a dramatic and populist move to the right which sought to punish the failings of a now delegitimated liberal-left establishment. Note, however, that although such a form of explanation might account for a significant change in the political sensitivities of everyday Germans, facilitating fascist mobilisation, it cannot, in itself, explain the form that fascism would take, nor indeed the capacity of the fascists to appropriate strategically this 'political opportunity structure' (Jenson 1995). This is, then, in essence a structural explanation in that

Table 3.1 *Context and conduct, structure and agency in the
rise of fascism in Germany*

Explanations emphasising context/structure	*Explanations emphasising conduct/ agency*
1. Social and economic context: the internal contradictions of the Weimar regime and the widespread sense of a governing crisis made the German population highly susceptible to a decisive move to the right which sought to punish the failings of the liberal-left establishment	1. Hitler himself: the charismatic leadership of Hitler mobilised and duped the population into an anti-semitic and xenophobic fascist mobilisation
2. Cultural context: a pervasive, deep-seated and distinctly German tradition of anti-Semitism pathologically predisposed the German population to fascist mobilisation	2. Groundswell resistance to Weimar: in the political vacuum following the demise of Weimar and the failure of the Communists to seize the moment, fascist tendencies and groupings organised themselves with considerable strategic skill, thereby crystallising and mobilising a popular and populist groundswell of resistance capable, eventually, of seizing the state apparatus
3. Historical context: the lingering legacy of defeat in 1918 predisposed the German people to the promise of military and economic ascendancy offered by the Nazis	

the context is seen to condition, if not entirely determine, the outcome. Given the context, the outcome was likely if not perhaps inevitable. Modes of analysis like this seek to establish *the conditions under which* particular outcomes become possible, even probable. To derive any greater predictive capacity from them would be to assume that actors are little more than simple extensions of their environment. This is but a small step from the ultra-determinist philosophy of predestination.

A second set of authors emphasise not so much the historical specificity of post-Weimar Germany, so much as the distinctiveness, indeed uniqueness, of German culture over a rather more extended period of time. Thus a currently extremely fashionable account emphasises the context provided by German culture and, in particular, German anti-Semitism. This reading is associated in particular with Daniel Goldhagen's highly emotive and deeply controversial book, *Hitler's Willing Executioners* (1996) – a book which began life as a Harvard PhD thesis and which has subsequently won its author a succession of accolades, from the American Political Science Association's prestigious Gabriel A. Almond Prize in comparative politics to the *Blätter für deutsche und internationale Politik's* Democracy Prize (awarded last in 1990).

It is important to note, however, that Goldhagen's work is not a direct attempt to explain the rise of fascism in the 1930s. Rather, he seeks to establish the motivations underpinning the perpetration of the Holocaust, an act of unprecedented barbarism and 'a radical break with everything know in human history' (1996: 4). The perpetration of the Holocaust by Germans, he argues, 'marked their departure from the community of civilised people' (1996: 419). Goldhagen's thesis can be summarised as follows. Germany was, for some centuries prior to the Nazi years, permeated by a particularly radical and vicious brand of anti-Semitism whose ultimate historical aim was the elimination of the Jews. This 'viral' and increasingly virulent strain of anti-Semitism, 'resided ultimately in the heart of German political culture, in German society itself' (1996: 428). Indeed, by the end of the nineteenth century, 'eliminationist anti-Semitism' (23–4) had come to dominate the German political scene; the Nazi machine only translated this ideology into a reality. The Holocaust, then, must be seen not so much as the product of Nazism, but as the culmination of an eliminationist anti-Semitism which long pre-dated fascism and was actively embraced by 'ordinary Germans', willing executors of Hitler's will. They had no need of special orders, coercion or pressure because their (distinctly German) 'cognitive models' showed them that the Jewish people were 'ultimately fit only to suffer and die' (316).

In sum, for Goldhagen, a pervasive, deep-seated and distinctively German tradition of anti-Semitism made the German public peculiarly, indeed pathologically, inclined to fascist mobilisation. Goldhagen's book, as noted above, is by no means uncontroversial (see, *inter alia*, Birn 1997; Finkelstein 1997; Shandley 1998; Stern 1996; and, for responses, Goldhagen 1997, 1998). Nor, for that matter, is it unproblematic. One might, for instance, point to other pervasive traditions of anti-Semitism in European countries in which Fascism did not take hold, to subjects other than the Jewish people against which a similar barbarism was perpetrated and to the direct participation of non-German subjects in the prosecution of the Holocaust. Yet whether or not his thesis is accepted, one thing is clear: this is a quite unambiguously contextual or structural explanation. Fascism, for Goldhagen, was in the most fundamental sense an expression of a pervasive yet, until then, repressed or latent but ultimately 'eliminationist' anti-Semitism waiting to find an explicit political voice. Consequently, the cultural context was a necessary (though, again, not in itself sufficient) condition of fascism and, indeed, the Holocaust.

Given the controversy which has come to surround Goldhagen's book – a controversy which at one point threatened to spill over into the courts – it is perhaps important to pay just a little more attention to the argument itself. For in certain key respects the widely identified weaknesses in the text derive from confusions over the question of structure and agency. Goldhagen's ostensible purpose is entirely laudable. It is to restore the conscious human subject to the perpetration of the Holocaust – in short, to restore a notion of human agency to a set of atrocities for too long accounted for in (comfortingly) structural terms. The deep irony, then, is that the logic of his thesis in fact largely serves to absolve German subjects of culpability for an act of barbarism he regards as at least latent in an 'exceptional' and 'eliminationist' anti-Semitism that pre-dates the rise of Fascism. If Hitler's willing executioners were indeed products of their (German cultural) environment, we must assume they could not have acted differently. Accordingly, they cannot be held culpable or even accountable for their actions. If, on the other hand, they were conscious, reflexive strategic actors who could have behaved differently but chose instead to indulge themselves in an orgy of violence, then their German identity is of no conceivable relevance. Goldhagen seems to dissolve the notion of human agency and subjectivity upon which notions of moral responsibility and culpability must surely be premised. The problem, to be clear, is not so much Goldhagen's tacit structuralism, but his inconsistency on the question of structure and agency – his vacillation between, on the one hand, an essentially contextual explanation of the Holocaust and, on the other, one which would attribute responsibility directly to the actors immediately implicated (for a more detailed exposition, see Hay 2000b).

As Norman Finkelstein notes:

> If Goldhagen's thesis is correct . . . Germans bear no individual or, for that matter, collective guilt. After all, German culture was 'radically different' from ours. It shared none of our basic values. Killing Jews could accordingly be done in 'good conscience'. Germans perceived Jews the way we perceive roaches. They did not know better. They could not know better . . . Touted as a searing indictment of Germans, Goldhagen's thesis is, in fact, their perfect alibi. Who can condemn a 'crazy' people?. (1997: 44)

If Goldhagen does indeed provide an unwitting alibi for Hitler's willing accomplices, then it is nonetheless crucial to note that he resolutely resists the logic of Finkelstein's move. That move – to reconceptualise the perpetrators not as exceptional characters (though everyday Germans) but as entirely unexceptional modern subjects, people like ourselves – Goldhagen categorically rejects. This is unsurprising. For it is an extremely disturbing move to make and one not easily accomplished in a work dedicated as an act of remembrance. Yet, if we are to come to terms with the Holocaust, and to assess its consequences for contemporary societies, we must surely pose the disturbing question of the latent potential for atrocities like the Holocaust in modernity itself. As Finkelstein again notes, 'lurid as Goldhagen's account is, the lesson [it] finally teaches us is . . . remarkably complacent: normal people – and most people, after all, are normal – would not do such things' (1997: 86). This contrasts sharply with the view of Primo Levi (himself an Auschwitz survivor): 'we must remember [that] the diligent executors of inhuman orders were not born torturers, were not (with few exceptions) monsters: they were ordinary men [and women]' (1965: 214).

A third, and altogether less controversial, set of structural explanations for the rise of fascism appeals neither to the immediate context of Weimar, nor to what are regarded as the historical specificities of Germanic culture, but to the legacy of defeat in 1918. Here the humiliating terms of the peace settlement loom large. A pervasive sense of economic crisis and decline together with the continuing ignominy of defeat in 1918, it is argued, made the German public prone to the promise of military and economic recovery and global ascendancy offered by the Nazis.

Turning to the more familiar agential explanations (again, see Table 3.1), we find two prominent, if rather different accounts.

The first emphasises Hitler himself. For many authors, the rise of fascism in Germany in the 1930s is unimaginable and hence inexplicable without appeal to the character of Hitler. The contextual factors are incidental. The argument is elegant in its simplicity. Exceptional outcomes require exceptional explanations. Consequently, what Goldhagen attributes to the exceptional nature of German anti-Semitism, other authors trace instead to the exceptional personal attributes of Hitler. The latter's charismatic leadership, it is argued, is the decisive factor of the mobilisation of the German population behind a nationalist, anti-Semitic and xenophobic ideology. This is, as clear as you get, an agential explanation.

Other agency-centred explanations draw their analytical brushstrokes more broadly, also arguing that history is made by conscious actors, but now drawing attention to a more extensive cast. Here the emphasis is placed on popular resistance. In the political vacuum following the demise of Weimar and the subsequent failure of the Communists to seize the moment, fascist tendencies and groupings came to mobilise a popular and populist groundswell of resistance, eventually seizing the state apparatus.

While the focus of this latter explanation is still, essentially, agential, it is quite clear that significant appeal is here made to the context in which specific agential factors came to acquire significance. Timing and the precise sequencing of events, is here crucial. The window of opportunity for fascist mobilisation may well have been small (an assumption which could only be defended through more sustained contextual analysis). Nonetheless, what is distinctive about this form of analysis is that it places the emphasis not upon the 'political opportunity structure' itself so much as the capacity of strategic actors to seize the opportunity with which they were presented.

Interestingly, this suggests that rather different standards of explanation are invoked by different authors and, more significantly, that these might depend upon prior ontological sensitivities. Thus, those more predisposed to structural explanations may define their analytical and explanatory task as one of seeking to establish the conditions under which a particular set of events might arise, while those predisposed to a more agential account might regard their task as that of elucidating the strategies required to realise a set of preferences within a given set of conditions. What this also suggests is that structural and agential factors need not be seen as oppositional. Indeed, it suggests the potential utility of seeking to combine the analysis of structure and agency and of recognising the complex interplay between the two in any given situation. It is to attempts to do precisely this that we turn presently. For now, however, it is important that we establish in rather greater detail the limitations of overly structural and overly agential analyses.

Positions in the structure–agency debate

As noted in the introduction to this chapter, there has been something of a (re)discovery and (re)turn to the question of structure and agency in political analysis in recent years. This has been accompanied by a quite conscious and concerted attempt to move beyond the widely identified limitations of the structural and agential extremes to which social and political theories seemed inexorably drawn in the 1970s. In this sense, and this sense alone, the renewed concern with the relationship between structure and agency has been impressively consensual. Scholars in political science and international relations have rounded on both *structuralist* and *intentionalist* tendencies with one voice (see, for instance, Adler 1997; Carlsnaes 1992; Cerny 1990; Dessler 1989; Kenny and Smith 1997; M. J. Smith 1998, 1999; Suganami 1999; Wendt 1987 and, for a review, Hay 1995b). In so doing they have drawn extensively and quite explicitly upon a prior strand of sociological and social theoretical work (see, for instance, Alexander 1988, 1989, 1995; Archer

1989, 1995; Bhaskar 1979, 1989, 1994; Bourdieu 1977, 1984, 1991; Giddens 1979, 1984). If we are, then, to understand the contemporary debate, it is first crucial that we identify what has been seen so troublesome about structuralist and intentionalist perspectives.

It is perhaps appropriate that we begin with the private language in which such discussions have tended to be couched. Those positions and bodies of theory that consistently privilege structural or contextual factors are referred to as *structuralist*; those that consistently privilege agential factors as *intentionalist* or *voluntarist*. Consider each in turn.

Structuralism

Structuralism is the explanation of political effects, outcomes and events exclusively in terms of structural or contextual factors. By such a definition, few if any pure forms of structuralism persist. Nonetheless, the term is widely deployed to point to the marginalisation of actors and agency in social and political analysis. As I have elsewhere noted, used in such a way structuralism is little more than a term of abuse (Hay 1995b: 193). To adapt Terry Eagleton's characteristically memorable phrase, nobody would claim that their own thinking was structuralist, 'just as noone would habitually refer to themselves as Fatso'. Structuralism 'like halitosis is what the other person has' (1991: 2).

Yet despite the bad odour that the term now seems to convey, structuralist tendencies have by no means been totally excised from political science and international relations. Thus, although rarely explicitly identified and defended *as structuralist*, structuralism lives on in various forms of systems theory. Such approaches seek to account for regularities in observed patterns of political behaviour (for instance, the behaviour of states within an international system) by appeal to the operation of systemic logics (logics operating at the level of the system as a whole). In so far as these logics are seen to operate in some sense independently of – and over the heads of – the actors themselves, recourse is being made to a structuralist mode of argument. Within international relations theory, neo- or structural realism and world systems theory might both be regarded as systemic in this sense (on the former see Buzan, Jones and Little 1993; Waltz 1979: 38–59; Wendt 1999: 11–12; and, on the latter, Hopkins and Wallerstein 1980, 1983; Wallerstein 1974, 1980, 1989; for a useful critique, Hobden 1999).

Moreover, in a related if nonetheless distinct sense, the now familiar appeal to notions like globalisation itself frequently implies a form of structuralism. For, insofar as globalisation is seen to imply a developmental logic unfolding over time in a largely irreversible fashion, and in so far as such a logic is seen as circumscribing the parameters of what is possible politically and economically, the analysis is structuralist (for instance, Barnet and Cavanagh 1994; O'Brien 1992; Ohmae 1990, 1995; Teeple 1995). The same might be said more generally of all appeals to seemingly inexorable 'processes without subjects' (Hay 1999b; Hay and Marsh 2000; Wincott 2000) or, as Peter J. Taylor has it, '-isations' (2000).

Yet this by no means exhausts the prevalence of structuralist tendencies within contemporary political analysis. Structuralism lurks in the most unlikely places. For, as hinted at in Chapter 4, even the most ostensibly agency-centred accounts, such as rational choice theory, often rely upon an implicit and underlying structuralism. Thus, although the form of rational choice is clearly agent-centred in the emphasis it places upon individual choice, its form is nonetheless inherently structuralist.

The paradoxical structuralism of rational choice

This potentially paradoxical remark perhaps requires some explanation. The point is, in essence, a simple one. The most basic assumption upon which rational choice theory is premised is that individuals are egoistic and self-regarding utility-maximisers who behave rationally in pursuit of their preferences. Moreover, in most cases these actors are assumed to have perfect (or near-perfect) knowledge of the environment in which they find themselves. Additionally, in any particular situation there is only one rational course of action consistent with a specific preference set. Consequently, if the actor is indeed 'the very model of a modern individual' (Hollis 1998: 16), then she or he will behave in any given situation in a manner determined (and thereby rendered predictable) by the context itself.

The implications of this are clear. We need know nothing about the actor to predict the outcome of political behaviour. For it is independent of the actor in question. Indeed, it is precisely this which gives rationalist modes of explanation their (much cherished) predictive capacity.

While it may seem somewhat perverse to detect in rational choice theory a basic structuralism, this is by no means as contentious as it might at first seem. For one of its principal protagonists, George Tsebelis, notes precisely this paradox:

That the rational-choice approach is unconcerned with individuals seems paradoxical. The reason for this paradox is simple: individual action is assumed to be an optimal adaptation to an institutional environment, and the interaction between individuals is assumed to be an optimal response to one another. Therefore, the prevailing institutions (rules of the game) *determine* the behaviour of the actors, which in turn produces political or social outcomes. (1990: 4, emphasis mine)

Yet this is not just any form of structuralism. In one key respect it is a highly unusual form of structuralism. For whereas, conventionally, structuralism is associated with the claim that the actor is a prisoner of her environment, in rational choice theory (as the name would perhaps imply), the actor is deemed autonomous and free to choose – if only to choose the sole 'rational' option in any given context. It is this, in the end, that is the genuine paradox. Yet, it should be noted, it is in the conflation of choice and structural determination which this paradox implies that rational choice theory's particular appeal resides. For it allows rationalists to deal (ostensibly) with questions of choice and agency, which would normally entail some recognition of the indeterminacy of political outcomes, without ever having to concede the open-ended nature of political processes. In short, it allows a quasi-natural scientific notion of prediction to be retained despite the theoretical incorporation of human agency, for which there is no natural scientific analogue. In the end, however, this is a façade. For what sense does it make to speak of a rational actor's *choice* in a context which is assumed to provide only one rational option? This is rather reminiscent of Henry Ford's (no doubt apocryphal) comment about the Model T, 'you can have any colour you like, so long as it's black'.

This final observation raises a crucial issue, one we have thus far tiptoed cautiously around. Since there is no analogue of human agency in the natural sciences,[7] structuralism might be seen to have strong affinities with naturalism.[8] While structuralists have certainly not held a monopoly on claims to a naturalist mandate for their 'scientific' conclusions, there is surely some substance to this connection. For in systems theory, as in rationalist approaches, the social sciences most closely resemble their natural scientific role-models. If the utility of an aspirant science is to be judged in terms of its ability to formulate testable hypotheses (predictions), then structuralism may hold the key to such a scientific status. This is, of course, neither to suggest that the utility of social and political theories *should* be assessed in such terms, nor that there are not considerable difficulties in squeezing social scientific problems into analytical categories derived from the natural sciences. It is, however, to suggest that naturalism may only be credible to those prepared to dispense with the notion of agency – whether explicitly (as in systems theory) or (as in rational choice theory) by appeal to the fallacy of fully determined free choice. If warranted, this makes the clear reticence of contemporary social and political theorists to label themselves structuralist (Tsebelis' candour notwithstanding) somewhat surprising.

The structuralist tendencies of the new institutionalism

If rational choice theory is perhaps a rather unexpected, and largely unacknowledged, devotee of structuralism, then the same cannot be said of the new institutionalism. In a sense the new institutionalism's oft-remarked structuralism can be traced to its very origins as a response to and rejection of the society-centred or input-weighted theories which had come to dominate political science (especially in the USA) since the 'behavioural revolution'. Where these emphasised the decision-making capacity of actors to determine outcomes, the new institutionalism emphasised the mediating and constraining role of the institutional settings within which such outcomes were to be realised. The former's tendencies to intentionalism were almost directly mirrored in the corrective structuralism of the latter. Indeed, the term 'institutionalism' itself implies such a certain structuralism. For if institutions are structures then institutionalism is a form of structuralism.

In this way, the new institutionalism emphasises the ordering (or structuring) of social and political relations in and through the operation of institutions and institutional constraints. Such constraints operate in a variety of ways and might be summarised as follows:

1. The 'density' of the existing institutional fabric in any given social or political context renders established practices, processes and tendencies difficult to reform and steer (P. Pierson 2000)
2. Institutions are normalising in the sense that they tend to embody shared codes, rules and conventions, thereby imposing upon political subjects value-systems which may serve to constrain behaviour (Brinton and Nee 1998: Part I)
3. Institutions are also normalising in the sense that they may come to define logics of appropriate behaviour in a given institutional setting to which actors conform in anticipation of the sanctions or opprobrium to which non-compliance is likely to give rise (March and Olsen 1984, 1989)
4. Institutions serve to embody sets of ideas about that which is possible, feasible and desirable and the means, tools and techniques appropriate to realise a given set of policy goals (Hall 1989, 1993)
5. Institutional creation may be constrained by a reliance upon existing institutional templates (DiMaggio and Powell 1991).

In the emphasis it places on each of these mechanisms of institutional constraint, the new institutionalism might be regarded as structuralist. This structuralism, however, is somewhat softer and more flexible than that of rational choice theory and has been tempered somewhat since the initial attempts to 'bring the state back into' political analysis in the

1980s (for instance, Evans, Rueschemeyer and Skocpol 1985). Indeed, the question of the relationship between structure and agency has emerged as a key focus of analytical attention in recent years among historical institutionalists in particular (Hall and Taylor 1998; Thelen 1999; Thelen and Steinmo 1992: 7–9; see also Hay and Wincott 1998; Hay 2001b).

The notion of structure to which it appeals is also distinctive and worthy of comment. In all of the positions we have thus far considered structures are principally appealed to as material factors constraining behaviour. Yet institutionalism, like constructivism, draws attention to the *intersubjective* nature of structure and hence to the role of agents in the constitution of the very contexts within which their political conduct occurs and acquires significance. Even if the explanatory weight tends to be placed upon the structures thereby created, this already implies a rather more complex view of the relationship between structure and agency than we have thus far seen. This is nowhere more clear than in the appeal to institutions in political explanation. For institutions tend to be defined in terms of rules, norms and conventions (Hall 1986: 6; March and Olsen 1984, 1989). In so far as such rules and conventions are upheld without the resort to force, sanctions or other forms of direct imposition and constraint, such institutions are *intersubjective*. They emerge and evolve out of human behaviour. The new institutionalism, particularly in its more historical and sociological variants, thus tends to replace rational choice theory's 'logic of calculus' with a 'logic of appropriateness'.[9] Conduct is context-dependent not because it is rational, in pursuit of a given set of preferences, for actors to behave in a particular manner in a given context, but because it becomes habitual so to do. In this way, the parameters of the possible become confined through the emergence of (intersubjective) habits and norms and their reinforcement over time such that rituals become *normalised* (DiMaggio and Powell 1991). We behave the way we do because we have become habituated to behaving in particular ways in particular contexts and because it is difficult and potentially risky, as a consequence, to imagine ourselves behaving in any other way. Context-dependent norms of behaviour thus emerge to which, by and large, we conform out of habit and of our own volition. In essence, we become self-constraining, as we put on a jacket on a hot summer's day to go to a meeting or troop en masse to the canteen on the stroke of 1 p.m. when it might be rather more 'rational' to dress in keeping with the weather and to stagger our lunch breaks.

For institutionalists, then, it is unremarkable that policy-makers in a Keynesian treasury department or finance ministry will tend to confine themselves to thoughts and policy proposals consistent with that

Keynesian orthodoxy, even when a more utility-maximising course might be open to them (Hall 1989, 1993). While it might well be rational to consider and, arguably, to pursue different policy solutions, utility-maximisation has little or nothing to do with it. Until such time as an economic paradigm such as Keynesianism reveals itself incapable of throwing up 'solutions' to the policy dilemmas its implementation periodically generates – until, in short, its crisis is announced – it is likely to circumscribe the parameters of policy choice (Hay 2001).

It is in this emphasis upon institutions as constraining the parameters of political possibility that the new institutionalism's strengths and weaknesses lie. On the positive side, it is highly sensitive to the difficulties in bringing about significant institutional and programmatic change and to the irreversibility of paths once taken. Yet, on the negative side of the balance sheet, its ability to account for the degree of institutional change that is observed is rather limited. Precisely by virtue of the emphasis it places on processes of institutionalisation and normalisation, then, it is far better at accounting for institutional stability than it is institutional change.

Critiques of structuralism

That structuralism, like halitosis, is something the other theorist exhibits is testament to the barrage of critiques to which it has been exposed over the years.[10] Nonetheless, as we shall see, while there may be good reasons for exercising a preference for views of the structure–agency relationship other than structuralism, the conventional critiques are less than totally devastating. Moreover, they tend to be critiques of a rather more totalising and debilitating form of structuralism than that which characterises either rational choice theory or the new institutionalism. Four common challenges are worthy of particular attention.

The first is little more than an expression of exasperation. Structuralism here stands accused of a systematic failure to acknowledge the influence of actors (individual or collective) upon the course of political events. In the last instance, the detractors and critics argue, it is actors that make history. Without them nothing changes; without them there is nothing to explain. An account which argues that political subjects simply make no difference is, then, nonsensical.

We might well empathise with the sentiments expressed here. Yet that such a critique is somewhat less than devastating is not difficult to see. For, quite simply, this is a charge to which any genuine structuralist could quite happily plead guilty. Structuralism fails to acknowledge the influence of actors upon events because, for structuralists, almost by definition, actors have no (independent causal) influence upon events. Agency is merely a medium through which structural logics unfold over time. To this there is simply no response, save to reiterate the alternate view. This is less a critique of structuralism than a tracing of its logical implications.

A second, related, criticism takes us a little further. Here it is suggested that structuralism presents the depressing image of a world populated by mere automatons whose behaviour is entirely predictable given the context in which they find themselves. Human subjects, in such a schema, are little more than functional relays for processes which are beyond their control, influence or comprehension. Exasperating though this may be for the critic (who fails to recognise this as a description of her experience), the critique does not stop here. Rather it seeks to trace the implications of such an assertion. In particular, it is noted, such an essentially hollow conception of human subjectivity is incapable of recognising any difference between, say, a fascist dictatorship whose ether might be penetrated to a considerable extent by processes of ideological indoctrination and social control and a liberal democracy in which the subject might be regarded as enjoying a rather greater degree of autonomy.

Two points might here be noted. First, this may indeed be a logical implication of the ultra-structuralist position. On such a reading there is nothing (or precious little) to choose between a fascist dictatorship and a liberal democracy in terms of the autonomy they accord the subject. Note, however, that this is only a problem for those who suggest that there is – those who hold out the prospect of actors reclaiming their freedom from the structural prison house they currently inhabit. For a genuine structuralist, neither condition is likely to be satisfied. Consequently, while this line of critique may again draw out the implications of an ultra-structuralism and might, as such, motivate a normative rejection of structuralism it, too, is less than totally devastating.

Relatedly, structuralism stands accused of (often unwittingly) promoting fatalism and passivity. For if the course of human history is ultimately pre-destined and pre-determined, then it makes no difference what we (as mere agents) do. Consequently, we might as well sit back and wait for the inevitable unfolding of history's inner logic. The irony, of course, is that by so doing the anticipated future might be put on permanent hold. If the transition from capitalism is inevitable, then there is no need to devote ourselves to the promotion of a revolution whose form, function and (perhaps) date is etched into the archaeology of historical time. A confidence in historical teleology[11] simply leaves no room for political intervention. Here again, the only problem is one of consistency. In so far as authors who espouse a teleological view of history subscribe also to a notion of transformative political agency, they are committing a logical fallacy. This is not likely to be a problem for pure structuralists, however dull their political lives, as a consequence, might be.

Finally, and perhaps of rather greater significance, many authors suggest that there is a fundamental contradiction at the heart of the structuralist position. It is simply stated. If the structuralist view were indeed valid, could structuralism ever be expressed? Put differently, if we are indeed all simply expressions of the structures we bear, how could we hope to know? How, in particular, is it that structuralist scholars, by climbing to a high perch in the ivory tower, can seemingly gain a vantage point from which to observe the structures which constrain the rest of us? In the end structuralism seems to rely on a patronising distinction between the 'enlightened' theorist and the rest of us which is logically inconsistent. This is a point to which we return in discussing Steven Lukes' 'three-dimensional' conception of power in Chapter 5.

This final line of critique does rather more damage to the structuralist position than the others combined. Once again, it points to a problem of inconsistency. If, as for purist structuralists, human subjects are products of their environment to the extent to which the ideas they hold are not their own but those they imbibe from the context in which they find themselves (as, for instance, in Althusser 1971), then what capacity does this give the structuralist to analyse the process? In short, unless the structuralist ideology critic is accorded rather greater autonomy, agency and insight than the rest of us (a proposition inconsistent with a structuralist ontology), then we should surely dismiss her theories as the product of a consciousness no less distorted than our own. What this suggests, in the end, is the difficulties of a pure and logically consistent structuralism. Note, however, that this is not the basis for a refutation of structuralism *per se* – merely particular forms of structuralism (those which imply a privileged position for the critic). The structuralist ontology may well be 'correct'. But, we can only hope that it is not. For if it is, there is precious little than we can hope to say about the environment in which we find ourselves.

Intentionalism

While the exasperation which the above critiques express has tended to put pay to the open declaration and defence of structuralism, its antithesis – intentionalism (or voluntarism) – has survived the years rather better.

The term 'intentionalism' itself implies that actors are able to realise their intentions. Accordingly, we can explain political outcomes simply by referring to the intentions of the actors directly implicated. Intentionalists tend to view the social and political world from the perspective of the participants in social and political processes, climbing down from their high perch in the ivory tower to adopt a position somewhat closer to the action. Like structuralism, intentionalism presents a simple view of the relationship between structure and agency. For, in the same way that pure structuralism effectively dispenses with agency, so pure intentionalism disavows notions of structure.

The concepts of structure, constraint and context are, then, largely absent from such accounts. Instead, intentionalists tend to take issues of social and political interaction at face value, 'constructing explanations out of the direct intentions, motivations and self-understandings of the actors involved and using explanatory concepts which the actors themselves might use to account for their actions' (Hay 1995b: 195). The world, it is argued, presents itself to us as really it is and should, consequently, be conceptualised in such terms. There is no need to import complex theoretical abstractions such as those associated with more structuralist analytical strategies.

The result is a form of analysis which tends to be highly descriptive. It is rich on detail; low on explanation. An intentionalist account of the reform of European social democratic parties in recent years, for instance, might adopt a 'fly on the wall' approach to the internal workings of such parties in developing a detailed account of this 'modernisation' process. It is less likely to account for the (perceived) need for modernisation in the first place or to situate it in terms of any broader context allowing wider lessons to be drawn.

Like structuralism, however, virtually no pure forms of intentionalism persist to the present day.[12] Intentionalism is perhaps best seen as a tendency present in certain modes of analysis rather than as a distinct and clearly defended position in its own right. It is not difficult to see why. For, without some conception of context it is almost impossible to deal with the differential capacity of actors to influence political processes and outcomes or, more prosaically still, to account for the inability of actors to realise their intentions in contexts in which they simply lack the resources to do so. It might be rather harsh, for instance, to attribute the failure of any Green Party to win a national election in a liberal democracy to purely agential factors.

It is perhaps not then surprising that most ostensibly intentionalist forms of analysis tend to contain submerged assumptions about the impact of context which remain unacknowledged, undefended and uninterrogated. Thus, for instance, an agency-centred account of the 'modernisation' of European social democratic parties in recent years is likely to accord far greater significance to the actions of those holding (structural) positions of power and authority within the party than to random passengers on the Clapham Omnibus or the Paris Métro. Moreover, even where causal significance is attached (as well it might be) to the ideas held by those on the Clapham Omnibus or Paris Métro, such an appeal is likely to refer to the structuring of societal preferences. As this example hopefully demonstrates, it is an extremely difficult exercise to formulate an explanation for a given social and political outcome with a lexicon restricted exclusively to agential terms. That this is so is due in no small part to the fact that actors themselves routinely appeal to the structured nature of their behaviour, their experience and the contexts in which they find themselves.

A purist intentionalist might well at this point interject by noting that the 'structure' routinely appealed to by actors is, in fact, the behaviour of others (or, at least, a consequence of the behaviour of others). Nonetheless, even this represents a considerable concession. For, from the perspective of the actor being considered (the preferred vantage point of the intentionalist, it should be recalled), the behaviour of others is a relevant contextual factor. It is, after all, the anticipated response of others, a factor beyond by control, that leads me to put on a jacket for the meeting or leave the office at 1 p.m. for the canteen. In this way, and numerous others, the behaviour of others causes actors to reconsider what they would otherwise do. Yet, even were we to regard the appeal to the structured behaviour of others as an agential factor, this does not exhaust the analytical poverty of a narrowly intentionalist position. For it does not deal with the fact that Lionel Jospin, for instance, by virtue of his structural position as leader of the Parti Socialiste, could exert a more direct influence over the course of the party's policy trajectory than any of his (not so similarly elevated) constituents.

Pure intentionalism tends to imply a condition of near anarchy in which all outcomes are entirely contingent upon the immediate conduct of the direct participants and in which, consequently, all outcomes are entirely indeterminent. Moreover, it would seem to imply, additionally, that no particular actor is likely to be able to exert any greater influence than any other – or, more accurately, that insofar as certain actors' conduct comes to acquire greater significance this, in itself, is a contingent outcome. Again, however, it should be noted that even the seemingly most intentionalist accounts tend to shy away from this logic of pure indeterminacy, just as structuralist accounts tend to shy away from a logic of pure determination.

If intentionalism is best seen, then, as a tendency, it is important to consider with what other tendencies it might be associated. Two, in particular, might usefully be identified. The first of these is what might be called *chronocentrism* or, more prosaically, *presentism*. It is the tendency to concentrate upon the present moment and, in so doing, to remove that moment from its historical context and, in particular, from its relation to both past and future. It is not difficult to see why intentionalism might tend to be associated with presentism. For if there is no conception of context or structure and hence no notion of strategic resources, strategic opportunities or strategic constraints, then there is effectively no relationship between the past and the present. Without a notion of the opportunities and constraints the past might bequeath actors in the present, there is simply no need to historicise action – nor, for that matter, any capacity to contextualise it historically. Similarly, if the determinants of all political outcomes are contained in the instant in which political action occurs, then there is no legacy passed on into the future (save, perhaps, for the memories of the actors themselves). Consequently, a purely intentionalist account can say nothing about the process of social and political change over time, save that it is indeterminant and explicable in purely intentional terms (a statement which amounts to no more than the reassertion of an ontological assumption).

The second tendency arises directly from the first. It is what might be termed *contextual parochialism* or what Richard Rose terms 'false particularisation' (1991: 450) – the tendency to restrict one's analysis to a tightly specified situation, to analyse that situation in its own terms and resolutely to resist the attempt to draw general or even transferable conclusions.[13] In some respects chronocentrism is merely a particular form of contextual parochialism in which the context to be analysed is specified temporally. Again, it is not difficult to see why intentionalism should result in a reluctance to draw conclusions from one situation and to apply them to another. For, like some postmodernist strands, its logic is that each and every event or occurrence must be understood in its own terms, since the way in which actors behave in any given situation is both unique and unpredictable. Consequently, we can make no appeal to general concepts and there are no lessons to be drawn from one context to another.

Like structuralism, it would seem, pure intentionalism is extremely limiting. Observations like those above have led many authors to suggest that if structuralist accounts tilt the stick too far towards the pole of structure in the structure–agency relationship, then intentionalism is guilty of the converse, failing to consider both the structural constraints on the ability of actors to realise their intentions and the structural consequences of their actions. Again, it is not so much wrong as profoundly limited and limiting, confining and consigning political analysis to a largely descriptive as opposed to an explanatory role.

The centrality of structure and agency to political explanation

The widely identified problems – or, perhaps more accurately, limitations – of both structuralism and intentionalism have suggested for many the need to move beyond these extremes to some middle ground (for perhaps the most explicit statement of this, see Adler 1997). What is required, it is argued, is a mode of analysis (and corresponding social ontology) capable of reconciling structural and agential factors within a single explanation; an account which is neither structuralist nor intentionalist yet an account which does not simply vacillate between these two poles. In recent years there has been a proliferation of contending accounts. These we will review presently. Before doing so, however, it is first important to establish some general principles from the discussion thus far.

As the example of the rise of fascism in Germany in the 1930s demonstrates well, concepts of structure and agency are implicit in every explanation we offer. Consequently, we can benefit from rendering them explicit and exposing them to critical scrutiny. In so doing it is, above all, consistency to which we must aspire. Yet we need to be clear about what precisely is entailed – and what is not entailed – by consistency in this context. As Martin Hollis and Steve Smith note, 'the agent–structure problem is not settled by deciding what proportions to put in the blender' (1990a: 393). By consistency, then, I do not have in mind a particular proportion of structural and agential factors (say, two parts agency for every one part structure) that must be appealed to in any set of explanations which might be seen as sharing a common ontology.

'Consistency' here means something rather different. What it entails is being able to demonstrate how a common social ontology is applied in each case considered and how this reveals the relative primacy of structural or agential factors in a given situation. A social ontology, as this makes clear, is not a guide to the correct proportion of structural and agential ingredients in any adequate explanation. It is, instead, a general statement of the manner in which agents are believed to appropriate their context and the consequences of that appropriation for their development as agents and for that of the context itself.

In seeking consistency in our appeal to the relationship between structure and agency we can benefit from interrogating the explanations we formulate by asking ourselves a series of questions (Box 3.1).

Box 3.1   Interrogating structure and agency in political analysis

1. Have we identified an agent or agents?
2. Is our agent individual or collective?
3. If collective, can we account for how this collective agency has been accomplished?
5. Have we contextualised our agent(s) within the broader context?
6. How relevant is the context we have chosen?
7. Are there other relevant contexts we have omitted?

Source: Adapted from Hay (1995b: 191).

The value of posing such questions can perhaps been seen if we consider the example of globalisation (a topic which could well benefit from an injection of analytical clarity). Consider the following statement, familiar from both the academic literature and the pronouncements of politicians on the subject:

> *Globalisation places pressures on western states to roll back their welfare provision.*

Statements such as this imply a loosely articulated explanation for welfare retrenchment along the lines, 'globalisation causes (or necessitates) welfare retrenchment'. Here, as is so often the case, globalisation is invoked as a process without a subject; no agent is identified. Consequently, we fail to get beyond the first question. Yet if we seek to restore active subjects to this hypothesised process, its logic of inevitability is rapidly tempered. Immediate progress, then, is made by replacing the initial statement with the following:

> *The ability of foreign investors to move capital and assets rapidly from one national context to another undermines the state's capacity to raise revenue to fund the welfare state through corporate taxation.*

Such a statement has the clear benefit of identifying a series of agents with the capacity to act; it also replaces the abstract and potentially obfuscating appeal to globalisation with a rather more specific process. Yet there is still no direct attribution of causal agency to identifiable subjects. Moving further to restore actors to this process without a subject, we might suggest a second modification:

> *The perception on the part of many western governments that investors are mobile and will exit high taxation environments has*

driven a process of corporate tax cutting, thereby undermining the revenue basis of the welfare state.

This is, once again, an improvement. We have now identified a rather different set of potential actors rather closer to decisions relating to welfare expenditure and we have introduced their perceptions into the equation. It is but a short step from perceptions to actions. Yet we have still not directly attributed welfare reform to identifiable subjects in a genuinely causal fashion. One final step fully restores agency to the (now considerably weakened) relationship between globalisation and welfare retrenchment:

Government X, acting on its belief that investors will leave high-taxation environments for low-taxation environments, has reduced the rate of corporate tax, with consequent effects for the revenue basis of the welfare state.

This is by no means a neutral example. Indeed, there are many ways of restoring a notion of agency to our initial statement in such a way as to identify different groups of significant actors and, no doubt, in such a way as to retain a more direct relationship between globalisation and welfare retrenchment. Now is not the place to review the argument that this relationship is, at best, a contingent one (though see Hay 2001c). Suffice it to note that attempts, such as this, to restore notions of agency to processes, like globalisation, without subjects, do serve to problematise the logics of inevitability such processes are frequently seen to imply.

Beyond structure versus agency

In recent years, as noted above, considerable attention has been devoted to the question or 'problem' of structure and agency. Invariably that attention has sought to diagnose the need for an approach to the question of structure and agency – in some accounts a 'solution' to the 'problem' – that transcends the unhelpful and polarising opposition of structure and agency. This opposition or *dualism*, it is argued, has tended to resolve itself into fruitless exchanges between structuralists and intentionalists. Here the ill-tempered debate, internal to Marxist theory, between the humanist and historicist Marxism of E. P. Thompson on the one hand and the structural Marxism of Louis Althusser is often seen as emblematic (see, for instance, McAnulla 1999). The debate was initiated by Thompson, whose blistering *ad hominem* critique, *The Poverty of Theory* (1978) was provoked by the (alleged) 'structural super-determinism' (Miliband 1970) of Althusser's anti-humanist Marxism (Althusser 1969, 1971; Althusser and Balibar 1970).[14] In what might be seen as an ironic victory for the structuralist view, Althusser's position is defended not by its author but by a range of Althusserian sympathisers presumably allured and 'interpellated' by its seeming logic (principally Anderson 1980; Hirst 1979; Nield and Seed 1979). Whether such exchanges were genuinely representative of the state of Marxist thought at the time is a moot point. For, arguably, the heat of the confrontation itself drove the protagonists to adopt and to seek to defend positions somewhat more entrenched than those they held at the outset. Moreover, however influential, the work of Althusser was by no means typical of Marxism at the time, lying, as it did, far to one end of the humanism versus anti-humanism continuum. Nonetheless, it is perhaps fair to suggest that the theoretical extremes of the time (whether Althusser's structural Marxism or the intentionalism of ethnomethodology) attracted rather greater attention (from proponents and detractors alike) than the more densely populated but seldom explicitly defended middle ground.

From the late 1970s onwards, however, things were to change as a younger generation of social theorists sought to resist the centrifugal pull of existing social theory. Principal among them was Anthony Giddens (then a recently appointed fellow of King's College, Cambridge, now director of the London School of Economics). Giddens, and others like him (notably Jeffrey Alexander, Margaret Archer, Roy Bhaskar, Pierre Bourdieu and Piotr Sztompka), effectively argued that structuralism and intentionalism had failed to deal with the relationship between structure and agency, by simply reducing one to the other. What was required was a return to the most basic of ontological principles, those concerning the relationship between the actor and the context in which she finds herself.

On the basis of this 'return to ontology', we have seen a proliferation of positions which allow us to move beyond structuralism and intentionalism, beyond the opposition of structure and agency. If, for structuralists, structure determines agency, and, for intentionalists, agency causes structure, then for this new group of authors, structure and agency both influence each other. Indeed, they are inherently and inexorably related and intertwined.

There is much on which these authors concur. This extends beyond a shared critique of the theoretical poverty of structuralist and intentionalist tendencies, to the nature of the relationship between conduct and context, agency and structure.[15] In short, each accepts the view that agents are situated within a structured context which presents an uneven distribution of opportunities and constraints to them. Actors influence the development of that context over time through the consequences of their actions. Yet, at any given time, the ability of actors to realise their intentions is set by the context itself.

Despite this common ontological core, however, the precise view of the relationship between structure and agency and the implications one might draw from it for political analysis vary considerably from author to author. In the pages which follow, we concentrate on the two approaches most frequently identified as 'solutions' to the problem of structure and agency, namely Giddens' *structuration theory* and the *critical realism* of Bhaskar and Archer. Through a critical engagement with these highly influential positions, we establish a point of departure for the preferred *strategic–relational approach* which is outlined and defended in the rest of this volume.

Before doing so, however, it is perhaps first worth noting that Giddens, Archer and Bhaskar were by no means the first to suggest the utility of a dynamic and dialectical understanding of the relationship between structure and agency.

Ironically perhaps, given the structuralism more usually attributed to him (a structuralism which certainly characterises many of his most important works), it is Marx who, in the opening passage of *The Eighteenth Brumaire of Louis Bonaparte* famously declares, 'men make their own history, but not of their own free will; not under circumstances they themselves have chosen' (1852[1960]: 115). This brief passage, though frequently cited, is often dismissed as unrepresentative of Marx's writings along the lines that if you write enough you will invariably stumble across insights more profound than the schema within which you are working. This is to do Marx a considerable disservice. For while it would perhaps be wrong to follow John-Paul Sartre in viewing this statement as the central thesis of historical materialism itself (1968), it is far from unrepresentative of Marx's historical writings. Indeed, similar sentiments are expressed in the third of Marx's *Theses on Feuerbach* of 1845, perhaps his clearest denunciation of structuralism:

> The materialist doctrine concerning the changing of circumstances and upbringing forgets that circumstances are changed by man and that it is essential to educate the educator himself . . . The coincidence of the changing of circumstance and of human activity or self-changing can be conceived and rationally understood only as *revolutionary practice* (1845[1975]: 422, emphasis in the original).

The Theses, it should be noted, culminate in another of Marx's oft-cited aphorisms which puts paid to his image as a structuralist, 'the philosophers have only *interpreted* the world in various ways; the point is to *change* it' (*ibid.*: 423, emphasis in the original).

In each of these passages, Marx seems to be suggesting that while agents do indeed fashion the world they inhabit (agency causes structure), the context or circumstances in which this occurs affects their ability to do so (structure constrains or conditions agency). It is precisely this sense of the dynamic interplay of structure and agency over time that authors like Giddens struggle – and, as we shall see, in certain respects fail – to emulate. Arguably, the profusion of recent literature notwithstanding, there is little to the question of structure and agency which is not already well (even better) captured by Marx in the opening paragraphs of the *The Eighteenth Brumaire*.

Giddens' theory of structuration

Whatever the merits of Marx's more humanist and historical writings, it is without doubt Giddens who has done more than any contemporary theorist to restore the question of structure and agency to centre stage. His ambitious theory of structuration, developed over many years, has rightly led him to become the most influential social theorist of the times, perhaps of the entire post-war period. Giddens' formulation is, as perhaps all social ontologies should be, appealing in its disarming simplicity. He sets out to transcend the dualism of structure and agency in existing social theory and, in so doing, stumbles upon a logic to which he can now attribute his considerable reputation. His approach to such questions is essentially dialectical: he notes the opposition between the entrenched positions which constitute the terms of a dualism, seeks to demonstrate the poverty of each, and transcends the dualism by offering a qualitatively novel 'third way'. Where there were dualisms, Giddens sows the seeds of duality. Thus, where, in his most recent work, Giddens sets out to transcend the dualism of old left and new right, social democracy and Thatcherism, in forging a 'third way' (1998) which claims to be 'beyond left and right' (1994), so in the theory of structuration he proposes what might be seen as a 'third ontology' beyond both structuralism and intentionalism (1976, 1979, 1981: 26–48, 1984).

As I have elsewhere noted, Giddens' aim 'has been to develop a hybrid theory capable of reconciling, on the one hand, a focus on the structures which are the very condition of social and political interaction, with, on the other hand, a sensitivity to the intentionality, reflexivity, autonomy and agency of actors' (Hay 1995b: 197). Structure and agency are, then, for Giddens, internally related or ontologically intertwined. They comprise a *duality*. The analogy he deploys is that of a coin: structure and agency are opposite faces. The analogy is telling and has implications to which we shall return presently. Note, however, that it implies an internal rather than an external relationship between structure and agency –

they are mutually dependent, indeed mutually constitutive. This clearly sets the theory of structuration apart from its structuralist and intentionalist precursors in which, at best, structure and agency are coins of greatly unequal weights which periodically collide.

The keys to Giddens' theoretical toolbox are the twin concepts *structuration* and the *duality of structure*. These are defined, in the useful glossary to *The Constitution of Society*, in the following terms:

Duality of structure	Structure as the medium and outcome of the conduct it recursively organises; the structural properties of social systems do not exist outside of action but are chronically implicated in its production and reproduction. (1984: 374)
Structuration	The structuring of social relations across time and space, in virtue of the duality of structure. (1984: 376)

With the notion of structuration, Giddens extends the symbolic interactionists' emphasis upon the skilled accomplishment of everyday interaction (Goffman 1959, 1963, 1972) to the macro-level, coming to conceive of the dynamic reproduction of social structures over time as a skilled accomplishment on the part of social actors. His focus is thus upon the process of change, in which structure and agent are mutually and directly implicated, rather than upon the context in which that change occurs or upon the actors inhabiting that context. This emphasis upon process is, as we shall see, crucial to any attempt genuinely to transcend the dualism of structure and agency as it is to the analysis of social and political change (see Chapter 4). It is particularly central to the 'praxiological' approach of Piotr Sztompka which focuses particular attention upon the interplay of agency, practice (or praxis) and what is termed 'social becoming' (1991, 1993). As Giddens himself suggests, social processes are 'brought about by the active constitutive skills of . . . historically located actors' and, he adds, 'not under conditions of their own choosing' (1976: 157). This scarcely veiled reference to Marx is highly significant, suggesting as it does that even in its earliest formulations, Giddens' theory of structuration owed much to Marx's timeless insight.

Surprisingly, given his emphasis upon the need to transcend the dualism of structure and agency, Giddens chooses to highlight not the duality of structure and agency (and hence the analytical nature of the distinction between the two), but what he terms the *duality of structure*.[16] By this Giddens refers to the (ontological) claim that 'social structures are both constituted by human agency, and yet at the same time are the very medium of its constitution' (1976: 121). Again he is close to echoing Marx – agents make structures, but, their autonomy is limited by the (always) already structured context in which they find themselves. That Giddens seeks to transcend the dualism of structure *and agency* by pointing to the duality of structure alone has troubled many commentators. Yet, strange though it might at first seem, it provides a clue to the distinctiveness – and possibly to the problematic nature – of his chosen 'solution' to the structure–agency conundrum.

Recall Giddens' coin analogy. Structure and agency are flip sides of the same coin. Consequently, we can view only one at a time. It is surely for this reason that he is reluctant to investigate the duality of structure and agency that his initial ontological interventions perhaps imply. What Giddens seems to suggest is that while structure and agency may indeed be ontologically intertwined, we as analysts are incapable of capturing that 'real' duality of structure and agency, confined as we are to view the world from one side of the coin or the other at any given moment. We may alter our viewpoint to capture the other side, but we cannot view both simultaneously. Accordingly, the best we can perhaps hope for is to recognise in the duality of structure and, presumably, the duality of agency (a term Giddens does not invoke), traces of the dialectical relationship between structure and agency.[17] The irony, then, is that while Giddens appeals to an ontological duality (interlinking) of structure and agency, he delivers an analytical dualism (separation). Although this is capable of capturing the Janus-face of structure and perhaps that of agency or praxis, it is incapable of interrogating the internal relationship between structure and agency which Giddens posits.

This analytical dualism is reflected in the 'methodological bracketing' of structure and agency that he proposes (1984: 281–372, esp. 288–93). This is simply grasped. In practice, he suggests, it is seldom if ever possible to capture simultaneously both the strategic (agential) and institutional (structural/systemic) aspects of a given situation. Consequently, when engaged in an analysis of 'strategic conduct' we must temporarily suspend or 'bracket off' our concern with the institutional context, for we cannot hope to view both sides of the coin simultaneously. Similarly, when engaged in an 'institutional analysis' we must 'bracket off' our concern with strategic conduct. The clear danger is a simple alternation between structuralist and intentionalist accounts which can only belie the sophistication of the structurationist ontology. Sadly, this tendency is closely replicated in Giddens' more substantive contributions in which he seems to vacillate between, on the one hand, structuralist accounts in which processes seem to operate without subjects (as, for instance, in his depiction of the 'juggernaut' of globalising 'late modernity' (1990, 1998, 1999) and, on the other, intentionalist accounts in which the reflexivity and creativity of subjects is emphasised with little consideration to the context in which they find themselves (as, for instance, in his reflections on self-identity and the 'pure relationship' (1991, 1992, 1994).[18] As Derek Layder notes, 'methodological bracketing ... has the paradoxical effect of enforcing an artificial separation between lifeworld and system elements and this is, of course, an outcome which is directly counter to the explicit objectives of structuration theory' (1998: 100).

This is by no means the only problem with Giddens' formulation. It is, nonetheless, intimately connected to the others. If the (undoubted) appeal of structuration theory lies in its promise (finally) to transcend the dualism of structure and agency, as I think it does, then it should be noted that this promise remains largely unrealised. That this is so is due, in no small part, to Giddens' reformulation and redefinition of the terms of that dualism.

Throughout this chapter we have tended to assume a common (and generally unproblematic) understanding of structure as the context in which action occurs. Yet this is not what Giddens means by the term. In fact, this latter sense of structure is far closer to Giddens' notion of system – which he defines as 'the patterning of social relations across time–space, understood as reproduced practices' (1984: 377). Structure is (re)defined, rather ideosyncratically, as 'the rules and resources recursively implicated in the reproduction of social systems'. He continues, 'structure exists only as memory traces, the organic basis of human knowledgeability, and as instantiated in action' (1984: 377). There are three things to note here. First, as Layder observes, in this formulation 'structure does not mean anything like the same thing as it does in conventional approaches' (1994: 138). Consequently, at best Giddens has transcended a rather different dualism to that which now attracts attention to the theory of structuration. The theory of structuration may well be regarded as a solution to a particular problem (though note again the dangers of the 'problem–solution' terminology), but it is not a solution to the conventional 'problem of structure and agency'. Second, on closer inspection there was no dualism between the terms Giddens deploys (Hay 1995b: 198). If agency is understood as the actor's 'capability of doing things' (Giddens 1984: 9) and structure as 'memory traces ... instantiated in action' (1984: 377), then there would seem little distance to bridge theoretically between them; these terms naturally imply a duality. Accordingly, it would seem, the dualism of structure and agency is resolved less by theoretical innovation than by definitional sleight of hand. Finally, and rather ironically, the genuine dualism between context and conduct (or, in Giddens' terms, system and agency) lives on. Indeed, as we have seen, it is replicated in the methodological bracketing the theory of structuration recommends. Far from providing a solution to the 'problem', Giddens may well compound it.

Critical realism and the morphogenetic approach

This brings us to the other much-touted 'solution' to the problem of structure and agency, namely the critical realism of Roy Bhaskar. Given the sheer volume of references to his work in this area, Bhaskar has written remarkably little which pertains directly to the question of structure and agency (though see especially Bhaskar 1979: 34–56, 106–37, 1989: 89–115, 1994: 100–7). Moreover, what he has written is both sufficiently general and, at times, sufficiently inpenetrable to sustain a diverse range of often mutually incompatible readings (compare, say, Archer 1989, 1995; Collier 1994; Outhwaite 1987; Sayer 1992, 2000 and the various contributions to Archer *et al.* 1998). Consequently, rather than present yet another variant in the pages which follow I focus instead on Margaret Archer's rather more systematic and exhaustive attempt to trace the implications of Bhaskar's critical realism for the question of structure and agency. This she advances in her distinctive, and now increasingly influential, 'morphogenetic approach' (1989, 1995, 1998). Although this, too, is based upon a particular reading of Bhaskar (and a not uncontentious reading at that), it is a reading that he would seem to endorse (Bhaskar 1998: xvi; see also Archer 1995: xii). Moreover, it is a reading which addresses the issues which concern us here in a more direct and systematic fashion than does the work of Bhaskar himself.

On the face of it the critical realist position is very similar to that advanced by Giddens. As philosophical realists, however, Bhaskar and Archer approach the analysis of social and political processes from a somewhat different starting point.[19] The world, they claim is structured in such a way that it exhibits a separation of appearance and reality. As Archer herself notes, 'there is no direct access to the "hard facts" of social life, at least for the vast majority of us who cannot subscribe to the discredited doctrine of immaculate perception' (1995: 17). Clearly such an ontological claim is untestable. Yet it serves as the very condition of a (critical) realist approach to social enquiry. The world does not present itself to us as it really is. Accordingly, if we are to reveal the structured reality of the world we inhabit, we must cast our gaze beyond the superficial realm of appearances, deploying theory as a sensitising device to reveal the structured reality beneath the surface. It is this 'depth ontology' which underpins critical realism. As this already makes clear, Bhaskar and Archer rely upon a rather more familiar conception of structure to that developed by Giddens. Despite this, what is said about the relationship between structure and agency is remarkably similar to the theory of structuration. Indeed, as already noted, Bhaskar goes so far as to use Giddens' notion of the duality of structure, arguing, in an uncharacteristically accessible moment, that 'society is both the ever-present *condition* and the continually reproduced *outcome* of human agency' (1979: 43, 1989: 92, emphasis in the original).

On the basis of the above observations it might be tempting to suggest that critical realism offers fresh promise of transcending the dualism of structure and agency and, in effect, of delivering what Giddens set out to achieve in the theory of structuration. Yet, as Margaret Archer's critique of Giddens makes clear, this is far from being the case.[20] Her critique is, in certain key respects, the very antithesis of that presented in the previous section. Archer takes Giddens' claim to have transcended the dualism of structure and agency at face value, and takes issue with it. For Archer it is not so much Giddens' ability to deliver what he promises that is at issue, so much as what he sets out to deliver in the first place. Quite simply, structuration theory is premised upon a dangerous and false assumption – that structure and agency comprise a duality and not a dualism. As she argues, 'the two have to be related rather than conflated' (1995: 6). For Archer, then, structure and agency are ontologically independent, capable of exercising 'autonomous influences' (*ibid.*).

This critique of Giddens provides the basis for Archer's more general distinction between what she terms *elisionist* and *emergentist* theoretical orientations (60–1). In pointing to the need to transcend the dualism of structure and agency, Giddens is an elisionist, dangerously (as Archer sees it) conflating structure and agency by denying their separability. Archer and, presumably by implication Bhaskar, are emergentists, for whom structure and agency 'are both regarded as emergent strata of social reality' (60).[21] Whereas elisionists concern themselves with the mutual constitution of structure and agency, emergentists concentrate instead upon the interplay of structure and agency over time.

It is the issue of the separability of structure and agency which is the crux of the matter. Archer's position, at least as expressed in *Realist Social Theory* (1995), is that structure and agency are not only analytically separable but ontologically separate. In this sense, an analytical dualism hardens into an ontological dualism. For Giddens, by contrast, while structure and agency may be separable analytically, they are not separate ontologically.

At this point it is important to note that Archer disputes this reading of structuration theory, arguing that Giddens endorses an 'inseparability thesis' in which structure and agency become entirely indistinct and irresolvable analytically. This seems a particularly harsh judgement. For while Giddens clearly defines structure (as rules and resources) and agency (as the capability to act) such that they are inextricably interlinked, the very fact that they are defined differently would seem to indicate that they are seen as separable analytically. To talk of rules and resources is not to talk of the capability to act. The suggestion that Giddens, and other (unnamed) critics of analytical dualism, cannot tell the difference between chickens and eggs (75), is something of a cheap shot. Moreover, as already noted, when it comes to operationalise the theory of structuration, Giddens invokes a 'methodological bracketing' which effectively serves to reimpose a rigid analytical and methodological separation of structure and agency. The irony, then, is that despite Archer's sustained critique, the morphogenetic approach and the theory of structuration, albeit for very different reasons, tend to replicate the dualism of structure and agency which Archer proposes. Archer, nonetheless, does have the benefit of consistency.

It is with respect to temporality, however, that the distinctiveness of the morphogenetic approach is established. Archer's central thesis is stated simply in the following terms: 'structure and agency can only be linked by explaining the interplay between them over time . . . without the proper incorporation of time the problem of structure and agency can never be satisfactorily resolved' (65). Here again the ontological separation of structure and agency is key. For Archer insists that structure and agency reside in different temporal domains, such that the pre-existence of structure is a condition of individual action: 'structures (as emergent entities) are not only irreducible to people, they pre-exist them, and people are not puppets of structures because they have their own emergent properties which mean they either reproduce or transform social structure, rather then creating it' (71). Interestingly, however, as Anthony King notes, Archer's own position on this question seems to have shifted over time (1999: 199–201). For, in her first book, *Culture and Agency* (1989), she refers to this temporal divide as purely 'analytical', whereas in *Realist Social Theory* (1995) it acquires the characteristics of a profound ontological dualism. Archer's view, at least in her more recent works, then, is that structures pre-exist agents (or subjects).

This ontological premise provides the basis upon which Archer builds her distinctive conception of 'the morphogenetic sequence' (for practical elaboration see also McAnulla 1999; Wilmott 1999).

Structure, here understood as ontologically separate from agency, necessarily pre-dates the actions which either serve to transform or to reproduce it – to produce its morphogenesis or its morphostasis (Archer 1995: 295–7). That action or interaction occurs over a particular (and finite) period of time. Its consequences, both intended and unintended, necessarily post-date such action and are captured in Archer's term structural elaboration. This, then, establishes a simple temporal sequence through which 'morphogenesis of structure' occurs.

There is much to commend this attractive theoretical schema. It seems to capture well the practical consciousness of engaging with a densely structured social and political environment. When orienting ourselves to the realisation of a particular goal we do indeed seem to encounter and engage with an external and pre-existing structural context. Our attempts to realise out intentions tend to be limited temporally, though the consequences of our actions may take some time to realise themselves. Moreover, that process of structural elaboration is one over which we effectively lose control once we have acted.

Yet what this serves to indicate, despite the ostensible concern with the complex interplay of structure and agency, is that such a temporal sequence presents a rather agent-centred and individualistic view of morphogenesis. From the vantage-point of a particular actor, the world does indeed appear to be pre-structured, such that structure and agent inhabit different temporal domains. The problem here is a perspectival one. From the vantage-point of a singular actor, social structures do indeed appear external and temporally independent. Yet, a subtle change in vantage-point alters this. As King explains,

> the key error which Archer makes in her derivation of social structure is to draw the sociological conclusion of the existence of a social structure from the perspective of a single individual . . . if she had de-centred her perspective to see that the constraint which I face is other individuals – and no less serious for that – just as I form some of the social conditions which mutually constrain these others, she would not have fallen into ontological dualism. (1999: 217)

This is an important point and will serve as a crucial point of departure for what is to follow. Yet it is crucial that we first clear up a potential misinterpretation. While the structured nature of social and political reality is indeed the product of human agency, it is not simply reducible to it (as King here seems to imply). The relationship between actors and their environment is an organic one. As such, the product of human action is, in key respects, greater than the sum of its component parts. It is this that gives structures what Archer terms 'emergent properties'. The key point, however, is that such emergent properties are not exclusively properties of the structure itself. To speak, as Archer does, of structural elaboration is to speak of a process by which forms of conduct and hence human agency are transformed over time, just as to invoke a notion of social structure in the first place is to appeal to the structuring of such conduct. Thus conceptualised, structure and agency do not exist in different temporal domains. Indeed, the very distinction between structure and agency is revealed as purely analytical. To speak of the different temporal domains of structure and agency is, then, to reify and ontologise an analytical distinction.

What it more, this ontological dualism of structure and agency seems somewhat at odds with Bhaskar's critical realism. In the end, Archer's position is too important to be adjudicated on the basis of whether it presents a credible reading and elaboration of Bhaskar. Nonetheless, it is surely instructive to note the tension between Archer's insistence that structure and agency exhibit an ontological (and temporal) dualism and Bhaskar's comment that structures can be said to exist only by virtue of their mediation of human conduct – structures constitute both the medium and condition of human agency (Bhaskar 1979: 43, 1989: 92; cf. Giddens 1984). This would certainly seem to imply that structure and agency are (temporally) coextensive.

As this perhaps suggests, the central limitation of Archer's approach is the rather episodic, disjointed and discontinuous view of agency it seems to imply. Despite her comment that 'action itself is undeniably continuous' (1995: 73), there is precious little room to acknowledge this within the morphogenetic sequence Archer identifies. The impression she seems to give is of structure as distant, external and long-enduring, while agency is conceptualised, in contrast, as an ephemeral or fleeting moment. This seems to imply a residual structuralism punctuated only periodically yet infrequently by a largely unexplicated conception of agency. This appears from the shadows and returns swiftly from whence it came, a perturbation or disruption in the otherwise pristine logic of structural reproduction.

The methodological implications of Archer's morphogenetic approach, as I have already hinted, may well be to reproduce precisely the bracketing of structure and agency which Giddens proposes.

Towards a strategic–relational approach

The above discussion suggests that any genuine attempt to transcend the dualism of structure and agency is only likely to be frustrated by adopting either the theory of structuration or the morphogenetic approach. Giddens' theory of structuration sets out in pursuit of this illusive goal but comes up short, ultimately capitulating in a methodological bracketing which seems to legitimate an alternation between structuralism and intentionalism. Arguably precisely this tendency is exhibited in his more substantive writings (Hay, O'Brien and Penna 1994: 51–61; Stones 1991; Thrift 1985). Archer's morphogenetic approach gets us no further since it is premised upon precisely the ontological dualism we are seeking to transcend. Archer, then, seeks to make a virtue out of the dualism of structure and agency which Giddens seeks but fails to overturn.

Altogether more promising is the strategic–relational approach developed by Bob Jessop (1990a, 1996; Hay 1999b; Hay and Jessop 1995). Like Giddens' theory of structuration, the strategic–relational approach sets out to transcend the artificial dualism of structure and agency; like Archer it draws upon the critical realism of Bhaskar.[22] Yet in other respects it differs significantly from each of these positions. It is important, then, that we begin by establishing its principal ontological premises.

The first of these, which places the strategic–relational approach in opposition to much of the existing literature is that the distinction between structure and agency is taken to be a purely analytical one. This assumption renders redundant Archer's insistence, for instance, that structure and agency reside in different temporal domains, such that the pre-existence of structure is a condition of individual action. For if the distinction is analytical, structure and agency must be present simultaneously in any given situation. Whether we can speak of structure and agency as exhibiting different temporal characteristics is an interesting and contentious point to which we return. Stated most simply, then, neither agents nor structures are real, since neither has an existence in isolation from the other – their existence is relational (structure and agency are mutually constitutive) and dialectical (their interaction is not reducible to the sum of structural and agential factors treated separately). While it may be useful analytically to differentiate between structural and agential factors, then, it is important that this analytical distinction is not reified and hardened into a rigid ontological dualism. As I have argued elsewhere, structure and agency are best seen, not so much (*à la* Giddens) as flip-sides of the same coin, as metals in the alloy from which the coin is forged. From our vantage-point they do not exist as themselves but through their relational interaction. Structure and agency, though analytically separable, 'are in practice completely interwoven (we cannot see either metal in the alloy only the product of their fusion)' (Hay 1995b: 200).

As this perhaps suggests, a strategic–relational approach offers the potential to transcend the dualism between structure and agency. It does so by suggesting that rather than consign ourselves to references to structure and agency which are, after all, merely theoretical abstractions, we concentrate instead upon the dialectical interplay of structure and agency in real contexts of social and political interaction. Thus ultimately more useful than the abstract and arbitrary analytical distinction between structure and agency is that between *strategic action* on the one hand, and the *strategically selective context* within which it is formulated and upon which it impacts on the other.

Consequently, for exponents of the strategic–relational approach part of the problem of the structure–agency debate is the language in which it has been conducted. Put simply, the very terms structure and agency themselves seem to imply an analytical *and* ontological separability at odds with the ontological assumptions of the strategic–relational approach. What is required is an attempt to devise a new conceptual language which might better reflect the relational and dialectical qualities of the ongoing interaction of structure and agency. This Jessop has sought to provide by drawing our attention to a range of second- and third-order concepts in which structure and agency are already mutually implicated. His strategy is straightforward. Starting with structure and agency, a pairing which seems automatically to invoke a conceptual dualism, Jessop seeks to bring agency into structure – producing a structured context (an action setting) – and to bring structure into agency – producing a contextualised actor (a situated agent). In moving to this new pairing of concepts, the conceptual dualism has been partially overcome.[23] Yet Jessop does not stop here. A repeat move – bringing the situated actor back into the structured context and the structural context to the situated actor – yields a new conceptual pairing in which the dualism of structure and agency has been dissolved. Jessop now identifies a *strategic actor* within a *strategically selective context*. No dualism exists between these concepts which, as a consequence, far better reflect both the manner in which actors appropriate the environment in which they are situated and the manner in which that context circumscribes the parameters of possible actions for them. The path from abstract to concrete, conceptual dualism to conceptual duality is traced in Figure 3.1.

The key relationship in the strategic–relational approach, then, is not that between structure and agency, but rather the more immediate interaction of strategic actors and the strategic context in which they find themselves. In emphasising the strategic content of action, this approach

Figure 3.1   *From dualism to duality: the strategic–relational approach*

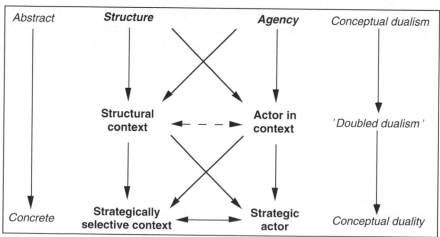

acknowledges that agents both internalise perceptions of their context and consciously orient themselves towards that context in choosing between potential courses of action. Strategy is intentional conduct oriented towards the environment in which it is to occur. It is the intention to realise certain outcomes and objectives which motivates action. Yet for that action to have any chance of realising such intentions, it must be informed by a strategic assessment of the relevant context in which strategy occurs and upon which it subsequently impinges.

Jessop's contribution is not merely to recognise, in strategic action, the orientation of actors towards an environment. Equally significant is his insight that the strategic environment itself is *strategically selective* – in other words, it favours certain strategies over others as means to realise a given set of intentions or preferences. In one sense this is obvious. A government seeking re-election is likely to find itself in a position of strategic choice as the election approaches (relating not only to the campaign it might fight, but also, for instance, to whether it should seek to engineer a pre-election economic boom). Yet, given the nature of the (strategically selective) environment in which it finds itself (given what we know, for instance, about its tenure in office, the state of the economy, the phase of the business cycle, the existing preferences of the electorate, the strategic choices made by contending parties and so forth), certain strategies are more likely to be rewarded at the polls than others. If this is obvious, then we should nonetheless note that it is scarcely acknowledged in the existing literature on structure and agency which gives us little insight into the selectivity of contexts. That many of Jessop's theoretical statements are little more than sociological truisms (at least once stripped of their terminological complexity) might be seen as a sign of their strength, not their weakness. Good political analysis is often a case of stating and re-stating that which is obvious but all too rarely reflected upon.

Clearly not all outcomes are possible in any given situation. It may well be that by the time of the election, the incumbent administration has become unelectable, for instance. Yet whatever the context, the outcome is not determined by the structure of the situation itself. Outcomes, then, are structurally underdetermined. This is by no means an unfamiliar suggestion. Indeed, it would surely be accepted by all but the most ardent of structuralists. Yet Jessop takes us further. Indeed, what differentiates his position from those we have thus far considered is his suggestion that although, in the final analysis, social and political outcomes are contingent upon strategic choices, the context itself presents an unevenly contoured terrain which favours certain strategies over others and hence selects for certain outcomes while militating against others. Over time, such strategic selectivity will throw up a series of systematically structured outcomes. Parties capable of engineering an electorally expedient or 'political' business cycle may be more likely to extend their tenure in office (see, for instance, Alesina 1987, 1989). Consequently, while the outcome of any particular strategic intervention is unpredictable, the distribution of outcomes over a longer time frame will exhibit a characteristic regularity (given some degree of structural stability over the time frame considered). A couple of examples may help to reveal the significance of this insight.

Consider first the prospects for labour market reform in Britain today, particularly the likelihood of reforms – such as the provision of comprehensive state-funded child-care facilities – designed to increase the labour market participation of women. An applied strategic–relational approach to such issues would perhaps suggest that given the existing institutions, traditions, culture, selections mechanisms and personnel of the British state, it is more likely than not that the state will continue to fail to pass legislation which might project a Scandinavian future (of greater labour market participation on more equitable terms) for British women (Esping-Andersen 1999: 57–60; Jenson, Hagen and Reddy 1988; Klausen 1999). Though by no means entirely determined, the outcome is strategically selected for.

A second, and rather different example comes from the political economy of globalisation, discussed above (see pp. 114–15). Given near-universal perceptions amongst policy-making elites of the increased mobility of capital, it is unlikely (though, again, by no means impossible) that liberal-democratic states will increase the tax burden on corporations. The outcome is, again, strategically selected for. Heightened capital mobility, it is widely believed, makes credible previously implausible capital exit strategies. Consequently, states which wish to retain their revenue base will find themselves having to internalise the preference of capital for lower rates of taxation and more deregulated ('flexible') labour markets (Przeworski and Wallerstein 1988; Wickham-Jones 1995). Interestingly, the empirical evidence lends a further complexity to this strategic–relational logic. For, given what we know about the difficulty of systematic welfare retrenchment (see, for instance, P. Pierson 1994, 1996a, 2001), we might expect to find states cutting headline rates of corporate taxation while, at the same time, clawing back various subsidies and incentives offered as tax concessions to business. This, again, is strategically selected for. As the empirical evidence reveals, while corporate taxation has fallen across OECD nations, aggregate tax burdens on capital have remained relatively stable (Swank 1996, 2001).

In both of these cases the outcome is 'strategically selected for', though by no means inevitable.

The concepts of strategy and strategic selectivity thus provide the

Figure 3.2   *Structure, strategy and agency in the strategic–relational approach*

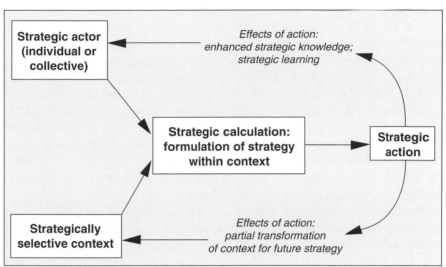

Source: Adapted from Hay (1995b: 202).

building blocks of the strategic–relational approach. It is this approach that underpins the argument of subsequent chapters. It is briefly elaborated in the pages which follow and outlined schematically in Figure 3.2.

Actors are conceptualised as conscious, reflexive and strategic. They are, broadly, intentional in the sense that they may act purposively in the attempt to realise their intentions and preferences. However, they may also act intuitively and/or out of habit. Nonetheless, even when acting routinely they are assumed to be able to render explicit their intentions and their motivations. Actors are assumed to monitor the immediate consequences of their actions, whether intuitively or more deliberately, and to be capable of monitoring the longer-term consequences of their actions. Though actors are conceptualised as intentional and strategic, their preferences are not assumed to be fixed, nor to be determined by the material circumstances in which they find themselves. Different actors in similar material circumstances (exposed, perhaps to different influences and experiences) will construct their interests and preferences differently. In a similar manner, the same actors will review, revise and reform their perceived interests and preferences over time (as material circumstances and ideational influences change). Accordingly, in monitoring the consequences (both intended and unintended) of their actions, actors may come to modify, revise or reject their chosen means to realise their intentions as, indeed, they may also come to modify, revise or reject their original intentions and the conception of interest upon which they were predicated.

Actors, as discussed above, are presumed to be strategic – to be capable of devising and revising means to realise their intentions. This immediately implies a relationship, and a dynamic relationship at that, between the actor (individual or collective) and the context in which she finds herself. For, to act strategically, is to project the likely consequences of different courses of action and, in turn, to judge the contours of the terrain. It is, in short, to orient potential courses of action to perceptions of the relevant strategic context and to use such an exercise as a means to select the particular course of action to be pursued. On such an understanding, the ability to formulate strategy (whether explicitly recognised as such or not) is the very condition of action.

At this point it is important to deal with a potential objection. For, it might be suggested, there is a certain danger here of so closely eliding strategy and agency as to imply that all action is the product of overt and explicit strategic calculation (just as rational choice theorists attribute an instrumental utility-maximising means–end rationality to all actors). The argument being made here is, in fact, somewhat different. What I am suggesting is that all action contains at least a residual strategic moment though this need not be rendered conscious. This makes it important to differentiate clearly between intuitively and explicitly strategic action:

1. *Intuitive, routine or habitual strategies and practices* are based upon perceptions (accurate or otherwise) of the strategic context and the likely consequences of specific actions. As such they can be regarded as strategic insofar as such practices are oriented towards the context in which they occur. However intuitive, the act of crossing the road so as to avoid oncoming cars and other pedestrians contains an inherently strategic moment. Although such an understanding and lay knowledge can be rendered explicit, invariably it remains unarticulated and unchallenged. Note, however, how effectively a close shave on a zebra crossing brings to the surface previously unquestioned strategic calculations. Insofar as the assumptions which implicitly inform such routines, habits, rituals and other forms of unreflexive action can be rendered explicit, these practices contain a significant strategic component. Such strategy is manifest in 'practical consciousness' (cf. Giddens 1984: 21–2).
2. *Explicitly strategic action* also relies upon perceptions of the strategic context and the configuration of constraints and opportunities that it provides. Yet here such calculations and attempts to map the

contours of the context are rendered explicit and are subjected to interrogation and contestation (particularly in the formulation and reformulation of collective strategies) in an overt and conscious attempt to identify options most likely to realise intentions and objectives (whether individual or collective).

These are, of course, ideal types. Any specific action is likely to combine both intuitive and explicit strategic aspects, though to differing degrees. Even the most explicit strategic calculation is likely to be infused with intuitive assumptions at the level of 'practical consciousness'.

Within this account, strategies, once formulated, are operationalised in action. Such action yields effects, both intended and unintended. Since individuals (and groups of individuals) are knowledgeable and reflexive, they routinely monitor the consequences of their action (assessing the impact of previous strategies, and their success or failure in securing prior objectives). Strategic action thus yields:

1. *Direct effects* upon the structured contexts within which it takes place and within which future action occurs – producing a partial (however minimal) transformation of the structured context (though not necessarily as anticipated), and
2. *Strategic learning* on the part of the actor(s) involved, enhancing awareness of structures and the constraints/opportunities they impose, providing the basis from which subsequent strategy might be formulated and perhaps prove more successful.

An example will perhaps serve to demonstrate the point. Consider, once again, a government seeking re-election. The consequences (both intended and unintended) of its strategic actions in the election campaign itself are likely to impact significantly upon the environment in which the party finds itself after the election – reflected, most directly, in the number of seats the party wins, whether it finds itself in office once again and, if so, with which collection of coalition partners. These are direct effects of its strategic choices, even if they contain significant unintended aspects. It may well be, for instance, that the (unintended) consequence of seeking to engineer a pre-election economic upturn (at whatever longer-term cost to economic performance) was to discredit the incumbent administration, contributing to its poor electoral showing. Whether intended or unintended, however, such effects are direct. Yet the process of electoral competition also throws up a series of more indirect effects. These relate, in particular, to the lessons drawn from a reflection upon strategic success and failure during the campaign. An administration expelled from office on the basis of an exposé of its attempt to sacrifice the long-term health of the economy for short-term electoral gain might come to re-evaluate the opportunity cost of such a strategy in future. In this way, the interaction of strategy and context serves to shape both the development of that context and the very conduct and identity of strategic actors after the event.

What the strategic relational approach offers us, then, is a dynamic understanding of the relationship of structure and agency which resolutely refuses to privilege either moment (structure or agency) in this dialectical and relational interaction. As we shall see in later chapters, this provides a range of crucial insights into the analysis of political power and political change, whilst exhibiting a particular sensitivity to the role of ideas (ideational factors) in the understanding of political dynamics.

Chapter 4

Continuity and Discontinuity in the Analysis of Political Change

That political analysts have increasingly turned to the question of structure and agency derives in no small part from concerns about the capacity of existing approaches to deal with complex issues of social and political change. To posit a world in which structuralist analysis will suffice is to assume that political change is effectively confined to relatively marginal modifications of behaviour set within the context of a definitive set of structuring rules or laws which remain essentially static over time. Though such an assumption renders more plausible a conception of political analysis as a social *science* couched in the image of the natural sciences (as argued in Chapter 2), it is increasingly difficult to reconcile with a world in which the 'rules of the game' seem to be in a state of near-constant flux. Though itself hotly disputed, the globalisation thesis would, for instance, suggest that many of the most cherished of political analytical assumptions (of tightly delimited political territories governed by sovereign states, of nation states and national economies as the natural units of political and political economic analysis respectively) are in a process of being transcended (for a flavour of the debate compare Held *et al.* 1999 with Hirst and Thompson 1999). However sceptical one might (and perhaps *should*) be about the new globalisation orthodoxy, the point is that were it ever plausible to posit a world in which the rules of the game remained constant over time and were immune from human intervention, it is no longer.

If structuralism is inadequate to the task of explaining complex social and political change, then intentionalism is no less problematic. Here, however, the problem is somewhat different. Structuralism implies a world of stability, even stasis – a world in which actors are weighed down by the structural constraints they bear. Intentionalism, by contrast, implies the absence of constraint – a world, in short, in which there are essentially no rules of the game and in which there is a close correspondence between observed and intended outcomes. Intentionalism certainly posits a world of flux, yet it is no better placed to capture the complexity of social and political change. The example of globalisation is again instructive. If globalisation is understood as a process by which the interconnections between distant places and events at the same moment in time are intensified – in which, in essence, the distant becomes proximate in a process of 'time–space compression' (Harvey 1989) – then the world it conjures is not an intentionalist world. Interconnectedness brings opportunities but it also brings constraints. Indeed, in an environment in which local outcomes are shaped not only by local interventions but by the (often unintended) consequences of actions in distant locations, it is far more difficult to ensure a simple correspondence between actors' intentions and outcomes. Local interventions may well be a necessary condition for the realisation of specific objectives, but they are unlikely to be sufficient in themselves. If we are to understand the changing social and political environment in which we find ourselves, then, we must move beyond the superficial appeal of both structuralism and intentionalism. This, at any rate, is the conclusion that political analysts have increasingly come to draw. Its consequence has been a more conscious and reflexive consideration of the question of structure and agency and a more sustained reflection on the conditions of social and political change. It is to the relationship between these issues that we turn in this chapter.

The chapter proceeds in three sections. In the first of these we consider the centrality of questions of political change to political analysis, particularly normative political analysis. We then turn in the second to the variety of analytical strategies which have been advanced to deal with issues of political change, before considering, in the final section, alternative models and conceptualisations of political change and the 'shape' of political time.

Time for change?

As the above discussion already serves to indicate, the analysis and interpretation of political change is one of the more difficult tasks that political analysts face. Change is complex, often unpredictable and invariably the result of a multiplicity of factors. Consequently, it is far easier to assume that political structures, institutions, codes, conventions and norms exhibit some regularity over time than it is to describe, and explain their transformation over time. Herein lies the appeal of structuralist modes of analysis. The obvious casualty, however, is the analysis of political change. All too frequently this is reflected in the temptation to make political analysis an essentially descriptive exercise in mapping a static terrain.

Examples are legion, but include those accounts of the development of the liberal-democratic state which either assume essential continuity over time (captured, for instance, in the notion of the perpetuation of distinct national political models, cultures or traditions) or, conversely, which periodise political development into a series of rigid stages (phases of capitalist development, say) whose internal structure can be charted and mapped without having to consider the temporal dimension (compare, for instance, Badie and Birnbaum 1983 with Cerny 1997; Rostow 1960). Equally problematic, at least for those who regard the analysis of political change as an integral component of any adequate form of political inquiry, is the appeal to trans-historical and universal concepts (such as rationality) abstracted from space and time and, conversely, the attempt to derive trans-historical laws and generalisations (for instance those relating to the determinants of electoral success) from a (statistical) analysis of events at different points in time. Finally, we might note the still highly influential tendency to confine political science to an analysis of a present from which all temporal traces have been removed. Such an approach tends to characterise much (though by no means all) rational choice and behaviouralist political analysis which claims a scientific pedigree.[1] It serves, essentially, to freeze a moment in time as the basis from which either to derive (as in rational choice theory) or to induce through empirical investigation (as in behaviouralism) the rules which structure political behaviour. Frequently, such analyses do not confine their conclusions to the present, offering predictive hypotheses on the basis of the (naturalist) assumption that the rules of the game derived from the analysis of the present will continue to hold in the future.

The principal purpose of this chapter, however, is not to expose the limitations of certain dominant strands of political analysis when it comes to interrogating processes of social and political change. Rather, its aim is to evaluate the potential promise of recent theoretical innovations which have both identified and sought to respond to such limitations.

Before turning directly to these perspectives, however, it will prove instructive to consider why it is that normative political analysis, in particular, should have so much invested in the analysis of political change.

The centrality of political change to normative political analysis

For those wishing to engage in a dispassionate, neutral and, preferably, scientific analysis of the political, the issue of political change is a complicating distraction. The political world would be far easier to analyse were one able to assume that change was confined to fairly marginal modifications of behaviour consistent with general, universal and trans-historical political truths (akin to scientific laws). For avowed political scientists this presents a highly significant three-way choice:

1. Accept – whether as a simplifying assumption and a necessary condition of a genuine science of the political, or as a simple matter of fact (or faith) – that observable political change is indeed of this form and is, as such, consistent with a naturalist political science
2. Defer and displace this disarming question by confining one's focus of analysis to situations in which this assumption appears most plausible, and proceed – on the basis that it is accurate – to develop a naturalist political science of this delimited political sphere, or
3. Acknowledge that there are indeed qualitative differences between the subject matters of the natural and social sciences sufficient to render naturalism (a pan-scientific unity of method) impossible and hence undesirable.

As I have thus far sought to suggest, among those reluctant to surrender their badges of scientific self-identification, very few have pursued the third option, dividing themselves almost equally between the first and second. Nonetheless, confidence in the scientific certainties which were once taken for granted has waned significantly in recent years. Thus, while it is certainly true that the majority of self-proclaimed political scientists proceed *as if* a natural science of the political were possible, far fewer would now regard this as much more than a convenient, simplifying and perhaps a necessary assumption; fewer still would not also wish to acknowledge the inherent fallibility of the knowledge claims they make on the basis of such an assumption (for a particularly clear statement of this see Sanders 1995: 64–8; see also Hinich and Munger 1997: 3–6; Stoker 1995). This disarming candour can only be welcomed. It surely reflects both a far greater acquaintance among practising political scientists with the philosophy of the natural and social sciences and a far greater acknowledgement of the 'fallacy of infallibility' in the latter.

If naturalism – albeit in this significantly qualified form – is still the norm for self-proclaimed political scientists, it is far more difficult to sustain for normatively motivated political analysts (whether critical or conservative).

For any *normative* and *critical political* analyst, the question of change is far from a complicating distraction – it is, in essence, the very *raison d'être* of political inquiry. Stated bluntly, critical political analysis is motivated by the desire for change. Its aim is to expose existing institutions, relations and practices to critical scrutiny as a means of promoting alternatives and bringing those alternatives to fruition. Confidence that the political environment is potentially amenable to conscious political intervention and hence substantive transformation would, then, seem a most basic and fundamental assumption. Without it there would be little purpose in developing a systematic critique of the limitations of existing political institutions and practices. If, to paraphrase Marx, the purpose of critical political analysis is not merely to interpret but to change the world, then above all else critical theorists need to know the conditions under which change occurs. They must retain the capacity to think, in Theodore Adorno's memorable terms, that 'things might be different'.

For conservative political analysts the task is one of vigilance. If they are to defend the status quo, they too must accept the possibility of structural transformation and must be aware and sensitive to the conditions under which it is likely to arise. In this respect they are no less interested than radical political theorists in the mechanisms in and through which change occurs. In particular they are concerned to establish the conditions under which pressures for reform arise, develop and crystallise into genuinely revolutionary threats.

The period from the French Revolution of 1789 to the passing of the Reform Act in Britain in 1832 provides an interesting example. For, arguably, the 1832 Reform Act might be seen as a pre-emptive response by normative defenders of the status quo to the perceived threat of revolution – real or imagined – in the wake of the French Revolution (for such an interpretation, see Finlayson 1970; Thomas and Holt 1977; Tilly 1995). The conservatively motivated political vigilance of the time is well expressed by Edmund Burke (1790). As this suggests, normatively inspired social and political thought, if it is to defend and/or promote the norms for which it stands, must accept the possibility of profound changes to the existing state of affairs in a way that more professedly neutral political analysis need not.

Historical political analysis

Yet it would be wrong to give the impression that it is only normatively motivated political analysts who are interested in questions of change and transformation. While a political science of the present might only be considered plausible in the context of the assumption that the 'rules of the game' are essentially static, such an assumption is in fact rarely held by those engaged in historical political enquiry. For some, this is reason enough to dispense with naturalism and with it any pretensions to a scientific status for the analysis of things political. Yet for others, a social science of historical political development is by no means oxymoronic. They are in good historical company (for excellent discussions of the historians' debate on these issues, see P. Burke 1992: 130–66; Tilly 1991).

Three solutions to the 'problem' of historical variability for the scientific status of political analysis fairly naturally present themselves. The first, and arguably the most influential, has been to adopt what might be termed a 'metahistorical' approach. Here the structural transformation of social, political and economic systems over time is openly acknowledged and embraced. Indeed, it is this which becomes the focus of the analyst's attentions. The laws which govern micro-historical processes and specific political events may be time- and context-dependent, but the laws of motion of history itself are here assumed universal and trans-historical. It is with the (scientific) elucidation of such general laws of societal development that proponents of such a view are concerned. Invariably such metahistorical accounts are also metaphorical in the sense that they are constructed in *evolutionary* terms.

Though, strictly speaking, a biological analogy, it is important to acknowledge that the evolutionary model which came to dominate the social sciences from their very inception was not Darwinian. Indeed, it both predated and differed significantly from that of Darwin (Sztompka 1993: 100). Its founders were Comte and Spencer and, in a dazzling variety of forms, it would come to capture the imagination of such social scientific luminaries as Durkheim, Tönnies and, ultimately, though here in more Darwinian tones, Marx.[2] Such evolutionary theorists seek to identify the underlying form or architecture of history itself. This, for Herbert Spencer, reflects the essential unity of social and natural processes:

> In its primary stage, every germ consists of a substance that is uniform throughout, both in texture and chemical composition. The first step is the appearance of a difference between two parts of this substance; or, as the phenomenon is called in physiological language, a differentiation. Each of these differentiated divisions presently begins itself to exhibit some contrast of parts; and by and by these secondary differentiations become as definite as the original one . . . By endless such differentiations there is finally produced that complex combination of tissues and organs constituting the adult animal or plant. This is the history of all organisms whatever. (Spencer 1972: 39; cited in Sztompka 1993: 102)

Differentiation, Spencer suggests, is essential to life itself and is conserved between biological and social/political systems. What is immediately interesting about this conceptual schema and the analogy upon which it is predicated is that it renders the science of history an essentially agentless affair. Thus, in the same way that a geologist might chart the clash of tectonic plates in reconstructing (after the fact) the history of a given geological form or landmass, so might the metahistorical political analyst detail the unfolding logic of organic differentiation or natural selection that constitutes and reconstitutes the body politic over time. A science of political change is thus rendered possible by removing the contingency and indeterminacy entailed by any recognition that history is *made*. History is thus reduced to the temporal unfolding of a sequence of events which might be catalogued, detailed and cross-correlated. Such an approach is directly analogous to that which enables a (behaviouralist) political science of the present. On the basis of such assumptions historical political analysis presents no greater difficulty to the political scientist than the analysis of the present. Such a view implies a logical unfolding of history in an almost predestined manner. This bloodless conception of political history is increasingly resisted.

More conventional today is Charles Tilly's disarmingly simple but profoundly significant maxim, 'we now live in one of many possible worlds' (1991: 86). Things, in other words, could have been different. It is but a small step to the conclusion that an account incapable of acknowledging this essential indeterminacy of social practice is inadequate to the complexity of history itself. If accepted this would seem sufficient grounds for rejecting an agentless conception of history.[3]

A second, and altogether different, response to the challenge posed by the historicity of political processes for political science is to acknowledge that in so far as rules can be held to govern social and political interaction, those rules are context-dependent. Consequently, to claim universal and trans-historical status for historical/political propositions is to commit a category error – extrapolating from the specific (and familiar) to the general, thereby mistaking parochial truths for trans-historical certainties, historical contingencies for structural necessities. For authors quick to point to the relevance of the vantage-point from which we write for the content of that we write, there can be no general social science of historical development. This is a view now accepted by many contemporary historians and political analysts. It implies a form of qualified naturalism – a science of political change, yes, but one with certain provisos. Since political actors are ultimately capable of transforming the context in which they find themselves, there are no general laws of societal evolution to be elucidated. Consequently, any social science of political development must be restricted to specific contexts and periods of time for which the assumption that the rules of the game remain essentially static is most plausible. One might, for instance, speak more plausibly of the laws governing the accumulation of capital in a particular capitalist economy in the latter part of the nineteenth century than one might of the general laws governing economic exchange in all times and in all places (see also Tilly 1991: 87). What such a view does seem to concede is an essential difference between the subject matters of the social and natural sciences (as discussed in Chapter 2), such that the degree of fit between the methods of the respective sciences is at best partial and is itself dependent upon the question being asked, the context within which it is being asked and the time frame over which it is being asked. Moreover, it implies that while trans-historical and universal claims might be appropriate to the natural sciences they can never be justified in the social sciences.

More radically hermeneutic or interpretativist historians and political analysts have, however, taken their epistemological scepticism considerably further. All knowledge, they suggest, is contextual. Moreover, convenient though it may well be, we cannot simply assume that if we choose our context and time frame with care we can proceed to a scientific analysis of this more delimited arena. For change is ongoing. Consequently, the 'rules of the game' can never be assumed static. Similarly, each context can be disaggregated further (either spatially or temporally) into constituent units, each of which is unique and must be understood in its own terms. This heightened sensitivity to the specificity and distinctiveness of each instant, event, setting or behaviour is characteristic of postmodernism and forms the focus of our attention in Chapter 7. Suffice it for now to note that, taken to its logical conclusion, it entails not only a disavowal of science and any privileged access to knowledge but a rather paradoxical manifesto for silencing historical and political analysts. This Andrew Sayer usefully terms 'defeatist postmodernism' (2000: 6, 67–80). In its less extreme variants, however, the postmodernist sensibility both implies and demands an approach to political and historical analysis which is conceptually cautious, reflexive about the normative and conceptual baggage it bears and acutely aware of its epistemological limitations. As Sayer himself suggests (*ibid.*: 6) this more modest and reflexive approach to the complexity and contingency of political change is by no means incompatible with the critical realist/strategic–relational perspective developed in Chapter 3.

A political science of political change may be very difficult to systematise, as the above discussion perhaps suggests. But this has not prevented a range of historical political analysts, especially those happy to leave scientific claims to others, from seeking to elucidate processes of political change over time. In the case of historical institutionalists, the aim has been to demonstrate the existence and effect of historical legacies in the political processes and institutions of the present (see, for instance, Thelen and Steinmo 1992; P. Pierson 1996a; for useful reviews see, especially, Hall and Taylor 1996; Peters 1999: Ch. 4). For them, quite simply, history matters; to understand the present is to understand how it has evolved from the past and to trace the legacies of that evolution. What this in turn suggests is the following. Even an avowedly neutral and purely descriptive political analysis of the present cannot but afford to acknowledge that the behaviours, practices, processes, institutions and structures it describes are not trans-historical givens transmitted from the past and bequeathed to the future, but are, instead, fluid, dynamic and ever-changing.

Analytical strategies for conceptualising change

As the above paragraphs reveal, issues of transformation and change raise some fairly fundamental questions about the scope, legitimate content, scientific status and limits of political analysis. Yet despite the seeming centrality of political change to political enquiry, remarkably little systematic attention has been devoted to its analysis and, in particular, to the theoretical and conceptual issues it raises. Consequently, political analysts tend to deal very poorly with questions of change, history and temporality where they deal explicitly with them at all.

Yet if there has been little systematic theoretical attention addressed to the problem of political change, this is not to imply that political analysts do not routinely deal with political change in their more substantive work. It is, however, to suggest that we might benefit from considering in a more explicit manner issues which tend to be addressed in a rather *ad hoc*, undertheorised and often inconsistent fashion.

Consider a political system, say a state, developing over time (from time 1 through time 2 to time 3) as follows (see Figure 4.1).

It changes its form over time from, say, a colonial monarchy with limited democratic accountability and participation (*A*), to a more inclusive liberal democratic welfare state in the initial post-war period (*B*) to a more neoliberal workfare/welfare state today (*C*). As political analysts we might be interested in this process of transition over time. More

Figure 4.1 *The development of a state system over time*

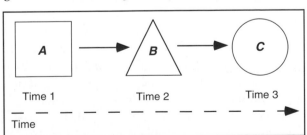

specifically, we might be concerned to identify the distinctive form and structure of the state at various points in this process and to assess the extent of the transformation that the state has undergone over this period of time, the more or less punctuated nature of that process of change and the mechanisms producing such a trajectory. Were we to examine the existing literature we would find a variety of approaches to a period of identified political transformation such as this, some more likely to yield answers to these concerns than others.

Three analytical strategies for dealing with (or, as we shall see, *not* dealing with) the process of political change over time naturally present themselves. They might be labelled the *synchronic*, the *comparative static* and the *diachronic*. Consider each in turn.

Synchronic analysis

The first, certainly the simplest and arguably the most problematic approach to the analysis of political change is the synchronic approach. A synchronic analysis is one which effectively freezes the object of analysis in time, thereby focusing attention on the structure of social or political relations at a specific instant. Indeed, in many respects it removes the object of analysis from the temporal domain altogether. As Peter Osborne notes in an admirable, if somewhat technical, discussion, 'synchrony is not con-temporality, but a-temporality; a purely analytical space in which the temporality immanent in the objects of inquiry is repressed' (1995: 27–8). In other words, a synchronic analysis is one which removes its subject from the temporal sequence of events, relocating it in an abstract theoretical realm outside of the temporal domain from whence it can be exposed to a more detailed structural interrogation. Unremarkably, there are limits to what such an analysis can yield about the process of change itself.

This is all rather abstract. What would a synchronic analysis look like in practice? Well, to return to our earlier example, say we are particularly interested in the structure and form of a state system in the initial post-war period (period *B*). Keen to pursue a synchronic analysis, we would effectively freeze the state at a particular point in time, say 1 November 1964 (during period *B*) in order to describe and detail its structure and form at that instant. Our analysis, a structural analysis in which the temporal dimension plays no part, we would assume to supply us with a general account of the structure and form of the state in question which might be generalised to the entire post-war period. This analytical strategy is presented schematically in Figure 4.2.

Synchronic analysis is, effectively, the equivalent of taking a photograph of a moving object. The result is an image of the object whose

Figure 4.2 *The synchronic or 'snapshot' approach*

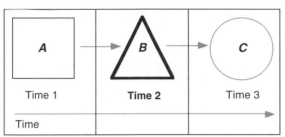

accuracy depends upon the sharpness of our analytical skills and the quality of our access to the relevant information (analogous to the precision and focal distance of the lens). Yet however sharp an image we create, it will tell us nothing about the motion of its object. At best this tells us something about the form of the state at a specific moment in time. It can tell us nothing about the process or even the extent of change; in fact it can tell us nothing about change at all, operating as it does in an artificial analytical realm from which temporality has been abstracted.

Given such comments the synchronic may seem like a rather strange mode of analysis to adopt. Yet a moment's reflection reveals that it is in fact remarkably common. Much political analysis (perhaps the majority) takes this form – describing political relations and behaviour at a particular moment in time in isolation from any consideration of political change over time. Empirical evidence – say in the form of elite interviews with ministers, advisors and senior public officials conducted over the space of a few days or weeks in the life of a government – is invariably taken as indicative of the character of an administration which may endure for several years. In this way, general statements about a particular period of time are generated on the basis of evidence sampled at a specific instant. While such a strategy is incapable, on its own, of giving insight into the process of political change it does have the compensating appeal of simplicity.

Comparative statics

Though in some sense little more than a variation on an essentially synchronic theme, the comparative statics approach represents a considerable improvement upon the narrowly synchronic approach described above, at least with respect to the analysis of political change. Nonetheless, it is important to note that the term is usually one of critique and is seldom a badge of self-identification. It tends to imply an approach

Figure 4.3   *Comparative statics as an analytical strategy*

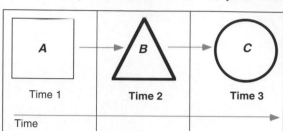

which, however sensitive to political dynamics, still fails to examine the process of change itself. Nonetheless, much ostensibly historical political analysis proceeds on the basis of such an analytical strategy.

Comparative statics is essentially a variant of synchronic analysis in which the analyst compares and contrasts synchronic analyses conducted at different moments in time, thereby comparing the form and structure of the system in question at various points in its development. Were we interested in the development of the state in the post-war period (with B and C), we might freeze the state in, say, 1964 (B) and again today (C) to compare and contrast the two. To do so would be to engage in an exercise in comparative statics. This strategy is depicted schematically in Figure 4.3.

While such a mode of analysis can clearly tell us something about the extent and direction of change over a particular period of time, it gives us no real clue as to the process of change itself. It tells us, for instance, nothing about the character, pace or temporality of change over the post-war period. For if we simply counterpose two structural (synchronic) analyses of the institutional architecture of the state at distinct moments in time (t_2 and t_3) we put ourselves in no position to adjudicate between contending accounts of the process by which that architecture has travelled from where it was at t_2 to where is has come to be by t_3. Is the process one of continuous and incremental evolution or is it characterised by a period of stasis punctuated by sudden and rapid institutional transformation? Or, indeed, is it better captured by some combination of the two? We simply lack the evidence to discriminate between these contending accounts.

More substantively, were we to engage in a comparative static analysis of the state, say, at the time of the great depression in 1929 and again in 1946 we would clearly identify substantial institutional changes. Yet without some knowledge of the intervening period, we would be incapable of adjudicating between contending accounts which attributed this observed transformation to a punctuating external shock (such as the

Second World War) or to an incremental and cumulative process of institutional change (associated, say, with a secular tendency for the scope and scale of the state's influence to rise over time). It is likely that additional information and the research of others may help us to assess the relative plausibility of such contending accounts of the evidence we generate. Nonetheless, in the absence of such additional information, the comparative static approach is itself incapable of contributing to our understanding of the process of change.

Given this, it is perhaps unremarkable that comparative static analysis has tended to result in approaches to the question of institutional change that emphasise historical oppositions or dualisms. Accounts of social and political change which employ comparative static methodologies are invariably couched in terms of a step-wise of 'stage'-ist conception of systemic change, contrasting the form of the system at an earlier stage of development (t_1) with its form at a later development stage (t_2). Comparative statics thus tends to be associated with conceptual pairings and oppositions such as modernity versus postmodernity, fordism versus post-fordism, closed national economies versus an open global economy, and, so forth. As suggested above, this counterposing of static snapshots taken as reflective of stages of development of the system in question in fact tends to prejudge and foreclose any discussion and analysis of the process and hence the temporality of change.

Yet it would be wrong to present comparative statics as always the methodological *cause* of such a discontinuous or step-wise conception of social and political change. For it might just as easily be the methodological *effect* of having already assumed a step-wise conception of institutional change. Thus, for historical materialists committed to an account of the course of human history in terms of the revolutionary progression from one mode of production to another, a comparative static approach (contrasting, say, exchange and productive relations under feudalism and capitalism) entails no necessary loss of insight. Since the logic of accumulation of capital is assumed to be constant for the duration of the capitalist mode of production, it does not need to be analysed over time. A synchronic analysis will suffice. Thus, if it can be assumed that for the duration of a given mode of production (t_0 to t_1, or t_2 to t_3 in Figure 4.4) the nature of the accumulation process is essentially invariant, then a synchronic analysis will serve to capture the logic of production and exchange.

In a similar vein, for those authors committed theoretically to a step-wise conception of institutional change, a comparative static approach is likely to prove entirely sufficient. Thus, for so-called regulation theorists committed to an account of capitalist development in terms of a succession of relatively stable phases of capitalist accumulation inter-

Figure 4.4   *Comparative statics in historical materialism*

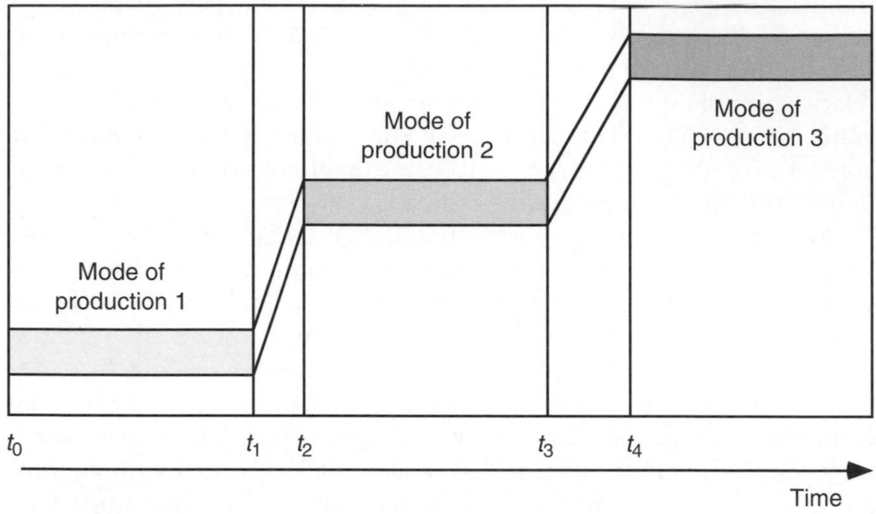

rupted periodically by punctuating crises, a comparative static counter-posing of one regime of accumulation (say, fordism) with its successor (post-fordism) is both theoretically consistent and empirically illuminating.[4]

What examples like this demonstrate, however, is that while comparative static methodologies themselves offer no insight into the process of change over time, they do imply, as they rely upon, certain assumptions about that process of change. As both regulation theory and the Marxist philosophy of historical materialism demonstrate, such assumptions may be explicit and theoretically informed. Yet, more frequently, they are implicit, unacknowledged and undefended. Either way they may impede and prejudge an empirical assessment of the pace, direction and temporality of the process of social and political change.

Diachronic analysis

With diachronic analysis we come, eventually, to a form of analysis which does not prejudge the issue of change over time and for which, consequently, the pace and timing of political change are empirical issues. *A diachronic analysis emphasises the process of change over time.* Rather than assume that the development of the system in question, say the state, can be split up into phases during which its structure and form can be assumed static (as in the comparative static approach), the devel-

Figure 4.5 *The diachronic approach to systemic change*

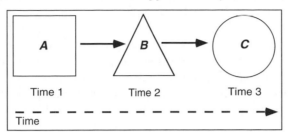

opmental path and the pace of change is treated as a matter for empirical investigation.

The analysis proceeds historically, emphasising the process of change over time. If the synchronic approach is analogous to the taking of a photograph at a particular instant and the comparative static approach to the taking of photographs at different points in time, the diachronic approach is the equivalent of a video 'panning' shot which follows the motion of the object in question. This is represented schematically in Figure 4.5.

This type of approach has been advocated most consistently in recent years by historical institutionalists who see their task as one of 'process tracing' (Krasner 1984; see also Hall 1993; Hay 2001b; P. Pierson 1996b; Thelen and Steinmo 1992), evolutionary economists who reject the rather static approach adopted by the neoclassical mainstream (Hodgson 1988, 1991, 1993; see also Carrier and Miller 1998; Rutherford 1996) and some neo-Marxists for whom the process of change is both complex and contingent (see, for instance, Jessop 1990a; Kerr 2001). What each approach shares is a desire to trace and chart the complex interaction of causal processes to produce structural and behavioural change – whether continuous or discontinuous, incremental or punctuating, evolutionary or revolutionary.

The diachronic approach has the clear benefit of allowing the political analyst to build empirically a picture of the process of change – such that we can assess the pace and timing of change without having to assume the form it takes in advance. In this way it allows us either inductively and empirically to advance theoretical statements about the temporal aspects (the time, timing and temporality) of the process of change under consideration or to test deductively derived theoretical hypotheses about that process of change.

This empirical emphasis upon the unfolding dynamic of institutional and behavioural change often tends to dispel or at least qualify significantly the sharp and dualistic periodisations which tend to be associated with comparative static methodologies. An empirical and historical analysis of the changing contours of European capitalism in the post-war period may, for instance, lead one to challenge significantly the notion of a rapid shift from fordism to post-fordism originating some time in the 1970s and impacting with equal force across the advanced capitalist world. Similarly, the notion of simple and epochal shifts from, say, modernity to postmodernity, national to global capitalism, and Keynesianism to monetarism are likely to emerge as casualties of a more diachronic or genuinely historical analysis which does not seek to privilege specific instants in the overall process of change.

It is tempting on the basis of the above discussion to conclude that if we are genuinely interested in the process of change we should confine our analysis to the diachronic, tracing processes over time. Yet it is important to acknowledge that here, as ever, trade-offs are involved. For while the use of synchronic snapshots offers us a relatively simple and convenient analytical tool, conducting a diachronic analysis in any rigorous fashion is a laborious and time-consuming exercise. Given such logistical considerations it is not terribly surprising that where synchronic or comparative static methodologies will suffice (where, for instance, the temporality of change can be assumed) and sometimes where they will not, political analysts have tended to exhibit a preference for such techniques.

Time, timing and temporality

As the above paragraphs have hopefully demonstrated, of the three perspectives considered, diachronic analysis has the potential to offer us the greatest insight into the complex and often unpredictable process of social and political change.

Yet even among those who engage in such analyses, there is little agreement as to the tempo, temporality and resulting 'shape' or pattern of social and political change over time. A variety of models of change can nonetheless be identified, appropriate perhaps to different contexts. This latter point is crucial. For there may be very good reasons to suggest that change displays a step-wise or punctuated path in certain social and political environments yet a more incremental and evolutionary trajectory in others. It is, then, important to consider the conditions under which change exhibits different rhythms and temporalities. Here the distinction between evolutionary and revolutionary temporalities is particularly significant.

Revolutionary change

The concept of revolution refers, in is broadest sense, to the abrupt – in some accounts near-instantaneous – process of institutional/systemic change in which the defining features of the social and political system are significantly recast. It can be, and invariably is, counterposed to evolution in which a more gradual, long-term and yet cumulative and directional process of change is proposed. A revolutionary process of change is one of discontinuity, in which, conventionally, periods of stability (or stasis) are punctuated by abrupt, intense and rapid moments of profound transformation.

In addition to this more general conception, revolution may be more precisely and specifically defined as, for instance, by Samuel Huntingdon as 'a rapid, fundamental and violent domestic change in the dominant values and myths of a society, in its political institutions, social structure, leadership, government activity and policies' (1968: 264). However, for present purposes I am less concerned with imposing an exacting and exclusive definition (insistent, say, on the violent and/or self-consciously revolutionary nature of the process of change being considered) than I am in exploring the opposition between revolution and evolution.

The preference for a revolutionary as distinct from an evolutionary conception of social and political change may arise in different ways. Here it is important to differentiate between those authors drawn theoretically to an account of history as a succession of stages punctuated periodically by abrupt moments of revolutionary transformation and those whose (revolutionary) account of the process of change is based more on observed empirical regularities. Among the former more deductive approach, we find Marxists and indeed neo/post-Marxist regulation theorists, both of whose theoretical schemas lead them to anticipate an alternation throughout history between periods of comparative tranquillity and rapid moments of structural transformation (whether the violent transition from one mode of production to another or the more peaceful replacement of one regime of accumulation with another within the capitalist mode of production). In addition, we also find a range of authors who seek to chart, in a sequential and rather agentless manner, what they see as the 'natural history' of a revolutionary cycle that is both inevitable and irreversible (Brinton 1965[1938]; Edwards 1927; Pettee 1938; see also Goldstone 1982). As Michael S. Kimmel notes, within this framework, 'as in classical tragedy, different social groups take various unalterable parts in the unfolding drama, which moves through a vicious cathartic bloodbath before the orderly passing on to a new regime' (1990: 47). In contrast to such deductive approaches, the induc-

Figure 4.6   *The revolutionary conception of political time*

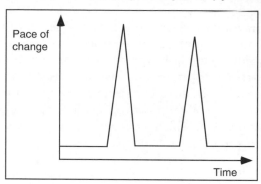

tive approach to revolutions is altogether more diverse. It encompasses a broad spectrum from normative political theorists, such as Edmund Burke (1968[1790]) and Alexis de Tocqueville (1955[1856]), anxious to protect the existing state of affairs from the threat of revolution, via those contemporary historical sociologists interested in tracing the process of institutional change over time whatever its observed temporality (for instance, Skocpol 1979, 1994; Tilly 1978, 1993; Tilly, Tilly and Tilly 1975) to those behaviouralists seeking to uncover empirically the causal factors which precipitate revolutionary change (for instance, Davies 1962, 1971; Gurr 1968, 1970a, 1970b). Whether empirically observed or theoretically derived, however, what this impressive diversity of authors share is a conception of social and political change in which revolution plays a key role, punctuating longer periods of relative stability. This conception is represented schematically in Figure 4.6.

Frequently this cycling between periods of stasis and periods of revolutionary transformation is assumed to be linked to similarly cyclical fluctuations in the level of relative deprivation, as reflected in levels of organised social protest. The classic analysis is the 'relative deprivation thesis' advanced by James C. Davies (1962) and Ted Gurr (1970b). This seeks to operationalise Tocqueville's observation that

> it is not always when things are going from bad to worse that revolutions break out. On the contrary, it often happens that when a people which has put up with an oppressive rule over a long period without protest suddenly finds the government relaxing its pressure, it takes up arms against it. Thus the social order overthrown by a revolution is almost always better than the one immediately preceding it, and experience teaches that us that, generally speaking, the most perilous moment for a bad government is when it seeks to mend its ways. (1955[1856]: 176–7)

The idea is a simple one. In a context characterised by improvements in material well-being, societal expectations will tend to increase – indeed, they will often tend to outstrip the capacity of the system to satisfy them. Such a scenario is likely to be stable while the disparity between anticipated and observed performance remains low and material well-being continues to rise (even if at a modest pace). However, any marked downturn in the capacity of the state to sustain improvements in material wellbeing is now likely to precipitate a revolutionary juncture. This is the so-called 'J-curve' model of revolution (Davies 1969). It assumes escalating societal expectations and the state's increasing inability to satisfy such expectations. Yet, as Gurr goes on to argue, this is but one of a number of potential scenarios in which relative deprivation might lead to revolutionary mobilisation. He defines relative deprivation as 'the perceived discrepancy between men's [*sic*] value expectations and value capabilities' (1970b: 13), arguing that this is directly correlated with both the intensity and scope of political violence. Unlike Davies before him, however, he differentiates between a variety of paths to relative deprivation and hence to revolution:

1. 'Decremental deprivation' – in which expectations remains constant but the state's ability to satisfy them falls
2. 'Aspirational deprivation' – in which the state's capacity to satisfy expectations remains constant while those expectations rise
3. 'Progressive deprivation' – in which expectations rise while state capacity declines (Davies' J-curve model), and
4. 'Accelerated deprivation' – in which expectations and the state's capacity to deliver material benefits both rise but at different rates such that the latter fails to keep pace with the former (1970b: 47–56).

Despite this differentiation between paths to revolutionary transformation borne of political protest, however, the central mechanism is the same. It is represented schematically in Figure 4.7.

Figure 4.7 presents the simplest scenario (corresponding to Gurr's model of decremental deprivation) in which the expected performance of the state remains constant. The logic of the model rests on the extent of the disparity between the expected and observed performance of the state (P_e and P_0, respectively). Once this disparity ($P_e - P_0$) reaches a critical level (r), a revolutionary juncture exists. At time t_1, the polity is stable since, although there is a disparity between the observed and expected performance of the state (and hence a condition of relative deprivation), $P_e - P_0 < r$. By time t_r, however, the disparity has grown (and with it the extent of relative deprivation) such that $P_e - P_0 > r$. A revolutionary scenario now exists. The value of r (the level of relative deprivation sufficient to precipitate revolution) will vary from political

Figure 4.7 *Gurr's relative deprivation thesis*

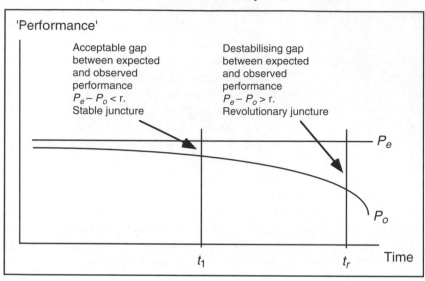

'Performance'

Acceptable gap
between expected
and observed
performance
$P_e - P_o < r$.
Stable juncture

Destabilising gap
between expected
and observed
performance
$P_e - P_o > r$.
Revolutionary juncture

P_e

P_o

t_1 t_r Time

system to political system and, for the same political system, over time. This reflects a range of mediating contextual factors, such as the existence of permitted and effective channels of political protest, the cogency of dissident organisations, the existence of means of channeling and diverting aggressive behaviour and of compensating distractions from revolutionary activity.

In models such as this, revolutions act like pressure release valves (cf. Tilly 1978: 218), restabilising the political system.

Protest and pressure builds exponentially as societal expectations remain unsatisfied. At a certain point the status quo is shattered by revolutionary mobilisation resulting in a rapid and intense period of systematic systemic transformation. The process is cathartic, cleansing the body politic of protest and dissension until such time as the pressure builds again (see Figure 4.8).

The revolutionary conception of social and political change thus posits an uneven unfolding of political change over time. Political history is depicted as an alternation between relatively lengthy periods of stasis and abrupt and condensed moments of fundamental transformation. Though perhaps most closely associated with the Marxist philosophy of historical materialism and, before that the Hegelian dialectic, it is by no means a necessarily Marxian or Hegelian conception of social and political change. Indeed, it has obvious affinities with theoretical schemas as varied as Vilfredo Pareto's account of the 'circulation of

Figure 4.8 *Revolutions as pressure-release valves*

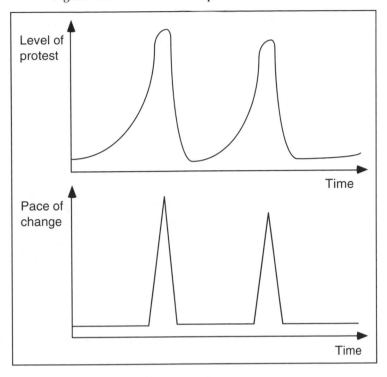

elites' (1935, 1966), the so-called war-centred theories of state development advanced by a range of Weberian and neo-Weberian authors (Mann 1985, 1988; Shaw 1984; Tilly 1973), and Kondratiev and Kuznets' theories of 'long-waves' of economic development (Kondratiev 1925, 1935, 1984 [1928]; Kuznets 1953; for a commentary, Berry 1991).

Those who advance a punctuated and revolutionary rather than an incremental and evolutionary conception of political change tend in general to view such a discontinuous political temporality as a universal human condition. However, one might plausibly suggest that such a punctuated model of social and political change is likely to prove most appropriate in certain types of political system and rather less so in others. Thus, non-democratic political systems, where there are few pressure-release valves other than state repression and the revolutionary transformation of the state, are perhaps more likely to exhibit a punctuated political development than more participatory and democratic political systems which are more able to respond constructively to societal discontents.

Evolutionary change

In key respects the evolutionary model of change is the very antithesis of the revolutionary model. Where conceptions of revolutionary change emphasise discontinuity, evolutionary accounts identify continuous processes of social and political change which are incremental yet nonetheless directional and hence cumulative over time. Or so one might think. For, to complicate things somewhat, much contemporary evolutionary biology has now come to embrace the notion of 'punctuated equilibrium', implying a rather discontinuous conception of change over time (see, for instance, Somit and Peterson 1989b). Moreover, this model has become increasingly influential in political analysis.

Yet, if it is perhaps increasingly difficult to differentiate between evolutionary and revolutionary accounts of systemic change (biological or political), this was by no means always the case. Classically, evolutionary perspectives posit gradual yet directional change. While the specific pace of change may well fluctuate periodically, it is never more than moderate. Moreover, the mechanism of change is one of adaptation and selection rather than one linked with the mobilisation of political protest and the build-up of pressure upon a centralised state apparatus (see Figure 4.9).

Classical evolutionary perspectives are distinguished by a series of common themes, highly conserved between different evolutionary theorists. These, as has already been noted, derive not from Darwinian evolutionary biology as is frequently assumed, but from a tradition of social evolutionism associated with Auguste Comte and, in particular, Herbert Spencer which in fact pre-dates the development of evolutionary theory in biology (Sztompka 1993: 125). Its core features are those of structural/functional differentiation and the growing complexity of the social/political system over time. Classic evolutionary theory thus posits a trans-historical process of societal development in which the growing

Figure 4.9   *The evolutionary conception of political time*

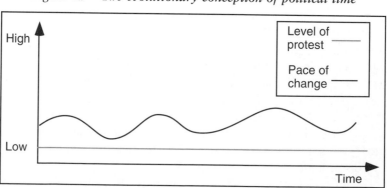

scope, scale and complexity of the social and political system is reflected in an ever more elaborate division of social, political and economic functions – just as the growing complexity of organisms is reflected in their internal differentiation into organelles, cells and organs. As C. R. Hallpike notes, 'for Spencer . . . societies are like organisms in all essential respects, in which every part has some essential function in relation to the well-being of the whole and whose evolution is a series of adaptive responses to the pressures of competition, the whole of the process exemplifying the famous principle of the Survival of the Fittest' (1986: 83–4; Spencer 1891, Part I: 272–7).[5] Spencer, in particular, argues that as society develops an entirely homogeneous mass culture becomes ever more unsustainable (1972). Innate inequalities of human endowment, a range of contingent factors and environmental conditions result in a differentiation of roles which, in turn, become more highly specialised such that the return to a 'primitive' condition of cultural uniformity becomes ever more difficult to effect. Functional differentiation is, then, an irreversible process. This is the basis from which the distinctive characteristics and attendant assumptions of evolutionary theory develop (Box 4.1).

Box 4.1   The defining characteristics of classical evolutionary thought

1.   The object of evolutionary explanation is assumed to be human society in its entirety. This is understood in organic terms, with the product being qualitatively greater than the sum of its component parts.
2.   Human history is assumed to display a distinct logic or pattern which is, in principle, knowable and which it is the task of evolutionary theory to elucidate.
3.   Change is assumed inescapable and irreversible but also directional – society evolves from the primitive to the developed, the simple to the complex, the homogeneous to the heterogeneous, the chaotic to the organised, the uniform to the differentiated. Such change, and the (evolutionary) mechanisms underpinning it, are understood to operate at the level of the system as a whole. It is reflected in, but not derivable from, the development of the system's constituent parts. Change is assumed to be unilinear, following a distinct and, in many accounts, a pre-destined path.
4.   The path of evolution is assumed to be divisible into stages, forming a 'natural' developmental path which cannot be altered – no stage can be by-passed.
5.   Change is assumed to be gradual, incremental and cumulative.
6.   Change is progressive (see also Hallpike 1986: 81–145; Hirst 1976: 14–48; Noble 2000: 40–70; Sztompka 1993: 99–112).

Understood in such strict and exacting terms, very few classically evolutionary perspectives persist. Indeed, contemporary evolutionary theorists reject almost all aspects of the above list. Where their classical forebears (such as Comte, Spencer, Tönnies and Durkheim) were motivated by a desire to chart the evolutionary logic of human history itself and their less distant neo-classical progenitors (such as Parsons, Sahlins and Service, Smelser and Rostow) were similarly motivated by the attempt to chart the evolution of specific societies through a succession of developmental stages, contemporary evolutionary theorists are altogether more modest in their theoretical endeavours.[6] Resistant to assumptions of common and inexorable developmental trajectories, of necessary stages of development through which societies must pass, of the value of 'agentless' natural histories of societal development and, above all, of the progressive nature of evolutionary change, they concern themselves with the elucidation of the complex and contingent mechanisms and processes of adaptation and selection which serve to give a directional character to institutional change. Thus, of the six central tenets of evolutionary theory outlined above, perhaps only the fifth survives.

Contemporary evolutionary thought must, then, be characterised rather differently. Whereas classical evolutionary theory, taking its inspiration from developmental biology, emphasises the growing complexity and differentiation of the social system, more contemporary perspectives tend to take their evolutionary inspiration and terminology from Darwin, emphasising competition, selection and adaptation. As Randall Collins perceptively notes, the former 'takes embryology as the model and represents society as growing like an organism, becoming not only larger but differentiating into specialised organs and functions'. The latter, by contrast, draws an altogether different biological analogy, namely, 'the Darwinian theory of how species evolve through the variation and natural selection of those forms best adapted to their environments'. Moreover, where 'differentiation sees societies as analogous to single organisms, growing during their lifetime; natural selection sees societies as analogous to the variety of species (populations of organisms), some of which are selected as favourable adaptations, and some of which are not' (Collins 1988: 13). The result is a series of characteristic traits of contemporary evolutionary theory which serve to differentiate it quite clearly from its now distant ancestors. These core tenets and assumptions are well summarised by Peter Kerr and David Marsh (1999, see Box 4.2).

Box 4.2 Contemporary evolutionary theory – key assumptions

1. Contemporary evolutionary theory is centrally concerned with understanding the temporality of change, exhibiting a heightened sensitivity to ongoing processes of change over time.
2. It is concerned to elucidate the factors and mechanisms which generate change and which serve to give to it a directional character. It is particularly sensitive to the potential interaction between processes and tendencies of change and the contingencies of outcomes this suggests.
3. Evolutionary dynamics are seen to derive from the complex interaction of selective and adaptive processes and hence from the (dialectical) interplay of environmental (structural) and intentional (agential) factors.
4. Change is conceived, consequently, as both path-dependent and contingent. History, though not determinant of future outcomes, lends a selectivity to the subsequent course of historical events, selecting for certain outcomes over others (Kerr and Marsh 1999: 177; see also de Bresson 1987; Hodgson 1993: Part IV; R. R. Nelson 1995; Nelson and Winter 1982; Ward 1997).

Useful as this checklist of assumptions is, however, a note of caution should perhaps be registered. For, save except for the appeal to the language of adaptive and selective mechanisms and, possibly, to the notion of change as incremental and cumulative rather than abrupt and punctuated, there is little that would seem distinctively *evolutionary* about this set of assumptions. Nor, for that matter, would most of these assumptions be regarded as particularly contentious among a great variety of authors who do not choose to regard themselves as advancing an evolutionary perspective. We should be cautious, then, not to assume that any author keen to emphasise the contingency of social and political change, the complex or dialectical relationship of structure and agency and the articulation or interaction of causal processes in the unfolding of political dynamics over time can be classified an evolutionary theorist. Indeed, one might well go further to suggest that there is in fact something of a tension in the above list of core evolutionary assumptions, especially if evolutionary accounts are seen as committed to the notion of incremental and cumulative change over time. For if the process of change is genuinely contingent – arising out of the dynamic, complex and unpredictable interaction of structure and agency such that contextual constraints are 'negotiated' (Kerr and Marsh 1999: 177) –

then is not the temporality of change an empirical rather than a theoretical question? What guarantees that the contingency of social and political change is confined to that consistent with an evolutionary temporality? Arguably, the highly sophisticated theoretical assumptions mapped out by Kerr and Marsh in fact preclude an evolutionary theory if, by evolutionary theory, we mean a perspective wedded to the notion of change as incremental. For, in the end, the process of change *either* exhibits a necessary temporality (whether evolutionary or revolutionary) or a contingent and indeterminate logic.

Ironically, perhaps, contemporary evolutionary biology may well come to our rescue here. For, as earlier indicated, the commitment to a notion of evolution as a gradual yet directional process of change is one which is rejected by a growing number of evolutionary biologists, who now point to the often punctuated nature of species evolution and the significance of catastrophic events (see, especially, Berggren and Van Couvering 1984; Eldredge and Gould 1972; Gould and Eldredge 1977; Levins and Lewontin 1985). These contemporary developments are encapsulated in the term 'punctuated equilibrium' to which we turn in the next section. The key point, for now, is that for such authors the temporality of evolutionary change may vary.

Whether this presents a potential solution or not, what is clear is that self-proclaimed evolutionary political analysts retain a strong commitment to the notion of evolution as a gradual and cumulative process. What is also clear is that such a model of social and political change is likely to prove most applicable in contexts in which levels of social protest and relative deprivation are low and in which the state is responsive to societal pressures as and when they arise (if it cannot anticipate them and take pre-emptive action). For many authors (notably many pluralists) this presents an accurate description of social and political change in contemporary liberal democracies; for others it is something of an idealised view of such societies, assuming rather higher levels of responsiveness to societal pressures than is really the case. Nonetheless, one does not have to accept this rather idyllic and participatory depiction of the liberal-democratic polity to argue that such political systems tend to be characterised, at least in general terms, by evolutionary rather than revolutionary change. A range of Marxist and neo-Marxist authors, for instance, have pointed to the ability of the contemporary capitalist state to channel societal discontents in such a way that they can be responded to and incorporated within the broad parameters of a liberal capitalist social formation. Indeed, one might plausibly argue that contemporary Marxist scholarship is characterised by its various attempts both to come to terms with and to explain how the long-anticipated revolutionary crisis of capitalism has come to be indefinitely postponed – to be replaced by a process of iterative evolution and adaptation (see, for instance, Aglietta 1979; Boyer 1990; Kerr 2001; Marsh 1999b).

Punctuated evolution and punctuated equilibrium

As suggested above, the notion of punctuated equilibrium has its origins in contemporary evolutionary biology. Here it is associated with two claims: 'that evolutionary change (or at least very significant proportions thereof) occurs in rapid bursts over (geologically) short periods of time, and that there is relative stasis after the punctuational burst' (Somit and Peterson 1989b: 1). The term was first applied to similar developments in political analysis by Stephen D. Krasner in an important review of contemporary strands in state theory (1984: 242). Krasner identified similarities in the work of a number of institutionalist authors who pointed to the 'episodic and dramatic rather then continuous and incremental' nature of institutional change and hence to 'differential rates of change in social and political structures over time' (*ibid.*: 234, 240). The term has now come to be associated with two distinct theoretical perspectives – neo-statism and historical institutionalism (see, for instance, Hall 1986, 1993; Hay 1999d, 2001b; P. Pierson 1996a, 1996b; Skocpol and Ikenberry 1983; Thelen and Steinmo 1992). Yet it is also worth noting that these positions have clear affinities with a range of neo/post-Marxist theorists of the state (see, for instance, Block 1987; Debray 1973; Hay 1996; Jessop 1990a; Offe 1984). Finally, the term punctuated equilibrium has also come to be associated with a diverse range of perspectives in comparative political and public policy which stress the significance of 'critical junctures' (Collier and Collier 1991), 'crises' (Hay 1999d; Skowronek 1982) or 'critical institutional events' (Baumgartner and Jones 1993).

As the term would itself suggest, punctuated equilibrium refers to a discontinuous conception of political time in which periods of comparatively modest institutional change are interrupted by more rapid and intense moments of transformation. This view of social and political change, when applied to the development of the liberal-democratic state, is seen by many as a rather more sanguine account than the evolutionary perspective. It points to the ability of the liberal-democratic state to respond successfully to societal demands and to disarm opposition, but also to its proneness to periodic moments of crisis in which this ability is compromised and in which the pace of change accelerates significantly. As Régis Debray perceptively notes, 'time is clearly not a homogeneous continuum; each period of social development, each social development,

Figure 4.10   *Punctuated equilibrium*

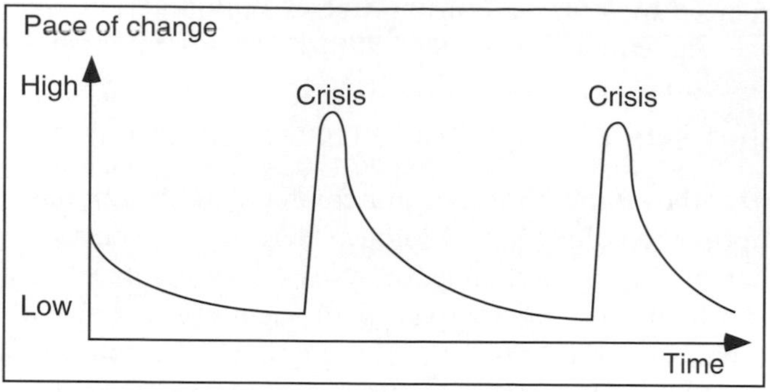

each social grouping has its ups and downs in time . . . political time moves faster in periods of crisis and stagnates in times of regression' (1973: 90).

This model of punctuated equilibrium combines aspects of both the revolutionary and evolutionary conception and is represented schematically in Figure 4.10. For long periods of historical time, change may appear incremental and entirely consistent with an evolutionary perspective. However, we cannot rule out the possibility that such periods of gradual change will be punctuated, however infrequently, by a dramatic quickening in the pace of change associated with moments of crisis. In such moments political regimes are overturned and governing paradigms replaced.

An example, though one not entirely undisputed in the existing literature, is the crisis of fordism and of the Keynesian welfare state in Western Europe in the late 1970s. This is widely interpreted as bringing to an end a period of sustained economic growth, political stability and policy continuity as the monetarist or neo-liberal paradigm of the 1980s came to replace the Keynesian, corporatist and welfarist paradigm of the post-war period (Gourevitch 1986; Hall 1993; Jessop 1992, 1994; Kitschelt 1994; Scharpf 1991).

Such a schema suggests that the development of the modern state is characterised by often lengthy periods of relative tranquillity in which consensus politics and an incremental or evolutionary form of development dominates. Here the pace of change is slower, though it is important to note that change nonetheless occurs. In moments of crisis, however, the pace of change quickens as one consensus is overturned and attempts are made to establish a new one (as Keynesian welfarism is replaced by monetarism or neo-liberalism, for instance). Such crises tend to be characterised by a growing frustration with the governing paradigm (the ruling ideas) and by the perceived need for an alternative.

While crises are identified as moments of great significance for the subsequent development of the social and political system in question, we cannot afford to dispense with an analysis of the intervening periods of relative calm. In this sense, the term punctuated equilibrium may be somewhat misleading, implying as it does an alternation between equilibrium or stasis in which little of significance occurs and disequilibrium or crisis in which the parameters of political possibility are fundamentally recast. Preferable, and a rather more accurate reflection of the views of historical institutionalists, is the term 'punctuated evolution' (Hay 2001a) which draws attention to the cumulative nature of often incremental change. While it is important, then, to emphasise the significance of punctuating moments of crisis, it is equally imperative that this is not achieved at the expense of a failure to acknowledge what goes on between crises (Kerr 2001).

Conclusion: structural, agential and ideational factors in the analysis of political change

In the same way that it is tempting to prefer a complex or dialectical view of the structure–agency relationship to its simple or one-dimensional alternatives, it is perhaps tempting to prefer the complex, punctuated evolutionary perspective to its simple, evolutionary and revolutionary alternatives. Yet, as with the question of structure and agency, some caution is required. For, here as elsewhere, trade-offs are involved. A punctuated evolutionary perspective is certainly versatile and, arguably, lends itself to rich and descriptively accurate accounts. Yet this versatility and descriptive accuracy is achieved at the price of theoretical complexity. Evolutionary and revolutionary perspectives, by contrast, are capable of providing us with highly parsimonious explanations, though they are, as a consequence, less likely to account for the nuances of complex social and political change.

Our preference for evolutionary, revolutionary or punctuated evolutionary perspectives on social and political change may, then, reflect our preference for parsimony or theoretical complexity. In a similar way, the extent to which we emphasise structural or agential factors in explanations of political change is likely to reflect our preference for structuralist, intentionalist or dialectical approaches to the structure–agency relationship. A range of distinctive structural, agential and, indeed, ideational factors can be identified. These might be woven together in a complex account of social and political change. In practice they are inextricably (indeed, ontologically) interwoven. Nonetheless, they are analytically separable. We consider each in turn.

Structural factors related to political change

If, as suggested above, political change is about the capacity of actors to shape their environment, about the ability of actors to make a difference, then this clearly depends upon the context in which they find themselves. Contextual factors are, then, likely to prove central to all but the most parsimonious and intentionalist explanations of social and political dynamics. A key challenge for those interested in the analysis of political change is to identify the extent to which, and the specific mechanisms through which, circumstances influence political behaviour and hence political outcomes.

If contexts might be seen as presenting actors with a range of opportunities and constraints, then it is important that we acknowledge the invariably uneven distribution of opportunities and constraints which they present to different actors. Differential access to strategic resources – such as knowledge and capital – may be a significant determinant of the capacity of actors to realise the opportunities inherent in any given social or political context. Thus, for those without capital or time (resources which might, in turn, be invested in knowledge), the opportunities for political protest, far less protest likely to result in the desired political outcome, are invariably extremely limited. As this suggests, access to resources is unevenly distributed in a structured manner – by virtue of class, ethnicity, gender, sexuality, kinship and so forth.

Structural or contextual factors thus present an unevenly contoured terrain, facilitating the strategic interventions of certain actors at the expense of others and selecting for certain outcomes over others. It is worth examining these in a little more detail.

In particular, we might differentiate between what might be termed *natural* and *social* structural factors. Both may limit the parameters of effective choice for political actors. An example of a natural constraint is the so-called 'half-life' of stratospheric chloro-fluoro-carbons (CFCs) – the length of time it takes for half of a given volume of CFCs to break down in the upper stratosphere. This gives us an indication of likely persistence of CFCs in the atmosphere. It is a natural constraint in the sense that it is not subject to human intervention. Yet it has profound political implications. If, as scientists have demonstrated, CFCs are likely to persist in the stratosphere for a considerable period of time and, as has been known since the early 1970s, their presence serves to catalyse ozone depletion, then ozone depletion cannot be halted for a considerable period of time even if all sources of stratospheric CFCs are eliminated. As Barbara Adam suggests, 'despite corrective action . . . there may be long periods of worsening effects before any sign of improvement can be registered' (1994: 100).

Yet if this is a natural constraint, there are as many social constraints in the politics of ozone depletion. As Adam again notes, 'the story of CFCs . . . is replete with time lags', very few of which are natural in origin:

> It is marked by time lags not merely between cause and effect, or between invention and recognition of the problem, but also between the identification of the problem, its multinational acceptance [as a problem] and the global agreement to take action. It entails time lags between the will to action and its collective execution, between actions and effects, between human corrective change and environmental recuperation. (1994: 100)

The vast majority of these constraints are social in origin.

As this example would perhaps suggest, the temporal aspects of structural or contextual factors are often highly significant. Opportunities absent for relatively long periods of political time may present themselves at others. During moments of perceived crisis, for instance, the opportunity for institutional and ideational change may be rather greater than at other moments of political time. Similarly, a particular hot summer or a severe storm may do more for the cause of environmental security than any number of academic reports charting the extent of ozone depletion or global warming.

Agential factors related to political change

Structural factors are certainly crucial to an understanding of social and political change. However, without some conception of human agency it is difficult to account for the seeming indeterminacy of social and political change. In the final analysis, after all, it is agents who make history. Consequently, if it is perhaps only arch intentionalists who would deny the significance of structural or contextual factors, it is only those committed to a purely deterministic conception of political development who would deny the significance of agential factors. Most obvious among these are the personal traits and characteristics of political subjects. Thus, prominent in descriptive histories of processes of political change are appeals to the charisma, personality, motivations and intentions of political subjects. While contexts present opportunities to actors, it is the conduct of those actors which determines the extent to which such opportunities are realised. Whether a revolution occurs or not depends not merely on the state of the economy or the harvest, but on the ability of actors to mobilise support for radical change – actors, in short, make a difference. Yet, if actors matter, they may matter in different ways and to different extents. The capacity of actors to engage in a strategic reconnaissance of their environment may facilitate their ability to promote change by opening up strategic avenues not seen by others. If resources such as capital, time and information are crucial to the ability of actors to realise their intentions, then it is important also that we acknowledge the capacity of actors to enhance the resources at their disposal.

Finally, the conduct of political subjects is crucial to the reproduction or transformation of existing social, political and economic structures and institutions. Agents acting in a routine manner will tend to reproduce existing structures and patterns of social and political relations over time, while actors rejecting norms and conventions will tend to transform existing institutions and practices.

Ideational factors related to political change

For political analysts not content merely to reel off a succession of structural or agential factors in formulating explanations for given social and political outcomes, the issue is not so much structure or agency *per se* as the dynamic relationship between the two. As we shall see in subsequent chapters, reflection on the relationship between structure and agency, context and conduct, reveals the crucial mediating role of ideas. It suggests the significance of ideational factors in the causation of political outcomes.

Actors must interpret their context in order to act strategically (indeed, to act at all). Consequently, interpretations of the environment in which they find themselves may play a crucial role in shaping actors' behaviour with consequent effects for the process of political change.

Moreover, empirically, changes in policy are often preceded by changes in ideas. Thatcherism and Reaganism are perhaps good examples. The adoption of the neoliberal economic policies associated with the Thatcher and Reagan administrations was proceeded by an ideological offensive and an attendant shift in the governing political/economic paradigm (see, for instance, Hall 1993; Hay 1996: Ch. 7; King 1987). The ability of actors to present a situation as one requiring a break with the past is often key to mobilising support for significant political change.

What examples like this suggest is that the ability to orchestrate a shift in societal and/or governmental preferences may be a key factor in delivering significant institutional change. Governments which are able to shape the preferences of the electorate (like those of Thatcher and Reagan) tend to be associated with more significant change than preference-accommodating administrations (like those of Blair and, perhaps, Clinton). The ability to mould societal perceptions would, then, seem a key facet of political power and a key determinant of political change. It is to these issues what we turn in Chapters 5 and 6.

Chapter 5

Divided by a Common Language? Conceptualising Power

That political scientists remain divided by the common language of power is perhaps testimony to the centrality of the concept to political analysis. Indeed, for many, political analysis can be defined quite simply as the analysis of the nature, exercise and distribution of power (Dahl 1963; Duverger 1964/66; Lasswell 1936/50; M. Weber 1919/46; and, for a more recent view, Goodin and Klingemann 1996). For those who adopt such a view the definition of power serves to circumscribe the parameters of political analysis. Given this, it is perhaps unremarkable that the concept of power has attracted quite so much attention, contention and controversy. How is power distributed? Is it repressive or constitutive? Is it best conceptualised in purely structural terms or as a capacity of agents? Or, indeed, is it better conceived as a resource conferred upon actors by the context in which they find themselves? Is the identification of a power relation an analytical or a normative exercise? Is the identification of an inequality of power itself sufficient to imply a normative critique of those identified as possessing 'power over'? Can power be exercised responsibly? Can the powerful be held to account? Should power be counterposed to freedom and autonomy? Is a liberation from relations of power possible and/or desirable? These and other fundamental questions continue to divide political analysts, as we shall see. They form the subject of this chapter.

For many, power specifies the sphere of the political: *power is to political analysis what the economy is to economics*. Such authors would be quick to embrace Terence Ball's suggestion that 'power is arguably the single most important organising concept in social and political theory' (1992: 14). Though perhaps increasingly prevalent, this should not lead us to overlook those authors who would challenge such a view and with it the centrality of the concept of power to political analysis. These authors are generally of the view that political *scientists* (often in contrast to less encumbered political *analysts* and *theorists*) cannot afford to define their analytical sphere so broadly as to include all real and potential power relations. For by so doing they would have to embrace a definition so all-encompassing as to exclude almost nothing (see, for instance, Heywood 1994: 25–6). However important the analysis of power to the conduct of political science, they suggest, the political domain cannot and should not be held coextensive with that of power itself. The result would be the in-discipline of an inchoate and unfocused discipline, unified not by its subject matter but by a power-centred approach to the analysis of the entire social sphere. As discussed in Chapter 2, such authors tend to advocate a relatively narrow and clearly delineated definition of the political as the *arena* of government as distinct from the *practice* or *exercise* of power.

This would perhaps suggest an irreconcilable gulf between proponents of an arena definition of the political, for whom an analysis of power is no more than a potentially useful aspect of the analysis of the political, and those advancing a process definition for whom power is to politics what time is to history. Yet this would be to present a somewhat misleading image. For there are a range of authors, many of them seminal figures in the development of political science as a discipline, who have sought to define power in such a way as to render it coextensive with the political while retaining an essentially arena definition of the latter. Chief among these is Robert Dahl himself (1957, 1963). What this suggests, a key theme of the present chapter, is that, like politics itself, power can be understood in a variety of more or less inclusive ways.

In this chapter I focus primarily on perhaps the key debate in the post-war period over the nature and definition of power – the so-called 'faces of power' controversy – before turning more briefly to a consideration of a very different exchange about the concept of power, the Foucault–Habermas debate. As we shall see, these debates reflect very different theoretical traditions and very different approaches to political analysis (Table 5.1).

The first, the faces of power or community studies controversy, is a classically anglophone (and Anglo-US) debate. It is concerned with the definition of the concept of power. Strangely, perhaps, it centres around the extent to which such definitional questions can and should be resolved methodologically – in short, whether power should be defined in such a way that it can be measured easily. The debate throws up a tension between, on the one hand, a definition of power so narrow, even banal, as to be uninteresting yet which is easy to operationalise in political analysis and, on the other, a more subtle and complex conception of power yet one which is almost impossible to measure and quantify. Throughout the debate, power is understood in rather pluralist and behaviouralist terms as an essentially inter-personal relationship.

The Foucault–Habermas debate is in fact something of a misnomer, as it was conducted for the most part, by protagonists other than

Table 5.1   *Divided by a common language*

	The 'faces of power' debate	The Foucault–Habermas debate
Protagonists	Political scientists – Dahl; Bachrach and Baratz; Lukes	Social and political theorists – Foucault and Habermas
Key issues of controversy	How should power be defined? Should power be defined such that it is measurable?	Is power ubiquitous? If so, is a liberation from power possible? If emancipation is impossible then what point critical theory?
Nature of the debate	Proceeds by way of a modification of pluralist understandings of power; primacy of methodology (for Dahl and Bachrach and Baratz)	Primacy of ontology (how does power function? is it ubiquitous?) over methodology (how might we measure it?)

Foucault and Habermas. As Samantha Ashenden and David Owen note, 'the history of this encounter is characterised by the marked absence of open dialogue' (1999: 1). For, as Michael Kelly comments:

> the amount of discussion by each philosopher about the other was unintentionally lopsided in Habermas' favour. He devoted two chapters of *The Philosophical Discourse of Modernity* (1987) to Foucault, but the book was published after Foucault's death and thus received no reply . . . the effect of this lopsidedness is that the debate is too often construed in Habermasian terms. (1994: 4)

In contrast to the faces of power controversy, this largely virtual exchange reflects a very different and more characteristically continental European intellectual tradition. The debate, such as it is, displays a perhaps remarkable disdain for methodological considerations, certainly when compared to its anglophone counterpart. It is almost entirely uninhibited by considerations as pragmatic or parochial (depending on one's loyalties) as whether one can 'measure' or catalogue the power relations one identifies. The tenor of the controversy is, consequently, much more philosophical, indeed, metaphysical. The debate concerns the extent to which power is ubiquitous and hence the very possibility of liberation or emancipation from power. As such it has clear implications for critical political analysis – for if there can be no possibility of liberation from power, then arguably critical theory loses its emancipatory potential. Finally, in contrast to the anglophone 'faces of power' controversy, power is understood to be social and structural rather than inter-personal.

The marked contrast in both the content and conduct of the two debates reveals much about the character and distinctiveness of anglophone political science. While the Anglo-US 'faces of power controversy' is concerned essentially with finding a definition of power which might be operationalised methodologically, the European debate is animated by rather more ethereal considerations – the extent to which the critique of, and emancipation from, power is possible given the ubiquity of power relations. The 'faces of power controversy', then, rests fundamentally on the tension between a concept of power that is simple, precise and potentially quantifiable and one which is more complex and intuitively appealing, yet which is much more difficult to catalogue and measure. For the majority of the protagonists, this essentially theoretical (indeed, ontological) controversy can and should be resolved by appeal to methodological concerns. Such a suggestion would be unthinkable in the context of the continental European debate.

The 'faces of power' controversy

As is by now clear, if the field of political analysis is, by the very political nature of its subject matter, profoundly contested, then within that field the concept of power is more profoundly contested than most. Yet this was not always the case. For in the early post-war years, when the practice of (anglophone) political science was assumed simple, there was but one 'face of power'. Debate may have raged between sociologists and political scientists as to the precise *locus* of power but, by and large, political scientists remained united and intransigent in their defence of a pluralist conception of power. Power was transparent, expressed in an unambiguous and empirically demonstrable way in the decision-making process.

This, at least, is the textbook orthodoxy. Arguably it is something of a myth. It is certainly true that influential political scientists in the 1940s and 1950s did not trouble themselves too much with conceptual disputes about the concept of power. Nonetheless, any but the most cursory treatment of anglophone political science in the early post-war years cannot fail to acknowledge the extent of the theoretical gulf (however implicit) which already divided pluralists and elite theorists in their efforts to operationalise the concept of power (compare, for instance,

Dahl 1956; Dahl and Lindblom 1953; Truman 1951; with Lynd and Lynd 1937/64; Hunter 1953; Lasswell 1936/50; Mills 1956; for a discussion see also Dunleavy and O'Leary 1987).

Decision-making: the first face of power

While the extent of its ascendancy even in the early post-war period might be questioned, then, the one-dimensional view of power was extremely influential. As its designation as the 'one-dimensional' view of power might suggest, it is relatively simply stated. Thus, for Dahl, one-time doyen of classic pluralism, A has power over B to the extent that she can 'get B to do something that B would not otherwise do' (1957: 201) *and*, crucially, where there is an overt conflict of *interests* (here assumed synonymous with *preferences*) between the actors involved. Thus, by virtue of A's power, B not only modifies her behaviour, but does so in full knowledge that her modified behaviour is contrary to her own genuine interests.

If Anna purchases Ben's car for £500 when they both know that it is in fact worth £800 – by threatening, say, to put a sledge-hammer to it if her less than generous offer is refused – then Anna might be said to exert power over Ben. Anna's power is mirrored in Ben's lack of power. Note, however, that were Ben unaware of the market value of his property and, consequently, were no threat required to facilitate the transaction, no power relation would have been exerted. This might seem rather strange and serves perhaps to highlight one of the key assumptions underpinning the (classic) pluralist conception of power. Actors are assumed to be blessed with perfect information and hence to know their real interests. Consequently, the preferences their behaviour exhibits can be assumed to reflect their genuine interests. What they want is what they really, really want. What's more, what they want is what's good for them. While it may certainly simplify matters to assume perfect information and the transparent quality of material interests, it may also seriously limit the utility of such a conception of power, as we shall see.

For now, suffice it to note that the pluralist conception of power is based on the idea of Anna getting Ben to do something that he would not otherwise do or, more generally, of A getting B to do something he or she would not otherwise do. This is operationalised by pluralists in a focus on decision-making. The powerful are those whose opinion holds sway in the decision-making arena, whether a parliament, cabinet or diplomatic negotiation.

There are four immediate things to note about such a definition of power:

1. Power is understood in terms of its *effects* – if Anna's actions have no effect on Ben, there is no power relation
2. Power is an attribute of *individuals*, exercised in their relations with other individuals – it is *behavioural*
3. Power is associated with *domination* or *power over* – it is not so much a capacity to affect outcomes, but to dominate others in so doing
4. Consequently, power is unproductive or zero-sum – some gain only to the extent that others lose out. If Anna has power, Ben does not; the extent of Anna's power is the extent of Ben's lack of power.

Such an approach had, and still has, an obvious appeal. Power is rendered transparent and can be catalogued, classified and tabulated in terms of the realisation of preferences in the heat of the decision-making process. An obvious and apparent object of analysis is identified (the arena of decision-making); a series of unproblematic methodological strictures naturally follow. For, as James L. Hyland explains, 'there is a radical distinction between having access to a political resource and successfully wielding that resource in the determination of a particular outcome'. Consequently:

> if we are attempting to establish who in reality wields actual power, the simple categorisation of people in terms of their access to potential political resources is wholly inadequate. We must try to decipher the actual lines of influence by identifying who was in favour of which alternative, which alternative was finally implemented and what the participants in the conflict actually did in the attempt to get their preferences realised. (1995: 197)

Thus, if we want to know *who* is powerful we tabulate exhibited patterns of influence in the decision-making process (Dahl 1961b; Polsby 1980).

Consider a tripartite political system. To ascertain the distribution of power we would monitor the outcome of the decision-making process over a given period of time, tallying the number of occasions in which particular parties' preferences were satisfied on controversial issues where a clear conflict of interest could be identified (see Table 5.2). In this scenario, Party *B* is revealed to hold the most power.

In sum, the classic pluralist conception of power is one-dimensional in its narrow focus on power as decision-making and analytically precise in unambiguously identifying what counts, and what does count, as power relations. It is also actor-centred in its focus on power as an interpersonal and zero-sum phenomenon. Finally, it implies an *instrumentalist* or *input* theory of the state which, as the term would perhaps

Table 5.2   *Operationalising power as decision-making*

	Vote 1	Vote 2	Vote 3	Vote 4	Vote 5	Total
Party A	WON	LOST	LOST	LOST	WON	2
Party B	WON	WON	WON	WON	LOST	4
Party C	LOST	LOST	LOST	LOST	WON	1

imply, conceives of the state as an instrument rather than a set of structures (on instrumentalism see Barrow 1993: 13–41; Finegold and Skocpol 1995: 176; Hay 1999c: 164–71; on input politics see Dunleavy and O'Leary 1987: 23–41). It focuses attention on those who inhabit positions of influence within the state apparatus rather than the nature, form and function of the state itself.

In so far as this classic pluralist conception of power was dominant in anglophone political science in the 1950s, the theoretical and empirical confidence it engendered among its proponents was not to last for long.

Agenda-setting: the second face of power

Enter Peter Bachrach and Morton S. Baratz. In two short but brilliant and highly significant methodological critiques (and later in more empirical detail), they proceeded to demolish the grand if fragile edifice of classical pluralism (Bachrach and Baratz 1962, 1963, 1970). Motivated, essentially, by a desire to defend elite theorists (such as Floyd Hunter) from the methodological critique of pluralists like Dahl (1958) and Nelson Polsby (1961), they took the offensive to the pluralists. Power, they argued, is Janus-faced, its complex nature merely obscured by a narrow concentration on the decision-making process. While decision-making is essentially and obviously a power relation in so far as the actions of the *A* affect *B*, this is not the end of the story. For power is also exercised in what they, rather cryptically termed, 'non-decision making'. Here, as they explained, 'A devotes his [*sic*] energies to creating or reinforcing social and political values and institutional practices that limit the scope of the political process to public considerations of only those issues which are comparatively innocuous to A' (1962: 948; see also 1963: 632). A non-decision is, then, 'a decision that results in the suppression or thwarting of a latent or manifest challenge to the values or interests of the decision-maker' (1970: 44).

Put in its most simple terms, power is exerted in *setting the agenda* for the decision-making process. The selection of what is and what is not subject to the formal process of political deliberation, they argued, is itself a highly political process – and one overlooked by pluralists. As James L. Hyland suggests, 'the common knowledge that certain decisions would be unacceptable to the local "godfather" is sufficient to remove whole ranges of potential options from the agenda of the town-meeting entirely' (1995: 194; see also Gambetta 1993, 1994).

What this suggests is that, even at this relatively early stage in proceedings, the faces of power controversy, though couched in the language of power, was essentially a dispute about the boundaries of the political. While pluralists restricted the concept of power, and in so doing their analysis of the political, to the content of the formal decision-making process, neo-elitists such as Bachrach and Baratz sought to broaden the concept of power, and with it the political, to encompass agenda-setting. Through the process of agenda-setting, they argued, powerful actors got to decide which issues became subject to (formal) deliberation (or decision-making) and which did not. Here they drew upon E. E. Schattschneider's concept of the 'mobilisation of bias' and the insight that power may be exercised by 'creating or reinforcing barriers to the airing of policy conflicts' (Bachrach and Baratz 1962: 949; Schattschneider 1960). The ability to shape agendas was, then, in one sense a more fundamental exercise of power than merely influencing decisions once the agenda had already been set. For the art of politics was to steer the agenda is such a way as to avoid the need for formal decision-making on issues where the desired outcome could not be guaranteed.

This suggests a more fundamental critique of pluralism. It is all very well to consider the exercise of power within the decision-making chamber, but if this is merely a talking shop from which consideration of all contentious issues has already been excluded, then the wood is being missed for the foliage on the trees. Indeed, such a narrow concern with decision-making is tantamount to an endorsement of systematic and deep-seated power relations. It is, in short, a normative legitimation of the political elite masquerading as a neutral and dispassionate science *of* the political. For, as Barry Hindess notes, 'it is the *covert* uses of power which make possible the benign public representation of power as serving the general interest . . . it is precisely because their power enables them to manipulate the agenda of political debate that the rule of unrepresentative elites meets so little opposition in such "democratic" communities as the US' (1996: 5, emphasis in the original).

It was the focus on agenda-setting as the second 'face' or dimension of power which served to differentiate Bachrach and Baratz's neo-elitism from Dahl's pluralism. Yet, it is important to emphasise that the neo-elitists sought not to supplant the pluralists' emphasis on decision-making with a similar concern for agenda-setting. Rather, they called for a more rounded and inclusive conception of power (and the political) capable of analysing *both* the decision-making and the agenda-setting (or non-decision-making) process. This revised definition of power extended the sphere of political analysis from the parliament or formal decision-making arena to include the corridors of power, the boardroom, the masonic lodge, the golf course and the clubs and pubs in which agenda-setting occurs behind the scenes.

Though certainly less naïve about the conduct and practice of political power, this extension of political analysis to the subterranean corridors of power did not come without a price. In short, it put paid to the methodological assuredness of the classic pluralists. It had been relatively simple to observe, catalogue and analyse the formal decision-making arena. But now that the locus of power was expanded to include the masonic lodge and now that power was seen to operate twenty-four hours a day, seven days a week rather than Monday to Friday, nine to five, the analysis of power was set to become an altogether more complex, exacting and, arguably, subjective task. This led a number of pluralist critiques to conclude that non-decision-making was simply unresearchable (Merelman 1968; Wolfinger 1971; though see Bachrach and Baratz 1970).

Important though the focus on agenda-setting clearly was, it did not exhaust Bachrach and Baratz's critique of classical pluralism. Even were one to accept its exclusive focus on decision-making, they argued, the classic pluralist approach was methodologically flawed. For, they suggested, Dahl, Polsby, and authors like them, provide no basis (objective or otherwise) for ascribing importance to specific issues and decisions.[1] Clearly some decisions are more significant than others and an approach which merely concentrates on the frequency with which different groups and actors get their way is likely to distort systematically the power relations involved. It may well be, for instance, that a strategic and hegemonic group will allow minority interests to prevail on certain issues which do not directly threaten its domination, reserving its influence for matters of greater significance. Indeed, such strategies may be crucial to the ability of an elite to maintain its hegemonic position. For pluralists, then, the buying off of particular constituencies (through, for instance, the targeted use of tax rebates), might be seen as an index of the power of those targeted; for neo-elitists is it further evidence of the power of those able to make such selective concessions. A simple tally of ostensible successes and defeats in the decision-making forum may, in such circumstances, hide more than it reveals.

Bachrach and Baratz's modified pluralism (or, as they would perhaps prefer, neo-elitism) implies two methodological innovations:

Table 5.3   *The power to make concessions*

Weighting	Vote 1 1	Vote 2 1	Vote 3 2	Vote 4 1	Vote 5 5	Total
Party A	WON	LOST	LOST	LOST	LOST	1
Party B	LOST	WON	WON	WON	LOST	4
Party C	LOST	LOST	LOST	LOST	WON	5

1. The need to consider the largely informal process of agenda-setting within the corridors of power before examining the formal decision-making process itself
2. The need to weight issues in the decision-making process in terms of their 'importance' in assessing the real distribution of power (this is illustrated in Table 5.3).

In its sensitivity to the selectivity of the decision-making agenda and the mechanisms by which significant issues may be filtered out and thereby excluded from the decision-making process, Bachrach and Baratz's 'two-dimensional' view of power represents a considerable advance on that of the classic pluralists. It is not, however, unproblematic. Like their pluralist forebears, Bachrach and Baratz assume that power relations exist only in so far as there is observable conflict between those exercising power and those over whom power is exercised (1970: 49). This excludes the possibility of power being exercised in situations in which the subordinated do not identify themselves as the subject of subordination – in which those subject to the negotiations and deliberations of agenda-setters and decision-makers do not perceive themselves as possessing an interest they are prevented from realising.

To return to our earlier example, for pluralists and neo-elitists alike, while Ben remains ignorant of the true market value of the car he has just sold to Anna for what she knows to be a paltry sum, he remains immune to Anna's power. This raises a problem of temporal inconsistency. For, if Ben subsequently meets Caroline who informs him that she would have paid over £800 for his car and that Anna exploited his naïvety in such matters, does this alter the situation? Does Anna's duplicitous offer now become a power relation retrospectively even if it were not a power relation when the offer was accepted?

The problem rests in the assumption, which Bachrach and Baratz share with Dahl, that actors' preferences are a direct representation of their material interests. As the above example perhaps suggests, perceived interests (or preferences) may vary independently of material circumstances as, for instance, actors' information of the context in which they find themselves changes. On the basis of the (limited) information available to him, Ben may regard his material interests to be served by selling his car to Anna only to come to re-evaluate that judgement, after the fact, once more complete information is available to him.

The result of this inability to differentiate between interests and exhibited preferences is that, for Bachrach and Baratz, as for Dahl, where there is no explicit conflict of (perceived) interest – where, in short, there is seeming consensus – no power can be said to be exercised. Despite their critique of classic pluralism, then, they retain a residual behaviouralism which they inherit from the pluralist tradition. In the concentration on the observable (and behavioural) phenomenon of agenda-setting, no consideration is given to the less visible processes by which *preferences* are shaped. This brings us to the intervention of Steven Lukes, and to the 'third dimension' of power.

The third dimension: preference-shaping

In outlining the limitations of Bachrach and Baratz's bold attempt to overcome the parochial pluralism of Dahl's early work, Lukes lays the basis for his own distinctive and important intervention in the debate. In what might at first seem like an exercise in one-upmanship, he calls for a radical *three*-dimensional conception of power – who, after all, could possibly prefer a one- or two-dimensional perspective when presented with a three-dimensional alternative? Where once there was only one face of power, there would now be three. Yet the significance of Lukes' intervention should not be understated. For in advancing the three-dimensional conception of power, Lukes offers us a route out of the behaviouralist impasse.

To restrict the use of the term 'power' to situations in which actual and observable conflict is present, he argues, is arbitrary, unrealistic and myopic. Anna certainly exercises power over Ben by getting him to do what he would not otherwise do. But power – and an altogether more effective and invidious form of power at that – is also exercised when she influences or shapes his very *preferences* – by convincing him, for instance, that £500 represents a good deal. As Lukes asks himself:

> is it not the most insidious exercise of power to prevent people, to whatever degree, from having grievances by shaping their perceptions, cognitions, and preferences in such a way that they accept their role in the existing order of things, either because they can see or imagine no alternative to it, or because they see it as natural or unchangeable,

or because they value it as divinely ordained and beneficial?. (1974: 24; see also 1978: 669)

As this passage perhaps suggests, Lukes is interested in rather more weighty issues than the price of second-hand cars. His analysis suggests that the societal consensus which pluralists and elitists would take as evidence of the absence of systematic inequalities of power is, in fact, the consequence of highly effective and insidious mechanisms of institutionalised persuasion. Here he draws implicitly on the work of the Italian Marxist, Antonio Gramsci (1971).

What is now required, Lukes suggests, is a framework capable of recognising: (i) the strategies, struggles and practices that characterise the decision-making process; (ii) the actions and *inactions* involved in shaping the agenda for the decision-making process; and (iii) the actions and *inactions* similarly implicated in the shaping of perceived interests and political preferences. This Lukes advances in his 'radical' three-dimensional conception of power. Its distinctiveness is summarised in Table 5.4.

Lukes' achievement is considerable, but his formulation is ultimately no less problematic for that. In expanding the notion of power to include preference-shaping, he is forced to draw the distinction between subjective or perceived interests on the one hand, and actual or 'real' interests on the other, suggesting that where power is exercised it involves the subversion of the latter. This is an important point and it is perhaps worth dwelling upon. To identify a power relationship within Lukes' schema is not merely to identify a situation in which Anna gets Ben to act in a manner he would not otherwise have done. It is also, crucially, to demonstrate that, regardless of Ben's preferences, his exhibited behaviour was indeed contrary to his genuine interests.

Yet who is to know what Ben's true interests are if he is capable of misperceiving them? This opens the Pandora's box that is the concept of *false consciousness* (Rosen 1996). The problem with such a formulation is the deeply condescending conception of the social subject as an ideological dupe that it conjures. Not only is this wretched individual incapable of perceiving her/his true interests, pacified as s/he is by the hallucinogenic effects of bourgeois (or other) indoctrination. But, to confound matters, rising above the ideological mists which tame the masses is the enlightened academic who from a high perch in the ivory tower may look down to discern the genuine interests of those not similarly privileged.

To most commentators such a formulation is now seen as both logically unsustainable and politically offensive, implying a privileged vantage-point for the enlightened academic which is difficult to sub-

Table 5.4 *The 'faces of power' controversy: political power in three dimensions*

	One-dimensional view	Two-dimensional view	Three-dimensional view
Proponents	Dahl, Polsby, classic pluralists	Bachrach and Baratz, neo-elitists	Lukes, Marxists, neo-Marxists and radical elitists/pluralists
Conception of power	Power as decision-making	Power as decision-making and agenda-setting	Power as decision-making, agenda-setting and preference-shaping
Focus of analysis	The formal political arena	The formal political arena and the informal processes surrounding it (the corridors of power)	Civil society more generally, especially the public sphere (in which preferences are shaped)
Methodological approach	'Counting' of votes and decisions in decision-making forums	Ethnography of the corridors of power to elucidate the informal processes through which the agenda is set	Ideology critique – to demonstrate how actors come to misperceive their own material interests
Nature of power	Visible, transparent and easily measured	Both visible and invisible (visible only to agenda-setters), but can be rendered visible through gaining inside information	Largely invisible – power distorts perceptions and shapes preference; it must be demystified

stantiate and for which no justification is offered, and a somewhat over-bearing paternalism towards the 'victims' of a distorted consciousness (Benton 1981; Clegg 1989: 95). To his considerable credit Lukes does, at times, acknowledge the difficulties of the distinction between false consciousness and real interests. Thus, whether A acts in a manner contrary to B's interests in any given situation is, he concedes, essentially 'an evaluative matter' (1974: 34; 1979). Later he remarks, 'any view of power rests on some normatively specific conception of interests' (1974: 35). Here Lukes is perilously close to accepting the logic of Hyland's perceptive critique, namely that 'a theory of human nature robust enough to ground a substantive conception of interests will necessarily be implicitly normative and hence will not be open to straightforward proof or disproof' (1995: 203). Yet if this is indeed the case then the convenient differentiation between real and perceived interests simply cannot be sustained.

Here Lukes relies on William E. Connolly's conception of 'objective interests': 'Policy x is more in A's interests than policy y if A, were he [*sic*] to experience the results of both x and y, would choose x as the result he would rather have for himself' (1972: 472; see also Habermas 1968; Isaac 1987: 35). Yet, while this certainly clarifies things, it merely compounds the problem. For such a definition is deliciously paradoxical, effectively conceding the essentially and irredeemably *perceptual* quality of supposedly 'objective' interests. There is nothing objective about the process by which one ascertains one's genuine interests, since one's objective interests are one's perceived interests under conditions of complete information. (Though, for an alternative view, see Dowding 1991: Chs 3 and 7). Moreover, since complete information is a purely hypothetical condition, objective interests are effectively recast by Connolly as the theorist's perception of how an actor *would* perceive her/his interests if blessed with perfect knowledge of past, present and *future*.[2] The concept is hardly robust.

It is not surprising, then, that Lukes is somewhat apologetic about the distinction he draws between real and perceived interests. Such obvious doubts, however, do not prevent Lukes from falling back on precisely such a distinction. Thus, when he asks himself 'can power be exercised by A over B in B's real interests?' he identifies two potential answers:

(1) that A might exercise 'short-term power' over B . . . but that if and when B recognises his [*sic*] real interests, the power relation ends: it is self-annihilating; (2) that . . . successful control by A over B . . . constitutes a violation of B's autonomy; that B has a real interest in his own autonomy; so that such an exercise of power cannot be in B's real interests. (1974: 33)

Lukes ultimately plumps for the former, albeit somewhat reluctantly and with the proviso than an empirical basis for identifying real interests must be insisted upon to 'obviate the potential dangers'. This may sound attractive. But since Lukes provides us with no suggestion as to how such an empirical basis can be established and, as already noted, concedes that identifying interests is essentially a *normative* task, it is not at all clear that a 'paternalist license for tyranny' has indeed been precluded (see also Clegg 1989: 103). While any doubt remains, the 'anarchist defence' against tyranny embodied in the second answer is perhaps to be preferred.

Power: analytical and critical perspectives

The above discussion raises two crucial questions. First, why, despite his obvious unease at the theoretical contradictions and normative dilemmas that it generates, does Lukes insist on premising his analysis of power on the distinction between real and perceived interests? And, relatedly, can a genuinely three-dimensional conception of power (that is, one sensitive to power as decision-making, agenda-setting *and* preference-shaping) be formulated that is not compromised by its reliance upon such a distinction?

Attributing power: analysis or critique?

Given Lukes' seeming inability to offer an objective, empirical, or even normative basis from which to assess the genuine interests of social subjects in a potential power relationship, and his evident reluctance (in the absence of such criteria) to position himself as the supreme arbiter of such interests, it seems obvious to ask why he makes the attribution of power dependent upon such an assessment. For might it not be, as Hyland has it, that 'the problem lies not with the thesis that there can be a form of power that operates through the moulding of consciousness, but with certain specific features of Lukes' account of such power' (1995: 203) – in particular, his reliance upon the notion of power as a subversion of real interests. The answer is revealing and suggests a potential route out of Lukes' theoretical dilemma.

Lukes, it should be recalled, is a self-professed *critical* theorist advancing a *radical* conception of power (see, especially, Hindess 1996: 86–93). What makes his conception both critical, and more specifically, radical is that to identify a power relationship is, for Lukes, to engage in critique. To identify *A* as exercising power over *B* is to identify a situation in which *B*'s (real) interests are being subverted, and to identify *A* as not

only responsible but culpable. It is, in short, to engage in a critique of
A – or, at least, of the social structure in and through which *A* comes to
exercise power.[3] Within such a schema power is not so much an analytical category as a critical category whose identification is reliant upon
an irredeemably normative judgement. At times Lukes is clearly aware
of this, as for instance when he refers to power as an essentially contested concept, and when he suggests that whether *B*'s real interests
are indeed subverted in any particular situation is, undeniably, an evaluative matter (1974: 34). Yet, at other times, as for instance when he
refers to the need to establish an empirical basis for identifying real interests, he seems to be referring to power as a purely analytical concept
(33). Lukes thus comes dangerously close to conflating analysis and critique. Indeed, much of the appeal of his argument resides in his ability
to present an essentially value-laden critical conception of power as a
neutral analytical category.

The practice of social and political critique (from whatever perspective) is inherently normative, ethical, evaluative and value-laden, as distinct from neutral, dispassionate, empirical and scientific. To engage in
critique is not to apply a scientific principle or analytical technique but
to compare real practices to an idealised (often utopian) alternative – in
Lukes' case, a world free from power relations. This requires (normative or value) judgements about the legitimacy of conduct which cannot
be grounded in claims to neutrality or objectivity.

If Lukes' analysis is ultimately somewhat frustrating then this is
because he smuggles the normative and ethical foundations for his
critical theory into his analysis of power. When it comes to identifying
a particular relationship as one of power Lukes, and those following his
schema, are forced to make an ethical judgement – what are the real
interests of both parties, and can they be adjudicated without consideration of their preferences? There is, and can be, no empirical, scientific
or analytical basis from which to answer such questions for, as ethical
dilemmas, they belong to an entirely different cognitive realm.

Once recognised for what it is then – an invitation to an ethical critique of power relations as distinct from an analytical technique for the
identification of power relations – Lukes' schema is not in itself contradictory. Nonetheless it should be noted that many of the things he says
about it are, and that Lukes' highly ambiguous acknowledgement of the
value-laden nature of his reformulation of the notion of power serves
only to confuse things further. Moreover, his failure to disentangle the
identification of power and the critique of its distribution and exercise
has a series of unfortunate consequences. First, power becomes a purely
pejorative concept. If to identify a power relationship is to engage in
a critique of that relationship, then it is clear that power cannot be

exercised responsibly or legitimately. The essence of power is negative, the purpose of critique to expose power relations as a potential means to their elimination. This is all very well, and indeed is logically entailed by Lukes' reformulation of the concept. Yet is serves to narrow our understanding of power such that it no longer refers to that familiar from pre-existing social and political theory, or from lay uses of the term. Moreover it suggests the need for a new conceptual repertoire to refer to all of those lay and theoretical uses of the term now eliminated at a definitional stroke. This Lukes fails to provide us with.

Secondly, by redefining power in this way Lukes generates a situation in which no two theorists are ever likely to agree on what constitutes a power relationship. For power is now understood as a departure from a utopian ideal in which the interests of all individuals are satisfied. Yet as Lukes himself notes, what an actor's real interests are is a matter of (ethical) judgement – and the likelihood of critics and theorists making identical judgements across the spectrum of potential social and political scenarios is remote. The concept of power is thus rendered relative. Moreover, power is now to be analysed not on the basis of how the social and political world *is*, but how it *ought* to be, or rather, how 'the real world' differs from the critic or theorists' idealised *projection* of how it ought to be. The casualty in all of this is the possibility of a dialogue about power, its distribution and its exercise, between those who do not share identical (ethical) perspectives for the adjudication of the validity of interests.

Redefining power

Need this be so? Does Lukes' bold attempt to extend the definition of power to include the shaping of perceived interests and preferences necessarily entail a purely negative yet relative conception of power? Perhaps not. For the above discussion would suggest that the theoretical confusions and ethical–political dilemmas that punctuate Lukes' discussion of power derive not from his conception of power as preference-shaping. Rather they have their origins in (1) his attempt to revise and modify (rather than reject and replace) the behavioural and actor-centred definition of power that he inherits from Dahl and Bachrach and Baratz, (2) the resulting need to differentiate between real and perceived interests and (3) the associated smuggling of normative criteria into an analytical definition. In short, the problems of Lukes' formulation reside in his failure to differentiate clearly between analytical questions concerning the *identification* of power within social and political settings, and normative questions concerning the *critique* of the distribution and exercise of power thus identified. While Dahl and Bachrach and Baratz simply assume that preferences and interests are identical, thereby dissolving a subjective question (what are *A*'s real interests?) into an empirical question (what does *A* perceive her/his interests to be?), Lukes problematises this by introducing the important observation that preferences may be shaped by the powerful. If he is not to reject altogether the behavioural conception of power (in which *A* gets *B* to do something that *B* would not otherwise do, and where there is a conflict of interest between the two), this obliges him to address the normative/subjective question which the pluralists conveniently side-step in the very definition of power itself. Yet this is precisely the problem. The alternative then is simple: we must reject the behavioural definition of power and redefine the concept in such a way as to separate out these distinct normative and analytical questions that Dahl, Bachrach and Baratz and Lukes conflate.

The task then is to disentangle the analysis and identification of power from its critique. This requires a definition of power that does not itself entail a value-judgement yet which is true to the spirit of Lukes' three-dimensional view. Such a conception of power must emphasise not only the consequences of *A*'s choices for the *actions* of *B*, but also, and perhaps primarily, their effects upon the *context* within which subsequent action must take place. Power then is about *context-shaping*, about the capacity of actors to redefine the parameters of what is socially, politically and economically possible for others. The ability to influence directly the actions and/or choices of another individual or group is but one special case of this more general capacity. More formally then we can define power as the ability of actors (whether individual or collective) to 'have an effect' upon the context which defines the range of possibilities of others (Hay 1995b: 191; for an alternative formulation see Dowding 1991). This is a *positive* conception of power – *power of* as opposed to *power over*. Yet it may also provide the basis for a *negative* conception of power – *power over* as opposed to *power of*. Thus actor *A* may be regarded as occupying a position of domination or power *over* *B* insofar as s/he has the capacity through intentional or strategic action to transform the context within which *B* finds her/himself; and where this is not a reciprocal relationship (i.e. where *B*'s actions would not have a similar effect on the context within which *A* finds her/himself).

It should be stressed that this is little more than the *analytical* basis of Lukes' third face of power rendered in definitional form. Yet this cannot be the end of the story. For to leave the redefinition of power here would be to replace a three-dimensional perspective with an (albeit expanded) one-dimensional account. To define power as context-shaping is to emphasise power relations in which structures, institutions and organisations are shaped by human action in such a way as to alter the parameters of subsequent action. This is an *indirect* form of power in which power is mediated by, and instantiated in, structures. Yet power is also exercised in a *direct* sense when *A* gets *B* to do something that s/he would not otherwise do (for our purposes, independently of their respective interests). Thus, to indirect power or *power as context-shaping* we must also add direct power or *power as conduct-shaping*. Indirect power is evidenced in the capacity of a government, say, to pass legislation. This does not directly and instantaneously effect the conduct of *B*, but once instantiated in statute serves to redefine the parameters within which *B* will continue to act while providing a power resource for the potential exercise of direct power by the law-enforcement agencies of the state. Direct power, by contrast, is immediate, visible and behavioural, and is manifest in such practices as physical and psychological coercion, persuasion and blackmail.

Such a reformulation of the concept of power has a number of significant consequences. First, it suggests that there are in fact two rather different conceptions of power submerged within the faces of power debate (direct and indirect power), and that Lukes fails to acknowledge the decisiveness of the break with Dahl and Bachrach and Baratz that his critique logically entails. In the first formulation, power is a behavioural phenomenon which is immediate, directly observable, and empirically verifiable; in the second, power refers to the capacity to redefine structured contexts and is indirect, latent and often an unintended consequence.

Second, and perhaps more significantly, the above reformulation of power as both context- and conduct-shaping does not rely in any sense on value-judgements about the interests (real or imagined) of the actors involved. To suggest that *A* exercises power over *B* is to make no claim, within this schema, about the subversion or violation of *B*'s 'true interests' (though such a claim is clearly not precluded by such a statement). Moreover, ascribing power in this way does not in any sense imply that the theorist occupies some privileged vantage-point from which the 'genuine' interests of social subjects can be ascertained. Though the identification of a power relationship (particularly one which is indirect) is still likely to be highly contestable, it does not imply that the political analyst need first engage in ethical judgements about the legitimacy of the conduct of those involved, or the interests of those likely to be effected. Ethical and normative judgements can thus be suspended temporarily while the analysis and identification of power takes place. Thus, although theorists and critics from divergent political and ethical stances are unlikely to agree upon the legitimacy of the actions of the powerful, they may at least be able to share a common analysis of the distribution and exercise of power within a given social and political context.

Accordingly, to attribute power on the basis of the above definition is to attribute neither responsibility nor culpability for particular effects as Lukes' purely pejorative conception of power would imply. The actor who unwittingly treads on a spider and kills it exercises a considerable power but one for which we may not wish to hold her/him responsible. Exercising power may be a necessary condition for being held responsible, but it is not a sufficient one. Moreover, the doctor who terminates the life of a patient in a consensual act of euthanasia clearly exercises a similar power, and one for which we may wish to hold her/him accountable and responsible. Yet in so doing we may well wish to absolve the responsible subject of culpability. This furnishes us with *an* answer to Lukes' final conundrum:

> Can A properly be said to exercise power over B where knowledge of the effects of A upon B is just not available to A? (1974: 51)

This is a telling example, for here Lukes clearly conflates power, responsibility and culpability. His assumption in the brief passage which follows this question is that the consequences of *A*'s actions must be negative such that to ascribe responsibility is to apportion blame, and to identify a power relation between *A* and *B* is to hold *A* responsible for its consequences. Yet if we follow the definition of power outlined above then clearly *A* exercises power in this situation. Whether we hold her/him responsible and, if so, culpable cannot be adjudicated in the abstract. It is certainly unfair to attribute responsibility and culpability to actors who we do not regard as exercising power; but it may be equally unfair to assume that all actors with power should be held responsible and culpable for the consequences of their action.

Is it likely that political scientists will remain divided by the common language of power. Yet we may be able to agree on what divides us. If so, it is first essential that we differentiate between the analytical questions concerning the identification of power, and the normative questions concerning the critique of the distribution and exercise of power thus identified. It is this, above all else, that is surely the lesson of the faces of power debate.

Foucault and the 'microphysics' of power

> In human relations . . . power is always present . . . these relationships of power are changeable relations, i.e., they can modify themselves, they are not given once and for all . . . The thought that there could

be a state of communication which would be such that the games of truth could circulate freely, without obstacles, without constraint and without coercive effects, seems to me to be utopian. It is being blind to the fact that relations of power are not something bad in themselves, from which one must free one's self. I don't believe there can be a society without relations of power. (Foucault 1988b: 11–12, 18)

Important and influential though it has certainly been, the faces of power controversy does not exhaust the analytical issues raised by the concept of power. Though space does not permit a detailed discussion of the issues in their full complexity, a brief postscript on the conceptual controversy surrounding the ubiquity and the very possibility of a critical theory of power casts an alternative light on many of the issues discussed above. It also prepares the way for the discussion of the realm of ideas and of the very possibility of critical political analysis in Chapters 6 and 7.

The continental European controversy over the concept of power revolves around the seminal contribution of Michel Foucault. Foucault's work poses, albeit implicitly, a significant challenge to the critical theory of Jürgen Habermas, Herbert Marcuse and, by extension, Lukes himself.[4] For the notion of critique which provides critical theory with its *raison d'être* is premised upon the possibility of a liberation or emancipation from power relations and, hence, of a world unencumbered or, in Habermas' terms, 'undistorted' by relations of power and domination. It is this that Foucault rejects, as in the passage above, where he points to the ubiquity of power.

Though Foucault's conception of power evolves and, in certain key respects, his later work on governmentality marks a significant departure from his earliest sustained reflections on power in *Discipline and Punish* (1977a) and the first volume of his *History of Sexuality* (1979), it is in these initial works that the spirit of his challenge to critical theory is most clearly stated.[5] It is with the first of these, *Discipline and Punish*, that I am principally concerned here.

Discipline and Punish opens, famously, with the graphic and almost indulgently fulsome description of the barbaric torture, drawing and execution of the regicide Damiens in the Place de Grève in Paris on 2 March 1757.[6] This is immediately counterposed to the regimentation, strandardisation, soulless efficiency and order of Léon Faucher's regime for a young offenders' institution of 1838. Though separated by little over 80 years, the contrast is staggering, epitomising, for Foucault, the profound nature of the shift from repressive to disciplinary 'power–knowledge regimes' underway in France at the turn of the nineteenth century.

Foucault's rhetorical strategy, reminding us perhaps of the power of the author, is to invoke in us an almost intuitive sense of revulsion and disgust at the brutality, incivility and barbarism of Damiens' execution and the lavish, gratuitous and yet disengaging and dispassionate tones in which it is described by a range of contemporary commentators. By contrast, the regimentation and order of Faucher's idealised carceral institution is reassuringly familiar, the epitome of civilisation and, indeed, progress – an index of our rise from mediaeval barbarism to modern civility. As Michel de Certeau suggests:

For the 'torture' of the *Ancien Régime*, a violent corporal ritual dramatising the triumph of royal order over felons chosen for their symbolic value, the reformist projects of the eighteenth century seek to substitute punishments applicable to all, in proportion to the crimes, useful to society, edifying for the condemned. (1984: 45–6)

Yet if the dramatic effect of Foucault's narrative rests on this contrast and relies on the sense of progress it invokes, the rest of the book is an attempt if not openly to question then certainly to problematise the ease with which this paradigmatic shift in the 'economy of punishment' (1977a: 7) might be read in such progressive terms. As his 'genealogical' account of the 'apparatuses', 'instrumentalities', 'techniques' and 'conditions of functioning' of this 'new age of penal justice' unfolds, a complex and disturbing picture is build up, frame by frame, of the cold functionality, efficacy and ruthless efficiency of the new penitentiary regime. The symbolic and public display of the sovereign's capacity to inflict pain and suffering upon his subjects is replaced by the far more covert, invisible and sinister capacity of a more decentred state to fashion, re-fashion and thereby constitute not merely the preferences, but the very soul and identity of modern subjects (Table 5.5). Foucault's model here is Jeremy Bentham's *Panopticon* (lit.: all-seeing). As he explains:

Bentham's *Panopticon* is the architectural figure of this composition. We know the principle on which it was based: at the periphery, an annular building; at the centre, a tower; this tower is pierced with wide windows that open onto the inner side of the ring; the peripheric building is divided into cells, each of which extends the whole width of the building; they have two windows, one on the inside, corresponding to the windows of the tower; the other, on the outside, allows the light to cross the cell from one end to the other. All that is needed, then, is to place a supervisor in a central tower and to shut up in each cell a madman, a patient, a condemned man, a worker or a schoolboy. By the effect of backlighting, one can observe from the

Table 5.5 *From Damiens to Bentham, from discipline to punish*

Punitive–repressive power–knowledge regime	Carceral–disciplinary power–knowledge regime
Epitomised in the execution of Damiens–Paris, 1757	Epitomised in Bentham's *Panopticon* – early nineteenth century
Display of force/sovereign power	Capacity of surveillance/control
Body as the site of power	Soul as the site of power
Repressive form of power	Educative form of power
Spectacular, collective, ceremonial and participatory	Invisible, individuated, andinternalised and non-participatory
Public	Private
Defence of the sovereign	Defence of collective society

tower, standing out precisely against the light, the small captive shadows in the cells of the periphery. They are like so many cages, so many small theatres, in which each actor is alone, perfectly individualised and constantly visible. (1977a: 200)

As he goes on to explain, the major effect of the *Panopticon* is 'to induce in the inmate a state of conscious and permanent visibility that assures the automatic functioning of power . . . the perfection of power should tend to render its actual exercise unnecessary' (201). In short, the perfection of power ensures that the individual disciplines herself.

Foucault's emphasis here, as elsewhere, is upon the body as a site upon which power relations are inscribed. He argues that though no longer the subject of physical repression and mutilation (as in the public spectacle of the execution of Damiens), the body nonetheless remains the stage upon which new discourses and power relations are played out. This may seem somewhat paradoxical, given Foucault's comment that:

a few decades saw the disappearance of the tortured, dismembered, amputated body, symbolically branded on face or shoulder, exposed alive or dead to public view. The body as the major target of penal repression disappeared. (1977a: 8)

Yet, although the direct hold on the body has in some sense been slackened in the move to a carceral society, the new power–knowledge regime of institutionalised regimentation and surveillance can be said to constitute and mould the body (and its conduct) to at least as great (and, perhaps, far greater) an extent, though now through the mediation of the soul. As Foucault suggests in a widely-cited passage:

Rather than seeing this soul as the reactivated remnants of an ideology, one would see it as the present correlative of a certain technology of power over the body. It would be wrong to say that the soul is an illusion, or an ideological effect. On the contrary, it exists, it has a reality, it is produced permanently around, on, within the body by the functioning of a power that is exercised on those punished – and, in a more general way, on those one supervises, trains and corrects, over madmen, children at home and at school, the colonised, over those who are stuck at a machine and supervised for the rest of their lives. (1977a: 29)

The architectural apparatus of the Panopticon is seen as a structural machine for the creation, sustenance and, quite literally, the *incorporation* of power relations. Within the Panopticon, 'it is not that the beautiful totality of the individual is amputated, repressed, altered by our social order; it is rather that the individual is carefully fabricated in it, according to a whole technique of forces and bodies . . . to increase both the docility and the utility of all elements of the system' (217). Essential to Foucault's analysis here is his claim that 'power produces knowledge . . . power and knowledge directly imply one another . . . there is no power relation without the correlative constitution of a field of knowledge, nor any knowledge that does not presuppose and constitute at the same time power relations' (27). Thus, it is the 'disciplines' of architecture and criminology and the knowledge claims they advance that are the very condition of existence of the regime of power–knowledge that is manifest in the carceral institutions of modern society.

Were this not itself sufficient to challenge our intuitive sense that the path from public torture to private surveillance is a progressive one, Foucault turns his attentions to the motivations underlying penal reform. As Lois McNay explains, though cast in terms of progress, humanity and civilisation, 'the main impetus underlying penal reform stems, in Foucault's view, from the necessity to ensure a more efficient and rationalised legal and social field' (1994: 92; Foucault 1977a: 80–2). In this way, Foucault suggests, the birth of the disciplinary regime of power–knowledge out of that epitomised by the execution of Damiens is less a process of progress than of the substitution of incommensurate and hence incomparable paradigms (cf. Kuhn 1970/96). History, then, is 'an endlessly repeated play of domination':

> Humanity does not gradually progress from combat to combat until it finally arrives at universal reciprocity, where the rule of law finally replaces warfare; humanity installs each of its violences in a system of rules and thus proceeds from domination to domination. (Foucault 1977b: 150–1)

There is, however, something of a tension in Foucault's argument here. As Axel Honneth perceptively notes, 'it is unclear whether the effectiveness of the means of social control is to be measured by criteria fixed by the institutional framework of a given social order or by the criteria set by a process of increasing social control that is independent of a specific social order' (1991: 183). If, in keeping with the spirit of the argument as a whole, power–knowledge regimes are, indeed, incommensurate and self-contained there can be no neutral language or narrative capable of adjudicating between them. Yet if this is so, how is it that Foucault can speak, in comparing the two regimes of power–knowledge, of 'an augmentation of social control' (1991: 184; Foucault 1977a: 80)? As in other parts of his work, the tension remains unresolved.

Such tensions notwithstanding, it is clear that for Foucault power is ubiquitous and that, consequently, there is no subject position beyond or outside power relations from which to cast a dispassionate gaze. Situated, as we are as modern subjects – subjects of and subjected to a carceral and disciplinary regime of power – the execution of Damiens does indeed appear primitive, inhumane and barbaric while Faucher's carceral regime appears the very model of a modern institution. Yet, socialised, indeed 'normalised' as we are within the confines of such a regime, who is to say that such a judgement is not itself the product of that normalisation?

Much of this is implicit in Foucault's almost self-consciously ambiguous narrative. Like many of the postmodernists whose ideas we consider in Chapter 7, Foucault's strategy is to problematise, disarm and *deconstruct*. He resists the temptation to supplant one 'grand narrative' of progress for another. Indeed, it is in this latter respect that his work has perhaps proved most influential. For Foucault not only challenges the ease with which we might attribute a progressive path to exhibited historical tendencies and trajectories *after the fact*. Crucially, he challenges our ability to project progressive *future* scenarios and with it, the very possibility of progressive or critical social and political theory. For if we are willing to accept that power is ubiquitous then there can be no prospect of a liberation or emancipation from power (such as that implicit in the critical theories of Marcuse, Habermas and Lukes). Consequently, the best that we can hope for it is to change the manner in which power is displayed. At the very least, then, the implications of this are that the critical theorist must bear responsibility for the 'power–knowledge regime' his or her reform agenda serves to constitute. Here Foucault equivocates – torn, it seems, between a sceptical and conservative position he is drawn to philosophically and a radical and reforming spirit which animates his work politically. The result, as I have elsewhere suggested, is 'an alternation which becomes increasingly frequent in his later work between a politically and normatively informed critique (reliant, albeit implicitly, upon some conception of emancipation), and an anti-foundationalist deconstruction of the very notion of progress upon which such a politics might be premised' (Hay 1994/95: 128; see also Best and Kellner 1991: 36, 72–3; Habermas 1989: 173–9). This is the 'postmodern tension' which, in Foucault, remains ultimately unresolved and to which we return in Chapter 7.

Chapter 6

The Discursive and the Ideational in Contemporary Political Analysis: Beyond Materialism and Idealism

It is, in many respects, remarkable that we have got this far without a systematic reflection on the role of ideas in political analysis. For such issues have rarely been far from the surface of previous chapters.

In Chapter 2, we concerned ourselves with the 'construction' of the sphere of the political in political analysis and hence with the significance of the labels we attach to the objects of our analytical attention. We went on to evaluate the possibility of, and limits to, a neutral or dispassionate 'science' of the political. If, as we suggested, the ideas of political analysts are *capable* of exerting an independent effect upon their object of analysis, this suggest the limits of a social science modelled upon the natural sciences. It surely also invites a consequent reassessment of the status of the knowledge claims we might be tempted to make as political analysts (though cf. Sayer 2000: 34–5).[1]

In Chapter 3, we explored the relationship between political conduct and political context, between agency and structure. While the language of structure and agency might at first appear to suggest an ideas-free realm, a moment's further reflection reveals that this is far from the case. This is a theme to which we return. Suffice it for now to note that strategy – in and through which an actor engages with the environment in which she finds herself – is an irredeemably perceptual matter, relating both to the extent and quality of the actor's information about, and the normative orientation of the actor towards, the context in which she is situated. Given the centrality of the concept of strategy to an understanding of the dynamic interplay of structure and agency, it is hardly surprising that Chapter 4, concerned as it was with the analysis of political change, should accord a key role to ideational factors. For ideas often hold the key to unlock political dynamics – as change in policy is often preceded by changes in the ideas informing policy and as the ability to orchestrate shifts in societal preferences may play a crucial role in quickening the pace, altering the trajectory or raising the stakes of institutional reform.

Finally, if questions of structure and agency are intimately connected to those concerning the realm of ideas, then the same is equally true of power. Central to the faces of power controversy reviewed in Chapter 5 are the categories of agenda-setting and preference-shaping both of which relate to the control which might be exercised over the framing of political action and hence to the ideational or discursive mediation of processes of political change. Moreover, underpinning the controversy surrounding the use of the concept of power in political analysis is the fundamental dispute over the utility of the distinction between 'real' and 'perceived' interests – are interests essentially material and objective or irreducibly ideational and subjective (Connolly 1972)?

As this would perhaps suggest, if we are to pose the most fundamental ontological and epistemological questions which divide political analysts today, it is difficult to avoid the relationship between the ideational and the material or, more specifically, the role of ideas in political explanation. It is to these issues that we turn directly in this chapter.

The chapter unfolds in three sections. In the first we consider the space accorded to ideas by different analytical traditions and perspectives in political science and international relations. We concentrate in particular on constructivism in international relations theory, an increasingly influential perspective which has sought consciously to acknowledge the role of ideas in processes of social and political change. We examine the distinctiveness of constructivism in contemporary international relations theory when set alongside a much older tradition of philosophical constructivism in the social sciences. In the second section we compare and contrast a variety of analytical strategies for dealing with the material–ideational relationship – idealism, materialism and both 'thin' and 'thick' constructivism. Finally we return to the question of structure and agency, examining the crucial but often unacknowledged role of ideas as the interface between actors and the contexts in which they find themselves. We explore the implications for political analysis of this insight.

The space for ideas in political analysis

There has, traditionally, been very limited space accorded to ideas as causal (or constitutive) factors in mainstream political science and international relations. And it is not difficult to see why. For those wedded to a predictive science of the political, ideas pose a considerable problem. If there is no analogue for agents in the natural sciences then there is also no analogue for the ideas actors hold and which motivate and animate their behaviour. As argued in earlier chapters, one convenient and influential way of dealing with this has been to assume that actors' behaviour is rendered predictable by the context in which they find themselves. If actors can be assumed rational and there is only one way in any given context to behave rationally in pursuit of a particular preference set, then an analysis of the context alone will provide us with all we need to predict political behaviour and hence political outcomes. This is the now familiar basis of rationalism. Within such a schema there is no room for ideas. Moreover, were we to create space for ideational effects by, for instance, acknowledging that actors informed by different sets of ideas will behave differently in the same context, the possibility of a predictive science of the political would rapidly fade.

In this way rationalism dispenses with the 'problem' of ideas in political analysis by making two convenient and parsimonious assumptions. The first is that actors have perfect or near-perfect information of the environment in which they find themselves, such that they know how to behave in such a way as to maximise their utility in any given context. As Sheri Berman perceptively notes, most rationalist explanations

> do not distinguish between reality and actors' perceptions of it. Instead, they assume that actors have access, if not to perfect information, then at least to relatively full and accurate information. If this were not the case . . . then it would be impossible to predict the behaviour of political actors based solely on knowledge of their material interests and an examination of their . . . environment. (1998: 31; see also Simon 1986: 210–11)

Second, rationalism assumes that material interests are given objectively in such a way that two identically positioned actors will not only share identical interests but will come to perceive of those interests in an identical fashion.

Such assumptions make a natural science of the political possible where one would otherwise not be possible. But they are, frankly, implausible. The key point for now is that any perspective which is not prepared to make such assumptions must, at pain of self-contradiction, accord an independent role for ideas in political explanation.

Behaviouralism is no less wary of ideas as causal factors and no less unenthusiastic about incorporating them within the political analysis it sanctions. Again, it is easy to see why. As Philip Converse notes:

> Belief systems have never surrendered easily to empirical study or quantification. Indeed, they have often served as primary exhibits for the doctrine that what is important to study cannot be measured and that which can be measured is not important to study. (1964: 206)

Sadly, perhaps, for classic behaviouralists a condition of being acknowledged as an important explanatory factor is measurability, indeed quantifiability. Consequently, however important many post-behaviouralists would now accept ideas to be, the analytical techniques they privilege do not avail themselves easily of ideational analysis. As Sheri Berman again observes, 'political scientists prefer to study things that they can see, measure and count and ideas seem to the opposite – vague, amorphous and constantly evolving' (1998: 16).

As this would perhaps already suggest, it is the movement from highly parsimonious forms of political analysis to those which value the realism and hence complexity of assumptions that has created space (once again) for ideational factors in political analysis. Just as it is easier to assume that the 'rules' governing social and political behaviour are essentially static and invariant over time, so it is easier to assume that actors have a direct and unmediated access to the strategic contours of the terrain in which they find themselves. In short, just as it is easier to assume that political analysis is an exercise in mapping a static object, it is easier to assume that the ideas of political subjects are irrelevant to an understanding of their behaviour. Accordingly, in a political science which values parsimony and predictive capacity, these are likely to be the very first assumptions.

In political science and international relations, then, it is the development of theoretical perspectives that value complexity and realism of assumptions over parsimony that have led to a reconsideration of the role of ideas in political analysis (among the more notable contributions, see Campbell and Pedersen 2001a; Checkel 1997; Goldstein and Keohane 1993; Hall 1989, 1993; Heclo 1974; McNamara 1998; Sikkink 1991; Wendt 1999 and for useful reviews, Blyth 1997a; Campbell 1998; Hall 1997; Jacobsen 1995). Chief among these in recent years has been constructivism in international relations theory. It is to the distinctive challenge it poses to the mainstream that we now turn.

Constructivism in and beyond international relations theory

In international relations theory attention in recent years has come to focus rather more explicitly on the relationship between the ideational (the realm of ideas) and the material. Thus, while for many contemporary institutionalists, the causal significance of ideas has been established *empirically*, for many contemporary international relations scholars the causal and/or constitutive role of ideas is an essentially theoretical – indeed, *ontological* – matter. This rather more consciously theoretical reflection on the role of ideas owes much to two crucial and related developments, the first empirical the second theoretical. Empirically, the end of the Cold War has had the effect of throwing international relations theory into a state of profound crisis (see, for instance, Baldwin 1993; Gaddis 1992; Keohane 1996; Schröder 1994). As John Ruggie rather ruefully acknowledges,

> The discipline of international relations failed to predict the collapse of the Soviet empire. A rupture of that kind was not part of the analytical domain of any major body of theory, though in many instances a scramble took place after the fact to retrofit theory to events. (1998: 102)

Such *post hoc* rationalisations notwithstanding, the ontological and epistemological complacency which once characterised mainstream international relations theory has long since evaporated (Tickner 1996). As Robert O. Keohane graciously concedes.

> The fact that we lack theories that would enable us to understand the effects of the end of the Cold War on world politics certainly should make us humble . . . Our present confusion also reveals the emptiness of claims that we possess a 'policy science' to which policy-makers refuse to listen 'at their peril'. (1996: 463)

In the wake of such assuredness debate has turned for the first time in a long time to the 'big questions': those of structure and agency, the material and the ideational, and the role of theory itself (Carlsnaes 1992; Dessler 1989; S. Smith 1995; Wendt 1987, 1999). As Keohane again suggests, 'our manifest inability to predict complex events, whether minor or earthshaking, should . . . teach us that although it is useful to seek to develop and test conditional generalisations, the accumulation of such generalisations is unlikely to lead to successful prediction of events that result from the conjuncture of multiple causal paths' (1996: 463). The result is a perhaps unprecedented degree of theoretical humility, reflexivity and openness to questions – such as the constitutive and causal role of ideas – previously deemed inadmissible in the lecture theatres, seminar rooms and hallowed journals of mainstream international relations theory (see, for instance, Adler and Barnett 1998; Campbell 1992; Der Derian 1995; Goldstein and Keohane 1993; Onuf 1989; Walker 1993; Wendt 1999).

Yet if the reassessment of the role of ideas in international relations theory owes much to the theoretical crisis of confidence inflicted by the end of the Cold War, it owes certainly as much to the emergence (or, more accurately, re-emergence) of constructivism as a theoretical approach.[2]

Constructivism in international relations theory

It is often the case that social scientists find themselves divided by a common language. That of constructivism is no exception. Conventionally, within the philosophy of the social sciences, constructivism refers to a relatively distinctive position which blends, at times, into relativism and has many similarities with what would now be termed postmodernism (see Chapter 7). Such philosophical constructivists tend to argue that 'reality' (if it is not too vulgar to speak in such terms) is not so much represented or misrepresented by ideas or discourse as constituted *as reality* in and through discourse (Berger and Luckmann 1966; Hacking 1999; Kukla 2000; A. Nelson 1994). In Jacques Derrida's memorable terms, there is nothing outside of the text (*'Il n'y a pas de horstexte'*) – and hence nothing outside of language itself (1976: 158). This philosophical constructivism is distinctly anti-realism in its rejection of the notion of an external reality independent of our knowledge and conceptions of it (on realism see Marsh 1999b: 12–14; Sayer 2000). Yet, in international relations theory nothing is as simple as it first appears. For although there are a range of ostensibly constructivist positions in the existing literature, some of which are avowedly anti-realist (for instance, Ashley 1984, 1987; Walker 1987, 1993), it is Alexander Wendt's particular variant of constructivism which is most frequently held to capture the essence of the constructivist challenge to mainstream international relations theory (Kratochvil 2000). Yet, by any conventional definition of constructivism, Wendt is no constructivist. Indeed, he seeks to defend a position which he labels, variously, as 'idealist', 'structuralist' and yet at the same time 'realist' (ontologically) and even 'positivist' (epistemologically).

While one might question the internal coherence of the hybrid position he has come to embrace, the motivation which underpins his apparent eclecticism is clear. Wendt is seeking to convince the mainstream that it has little to fear by taking ideas more seriously than it has been accustomed to doing. In particular, he suggests, constructivism (at least in this decidedly 'thin' variant he advances) need not be corrosive of many much cherished realist and neo-realist assumptions. Whether this is ultimately sustainable or not is beyond the scope of this chapter (though, for various opinions, see Alker 2000; Keohane 2000; Krasner 2000; Kratochvil 2000; Ringmar 1997; S. Smith 2000; and for a response to his critics, Wendt 2000). Suffice it for now to note that the particular constructivism he advances is highly distinctive. In what follows we shall refer to it as 'thin' constructivism in order to differentiate it clearly from the 'thick' constructivism introduced above. For Wendt:

Constructivism is a structural theory of the international system that makes the following core claims: (1) states are the principal units of analysis for international political theory; (2) the key structures in the state system are intersubjective rather than material; and (3) state identities and interests are in important part constructed by social structures, rather than given exogenously to the system by human nature or domestic politics. (1994: 385)

Of these supposedly core tenets of constructivism, the first is an unapologetic endorsement of the most fundamental of neo-realist assumptions which has little if anything to do with a philosophical constructivism.[3] True, it is what distinguishes Wendt's particular constructivism from others, but as this would suggest it is hardly constitutive of constructivism itself. The remaining two ontological assumptions are certainly more obviously constructivist – in their emphasis upon both the causal and constitutive significance of intersubjective and hence ideational factors. Nonetheless, many constructivists would see problems with the rigid demarcation of the realm of the material and the intersubjective or ideational implied in the second, preferring instead to explore the dynamic interaction of material and ideational, rather than privileging one moment of the dualism. Similarly, though on some readings a clear endorsement of philosophic constructivism, the precise significance of Wendt's third core assumption rests on the extent of the qualification implied in the phrase 'in important part'. Finally, despite Wendt's enduring concern with the 'structure–agency problematique' and his avowedly Giddensian approach to the relationship between conduct and context (1987, 1992, 1999; Shapiro and Wendt 1992; Wendt and Shapiro 1997), his constructivism does tend towards a 'structural idealism' (1999: 1). This emphasises the internalisation (by states) of intersubjective norms and conventions and hence is good at explaining constraint and continuity. Yet, it has all too little to say about the establishment and revision of such norms and conventions in the first place and hence little to inform an analysis of the dynamism of the international system and the states which comprise it. In short, it tends to view ideas more as 'the ever-present condition' rather than the 'continually reproduced outcome' of human agency (cf. Bhaskar 1979: 43).

In sum, although Wendt's thin constructivism has certainly served to draw attention to the role of ideas in international relations theory, his seeming desire not to offend the mainstream results in a peculiarly eclectic blend of constructivist insight and neo-realist convention. It is important, then, that we consider what a rather 'thicker' version of constructivism might entail. Here it is useful to look beyond contemporary international relations theory.

Constructivism beyond international relations theory

Altogether more representative of social constructivism within the social sciences is Ian Hacking's (1999) provocative and perceptive book, *The Social Construction of What?* In it, Hacking points to the proliferation of subjects, objects and processes – from authorship (Woodmansee and Jaszi 1994) to Zulu nationalism (Golan 1994), reality (Berger and Luckmann 1966) to emotions (Harré 1986) – identified as products of social construction in recent years. Yet in among this great diversity of objects of social construction, Hacking is able not only to identify a common sense of social construction – something by which each might be said to have been socially constructed – but, in addition, a common and *normative* purpose underpinning the claim that each has been socially constructed. Hacking characterises social constructivism as follows.

Social constructivists about X tend to argue that:

(1) X need not have existed, or need not be as it is. X, or X as it is at present, is not determined by the nature of things; it is not inevitable. (1999: 6)

Furthermore, for the most part their analysis either claims directly or tends also to imply that:

(2) X is quite bad as it is
(3) We would be much better off if X were done away with, or at least radically transformed. (1996: 6)

Later on, Hacking adds an additional clause by way of a precondition:

(0) In the present state of affairs, X is taken for granted; X appears to be inevitable. (1999: 12)

Hacking's attempt to capture the essence of constructivism is extremely compelling, conveying both the analytical and normative content of the rhetorical claim that 'X is socially constructed' (though see Kukla 2000: 1–6). What his account serves to emphasise, in particular, is the stress placed by constructivists upon the *contingent* or *open-ended* nature of social and political processes and dynamics – especially those conventionally seen as fixed. Particular constructions may serve to present a 'reality' which is static, immutable or inexorably unfolding in a given direction, but the recognition of the constructed nature of the reality we perceive implies that things could and can be different. Constructivism, then, despite Wendt's 'structural idealism', both seeks and serves to restore politics and agency to a world often constituted in such a way as to render it fixed and unyielding. It aims to reveal the contingency of social construction and hence the conditions under which things might, indeed, be different. A brief example will perhaps serve to clarify the argument.

Globalisation as a social construction

Globalisation has become a key referent of contemporary political discourse and, increasingly, a lens through which policy-makers view the context in which they find themselves. If we can assume that political actors have no more privileged vantage-point from which to understand their environment than anyone else and – as most commentators would surely concede – that one of the principal discourses through which that environment now comes to be understood is that of globalisation, then the content of such ideas is likely to affect significantly political dynamics. In short, the social or discursive construction of globalisation may have an effect on political and economic dynamics independently of the empirics of globalisation itself.

Consider tax competition between states, first discussed in Chapter 3. The conventional wisdom (whether of the so-called hyperglobalisation thesis or of open economy macroeconomics) suggests that in a globalised context characterised by the heightened (and in some accounts, the free) mobility of capital, vicious competition between states will serve to drive down the level of corporate taxation (for the hyperglobalisation thesis see Kitschelt 1994; Kurzer 1993; Scharpf 1991; Teeple 1995; and for the open economy macroeconomic perspective, Razin and Sadka 1991a, 1991b; Tanzi and Zee 1997; Tanzi and Schuknecht 1997).[4] Accordingly, any failure on the part of a state to render (and to continue to render) its corporate taxation levels competitive in comparative terms, through (a succession of) tax cuts, will result in a punitive depreciation in net revenue as capital exercises its mobility to exit.

However compelling the logic, there is precious little evidence to substantiate the thesis (Cooke and Noble 1998; Swank 2001), nor the parsimonious if implausible assumptions upon which it is based.[5] Yet, the crucial point for constructivists is that if governments believe it to be true, they will act in a manner consistent with its predictions, thereby contributing to an aggregate depreciation in corporate taxation – whether they are right to do so or not. The social construction of globalisation's effects is here revealed a crucial determinant of political and economic outcomes, whether or not such constructions are well-informed. The process is outlined schematically in Figure 6.1.

To elaborate, were we to envisage a (hypothetical) scenario in which the hyperglobalisation thesis were accurate, the free mobility of capital would indeed serve to establish tax competition between fiscal authori-

Figure 6.1   *The causal significance of ideas about globalisation*

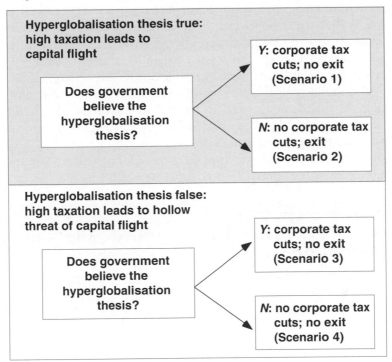

ties seeking to retain existing investment levels while enticing mobile foreign direct investors to relocate. The price of any attempt to buck the trend is immediate capital flight with consequent effects on budget revenue. In such a scenario any rational administration aware (or assuming itself to be aware) of the mobility of capital will cut corporate taxes with the effect that no exit will be observed (scenario 1 in Figure 6.1). Any administration foolish enough to discount or test the mobility of capital by retaining high levels of corporate taxation will be rudely awakened from its state of blissful ignorance or stubborn scepticism by a rapid exodus of capital (scenario 2). In a world of perfect capital mobility, then, the learning curve is likely to prove very steep indeed.

Yet, were we to assume instead that we inhabit a world in which the mobility of capital is much exaggerated and in which capital has a clear vested interest in threatening exit, and the scenario unfolds rather differently. Here, fiscal authorities lulled into accepting the hyperglobalisation thesis by the (ultimately hollow) exit threats of capital will cut rates of corporate tax, (falsely) attributing the lack of capital flight to their competitive taxation regime (scenario 3). Yet, were they to resist this logic by calling capital's bluff they might retain substantial taxation receipts without fear of capital flight (scenario 4). The crucial point, however, is that while politicians believe the hyperglobalisation thesis – and act upon it – we cannot differentiate between scenario 1 (in which the thesis is true) and scenario 3 (in which it is false). Though in the former scenario globalisation is a genuine constraint on political autonomy and in the latter it is merely a social construction, the outcomes are the same. As this demonstrates, in the end at least in this scenario it is ideas about globalisation (constructions) rather than globalisation *per se* which affects political and economic outcomes.

This social constructivist approach to globalisation, restated in Hacking's terms, is outlined in Box 6.1.

Box 6.1   Constructivism applied: the case of globalisation

1. Vicious tax competition between states (X) is bad, undermining the basis of the welfare state (Hacking's proposition 2)
2. In the present state of affairs, vicious tax competition between states it taken for granted as a direct consequence of globalisation (Hacking's proposition 0)
3. Globalisation, however, does not necessitate such tax competition, though it is frequently assumed to do so (Hacking's proposition 1)
4. Vicious tax competition between states is unnecessary and contingent; we would be better off without it (Hacking's proposition 3).

This is but one example. What it, and others like it, suggest is that the discursive construction of globalisation may play a crucial independent role in the generation of the effects invariably attributed to globalisation and invariably held to indicate its logic of inevitability (Hay and Watson 1998; Hay, Watson and Wincott 1999). In a context in which direct corporate tax rates have fallen over time – and in which that process has been linked publicly to the constraints imposed by globalisation (Blair and Schröder 1999: 167; Schwanhold and Pfender 1998; 21–2) – this is a not insignificant point. What it suggests is the importance of differentiating between the effects of globalisation and the effects of dominant discourses of globalisation that might be challenged and resisted. Drawing such a distinction is an integral aspect of restoring notions of political responsibility and accountability to contemporary political and economic dynamics. It is precisely the type of task that motivates social constructivism.

The difference that ideas (can) make

> It is a paradox that scholars whose entire existence is centred on the production and understanding of ideas, should grant ideas so little significance for explaining political life. (Sikkink 1991:3)

As we have seen, the role accorded to ideas in political analysis is highly contested. It varies considerably from analytical approach to analytical approach and tends to reflect deep-seated assumptions about, among other things, the role of theory, the value of parsimony and the status of the knowledge claims we can make as political analysts. Despite this, the controversy tends to resolve itself into the question of whether ideas should be accorded a causal role independent of material factors or not. Once framed in such terms, the principal positions in the debate can be identified relatively clearly. They are summarised in Figure 6.2.

Rather like the issue of structure and agency discussed in Chapter 3, positions on the relationship between the ideational and the material can be differentiated into those which privilege either moment in the process of social and political causation and those which explore the interaction between the two. Thus, in the same way that we can distinguish between simple and dialectical accounts of the relationship between structure and agency so we might differentiate between simple and dialectical accounts of the material–ideational relationship (see Table 6.1; cf. Hay 1995b: 193).

In certain respects the simplest of these positions is that adopted by contemporary idealists – postmodernists, deconstructivists, interpretivists, hermeneuticists and poststructuralist discourse analysts (on postmodernism as an idealist reincarnation see Eagleton 1996; Sayer 2000). Though it would be a travesty to label any of these positions simple, their stance on the relationship between the ideational and the material is far from complex, even if their proponents' motivations for holding it are not (see, for instance, the discussion in Howarth 2000). In essence, they suggest, there is no relationship between the material realm and that of ideas since, in Derrida's terms, all is language, there is nothing outside of the text (1976; Laclau and Mouffe 1985). As David Howarth explains, 'where discourse theory parts company with some versions of realism is, first, in its claim that there is no "extra-discursive" realm of *meaningful* objects and, second, in its rejection of the view that this independent realm of objects *determines* the meaning of those objects' (1995: 127; in the original emphasis).

This may sound simple enough, yet it is complicated significantly by a second key feature of this approach to political analysis. For contemporary forms of idealism tend also to reject a *causal* approach to social

Figure 6.2   *The role of ideational factors in political explanation*

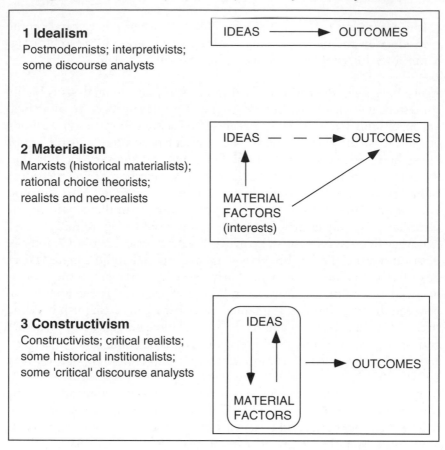

1 Idealism
Postmodernists; interpretivists;
some discourse analysts

IDEAS ⟶ OUTCOMES

2 Materialism
Marxists (historical materialists);
rational choice theorists;
realists and neo-realists

IDEAS — — ➤ OUTCOMES
↑
MATERIAL
FACTORS
(interests)

3 Constructivism
Constructivists; critical realists;
some historical institionalists;
some 'critical' discourse analysts

IDEAS
↓ ↑
MATERIAL
FACTORS
⟶ OUTCOMES

Table 6.1   *Positions in the material–ideational debate*

Account	Prioritises ideational factors and constitutive logics	Prioritises material factors and causal logics
Simple view of material–ideational	Idealism	Materialism
Dialectical view of material–ideational	'Thick' constructivism	'Thin' constructivism; critical realism

and political analysis in which the relative weight of material and ideational factors might be assessed. Rather, they emphasise *constitutive* logics and processes – the construction, in discourse, of those objects on which material status is more conventionally conferred (Howarth 2000: 100–4).[6] As such, and true to form, contemporary idealists tend to 'deconstruct' and dissolve the very distinction between the ideational and the material in the first place. Consequently, the schematic depiction of contemporary idealism in Figure 6.2 is not strictly accurate, in the sense that the purpose of such forms of analysis tends not to be the elucidation of the causal factors responsible for specific outcomes so much as the attempt to establish the (discursive) conditions of existence of specific social and political practices. Nonetheless, it is accurate in suggesting that contemporary idealists invariably confine their analyses to the discursive (which they see as coextensive with the social).

The materialist position is idealism's polar opposite and tends to characterise mainstream approaches in both political science and international relations. It also implies a relatively simple relationship between the material and the ideational. Here, however, the roles are reversed: the material is now dominant in the final analysis (and, in some accounts, in the first and every intervening instance). Contemporary materialism tends to take one of two forms. In the first, often associated with an aggressive and assertive behaviouralism, non-material factors are simply dismissed as irrelevant to a science of the political modelled closely on the natural sciences (for a critique of such positions see Marsh 1999b: 11–14). In such rigidly positivist accounts, the material circumscribes the realm of the real; the ideational realm is dismissed as a mere rhetorical distraction. For advocates of such a view, the purpose of a political science worthy of the label is the elucidation of the 'genuine' (for which read material) causal mechanisms responsible for specific political outcomes.

Though dominant throughout the post-war period in anglophone political science and international relations, recent years have seen a subtle shift in emphasis and a considerable softening in tone. Many contemporary materialists are prepared to concede the seeming dependence of political outcomes upon the ideas actors hold about the context in which they find themselves. This might seem like an obvious and significant concession to constructivism. However, as is so often the case, first appearances are deceptive. For such materialists make an important additional claim which significantly qualifies the extent of their apparent concession to constructivism and effectively restores, at a stroke, their materialism.

They argue that the ideas which animate and inform political behaviour are, in fact, shaped by material circumstances – principally material interests – and should not, as a consequence, be accorded any independent causal role (Goldstein and Keohane 1993; North 1990; North and Thomas 1973; for critiques see Blyth 1997a; Campbell 1998; Woods 1995). Any causal role constructivists might be tempted to attribute to ideas is, then, in fact better credited to the material interests which underpin those ideas.

Finally, there are the constructivists themselves. Of the three (somewhat stylised) positions considered here, theirs is certainly the most complex in its treatment of the relationship between the ideational and the material. Like the revised materialism of many rational choice institutionalists and neo-realists, constructivists start from the recognition that we cannot hope to understand political behaviour without understanding the ideas actors hold about the environment in which they find themselves. Yet here the materialists and the constructivists part company, with the latter refusing to see such ideas as themselves reducible to ultimately determinant material factors. Consequently, they accord ideas an independent causal role in political explanation. Nonetheless, while it is important not simply to reduce the ideational to a reflection, say, of underlying material interests, it is equally important not to subscribe to a voluntarist idealism in which political outcomes might be read off, more or less directly, from the desires, motivations and cognitions of the immediate actors themselves. What is required, instead, is a recognition of the complex interaction of material and ideational factors. Political outcomes are, in short, neither a simple reflection of actors' intentions and understandings nor of the contexts which give rise to such intentions and understandings. Rather, they are a product of the impact of the strategies actors devise as means to realise their intentions upon a context which favours certain strategies over others and does so irrespective of the intentions of the actors themselves.

Yet, constructivism, at least as outlined here, is a broad church, encompassing a diverse range of positions (see Table 6.1). At the idealist end of the spectrum we find varieties of 'thick' constructivism keen to privilege the constitutive role of ideas while not entirely denying the significance of material factors. At the other end of the spectrum we find varieties of critical realism whose rather 'thinner' constructivism tends to emphasise instead the constraints the material world places on such discursive constructions (for a variety of different positions within this spectrum compare the various contributions to Christiansen, Jørgensen and Wiener 2001). What each of these positions shares, however, is a complex or dialectical view of the relationship between the ideational and the material.

Structure, agency and ideas

As the above discussion demonstrates, it is difficult to reflect upon the relationship between the ideational and the material without invoking the structure–agency debate. Indeed, positions on these two core onto-logical relationships tend to be closely linked – with those adopting a complex or dialectical view of the relationship between structure and agency also tending to adopt such a view of the relationship between the ideational and the material. It is not difficult to see why.

For if we accept the dialectical view of the relationship between struc-ture and agency introduced and defended earlier, a similarly dialectical view of the relationship between the ideational and the material almost inevitably follows. Consider the strategic–relational approach discussed in Chapter 3. Fundamental to this particular approach to the question of structure and agency are the concepts of strategy and strategic selec-tivity. Actors are strategic. Moreover, structures are selective of strategy (imposing a strategic selectivity in Bob Jessop's terms) in the sense that, given a specific context, only certain courses of strategic action are avail-able to actors and only some of these are likely to see actors realise their intentions. Social, political and economic contexts are densely structured and highly contoured. As such they present an unevenly distributed con-figuration of opportunity and constraint to actors. Thus, while they may well facilitate the ability of resource- and capital-rich actors to further their strategic interests, they are equally likely to present significant obstacles to the realisation of the strategic intentions of those not simi-larly endowed. Those with time and capital at their disposal are likely to find it far easier to lobby the state for a renegotiation of the terms of their citizenship contract than those juggling child-care responsibilities with a number of poorly paid part-time jobs.

This is fine as far as it goes. But in one significant respect it is deeply suspect. For it tends to assume that strategic actors have a fairly direct and unmediated access to the contours of the terrain they inhabit, such that they can effectively 'read off' the likely consequences of their action from their knowledge of the context in which they find themselves. This, however, is a most dubious premise, akin to the perfect information assumption of much neoclassical economists, rational choice theory and neo-realism. Though convenient and parsimonious, it is ultimately unre-alistic. If one is prepared to accept this then a key role for ideas imme-diately opens up in the relationship between structure and agency. For if actors lack complete information, they have to *interpret* the world in which they find themselves in order to orient themselves strategically towards it. *Ideas provide the point of mediation between actors and their environment*. This is a crucial theoretical step. For, if it is accepted (and, as we have seen, there are many who resist such a move in the name of parsimony or science), it suggests that ideas simply have to be accorded an independent role in the causation of political outcomes. If such outcomes include material effects (as invariably they do) then it must follow that the material and the ideational are related dialectically, since the ideas actors hold have demonstrable material effects. In sum, *a dialectical understanding of the relationship between the ideational and the material is logically entailed by a dialectical understanding of the relationship between structure and agency*.

This is an important if complex point and warrants further elaboration. Within the strategic–relational approach, actors are conceptualised as reflexive and strategic, orienting themselves and their strategies towards the environment within which their strategic intentions must be realised. Yet they are by no means blessed with perfect information of that context. At best their knowledge of the terrain and the (strategic) selectivity it impose is partial; at worst it is demonstrably false. To return to an earlier example, domestic political elites may simply lack the information required to assess the validity of the hyperglobalisation thesis and with it the claim that capital flight can be prevented only by reductions in rates of corporate taxation. Under such circumstances they may well come to accept – as informed hunches – theories which are, or may subsequently prove to have been, empirically suspect.

Examples abound, though one of the more entertaining is surely Ronald Reagan's seeming confidence in the 'Laffer curve'. Based on the work of the maverick Californian economist Arthur Laffer, this predicted that a reduction in the rate of (income) tax would result in a net appreciation in revenue to the Treasury since the incentive to entrepreneurialism would be all the greater under a less punitive taxation regime (Laffer 1981; Wanniski 1978).[7] In short, the lower rate of taxation would be more than compensated by a boost in economic activity. Needless to say when Reagan put Laffer's theory to empirical test in office the result was a net depreciation in revenue and a doubling in the size of the fiscal deficit in the space of two years (King 1987; see also Alt and Crystal 1983; Henderson 1981; Tobin 1982).

While we might readily concede that political actors lack complete information, we might nonetheless point to their capacity to learn and, in so doing, to close in on an ever more accurate account of the context they inhabit. For, given that actors are reflexive, routinely monitoring the consequences of their action, we might expect their knowledge of the context to evolve over time – if not, perhaps, to a situation approximating complete information, then at least to one of relatively reliable reconnaissance. Yet a moment's reflection reveals that this too may be an unwarranted assumption. For while actors might well acquire cumulative knowledge over time in an environment that is essentially unchanging, this is rarely, if ever, the case in situations characterised by a density of existing institutions and practices and a proliferation of strategic actors (the subject matter of contemporary political analysis). Political actors certainly do draw lessons from past experience, but there is no guarantee that they will draw the 'right' lessons, nor any simple way of adjudicating between the 'right' and the 'wrong' lessons in the first place. Moreover, even were we to assume complete information of a current context (based, presumably, on extensive reconnaissance of prior strategic interventions), this would be insufficient to predict the likely consequences (even over the short term) of a particular course of strategic action. For the effects of a specific and given intervention are not merely determined by the structure of the context at the moment at which the action occurs. A range of additional and – from the vantage-point of the actor about to make such an intervention – unknowable factors are also relevant. These include strategic responses made to the intervention itself as well as the quite independent actions of others. In principle, this gives social and political interaction an inherently indeterminent, unpredictable and contingent quality. When the incomplete information of any given actor is also considered, it is hardly surprising that strategic action almost always includes unintended consequences.

In a world which exhibits such qualities, it should come as no surprise that actors routinely rely upon cognitive short-cuts in the form of more or less conventional mappings of the terrain in which they find themselves. Thus, for instance, policy-makers typically conceptualise the policy-making environment through the lens of a particular policy paradigm – such as Keynesian or monetarist economics (Hall 1993). Access to the context is thus mediated discursively. How actors behave – the strategies they consider in the first place, the strategies they discount, the strategies they deploy in the final instance and the policies they formulate – reflect their understanding of the context in which they find themselves. Moreover, that understanding may eliminate a whole range of realistic alternatives and may, in fact, prove in time to have been informed by a systematic misrepresentation of the context in question.

This suggests a very significant role for ideational factors in political analysis. Yet it should not lead us to overlook the constraints that the context places upon its discursive construction (Marsh 1999b: 15–16; Hay and Marsh 1999b: 218–20). After Reagan's first three years in office it was clear, after all, that the Laffer curve had failed to capture the complexities of taxation and economic incentives in 1980s America.[8] As this

Figure 6.3   *Discursive and strategic selectivity*

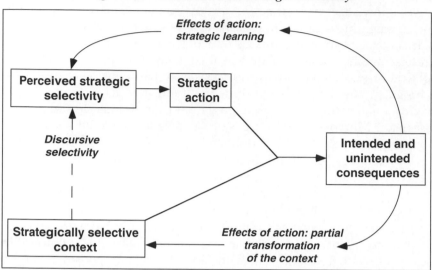

example and others like it suggest, for particular ideas, narratives and paradigms to continue to provide cognitive templates through which actors interpret the world, they must retain a certain resonance with those actors' direct and mediated experiences. In this sense the discursive or ideational is only ever relatively autonomous of the material. Just as it imposes a strategic selectivity, then, the context also imposes a *discursive selectivity*, selecting for and selecting against particular ideas, narratives and construction. This is outlined schematically in Figure 6.3.

Strategy is forged in a context which is strategically selective, favouring certain strategies over others as means to realise specific intentions. Yet, actors have no direct knowledge of the selectivity of the context they inhabit. Rather they must rely upon understandings of the context (and the selectivity it is likely to impose on strategy) which are, at best, fallible. Nonetheless, some understandings are likely to prove more credible given past experience than others. Under most circumstances, 'Reagonomics' notwithstanding, the idea that reductions in taxation will precipitate an increase in revenue is considered less plausible than that which suggests the opposite outcome. In this way the context comes to exert a discursive selectivity upon the understandings actors hold about it. Thus, although the relationship is never likely to be one of direct correspondence, there is always some relationship between the context itself and the ideas actors hold about that context. However accurate or inaccurate, such understandings inform strategy and that strategy in turn yields both intended and, inevitably, unintended consequences. Unintended consequences, in particular, provide an opportunity for strategic learning, offering a clue to the inadequacies of existing understandings of the context and inviting revisions. Presumably, Reagan's economic advisors rapidly came to rethink the validity of their interpretation of the Laffer curve – and perhaps the validity of the Laffer curve itself – as the budget deficit ballooned in the immediate wake of the Economic Recovery Tax Act of 1981.[9] In this way ideas about the context and the strategies they inform evolve over time. Whether this results in a process of cumulative learning, as might be reflected, say, in more effective policy-making, in an empirical question which can be answered only on a case-by-case basis.

Conclusion: paradigms and paradigm shifts

In this chapter I have sought to make and defend three central claims:

1. Ideas should be accorded a crucial role in political explanation, since actors behave the way they do because they hold certain views about the social and political environment they inhabit. Moreover, those ideas cannot simply be derived from the context itself.
2. We cannot assume that political actors are blessed with perfect information of their context. They have to make assumptions about their environment and about the future consequences of their actions and those of others if they are to act strategically. The ideas they hold about their environment are, then, crucial to the way they act and hence to political outcomes.
3. The distinction between the realm of ideas (the ideational) and the material should not be seen simply as that between the realm of the superficial or non-real (the ideational) and that of the real (the material). Ideas and beliefs are both real and have real effects.

What I hope to have demonstrated is the centrality of ideas to an understanding of the relationship between agent and structure, conduct and context. Actors appropriate a world which is always already structured, yet they are confined to do so through a lens of understanding and, inevitably, misunderstanding. The agent's point of access to the densely structured context in which they find themselves is, then, irreducibly ideational. This surely serves to place ideas at centre stage in political analysis for all but the most structuralist of positions. Yet less this be taken to imply a defence of an idealist approach to political analysis, it is immediately important to note that for our understandings and cognitions to continue to inform behaviour they must find and maintain a

Figure 6.4   *The material–ideational dialectic*

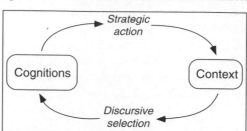

certain resonance with our experience. In this way the context itself exerts a strong *selective* effect upon the ideas we hold about it. Yet this is but half of the dialectical relationship between the ideational and the material. For it is not just the context which shapes our ideas. Those ideas, however misinformed they may prove to have been, exert their own effect upon the development of the context over time through the strategic action they inform. In this way, the ideational and material are related dialectically, as captured schematically in Figure 6.4.

Two important points follow from this, both of which return us to discussions in earlier chapters. First, the recognition of the (discursively) mediated nature of our experience of, and engagement with, the structured context in which we find ourselves suggests the power of those able to provide the cognitive filters, such as policy paradigms, through which actors interpret the strategic environment. As Steven Lukes and, before him, Antonio Gramsci were well aware, those able to shape cognitions, perceptions and preferences exert a very considerable and potentially malign influence over society and societal development (a key theme of Chapter 5).

What this in turn suggests is the need for a political analysis rather more attuned and sensitive to ideational, perceptual and discursive factors. More specifically, it suggests the need to consider the dominant paradigms and frames of reference through which actors come to understand the contexts in which they must act and, above all, the mechanisms and processes by which such paradigms emerge, become challenged and are ultimately replaced. Periods of perceived crisis – in which the disparities between previously unquestioned cognitive frameworks and the 'realities' they purport to represent are starkly revealed – here acquire a particular significance (Hay 1999d, 2001b). Yet, tempting though it may seem to see ideas as somehow more significant – as 'mattering more' – in the uncertainty and confusion of the moment of crisis (Berman 1998; Blyth 2000; Campbell 1998), this is a temptation we should resist. For it implies an ontological inconsistency – a variable relationship between the ideational and the material over time. Arguably more convincing, and certainly more consistent, is the view that the ideational and the material are always intimately connected but that the significance of that dialectical relationship is rather more obvious and immediate in a context in which one set of perceptions and cognitions is replaced by another. It is not that ideas matter more in times of crisis, then, so much that new ideas do. Once the crisis is resolved and a new paradigm installed, the ideas we hold may become internalised and unquestioned once again, but this does not mean that they cease to affect our behaviour.

Either way, and with respect to policy-making in particular, the ability to transform the institutional context of state, economy and society may reside less in access to governmental power and more in the ability to make the case for a shift in the dominant paradigm informing policy. The political power of ideas and the political power of economic ideas in particular (Hall 1989, 1993; see also Blyth 2000; Hay 2001b), though largely ignored within most conventional accounts, can scarcely be overemphasised.

Chapter 7

The Challenge of Postmodernism

Postmodernism is a dangerous term, used in dismissive tones and with increasing abandon by political analysts to refer to work they regard as all too keen to embrace the limits of a science of the political. In this sense it has tended to become a term of exasperation at the work of others rather than a badge of self-identification. Within the political analyst's lexicon, and like structuralism, functionalism and relativism before it, postmodernism is now principally employed as a term of abuse. Thus while many authors are declared 'postmodernist' by their critics, few openly embrace the term themselves. It is then important that if we are to do any kind of justice to the positions which might be labelled 'postmodernist' we are extremely careful in specifying what the term implies and what it does not imply.

What is certainly clear is that while the themes with which this volume has been principally concerned have come to acquire a certain kudos in contemporary political analysis, that respect has not been extended to postmodernism.[1] Yet of all approaches to the analysis (and the limits to the analysis) of the political, it is perhaps postmodernism which has most consistently addressed itself to such issues, albeit in a manner distinctly discomforting to the mainstream. It is thus important that we consider the nature of that challenge and the lessons which might be drawn from it. That is the purpose of this chapter.

Given the confusion and consternation which the term invariably engenders, to say nothing of the contempt in which its proponents are habitually held in mainstream political science and international relations, it is important at the outset that we establish what precisely is meant by postmodernism. As we shall see, while it is easily and frequently caricatured and, indeed, lends itself all too easily to such caricatures, the challenge it poses is rather more serious, subtle and significant than is generally assumed.[2]

Yet before turning directly to the matter of definition, it is perhaps important to say something about the attitude adopted to postmodernism in the pages that follow. As hinted in the very first chapter, I do not regard postmodernism as a distinctive analytical perspective in its own right on a par with, say, rationalism, behaviouralism, constructivism or the new institutionalism. We cannot speak of a postmodernist

approach to electoral competition in the same way that we might a rationalist approach to central bank independence or a constructivist
approach to international security. Its contribution, if any, to political
analysis has been to expose and challenge many of the taken-for-granted
assumptions which underpin more conventional theoretical approaches.
As such it problematises and draws attention to that previously regarded
as unproblematic and uncontentious. It shines a penetrating and often
unwelcome light into the murkier corners of the discipline. Its strategy
is *de*constructive – and, many would argue, destructive – rather than
*re*constructive. As such it should not – and perhaps cannot – be judged
in terms of its substantive contribution to political analysis; a contribution which is in fact quite modest (though see, for instance, Ashley 1987;
D. Campbell 1992; Walker 1993; C. Weber 1995).

Herein lies the frustration which postmodernism invariably prompts
from the mainstream. For, at its worst, postmodernism seems to entail
the rather sanctimonious one-upmanship that comes with the tireless
and nagging critique of whatever political analysts offer. What makes
this particularly galling is that by confining itself to deconstruction postmodernism never risks exposing itself to a similar critique by putting
something in place of that it deconstructs. It is unsurprising, then, that
it is often accused of critique for its own sake (Goldmann 1996: 408–9;
Jackson and Sørensen 1999: 237). That having been said, if one-upmanship implies a sense of smug self-satisfaction and intellectual superiority, then it is something that postmodernism cannot really be accused of.
For its deconstructive imperative, however misguided we may believe it
to be, is motivated by a disarming modesty and candour about the limits
of political analysis and an entirely laudable and deeply normative
respect for the subjects of that analysis.

As this perhaps already indicates, I have some considerable sympathy
for the sense of frustration and exasperation which postmodernism
invariably engenders among those who judge political analysis by the
substantive contribution it makes. Nonetheless, the challenge which
postmodernism poses cannot be so easily dismissed and deserves very
careful consideration. For if the postmodernists are right, contemporary
political analysis is, at best, a largely redundant and worthless exercise.
That, as will become clear, is not my view. However, there is much that
critical political analysts can learn from postmodernism in the process
of reassuring themselves that this is indeed not the case.

Yet, whatever else it is, *this book is not a work of postmodernist
political analysis*. For while postmodernism poses a series of important
challenges which deserve to be taken far more seriously than they have
to date, my central contention is that these challenges can be responded
to by the sort of critical political analysis I have thus far sought to defend

and will defend further in what follows. Such a mode of critical political inquiry, as Andrew Sayer notes, must be 'conceptually cautious and more reflexive about both its implicit philosophy and methodology and its social and political coordinates' (2000: 6). But it cannot afford to abandon its critical, political and analytical aspirations.

The chapter proceeds in three sections. In the first we trace the origins of postmodernism in the rejection of the modernist aesthetic sensibility in art and architecture in the late 1960s and early 1970s, examining postmodernism as an aesthetic sensibility in its own right. In the second section we explore the intellectual sensibility of postmodernism. This shares much with postmodernism's aesthetic sense. It can be characterised by a normative respect for others based upon what might be termed an 'ontology of difference'. Both are reflected in a certain epistemological scepticism informing a deconstructive methodolog. In the final section we consider the contribution of postmodernism to contemporary political analysis and examine its limitations and internal inconsistencies before assessing its implications for the critical political analysis that I have sought to defend in this volume.

Modernism and postmodernism as aesthetic sensibilities

Postmodernism is a relatively recent addition to the language of theoretical debate in the social sciences. If we are, then, to appreciate fully the nature of the challenge that it poses to contemporary political analysis it is important that we first establish the origins of the term in art, architecture and aesthetics. Postmodernism in political analysis, I will argue, it perhaps best seen as an intellectual sense and sensibility. As such, it owes much to the emergence of postmodernism as an artistic and aesthetic sensibility from the late 1960s. The very fact of this association with a distinctly avant-garde artistic movement, it need hardly be pointed out, has not enhanced its chances of a favourable reception from the political science mainstream. It is with that aesthetic movement, however, that we must begin.

While, as Jim McGuigan notes, 'the search for an original meaning is not only trivialising and probably futile but also seriously misleading' (1999: 8), accounts of postmodernism invariably begin with a search for the concept's first usage. More significant, as he goes on to suggest, is to understand why it was that, at a certain point during the late 1960s and early 1970s, 'postmodernist' became an important label of self-identification for countercultural movements in architecture and the arts (literature, poetry, painting and photography in particular).

Postmodernism was originally defined in oppositional terms (as *post-modernism*), to refer to a particular form of artistic expression – a particular aesthetic sensibility (Hassan 1982; Sontag 1966). It constituted, in short, a rejection of the literary and artistic movement of modernism, a rejection of the modernist aesthetic sensibility (for an excellent discussion see Connor 1997: 74–223). As Steven Best and Douglas Kellner explain, 'against modernist values of seriousness, purity and individuality, postmodern art exhibits a new insouciance, a new playfulness and a new eclecticism' (1991: 11).

If we are to understand the postmodernist aesthetic sensibility, then, it is important that we first seek to capture something of that which it sought to transcend – modernism. As Jim Powell suggests, 'modernism is a blanket term for an explosion of new styles and trends in the arts in the first half of the twentieth century' (1998: 8). In so far as this breathtaking profusion of artistic innovations was unified, that unity resided less in the modes of artistic expression to which it gave rise than in the motivations underpinning and informing this proliferation of artistic and aesthetic forms.

Modernism can be characterised by the attempt to rediscover eternal values, which might capture the essence of the human condition, amid the chaos of modern societies – societies in which the promise of science, religion, reason, emancipation and enlightenment had long-since proved illusory. Thus, Picasso's *Guernica* of 1937 sought to capture something of the universal brutality of war, just as Giacometti's attenuated, elongated and emaciated sculptures of the human form sought to speak to the isolation and anomie of the individual in contemporary societies. In a world of angst and alienation, modernism sought to create new value through artistic and aesthetic innovation, experimentation and creativity. This emphasis upon innovation, however, was in one sense to prove modernism's downfall as it came, over time, to be associated with a tendency to pure aesthetic self-indulgence – of art for art's sake (*l'art pour l'art*). Particularly notable, in this respect, was Schoenberg's endorsement (from 1908) of free atonality and his later adoption of a twelve-note scale which violated the long-standing relationships between one note and the next on the diatonic scale (Dahlhaus 1989). As this example perhaps suggests, the modernist experimental imperative served to establish over time an ever-more complex set of codes and conventions, requiring for their comprehension and appreciation ever-greater resources of cultural capital on the part of the audience. The result was a certain intellectual and aesthetic snobbery and a rigid demarcation between both high culture and pop culture and between the artist and audience. This characteristic valorisation of novelty and experimentation – again, often for its own sake – tended, then, to come at the price of increasing obscurity. Modernism, thus, tended towards high modernism, becoming ever more self-referential, esoteric, exclusive and elitist. It was this, in particular, which the postmodernists sought to reject.

That challenge came first in architecture and was encapsulated in Robert Venturi, Denise Scott Brown and Steven Izenour's seminal *Learning from Las Vegas* (first published in 1972, revised in 1977; see also Jencks 1977, 1986), described by Fredric Jameson as 'one of the classic texts of contemporary theory' (1991: 141). The perhaps uncharacteristic clarity of the distinction between modernism and postmodernism that they were able to draw derives at least in part from the specificity of architecture as a cultural practice. As Steven Connor rightly observes, within architecture 'movements and stylistic dominants are much more conspicuous and less arguable than elsewhere'. Moreover, as he goes on to note, 'the reason that postmodernism is provided with such a relatively unarguable definition in architecture turns out, interestingly, to rest upon the visible dominance in the twentieth-century experience of architectural modernism' (1997: 75). This makes architecture a particularly good point from which to begin an exploration of the postmodernist aesthetic sensibility.

Postmodernist architecture: learning from Las Vegas

In what sense, then, does postmodernist architecture depart from the modernism, say, of Le Corbusier, Lloyd Wright or the Bauhaus of Gropius or Mies van der Rohe? A number of points might here be made, but it is first important to establish what it was, precisely, that the postmodernists sought to reject.

The architecture of modernism was self-consciously an architecture of invention and novelty which sought to challenge existing conventions as a means of establishing its own and which sought to utilise new materials (limiting itself almost exclusively to sheet glass, concrete and steel) and new (industrial) construction techniques. It sought a purification of architectural practice emphasising functionality over form, content over decoration and ornamentation, thereby promoting what Venturi *et al.* term an 'abstract geometrical formalism'. Consequently, modernism was humourless, mathematical in its precision and cold, shunning what it saw as the clutter, confusion and frivolous ornamentation which had characterised pre-modern architectural genres (and hence many of the urban spaces into which it now sought to insert itself).

It was this that the postmodernists resisted. In a characteristically deconstructivist gesture, Venturi mocked Mies van der Rohe's defining statement of modernist architecture, 'less is more', mischievously retorting, 'less is a bore'. This neatly encapsulated the postmodernists' challenge. In a passionate polemic, the postmodernists charged their modernist forebears with culpability in, and responsibility for, the creation of a dehumanising, soulless and dystopic cityscape in which the victims of modernism were confined to live out their existence in boxes of concrete and glass. What they rejected in particular was the arrogance, complacency and, above all, the invasiveness of modernist architecture which had effectively imposed a uniform, and uniformly alienating, experience upon those subjected to its dystopic fantasies. The postmodernists sought to replace dull uniformity and univalence (the sense that there was only one 'correct' way to appreciate a given architectural form) with a playful and disrespectful multivalence. The aim was to present the citizen, now respected and cast in the mould of critic, with a proliferation of visual images and cues which might be interpreted creatively and which sought to engage with, rather than compensate for, the 'clutter' of the environment in which the building was situated. As Steven Connor suggests, in this way postmodernist architecture 'begins to mutate away from the geometric univalence of modernist architecture, as though allowing into its own form something of the multiplicity of ways of reading it, or, in a sense, reading itself in advance' (1997: 80). In John Docker's terms, 'the spectator, the participant, is not dominated by the expert, as with modernism, is not rendered passive, but . . . is allowed a space and freedom to interpret a variety of changing incongruous contradictory juxtaposed orders' (1995: 87–8). The architecture which Jencks and Venturi sought to promote was thus 'suddenly playful, whimsical, eclectic, jumbling together different architectural modes and languages and past and present styles . . . reintroducing elements of the ornamental, decorative and pictorial that modernism had for decades tried to purge and eliminate' (Docker 1995: 82). This was a plural architecture for a 'pluralist society' (Venturi, Scott Brown and Izenour 1977).

The defining feature of postmodernist architecture for Charles Jencks, however, was not its pluralism, humour, multivalence or eclecticism, but what he famously termed its 'double-coding' – the 'sampling' and juxtaposition of different styles of different periods to create the effect of parody, pastiche, ambiguity and paradox (1986: 14; see also Rose 1991: 101–49). It is out of such ambivalences and ambiguities that the multivalence and plurality of the architectural form as text arises. As McGuigan explains, in this way 'the postmodern text is not necessarily confined to just two meanings but, through various stylistic hybrids, it may suggest a multiplication of meanings resulting from an opening out of differences of interpretation' (1999: 16).

From modernism to postmodernism

In architecture, the distinction between modernism and postmodernism was particularly stark, as I have been at pains to demonstrate. Yet elsewhere the relationship between the two is rather more complex. As Terry Eagleton usefully suggests,

> postmodernism does not come after modernism in the sense that positivism comes after idealism, but in the sense that the recognition that the emperor has no clothes comes after gazing upon him. And so, just as it was true all along that the emperor was naked, so in a way post-modernism [to its advocates] was true even before it got started. It is, at one level at least, just the negative truth of modernity, an unmasking of its mythical pretensions. (1996: 29)

Postmodernism thus relies on, and is arguably parasitic upon, modernism. For, if there is no rigid distinction between high culture and pop culture then there is no shock value to be had by venerating kitsch as high culture or by placing off-the-shelf vacuum cleaners, in plexiglas vitrines, in the window of New York's New Museum of Contemporary Art, as in the controversial work of Jeff Koons (on which see Foster 1996: 99–124). It is modernist conventions which postmodernists seek to disrupt. Accordingly, without them it has neither meaning nor significance. Thus, however much a postmodernist intellectual sensibility might protest at the dualistic counterposing of modernism and postmodernism as aesthetic codes, such binary oppositions are in one sense the very condition of postmodernism.

This paradox is interestingly explored by Ihab Hassan. In the first edition of his seminal work, *The Dismemberment of Orpheus: Towards a Postmodern Literature*, Hassan resists such dualistic logics, insisting instead, rather like Eagleton above, that 'the postmodern spirit lies coiled within the great corpus of modernism' (1971: 139). Yet in a later revised edition, he adds a telling 'postface' in which the opposition between modernism and postmodernism is neatly summarised in terms of a series of dualistic distinctions (see Table 7.1). As Connor notes, in so doing Hassan relies upon a 'binary logic to promote the very things that appear to stand against binary logic, the ideas of dispersal, displacement and difference; he gives us difference *as opposed to* origin, irony *as opposed to* metaphysics, and so on, projecting the sense that these parallel lists of cultural symptoms could be extended infinitely without ever threatening the modernism/postmodernism opposition that sustains and produces them' (1997: 119, emphasis in the original). What this demonstrates yet again is the difficulty in pinning down postmodernism (here as an aesthetic sense) in terms which do not fall foul of its own heightened sensitivity to, and respect for, difference. Despite this, however, Hassan provides an extremely useful heuristic device, giving us an important set of cues as to the aesthetic specificity of postmodernism.

Modernism is concerned with the development of artistic and aesthetic

Table 7.1 *Modernism and postmodernism as aesthetic sensibilities*

Modernism	*Postmodernism*
Form (closed)	Antiform (open)
Purpose	Play
Design	Chance
Hierarchy	Anarchy
Art object/finished work	Process/performance
Narrative coherence/authenticity	Dissonance/multiple voices/collage/ pastiche
Originality/creativity/authorship	Death of the author/sampling
Depth/underlying reality	Surface/depthlessness

Source: Revised and adapted from Hassan (1982: 267–8).

codes and conventions, however subversive these may have been at the time of their development. It is this closure and associated emphasis upon *form* which makes, say, Magritte's *Ceci n'est pas un pipe* recognisably surrealist, just as it makes the Royal Festival Hall recognisably a work of modernist architecture. Modernism thus entails internal and hence self-referential systems and standards of judgement. This postmodernism rejects as both reactionary and pretentious. Instead it seeks to challenge and resist all codes and conventions, promoting a more inherently open and anarchic approach. This seeks to avoid the claustrophobic institutionalisation of artistic style and taste as convention. Whether postmodernism succeeds in this endeavour is something of a moot point. As Hal Foster concedes, with the appropriate air of contrition:

> I supported a postmodernism that contested this reactionary cultural politics and advocated artistic practices not only critical of institutional modernism but suggestive of alternative forms – of new ways to practice culture and politics. And we did not lose. In a sense a worse thing happened: treated as a fashion, postmodernism became *démodé*. (1996: 206)

What is clear, however, is that where modernism had embraced form and closure, postmodernism celebrates openness, anarchism and antiform. Modernist art is purposeful and serious – oriented to the achievement of specified goals such as the revelation of timeless truths about human nature or, in architecture, the facilitation of the flow of people through an urban space. Postmodernism, by contrast, is breathless, whimsical and playful, disrespectfully mocking the self-importance of a high-minded aesthetic elite of artists and art critics in a joyous celebration of kitsch and the banal. This contrast is reflected in modernism's studious emphasis upon control – upon care, precision and design – when set against the postmodernist embrace of chance, indeterminacy and contingency. Nowhere is this clearer than in the postmodernist penchant for installation art in which the contingent reaction and engagement of the spectator-come-participant is integral to the artwork itself (Foster 1996: 184, 199–202; Hopkins 2000: 228–31).

If modernism fetishises control, precision and design then in so doing it serves to construct and reinforce a series of binary hierarchies. Notable among these are those between high and popular culture, between good and bad art, and between the author or artist and the audience. Each of these postmodernism seeks to problematise, disrupt and deconstruct – in its attempts to 'bring the art gallery into the street and the street into the art gallery', in its reverence for kitsch and its disrespect for tradition and the 'aura' of classical texts, and in its inversion of the relationship between the artist and the audience in various forms of installation and performance art. As this suggests, postmodernism tends to conceive of art as an open-ended and ongoing process of performance and engagement which destabilises the artist–audience hierarchy, whereas modernism emphasises instead the art object or finished work – an object of veneration and respect and an expression of the creativity and skill of the artist or author.

In modernism the artist is central; art itself merely a medium for the expression of the artist's creativity. Consequently, modernism relies upon the authentic and original voice of the artist as author. The result is narrative coherence and a text which, if correctly appreciated, interpreted and decoded, reveals its author's message. This postmodernism rejects. In adopting techniques of collage, sampling and pastiche it acknowledges and draws attention to the variety of subject positions and vantage-points from which the world-as-text can be viewed, experienced and engaged with. It celebrates plurality, diversity and dissonance, bringing together a cacophony of multiple voices to explore the paradoxes and tensions thrown up by their juxtaposition. In place of modernism's cult of the artist, then, postmodernism joins with Roland Barthes in proclaiming 'the death of the author' (1977), shamelessly borrowing or 'sampling' and reassembling sounds, images and text.

The modernist and postmodernist aesthetic sensibilities exhibit rather different ontologies. Modernism is, in fact, profoundly realist in its ontological assumptions, implicitly positing a world whose surface appearance can be punctured through artistic creativity to reveal underlying realities and inner truths not apparent from the type of surface description characteristic of simpler aesthetics – such as those that gave rise to photo-realism (on modernism as philosophical realism, see Lunn 1985).

Postmodernism, by contrast, is deeply suspicious of claims as to the existence of underlying realities and inner essences, preferring instead to celebrate the superficial depthlessness of the world as it presents itself to us. As Patrick Bateman laments in Bret Easton Ellis's *American Psycho*, 'surface, surface, surface was all that anyone found meaning in . . . this was civilisation as I saw it, colossal and jagged' (1991: 374–5).

In sum, postmodernist art explores the realm of chance and contingency, emphasising the superficial (the surface) and resisting all artistic conventions and aesthetic norms (such as recognisable styles and genres). It is disrespectful of cultural and artistic traditions and of the artistic 'establishment', striving consistently to be heterodox rather then orthodox. It rejects the elitism of high modernism and seeks to take to the streets while returning the streets to the art gallery, thereby blurring and dissolving such conventionally rigid distinctions. It is playful and experimental. It appropriates, uses and 'samples' previous artistic expressions, often proceeding by way of collage, parody and pastiche. It challenges the creativity of the author, emphasising instead what is made of, and done with, the text by the spectator-as-participant, while down-playing the creation of the text itself. Its principal features can be summarised as in Box 7.1.

BOX 7.1 Characteristic features of postmodernism as an aesthetic sensibility

1. The effacement of boundaries between art and everyday life (bringing the street into the museum and the museum into the street)
2. The collapse of the hierarchical distinction between high and pop culture
3. Stylistic eclecticism and 'sampling' – the assumption that art is repetition
4. Parody, pastiche, irony, playfulness
5. A celebration of kitsch and the surface 'depthlessness' of culture
6. The decline in 'aura' of the artist as genius or author.

Postmodernism as an intellectual sensibility

Understood in such terms, there are clear affinities and similarities between postmodernism as an aesthetic sensibility and as an intellectual current. Indeed, in the same way that aesthetic and stylistic postmodernism is not reducible to any single essence or defining principle, academic postmodernism (for want of a better term) belies a simple definition. It, too, must be conceptualised as an intellectual sensibility rather than as a clearly defined position or perspective.

As such, I suggest, postmodernism is perhaps best seen as a heightened sensitivity to the opinions and worldviews of others – a respect for others and other perspectives. This emphasis may well prove controversial. For, conventionally within political science and international relations, postmodernism is understood as little more than an epistemological relativism – and dismissed accordingly. The extent to which postmodernism does indeed imply relativism is an important and interesting question to which we return. Suffice it for now to note that in so far as postmodernism does express an epistemological scepticism, this derives from prior normative and ethical commitments and indeed ontological assumptions. Thus, although sadly ignored in much of the existing literature on the subject, postmodernism is motivated by a deep normative respect for others, leading to a questioning of all universal (and universalising) claims. Seen in this way postmodernism is neither an end of epistemology nor the triumph of a relativist epistemology but, instead, a normatively motivated exploration of the limits of critical social and political inquiry (with certain epistemological implications).

What is clear, however, is that postmodernism, whether as an artistic, aesthetic or intellectual sensibility, is extremely evasive. That evasiveness, though deeply frustrating, is integral to the challenge it poses. For postmodernism is a form of interrogation – a mode of questioning – rather than a perspective in its own right. It is *de*constructivist rather than *re*constructivist. It poses a series of discomforting questions and resists simple answers. In this respect it is rather like the persistent child who repeatedly asks the difficult questions and refuses to be fobbed off with an evasive or gestural response. In particular, postmodernism is motivated by a normative suspicion of the legacy of modernist assumptions in contemporary thought. This is well captured by Terry Eagleton in the following terms:

> Postmodernism . . . is a style of thought which is suspicious of classical notions of truth, reason, identity and objectivity, of the idea of universal progress or emancipation, of single frameworks, grand narratives or ultimate grounds of explanation. Against these Enlightenment norms, it sees the world as contingent, ungrounded, diverse, unstable, indeterminate, a set of disunified cultures or interpretations which breed a degree of scepticism about the objectivity of truth, history and norms, the givenness of natures and the coherence of identities. (Eagleton 1996: vii)

This takes us far closer to a useful definition of postmodernism. Yet if we are to take the challenge that postmodernism poses to conventional

Figure 7.1 *Postmodernist ontology, epistemology and methodology*

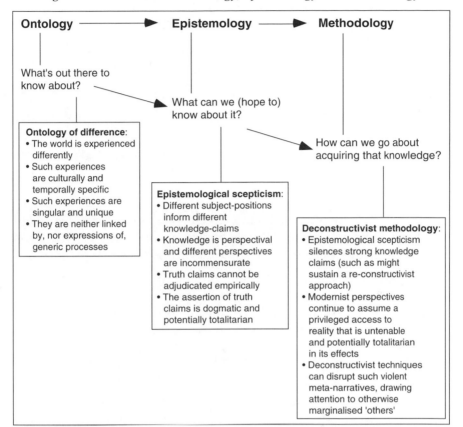

political analysis seriously, it is important to acknowledge that this challenge is ontological, epistemological and methodological. This suggests the utility of defining postmodernism explicitly in such terms.

Postmodernism is, then, perhaps most usefully conceptualised as the combination of *an ontology of difference and singularity, an epistemological scepticism and a deconstructivist methodology* (see Figure 7.1).

Postmodernism's ontology of difference

Understood in this way, postmodernism's most fundamental premises are ontological (see Table 7.2). The world, for postmodernists, is experienced differently – and from an almost infinite variety of vantage-points or subject-positions. Such experiences are culturally and temporally specific, since our access to the social and political universe we inhabit is discursively mediated. Moreover, our exposure to, and immersion in, such discourses varies, at the same time, between cultures

Table 7.2   *The ontologies of modernism and postmodernism*

Modernism's ontology of totality	Postmodernism's ontology of difference
Identity	Difference
Unity	Singularity
Generality	Specificity
Metonymy	Uniqueness
Connectedness	Diversity
Organicity	Individuation
Coherence	Dissonance
Totality	Fragmentation

and, over time, for the same culture. Our cognitions are, then, constructions which reflect the cultural context in which we are situated. As a consequence, as Clifford Geertz persuasively argues:

> Trying to understand people quite differently placed than ourselves, encased in different ambitions, possessed of different notions as to what life is all about, poses very similar problems, whether the conditions, ambitions, and notions be those of the Hanseatic League, the Solomon Islands, the Count-Duke of Olivares, or the Children of Sanchez. Dealing with a world elsewhere comes to much the same thing when elsewhere is long ago as when it is far away. (2000: 120)

While many postmodernists would wish to add to Geertz's 'worlds long ago' and 'far away' those 'here and now', the sentiment is essentially the same.

When one considers that cultures are internally differentiated the variety of potential subject-positions from which the world may be viewed proliferates further. Consequently, 'our' world (that of here and now) is also one of heterogeneity, 'Otherness' (with, as Geertz puts it 'postmodern capital letters and post-stucturalist shudder quotes' (2000: 120)), difference and diversity. Our experiences are singular and unique and are neither expressions of, nor even linked by, common or generic processes. This ontology of difference (and the normative respect for such difference which underpins it) is well captured in Lyotard's notion of the *differend*:

> The *differend* is the unstable state and instance of language wherein something that must be able to be put into phrases cannot yet be . . . What is at stake in a certain literature, in a philosophy, or perhaps even in a certain politics, is to bear witness to differends by finding idioms for them. (Lyotard 1988: 13)

As he further explains in slightly less cryptic terms.

> As distinguished from a litigation, a differend would be a case of conflict, between (at least) two parties, that cannot be equitably resolved for lack of a rule of judgement applicable to both arguments. One side's legitimacy does not imply the other's lack of legitimacy. However, applying a single rule of judgement to both in order to settle their differend as though it were merely a litigation would wrong (at least) one of them (and both of them if neither side admits this rule). (1988: xi)

A good example of this is the 'Salman Rushdie affair', a clash between parties inhabiting different worldviews or language-games and sharing no common standard for the resolution of their dispute (for interesting discussions, see Dubin 1992: 83–9; Jennings and Kemp-Welch 1997). If difference is to be respected, judgement must be indefinitely deferred.

Postmodernism is, then, characterised by an *ontology of difference and singularity* for which no two things are ever the same – nor even an instance of the same thing. Experiences are unique and must, consequently, be understood in their own terms. No generic, far less universal, accounts can be offered for no universal language or discourse exists. To posit a *lingua franca* (a common language which speakers of different tongues might share) is to deny – or, worse still, to acknowledge and yet fail to respect – singularity and difference. There are, in short, no trans-historical, trans-cultural, far less universal theories or truths.

Postmodernism's epistemological scepticism

As the above paragraph suggests, a postmodernist ontology of difference shades seamlessly into an *epistemological scepticism* which, at times, threatens to give way to a fully fledged relativism. It is this, as I have suggested, for which postmodernism is perhaps best known in political science and international relations (Vasquez 1998: 215). Animated by an ontological conviction that the world can be viewed from a multiplicity of (incommensurate) perspectives and a normative (indeed, pluralist) conviction that each of these should be accorded equal respect, postmodernism is drawn inexorably towards a suspicion of all epistemological foundations. For, in a world of difference, alternative and incompatible knowledge-claims can always be advanced from different subject-positions. Since, as in the Salman Rushdie affair discussed above, there is no available standard to adjudicate such contending claims which does not itself violate the internal norms of one, other or both subject-positions, a respect for difference logically entails epistemological quietism. Thus, as Andrew Sayer perceptively notes:

whatever the philosophers and social theorists have argued, among students who are attracted to relativism, the most common motive is a fear of absolutism, a fear that accepting the possibility of distinguishing truth from falsity will require one to pronounce the beliefs of others as false. Relativism appears to have the virtue of being egalitarian and open-minded, avoiding implications that others are 'falsely conscious'. (2000: 48)

A similar observation is made by Martin Hollis and Steven Lukes in the context of a rather earlier debate:

Relativism has always appealed to noble and worthy sentiments. Within anthropology a need and duty have long been felt not only to understand the worlds of other cultures from within, but also to respect them: here to interpret the world is not to change it. (1982: 2)

The similarity between the cultural relativism emergent in social anthropology in the 1970s and 1980s and the epistemological anxieties of present-day postmodernists is surely telling and is an issue to which we return presently. What the juxtaposition of these quotes again suggests is that postmodernism's epistemological scepticism is normatively motivated. It is a product not of an enthusiastic attempt to throw away the foundations on which objective knowledge claims might be made for its own sake but of the failure to discover such foundations after an exhaustive search. In the absence of standards about which we can be absolutely confident, the postmodernists effectively suggest, we owe it to others not to assert our 'truths' over theirs.

Whether such a normative motivation is defensible and whether, if it is, epistemological quietism is the best way to respect difference is another matter and an issue to which we will also return (see also Herzfeld 2001: 31–2). Suffice it for now to note that, for postmodernists, all knowledge is situated or perspectival (knowledge *from somewhere* as opposed to knowledge *per se*). The assertion of transcendent knowledge claims (such as might settle, one way or another, Lyotard's *differend* or the Salman Rushdie affair) is, then, dogmatic and, potentially, totalitarian. It is akin to outlawing the expression of religious freedom on the grounds that the positing of a deity constitutes an assault upon the authority of the sovereign state.

Postmodernism's deconstructivist methodology

Postmodernism thus entails a rejection of all claims to epistemic privilege on the grounds that if we cannot know with certainty – and hence do not possess a firm (epistemological) foundation for our assertions – then we should resist making strong knowledge claims altogether.

It is but a short step to postmodernism's *deconstructivist methodology*. To avoid any potential for confusion here, it is immediately important to signal two rather different senses of the term 'deconstruction' invoked by postmodernists. The first is more generically postmodernist in the sense that it might be held to apply to all postmodernists. Indeed, arguably it is logically entailed by the ontology and epistemology outlined above. It is, partly as a consequence, less precise and more negative in tone than the second, implying not so much the positive advocacy of a methodology that is distinctively deconstructivist as a rejection (on epistemological grounds) of any methodology which might be regarded as reconstructivist.

The second sense of deconstruction is by no means logically implied by a postmodernist epistemological scepticism (though it is consistent with it) and, as a methodology, is deployed by only a handful of postmodernists or, as they would tend to prefer, post-structuralists. It is, however, deconstructivist in both a more specific and a more positive sense, involving the adoption of the analytical techniques associated with the French post-structuralist Jacques Derrida.

In its most generic sense, postmodernism is deconstructivist by default. Lacking the confidence which a less sceptical and suspicious epistemology might engender, postmodernists deny themselves the voice with which to project a reconstructivist approach. As Andrew Sayer observes, 'in place of a paternalistic and imperialist presumption to speak for others, we have an extreme deference towards others, a reluctance to speak for them, even where doing so might help' (2000: 76). Wary of the 'violence' to difference that foundational claims necessarily entail, postmodernism restricts itself to a series of disruptive strategies and techniques. Its ambitions are, accordingly, modest – to interrogate and (however temporarily) to interrupt the violence of more confident modernist metanarratives, drawing attention to the otherwise silenced 'others' such narratives ignore. As Richard Ashley and R. B. J. Walker claim, the aims of postmodernism in international relations are 'to interrogate limits, to explore how they are imposed, to demonstrate their arbitrariness and to think *other*-wise' (1990: 263–4, emphasis in the original).

As this suggests, deconstructivism is, in essence, a methodology of self-denial – a disruption of modernist pretensions, certainly, but one which denies itself the authority to put anything in place of that it deconstructs. In this way, rather like its artistic and aesthetic namesake, academic postmodernism is highly parasitic upon modernism and, indeed, the prevalence of modernist assumptions which might be deconstructed (see also

Trouillot 1991: 21). Postmodernism is, then, a purely oppositional discourse. The implications of this are rather paradoxical. For, insofar as a postmodernist sensibility does indeed breed within society 'a degree of scepticism about the objectivity of truth, history and norms, the givenness of natures and the coherence of identities' (Eagleton 1996: vii), postmodernists will find themselves without anything to deconstruct; and without anything to deconstruct they will have nothing to do.

So much for a generic deconstructivism. Rather more substantive methodologically is Derrida's distinctive brand of deconstruction, which offers an altogether more specific armoury of analytical techniques. Deconstructivist theory, however, is notoriously impenetrable. As Steven Woolgar asks himself in a special issue of the journal *Current Anthropology*:

> Q: *What's the difference between the Mafia and a deconstructivist?*
> A: A deconstructivist makes you an offer you can't understand.
> (Cited in M. A. Rose 1991: 40)

It is not difficult to substantiate the claim which underpins Woolgar's pun. The following passage – taken, ironically, from a book entitled *Dissemination* – provides ample testimony:

> A writing that refers only to itself and a writing that refers indefinitely to some other writing might appear non-contradictory: the reflecting screen never captures anything but writing, indefinitely, stopping nowhere, and each reference still confines us within the element of reflection. Of course. But the difficulty arises in the relation between the medium of writing and the determination of each textual unit. It is necessary that while referring each time to another text, to another determinate system, each organism only refer to *itself* as a determinate structure; a structure that is open and closed *at the same time*. (Derrida 1982: 202; emphasis in the original)

At this point, you might well think, a definition may help. Yet, as Christopher Norris reminds us, things are not so simple. For deconstruction belies definition: 'to treat it as amenable to handy definition is to foster a misleadingly reductive account of that activity and hence to render one's text redundant as it originates' (1983: 6). Similarly, as Trevor J. Barnes remarks, 'writing about Derrida is unsettling because his aim is to question the very project of writing' (1996: 163). And, as Derrida himself concedes (if that is the appropriate term), 'deconstruction loses nothing from admitting that it is impossible' (1991: 209). Apparently impossible to define and, presumably, just as impossible to practice, deconstruction might seem a less than appealing methodology. Yet it does in fact offer postmodernists a set of techniques with which to operationalise their antipathy towards hierarchical dualisms in a manner consistent with their epistemological scepticism and their fear of traversing the deconstruction–reconstruction divide. As a methodology it has proved increasingly influential in international relations theory (see, for instance, Ashley 1988; Campbell 1992, 1998; Walker 1993).

At the risk of rendering the text, in Norris' terms, 'redundant as it originates', deconstruction might be seen (defined, even) as a form of immanent critique, 'an acute form of reflexive criticism, one that uses the meaning of a term to disrupt that meaning' (Barnes 1996: 165). As Jonathan Culler explains, 'deconstruction appeals to no higher logical principle or superior reason but uses the very principle it deconstructs' (1983: 87). In this sense, as in immanent critique, it does not seek to impose external standards or judgements upon an object of deconstruction (a text), but seeks to disturb those already expressed within the text, by exploring their internal inconsistencies and paradoxes.

Deconstruction proceeds by way of an interrogation of the often implicit binary oppositions which structure modernist texts (truth–falsity, justice–injustice, and so forth). Derrida sees the whole tradition of Western metaphysics from Plato as characterised by 'a thinking which makes privileged use of binary, oppositional structures, whereby a positively marked term is defined against a negatively marked one (presence against absence, the inside as against the outside, the soul as against the body, meaning as against its sign, the spirit as against the letter, the clear as against the obscure, the literal as against the figural, the rational as against the irrational, the serious as against the non-serious, and so on, indefinitely)' (Bennington 2000: 8). This takes us to the crux of deconstruction. For deconstructivists in the Derridean tradition seek to demonstrate the operation of such oppositional binaries within the texts they scrutinise. They argue that, though frequently unacknowledged and, where acknowledged, invariably presented as neutral and/or descriptive rather than hierarchical, such oppositions: (i) pervade Western thought (and Western cultural practices) and (ii) are necessarily and violently hierarchical. Western/modernist thought is thus structured by, and dependent upon, an endless succession of hierarchical dualisms which serve, in their privileging (or 'centring') of one term over the other (man over woman, reason over irrationality, and so forth), to repress, marginalise and silence others (the 'Other'). The purpose of deconstruction is to restore that 'Other' by unravelling and thereby disrupting the hierarchical nature of the binary opposition – questioning 'not just the *hierarchy* of the opposition, but its very *oppositionality*' (2000: 9, emphasis in the original).

As the above discussion perhaps suggests, Derrida's deconstructivist methodology is acutely sensitive both to difference and to the violence to difference that totalising modes of thought inflict. It is, moreover, deeply normative in its motivation. Accordingly, it sits extremely uncomfortably alongside the conventional view of postmodernism as 'a relativistic nihilism that rejects all knowledge claims and renders political and ethical commitment redundant' (Howarth 1995: 116).[3] As Richard J. Bernstein rightly notes, 'few contemporary thinkers have been so alert and perceptive about the temptations and dangers of violently crushing or silencing differences, otherness or alterity – in "others" or even the "other" in ourselves' (1991: 184). Thus, as a number of recent authors have sought to demonstrate, deconstruction is a deeply political act and one that is most definitely motivated normatively (Beardsworth 1996; Bennington 1994, 1999, 2000; Culler 1983; Lawson 1985; Norris 1987, 1991). Whether, in the end, it is a sufficiently political act is another matter. For, like postmodernism more generally, Derridean deconstruction would seem to refuse to sanction a more engaged and positive politics capable of institutionalising its undoubted respect for difference. Arguably, for that to occur, reconstruction is required.

This brings us to critiques of postmodernist excess. But before evaluating such critiques directly, it is important that we consider the contribution that postmodernism has made to contemporary political analysis. We start, then, with the positive side of the balance sheet.

The contribution of postmodernism to political analysis

It is perhaps first important to note that the contribution of postmodernism is very unevenly distributed between political science and international relations. For while it has yet to make much of an impact in political science, it has proved far more influential within international relations theory. This is reflected in the substantial secondary literature on postmodernism which now exists in the latter discipline (see, for instance, Devetek 2001; Keohane 1989; S. Smith 2001; Smith, Booth and Zalewski 1996; Vasquez 1998) and the almost complete absence of an equivalent literature in the former (though see the passing references in Goodin and Klingemann 1996; Marsh and Stoker 1995).

The uneven nature of this response to postmodernism probably owes much to the crisis of theoretical confidence which the end of the Cold War precipitated – something mainstream perspectives had simply failed to anticipate (P. Allan 1992; Bowker and Brown 1993; Gaddis 1992). As Kjell Goldmann has noted, international relations theory from the 1950s to the 1980s 'may be characterised as the accumulation of explanations of the Cold War's persistence' (1996: 408). Faced with a most stark and unexpected falsification of their most basic assumptions and the predictions they had given rise to, it is perhaps unsurprising that international relations theorists proved rather more receptive to radical theoretical alternatives than their more self-confident contemporaries in departments of political science. Nonetheless, whilst postmodernism may have been tolerated rather more by international relations theorists, it has hardly been enthusiastically embraced by either mainstream.

Its contribution to contemporary international relations theory, however, has been considerable – if still, perhaps, largely theoretical. It is well summarised in John A. Vasquez's sensitive and perceptive commentary. In this he points to five key insights from which, he argues, contemporary international relations theorists can learn much. Space does not permit a detailed exposition of each, so we will consider just two: (i) the demonstration of the arbitrary nature of modernity, modernisation and, indeed, 'progress', and (ii) the demonstration that conceptual frameworks are prone to self-fulfilling prophecies (Vasquez 1998: 216–20).

Of the two, the first is clearly the more authentically and explicitly *post*-modern. Unsurprisingly, perhaps, postmodernists draw attention to the invariably implicit, unacknowledged and ultimately indefensible modernist assumptions which they detect underpinning conventional western approaches to the study of international relations. In particular they seek to expose the reliance of such conceptual schemas on teleological notions of history and progress which posit a world unfolding over time towards a condition of civilisation, liberty and enlightenment. In Vasquez' terms:

> To postmodernism, the ideas of economic and political *development* are just so many modernist conceits in a litany of conceits that have been imposed on the weak and the defeated. Modernity is not progress. It is not optimal. It is not superior. It is culturally and ethically arbitrary. (1998: 217, emphasis in the original)

As is so often the case with postmodernism, it is difficult to point to a substantive contribution that is being made here. Indeed, such an exposé of modernist assumptions merely serves to make international relations, particularly critical international relations, more difficult. Nonetheless it is an important contribution.

Drawing inspiration from Foucault's genealogy of power–knowledge regimes discussed in Chapter 5, postmodernists reject metanarratives of progress in favour of accounts which emphasise discontinuity and incommensurability. The carceral and penal codes which discipline contemporary societies imply a profoundly different regime of power, knowledge and justice to those which dominated earlier decades or centuries. There is, moreover, no neutral ground 'beyond power–knowledge' from which to compare these contending regimes. They are simply incommensurate – what appears just under one regime will not (necessarily) appear just under another. We may well express a preference for one over another and we may well be able to justify this normatively. Indeed, it would be surprising were we not able to do so. But in the process of stating and defending such a preference are we not merely giving voice to the power–knowledge regime and attendant conception of justice within which we have been socialised? If so, or if we are prepared to concede that this is so, then the implications are considerable. For what applies to regimes of discipline and punishment applies elsewhere too . . . As Steve Smith asks himself, 'how can history have a truth if truth has a history?' (2001: 240).

Thus, whatever he may have thought at the time, there was nothing neutral or objective about Silvio Berlusconi's unfortunate claim, in the immediate wake of the terrorist attacks on New York and Washington of 11 September 2001, for the superiority of Western-Christian culture when compared to that he attributed to the perpetrators. Indeed, postmodernists would contend, there is simply no way of adjudicating neutrally or dispassionately between contending cultures, 'civilisations' or conceptions of justice.

In problematising the ease with which we might draw trans-historical or trans-cultural comparisons in this way, postmodernism reminds us of the inherently subjective and normative dimension of any notion of 'progress'. To describe the transition from dictatorship to democracy as progressive is entirely commonplace and is, of course, justifiable. But the point is that it is only justifiable with respect to, and in terms of, a particular ethic. There is nothing objective or absolute about the degree of 'progress' involved in the transition, nor anything inevitable about the transition itself. More problematic still would be to assume, as in many classically modernist accounts, that it is the progressive nature of the transition from dictatorship to democracy that renders it inevitable. All of this postmodernism rejects, and that is no bad thing.

It is important, however, to be clear about the implications of this. The point is not that we must abandon the appeal to notions of progress in political analysis, though that would perhaps be the postmodernist's natural response. What is implied, however, is that where we appeal to notions of progress we do so in a rather more cautious and self-conscious a manner. In particular, we must acknowledge that notions of progress answer to particular ethical judgements, that they are contestable, and that, as a consequence, they need to be defended normatively. If we are not prepared to advance an ethical justification for the inherently normative criteria to which we appeal when invoking notions such as progress or development then we should, indeed, take the post-modernists' self-imposed vow of (judgemental) silence.

Yet the postmodernist critique does not end here. For by pointing to the arbitrary nature of modernity in this way it draws attention to the power of those who get to specify the content of what might be termed 'mock universals' – progress, truth, justice, reason, rationality and so forth. This is – or should serve as – a chastening reminder to political analysts who like to think of themselves as doing good, of their respon-sibilities – and some time culpabilities – in pointing to 'progressive' paths, whether taken or untaken. It reminds us, in particular, of the context from which we write and of the role of contextualisation and the socialisation it reflects on both the content of what we write and on that we take for granted and do not feel the need to justify. Whilse this may make the practice of political analysis more difficult, throwing up a series of normative and ethical dilemmas which we must negotiate, it is a welcome and valuable contribution in its own right. It may serve to guard against the arrogance, self-assuredness and complacency which certainly characterised international relations before the end of the Cold War and arguably still characterises much political science today.

The second contribution identified by Vasquez is rather more sub-stantive and, perhaps, rather less distinctively postmodern – a point to which we return. Conceptual frameworks, indeed language more gen-erally, is prone to self-fulfilling prophecies against which contemporary political analysts should guard. As Vasquez suggests, 'whenever ideas spread and people behave and act on them, then that part of the world portrayed by these ideas actually comes into being' (1998: 218). This is, in fact, something of an exaggeration, as actions informed by dominant understandings do not serve *always* to reconstruct the world in the image of those ideas. Nonetheless, the basic point is an important and perceptive one – and, indeed, one perhaps already familiar from Chapter 6.

What the postmodernists here remind us of is both the causal and con-stitutive role of ideas in social and political systems. Consequently, the very conceptions of the world we advance and the assumptions on which they are premised *may come* to play a crucial role in reconfiguring the social and political landscape in which we find ourselves. As argued in Chapter 6, the internalisation by elected officials of conventional assumptions about globalisation may be sufficient to bring about out-comes consistent with the globalisation thesis, whether that thesis is true or false (see also Hay and Rosamond 2002; Watson 2000). Similarly, the perception of a military or terrorist threat, whether accurate or otherwise, may be sufficient to bring about pre-emptive action and con-sequent retaliation. This, in turn, is likely to be taken to 'confirm' the reality of the initial threat. In this way conceptions strongly held and acted upon may indeed become self-fulfilling prophecies (Campbell 1992, 1998; Wendt 1995). As Tariq Modood has noted, commenting in *The Observer* on Berlusconi's remarks on the attacks on Washington and New York, 'a "clash of civilisations" poses a danger of becoming a self-fulfilling prophecy at a time when we are all trying to make sense of an atrocity on such a large scale' (30 September 2001).

Vasquez's own example, which seems to draw implicitly on the work of Jim George (1994), is particularly instructive and adds an additional layer of complexity to such self-fulfilling logics. For, as he notes:

> The extent to which rational choice analysis can become a rigorous science will depend very much on the extent to which people or leaders accept its rules to guide their behaviour. In doing so, they will not only create a reality but people who are 'rationally-calculating individuals'. Such a science succeeds in explaining more and more of the variance *not because it is able to uncover the 'causes' of behaviour, but because it produces them.* (1998: 219, emphasis mine)

This is a very significant observation and applies not only to rationalist perspectives such as neo-classical economics, rational choice theory, realism and neo-realism but, potentially, to all conduct-shaping social, political and economic theories. Its logic is impeccable and, in essence, very simple. If political actors internalise assumptions, for instance about the limited parameters of political choice in an era of globalisation, they will act on the basis of such assumptions, however inaccurate they may be, to produce outcomes consistent with the theory's predictions. In so far, then, as the predictions of rational choice theory, neo-realism or neo-classical economics conform to political and economic practice it may well be because political and economic actors have internalised precisely such theories, incorporating them within their modes of calculation and practice.

Such reflections are, again, chastening and may serve to remind political analysts – particularly those with a direct or even indirect line to holders of public office – of their responsibilities to us all.

This is, again, a very significant contribution. However, as the references to the existing literature in proceeding paragraphs testify, this is a contribution which is by no means the exclusive preserve of post-modernists. As argued in Chapter 6, social constructivist approaches to international relations and ideationally sensitive variants of the new institutionalism within political science have, for some time, been interested in the self-fulfilling nature of conceptual frameworks, policy paradigms and, in short, the ideas influencing the strategic deliberations of public officials (see for instance Berman 1998; Blyth 2000; Hall 1993;

Hay 1999e; Hay and Rosamond 2002; McNamara 1998; Wendt 1995, 1999). What this, in turn, implies is that one can embrace the causal and constitutive role of ideas within social and political systems without having to embrace the excesses to which postmodernism seems, invariably, prone.

The postmodernist challenge to (critical) political analysis

Having sought to outline a conception of postmodernism as a normatively motivated ontology, epistemology and methodology and having sought to assess the nature of its contribution, we are now in a position to turn more directly to the challenge it might be seen to pose to political analysis – and critical political analysis in particular.

Here I will adopt what might at first appear a rather strange strategy, by examining the development of social and cultural anthropology – *as a form of political analysis* – in recent years. My argument is, in fact, relatively simple. First, in so far as social and cultural anthropology is concerned with the distribution, exercise and reproduction of relations of power, it is a form – albeit a distinctive form – of political analysis. By the definition advanced in Chapter 2, cultural anthropology is no less a form of political analysis than psephology or security studies. Whilst this first point is likely to prove controversial, it is the second that is more immediately significant. It is this. In its engagement with difference (in the form of cultures other than our own), and in its engagement with its own frequently colonialist past, anthropology has always posed in a most acute and intense way the challenge now represented by postmodernism. Moreover, and as a consequence, anthropologists have responded to that challenge in a rather more sensitive and sophisticated manner than has invariably been the case in (mainstream) political science and international relations. As Michael Herzfeld has recently suggested, 'anthropology has learned as much – and can teach as much – by attention to its mistakes as by the celebration of its achievements' (2001: 2). It would be nice to think that some day the same might be said of political analysis.

Anthropology: from barbarism to postmodernism and beyond

Anthropology is conventionally understood as the study of 'other' societies and 'other cultures'. Consider first its practices at the turn of the twentieth century. As a great number of more recent commentators have noted with the appropriate degree of embarrassed unease, guilt even, anthropology was dominated, at the time, by a view of the inexorable progression of societies and of 'man' from a condition of primitive barbarism to one of civilisation, enlightenment, freedom and, above all, modernity through secularisation, the 'mastery' of science, the subversion of ritual, myth and 'tribal' symbolism, and so forth (Asad 1991; Fabian 1983; Fanon 1963; Herzfeld 1987; Scott 1992, 1994). Social anthropology, as in Evans-Pritchard's classic text of the same name, was the study of 'primitive societies' (1951: 11) or, in Lévi-Strauss' terms, the elucidation of the structures of *The Savage Mind* (1966). It was, moreover, committed to an invariably evolutionary metanarrative of progress which drew somewhat dubious inspiration from physical anthropology – with the latter's notorious attempts to locate specific 'tribes' on the chart of evolutionary progress by gauging the size of their skulls (Kuper 1994). This integrated anthropology tended to regard the objects of its knowledge as 'specimens' rather than subjects in their own right (Fabian 1983; Herzfeld 2001: 35). A more classically modernist metanarrative is hard to imagine.

Were this not already sufficient to discredit the discipline in the eyes of contemporary commentators, such anthropology is now widely seen to have been dependent upon, and more or less complicit with, a deeply colonialist process of imposed 'Westernisation'. As Kathleen Gough argued in a symposium on the responsibilities of the anthropologist as early as 1968:

> Anthropology is a child of Western imperialism. It has roots in the humanist visions of the Enlightenment, but as a university discipline and a modern science, it came into its own in the last decades of the nineteenth and the early twentieth centuries. This was the period in which the Western nations were making their final push to bring practically the whole pre-industrial non-Western world under their political and economic control. (1968: 403)

While it would be wrong, then, to see anthropology as directly implicated in the imperialism which saw 'first contacts' rapidly followed by the mass transportations of the slave trade (on which see Huizer 1979: 5–6; Sombart 1924: 702, 708–9), it was nonetheless constructed on precisely the same opposition of barbarism and civility that provided the rationale for such violent exercises in colonial brutality. As Michel-Rolph Trouillot perceptively observes, it is precisely this

> construction of otherness upon which anthropology is premised ... Anthropology did not create the savage. Rather, the savage was the *raison d'être* of anthropology. (1991: 29, 40)

Something similar might be said of earlier variants of development theory. If such anthropology was not directly colonialist, it both relied upon and enjoyed colonial patronage (Asad 1979: 92).

Cast in this light, it is not surprising that much contemporary anthropology adopts a strangely apologetic, even confessional, tone, comforting itself with what Jonathan Benthall terms, 'the therapy of a searching self-examination' (1995: 2). It is perhaps for precisely this reason that it has responded so sensitively and directly to the challenges posed by postmodernism. Indeed, in many respects it might be argued that anthropology in fact pre-empted the challenge of postmodernism, responding to it before it was even formulated in its now familiar terms.

Returning, temporarily, to the first half of the twentieth century, the stylised role of the anthropologist as colonial traveller was to leave her or (more likely) his high perch in the ivory tower, to chart a ship and to sail off to some distant and primitive land. Here, armed only with a notepad and, perhaps, a camera, his task was to detail the barbarism, brutality and incivility of other societies and cultures when cast through the lens of the Enlightened western rationalist (on the modernist predilection for, and preoccupation with, the visual see Classen, Howes and Synnott 1994: 88–92; Herzfeld 2001: 34–8; Jay 1993). Such ethnography offered a glimpse of other cultures, cultures lower on the evolutionary rung of progress and civilisation than our own. Indeed, it offered a glimpse of ourselves – or, at least, our ancestors – at an earlier stage in the grand evolutionary scheme of things. As Gerrit Huizer suggests, for the vast majority of its history and 'with some notable exceptions' western anthropologists have tended to 'approach other cultures as more "savage" or "barbarian" or at least "less civilised" than their own' (1979: 7).

Contemporary anthropology, however, is an altogether different entity (with, again, the inevitable notable exceptions). The reasons for this are numerous and arise, at least in part, from changes to the environment in which anthropologists now find themselves. As Trouillot again notes, 'like many of the human sciences, [anthropology] now faces dramatically new historical conditions of performance' (1991: 18). Principal among these are the effects of decolonisation and the inevitable change in the relationship between ethnographic 'object' and anthropological 'observer' that this has entailed. The 'nervousness' engendered by a recognition of the anthropological 'object' as an agent and subject in her own right is now a common theme of contemporary anthropological-cum-philosophical reflection (Benthall 1995: 5; Trouillot 1991: 19). It is, as ever, brilliantly captured by Clifford Geertz:

> This inter-confusion of object and audience, as though Gibbon were to find himself suddenly with a Roman readership . . . leaves contemporary anthropologists in some uncertainty as to it rhetorical aim. Who is now to be persuaded? Africanists or Africans? Americanists or American Indians? Japanologists or Japanese? And of what: Factual accuracy? Theoretical sweep? Imaginative grasp? Moral depth? Is it easy enough to answer, 'all of the above'. It is not quite so easy to produce a text that responds. (1988: 133)

As he goes on,

> the very right to write – to write ethnography – seems at risk. The entrance of once colonialised or castaway peoples (wearing their own masks, speaking their own lines) onto the stage of global economy, international high politics, and world culture has made the claim of the anthropologist to be a tribune for the unheard, a representative of the unseen, a kenner of the misconstrued, increasingly difficult to sustain. (1988: 133)

For a discipline accustomed for so long to the silence of those about whom it spoke, the transformation of 'specimens' into agents and the sound of anthropological subjects talking back was discomforting indeed. As Geertz again suggests, in such a context the 'burdens of authorship' suddenly appear more arduous (1988: 138). It is not surprising, then, that postmodernism should have come to acquire a particular appeal within anthropology.

Inspired in the first instance if not perhaps by directly postmodernist ideas then certainly by a normative respect for the subjects of its knowledge claims, anthropologists from the 1970s onwards came increasingly to regard the assumptions and practices of their disciplinary forebears as barbaric, even totalitarian. Modernist anthropology, for want of a better term, had merely served to impose one distinct and partial view of the world – that informed by the norms and conventions of western civilisation – onto societies which worked rather differently. Thus, rather than seek to chart and detail the barbarism and primitivism of other cultures regarded as inferior to our own – or, worst still, lower on the evolutionary rung of progress and civilisation than our own – we should seek to suspend our judgements and understand such societies in their own terms (by adopting what Clifford Geertz (1983) famously terms the 'native point of view'). While many more self-consciously postmodernist authors might regard the (otherwise laudable) aim of seeking to 'understanding others as they understand themselves' as hopelessly naïve, what they would share with this more modest and reflexive anthropology is the implication that there is no neutral basis from which to judge others (see also Fay 1996). And in the absence of such a universal standards, we should perhaps resist the temptation to judge altogether – on the ground if we can't do it neutrally, we shouldn't do it at all (cf. Lyotard 1988).

This profound respect for difference, reflected in a desire to seek to treat the objects of social and political analysis in their own terms as opposed to those we bring with us, should by now be familiar. It suggests that, in significant respects, anthropology is the natural home of postmodernism – posing the question of difference in the starkest terms. As Michael Herzfeld notes, the very process of ethnography on which anthropology relies makes modernist metanarratives of evolutionary progress difficult to sustain:

> Knowing those about whom one writes as neighbours and friends makes lofty ideas about the hierarchy of cultures both untenable and distasteful. (2001: 3; see also Stocking 1995)

Geertz, again, takes the observation a little further, suggesting in a brilliant essay on 'anti-anti-relativism', that the 'relativist bent' is in one sense inherent in anthropology:

> One cannot read too long about Nayar matriliny, Aztec sacrifice, the Hopi verb, or the convolutions of the hominid transition and not begin to consider the possibility that, to quote Montaigne . . . 'each man calls barbarism whatever is not his own practice . . . for we have no other criterion of reason than the example and idea of the opinions and customs of the country we live in'. That notion, whatever its problems, and however more delicately expressed, is not likely to go entirely away unless anthropology does. (2000: 45; Montaigne 1978: 205)

This, in essence, is the challenge of postmodernism. Yet, interestingly, it is a challenge to which Geertz finds a response (Inglis 2000: 133–55). Though held by many to be a postmodernist – and here seen attacking the conventional critique of relativism, if not quite defending relativism itself – Geertz invariably appears in debates on postmodernism and anthropology in the postmodernists' dock (see, for instance, Clifford 1988; Clifford and Marcus 1986; Tyler 1987). The dispute between Geertz and self-styled postmodernist opponent of twentieth-century ethnography (and doyen of postmodernist anthropology), James Clifford, over the former's interpretation of the Balinese cockfight as social text (1973) is particularly revealing. In this debate, Geertz seeks to defend an analytical and ethnographic anthropology prepared to draw a distinction between social practices as they appear to *us* as external observers and as they are experienced (and hence, as they *are*) to culturally embedded social participants. As James Bohman explains, 'Geertz distinguished between what appears to be going on to us and what is going on for the Balinese; this sense need not be their own explicit self-interpretation, but is provided by putting the fight in the whole context of Balinese cultural practices and symbols' (1991: 127). This familiar practice of ethnographic anthropology Clifford rejects, challenging the authority Geertz seems implicitly to claim as an ethnographer and privileged interpreter of other cultures. Geertz's profoundly modernist arrogance, Clifford suggests, is reflected in his attempt to go beyond the interpretation offered by direct participants, presumably to reveal a more fundamental 'reality', and his insistence that the Balinese need not necessarily agree with the interpretation he offers. Clifford, in particular, takes issue with comments like the following:

> [I]t is only apparently cocks that are fighting. Actually it is men. (Geertz 1973: 417)

In passages like this Clifford detects an all-too-hasty attempt to speak for others without an acknowledgement both of the difficulties of so doing and, above all, of the necessarily 'dialogical and political context out of which ethnographic interpretation itself emerges' (Bohman 1991: 128–9). While Clifford may well have a valuable point about the general thrust of much ethnographic anthropology, Geertz seems a rather strange target for such a critique. For, while the postmodernists are surely right to challenge in much ethnography, whether historic or contemporary, a certain tendency to 'exoticism' and a rather curious fascination with the unusual and the unfamiliar, such a criticism does not easily encompass Geertz's 'depth hermeneutics'. For his work has consistently displayed a sensitivity to, respect for, and sense of responsibility towards, those about whom he writes which sets him apart from many of his contemporaries. Indeed, however disingenuous this might seem to Clifford, Geertz's interpretation of the Balinese cockfight begins with a sustained reflection on the difficulties of the anthropological first encounter – of 'being there' as a stranger in the very subject of your ethnographic study (1973: 412–17; see also, 1988: 1–24). Thus, although they draw somewhat different implications from their reflections on the practice, politics and poetics of ethnography, arguably both critic and accused display a common – and laudable – concern to respect the integrity and autonomy of the subjects of the anthropologist's gaze.

For his part, Clifford is drawn inexorably towards an anthropological paralysis in which the burden of authorship and responsibility is ultimately lifted as the author contents himself with scepticism and deconstruction. Yet Geertz refuses to take the postmodernist vow of silence, preferring instead to bear the political and ethical responsibility inherent in the interpretation of others. As Bohman asks himself:

> How does one responsibly and accurately portray other forms of life within one's hermeneutic circle? As correctly and responsibly as possible, subject to constant revision based on free and open dialogue with participants and with other interpreters. (1991: 130)

This is, perhaps, the best we can do whether as anthropologists or political analysts. If it is not good enough, if we do not perceive it to be good enough, or if we are not prepared to bear the ethical responsibilities it implies to those for whom we write and to those about whom we write, then we have no choice but to take the postmodernists' vow of silence. The implications of that are, I suggest, a suspension of political analysis and a suspension of political judgement. And the consequences of that, I would contend, are unthinkable. To reveal why, we need only turn from contemporary anthropology to the sphere of critical political inquiry and to the implications, for the latter, of a self-imposed postmodernist vow of silence.

In defence of critical political analysis: resisting postmodernism's vow of silence

> Playing with the pieces – that is postmodernism. (Baudrillard 1984: 24)

My aim in this chapter has been to present postmodernism as a profound ontological, epistemological and methodological challenge to the assumptions, rationale and practice of contemporary political analysis – a challenge to which the type of critical political inquiry that I have sought to defend in these pages can, and must, respond (see also Sayer 2000). I have also sought to draw attention to the deep normative respect for difference which underpins that challenge. As such I hope to have contributed, in however meagre a fashion, to an ongoing reappraisal of both postmodernism and of the conduct of contemporary political analysis.

Yet, in the end, and as the comments of previous sections will hopefully already have served to indicate, this is no work of postmodernist advocacy. Far from it. In this concluding section, then, my aim is to clarify my position, pointing to the dangers of what I have termed a self-imposed postmodernist vow of silence and seeking to indicate why critical political analysis must retain its voice in responding to the challenge of postmodernism.

My argument is simply stated – taken to its logical conclusion, post-modernism threatens to sacrifice, on the altar of a laudable respect for difference, the ability to defend political practice. As such, it has profoundly conservative implications. That this is so derives, I suggest, from the tension or 'performative contradiction' that has tended to characterise post-enlightenment social and political thought (on which see Habermas 1981, 1989). This finds its clearest and most self-conscious expression in the work of Michel Foucault, yet it characterises post-enlightenment social and political thought more generally. It can be summarised in terms of a clear tension between:

1. The position 'post-prefixed theorists' are *philosophically* drawn towards – a profound scepticism towards claims to objectivity and of a privileged access to knowledge, and
2. The position many of them remain *politically* sympathetic to – the advocacy of an engaged and 'emancipatory' politics premised upon critique and motivated by the desire to make the world a better place (see also Eagleton 1996).

In Foucault this tension remains largely unresolved. The result is an alternation, increasingly frequent in his later work, between a politically and normatively informed critique (reliant, albeit implicitly, upon some conception of emancipation), and an anti-foundationalist deconstruction of the very notion of 'progress' on which such a politics must, in the end, be premised (compare Foucault 1977a: 151 and 1982: 216, 1988b: 156; see also Best and Kellner 1991: 36, 72–3; Habermas 1989: 173–9; Larrain 1994).

In sharp contrast, more self-consciously postmodernist thinkers (most notably Lyotard and Baudrillard) have consistently resolved this tension by subordinating any political concerns they might have to a normatively inspired rejection of totalising metanarratives. In short, they remain philosophically pure by denying themselves a political voice and by refusing to allow themselves to imagine a world preferable to that we now experience. Not surprisingly this has proved profoundly debilitating politically, committing consistent postmodernists to an effective vow of political silence and, arguably, to complicity in the reproduction of the status quo. Herein lies postmodernism's innate conservatism.

The metanarrative to end all metanarratives?

Yet this is by no means postmodernism's only contradiction. Indeed, much more frequently challenged is the status of the postmodernist proclamation of the 'end of metanarratives' and its disavowal of the hopes of enlightenment, progress, and emancipation. Stated most bluntly: how can such a position be articulated? Is the pronouncement of the end of metanarratives not silenced by the very voice that expresses it? Are postmodernists not guilty of advancing the metanarrative to end all metanarratives?

Interestingly, Lyotard himself comes very perilously close at times to admitting as much. For in his self-styled (and, presumably, ironic) role as educator in *Le Postmoderne expliqué aux enfants*, Lyotard concedes:

> one is tempted to give credence to a grand narrative of the decline of the grand narrative. (1992: 40)

The rhetorical strategy deployed here invites a rejection of metanarratives on the basis that this might elevate us to a more 'enlightened' state. Such a reading may not sit uncomfortably with the stylised role Lyotard here adopts as educator, but it directly contradicts postmodernism's post-enlightenment credentials. We are lured into a temporary suspension of our 'incredulity towards metanarratives' so that we might 'learn' from this particular discourse. And for what purpose? So that we might further fuel our suspicion of *other* metanarratives. As André Kukla mischievously observes:

> The peculiarity of Lyotard's stance has often been remarked upon. Second-level discourses [metanarratives] are deemed to be reprehensible, but apparently third-order discourses like his own are okay. What would be Lyotard's opinion of fourth-level discourses like the one I'm engaged in right at this moment? Is there a problem with all even-numbered levels? It's hard to avoid the impression that Lyotard's stricture is a gerrymandered criterion designed to exclude something preconceived. (2000: 158)

As Kukla implies, this is no temporary aberration on Lyotard's part, no modernist *faux pas*, no one-off lapse into the totalitarian discourses of enlightenment rationalism. Indeed, in the passage that immediately precedes the offending extract, Lyotard engages in a classic exercise in 'enlightened' Popperian refutation – dismissing a catalogue of metanarratives on the basis of a list of 'invalidating' events:

> In the course of the last fifty years, each grand narrative of emancipation – regardless of the genre it privileges – has, as it were, had its principle invalidated. *All that is real is rational, all that is rational is real*: 'Auschwitz' refutes the speculative doctrine. At least this crime, which is real, is not rational. *All that is proletarian is communist, all that is communist is proletarian*: 'Berlin 1953', 'Budapest 1956', 'Czechoslovakia 1968', 'Poland 1980' (to name but a few) refute the doctrine of historical materialism: the workers rise up against the

Party. *All that is democratic is by the people and for the people, and vice versa*: 'May 1968' refutes the doctrine of parliamentary liberalism. Everyday society brings the representative institution to a halt. *Everything that promotes the free flow of supply and demand is good for general prosperity, and vice versa*: the 'crisis of 1911 and 1929' refute the doctrine of economic liberalism, and the 'crisis of 1974–79' refuted the post-Keynesian modification of that doctrine. (1992: 40; emphasis in the original; cf. Douzinas, Warrington and McVeigh 1991: 111–12)

This, too, may be intended as an ironic gesture; but there is surely only a certain amount of irony one can get away with. Irony or no irony, the rhetorical style is again distinctively rationalist. In passages like this the performative contradiction at the heart of Lyotard's work is cruelly exposed, as he slips into the refutation of metanarratives *by assertion* and engages in precisely the sort of distorting and totalising simplification of which he invariably accuses his opponents.

Politics as (meta)-narrative

If postmodernism, at least in Lyotard's formulation, is the metanarrative to end all meta-narratives, supposedly clearing the decks of homogenising and distorting discourses that do violence to difference, then it is perhaps important that we reflect on the nature of *meta*-narrativity itself. For clearly much hinges on how the apparently somewhat arbitrary distinction between narrative and metanarrative is drawn.

Here, again, we discover something of a paradox. For, as Jorge Larrain notes, despite the characteristic postmodernist concern to acknowledge and respect difference wherever it can be found:

in their onslaught against metanarratives and theories of universal application, poststructuralists and postmodernists feel nonetheless perfectly able to discriminate between the theories which fall under such labels and those which can be saved. (1994: 303)

So, when does a (presumably legitimate) narrative become a (totalising and distorting) metanarrative? If we are to view metanarratives as accounts which distort and do violence to difference then it is not difficult to see that all narratives are metanarrative in certain respects. For do not all narratives, all stories, all accounts involve simplification, distortion and the adoption of a subject position? Indeed, is this not precisely the point of the postmodernist critique? Narration involves abstraction as a plot is discerned from a complex series of events which has no innate or essential meaning or significance other than that attributed to it in the very process of narration. Moreover, such abstraction necessarily involves distortion and simplification of a more complex reality (if only as a means to render it intelligible). Hence narration necessarily entails the silencing of or 'doing of violence to', certain singularities, certain differences. In this respect, while some narratives are certainly worse than others, all narratives are guilty of some indifference to difference. And none is more indifferent to difference than that which makes possible postmodernism – the metanarrative to end all metanarratives! The distinction between narratives and metanarratives is, then, at best one of degree and, at worst, wholly arbitrary.

To be a consistent postmodernist, then, should we not dispense with narratives and metanarratives alike? If so, to be a postmodernist is, indeed, to take a self-imposed vow of absolute silence. For, as postmodernists would certainly be the first to point out, narrative is a condition of thought, strategy, action, communication, intervention and, indeed, politics.

The implications of this are profound indeed. First, it suggests that even postmodern political discourses, in as much as they take narrative form, necessarily impose their own violence of in-*difference*. There is no escape, irony notwithstanding. This merely reiterates the need to take ethical responsibility for the *others* whose voices and worldviews necessarily remain marginalised from the narratives which inform political strategy and practice.

Yet does that ethical responsibility not also extend to those trapped within the disciplining structures in whose reproduction we are complicit if we deny ourselves a political voice? In short, can we allow ourselves to be so sensitive to difference that we refuse to take action in the face of what we perceive to be obvious injustices, because of the potential violence to difference our actions might entail? As Sabina Lovibond perceptively notes:

> if there can be no systematic political approach to the questions of wealth, power and labour, how can there be any effective challenge to a social order which distributes its benefits and burdens in a systematically unequal way? (1991: 32)

Should we deny ourselves the capacity to identify, challenge and potentially overturn such inequalities and (perceived) injustices in the name of a respect for difference?

As this line of interrogation perhaps implies, there is a consistent and largely unacknowledged trade-off between the respect for difference and singularity on the one hand, and the political potential to challenge the broader processes and mechanisms which sustain relations of domination on the other. The respect for difference, if taken to its logical extreme, is profoundly debilitating politically, proffering an anti-politics of abstention. As Chris Brown pointedly notes, 'by refusing any task more positive than of undermining existing theory, [postmodernism] effectively leaves the world as it is' (1992: 218). More pointed still is Larrain:

> By suspecting those who suspect the established system, postmodernism explains away the problem of, and hence cannot but implicitly support, the status quo. (1994: 313)

For inhabitants of ivory towers that may well be a price worth paying for philosophical consistency and purity. But, for those for whom life is often nasty, brutish and short, philosophical purity is likely to provide limited solace.

(There's no) accounting for difference

How then can we reflect theoretically the uniqueness and singularity of specific relations of domination, while sustaining a politics of resistance and structural transformation?

The identification of difference need not result in the fallacy of theoretical and political singularity: the view that a world of difference dictates a parochialism of both theory and practice. For, it is one thing to reject totalising modes of thought which are incapable of recognising and accounting for the apparent singularity of particular social and political relations in particular contexts; it is another thing altogether to abandon attempts to identify broader *processes* which impinge upon a variety of contexts in different ways to produce disparate effects. The experience of patriarchy may vary from context to context and from individual to individual, but this does not render patriarchy any less regressive or totalising a set of social processes. Moreover, while patriarchy should be resisted in each and every context in which it arises in a manner sensitive to the specificity of its expression, this is no substitute for a more concerted and collective politics of resistance to patriarchy itself and the mechanisms in and though which it is reproduced. If such a politics entails a certain indifference to difference then so be it. For the cost of a respect for each and every difference is political paralysis; and that is simply too high a price to pay.

If we are to recognise our ethical responsibility to those who remain trapped within the disciplining structures of our profoundly inegalitarian societies, then, we must retain the possibility of systematic and 'progressive' political change. Tempting as it might be, we cannot afford to sacrifice critical political analysis, and with it the very possibility of progressive social and political change, on the altar of the respect for difference.

Critical–Political–Analytical

Postmodernism may appear as something of a black hole which threatens to expunge the very possibility of political analysis and into which all political science and international relations seems inexorably drawn, never to escape. For many, this is reason enough to avoid getting too close. It is, then, important to establish that, whatever physicists may say of black holes, in this case there is light on the other side. In the previous chapters we have travelled a long and, on occasions difficult, path and it is also important that having almost reached our destination we take stock of the journey undertaken. In this brief conclusion, then, my aim is to turn from the challenge of postmodernism to a rather more constructive or reconstructive agenda.

My aim in the pages that follow is to establish and to illustrate a number of features of the sort of critical political analysis that I have sought to defend in this volume – a critical political analysis responsive to each of the controversies we have dealt with in preceding chapters, a critical political analysis capable of responding without capitulation to the challenge of postmodernism outlined in Chapter 7. I illustrate the distinctiveness of this approach by considering its implications for the analysis of globalisation, demonstrating how the ideas discussed in previous chapters might be brought to bear upon the question of the limits of the political (and of political autonomy in particular) in an era of much-vaunted globalisation.

Critical political analysis, I argue, should be:

1. Empirical but without being empiricist
2. Balanced in its conception of the relationship between structure and agency
3. Inclusive in its conception of the political, inclusive in its incorporation of extra-political factors and attentive to the interaction of the domestic and the international
4. Sensitive to the potential causal and constitutive role of ideas in social, political and economic dynamics and, above all
5. Attentive to the contingency, open-endedness and inherent unpredictability of social, political and economic systems.

In the pages which follow I consider the implications for a critical political analysis of globalisation of each in turn.

Empirical but not empiricist

A key theme of this volume has been the qualitative difference in subject matter between the natural and social sciences and the difficulty, if this is acknowledged, of sustaining a credible and *naturalist* science of the political. In particular, I have argued, the object of the natural scientist's analytical attentions remains independent of the analytical process in a way which is simply not the case for the analysis of social and political systems. The latter are populated by conscious and reflective agents who are capable of revising their behaviour, often in the light of – and even in direct response to – the theories advanced by social and political analysts. There is no equivalent in the natural sciences. Matter cannot choose to disobey the laws of gravity. Thus, while one should not under-emphasise the difficulty of engaging in the dispassionate and neutral accumulation of objective truths for natural scientists, they are at least independent of the systems they analyse in a way that political analysts are not.

Yet, however tempting it may well be on the basis of such reflections to dismiss an empirical political analysis on the grounds that it aspires to a science of the political that is simply impossible, this is a temptation that we should resist. For while it is important to retain a cautious, even sceptical, attitude towards the empirical indices we use and to be sensitive to the fact that many of our most significant explanatory variables do not avail themselves of quantification or simple measurement, description is the basis from which interpretation and explanation must build. Indeed, it seems fair to suggest that while political analysts are always likely to remain divided by the interpretations and explanations they offer of particular events or processes, they do have a rather greater chance of agreeing on the description of their subject matter. That entails the accumulation of empirical evidence. Thus, while empirical evidence alone is never enough it is an important and necessary starting point.

This is nowhere more pertinent than with respect to the political economy of globalisation. To speak of economic globalisation, as many do, is, essentially, to make a descriptive and empirical claim. Yet what is immediately interesting to note is the 'casual empiricism' displayed by the highly influential proponents of the 'hyperglobalisation' thesis and the largely anecdotal nature of their appeal to empirical evidence (for a critique of this literature see Busch 2000). Those who have engaged in a more rigorous and systematically evidential assessment of patterns of economic integration invariably draw a rather different set of conclusions. Thus, on the basis of an exhaustive (if not entirely uncontroversial) assessment of the empirical evidence sceptics such as Paul Hirst and Grahame Thompson conclude that globalisation is, in fact, a rather inaccurate description of existing patterns of international economic integration (1999; for an important critical response to their work see Held *et al.* 1999). In so doing they point to five things (Box C.1)

Box C.1   The empirical case against globalisation

1. International flows of capital (such as foreign direct investment–FDI) tend to be extremely concentrated within the core 'triad' (of Europe, North America and Pacific Asia) providing evidence of regionalisation and 'triadisation' but hardly of globalisation (Hirst and Thompson 1999)
2. The pace of economic integration is higher *within* regions (such as Europe, North America or Pacific Asia) than it is *between* regions, suggesting that regionalisation rather than globalisation is the overriding dynamic in the process of international economic integration (Kleinknecht and ter Wengel 1998; Hay 2001d)
3. Although the period since the 1970s has seen the growing openness of national economies (such that imports plus exports account for a growing proportion of gross domestic product–GDP), there is still some considerable way to go before pre-First World War figures are likely to be exceeded (Bairoch 1996; Hirst and Thompson 1999)
4. Financial integration has failed to produce the anticipated convergence in interest rates which one would expect from a fully integrated global capital market (Hirst and Thompson 1999; Zevin 1992)
5. Financial integration has failed to produce the anticipated divergence between rates of domestic savings and rates of domestic investment which one would expect in a fully integrated global capital market – the so-called 'Feldstein–Horioka puzzle' (Watson 2001).

As this perhaps suggests, any critical political analysis of globalisation must surely start with the empirical evidence, however contested its interpretation may prove.

Structure and agency

As I have been at pains to demonstrate throughout this volume, what differentiates social and political analysis from the natural sciences is agency, the capacity of actors to shape the environment in which they find themselves. It is important, then, that we are capable of incorporating an active role for agents in the accounts we offer. This is particularly important for critical political analysis, interested as it is in the possibilities for progressive social and political change and in holding actors accountable for the consequences of their actions. At the same time, however, it is important to acknowledge that whilst it is indeed actors who make history, the parameters of their capacity to act is ultimately set by the structured context in which they find themselves. It is, then, the dynamic relationship between structure and agency that we must seek to interrogate, explore and ultimately reflect.

The implications of this for the literature on globalisation are again profound and are explored briefly in the following paragraphs.

As argued in Chapter 3, self-declared 'solutions' to the 'problem' of structure and agency tend to draw attention, rightly, to the operation of *processes* in which both actors and structures are implicated in a dynamic way. They place the emphasis not upon the explication of deterministic structural logics or the identification of hegemonic intentional actors but upon the elucidation of processes, in which structure and agent and intimately interwoven, over time. Given that globalisation is a process term, one might be forgiven for thinking that its analysis naturally lends itself to a subtle and complex rendition of the structure–agency relationship to elucidate the causal mechanisms involved. Sadly, nothing could be further from the truth.

This is because, while globalisation may masquerade as a process term in both the popular and academic vernacular, it is a 'process without a subject' – a process to which no actors are linked. Accordingly, the term globalisation as used in most popular and academic debate is an obfuscation, and a potentially dangerous one at that. For it tends to conjure a sense of inexorability, inevitability and immutability, mapping a path to an end-state (a condition of pure globalisation) never fully realised yet always in the process of being realised. This represents a dangerous conflation of process and outcome which can serve only to hide the complex, contested and contingent causal dynamics which generate the evidence frequently cited in support of the globalisation thesis. The task for a critical political analysis of globalisation, then, is to restore actors and agency to a process without a subject.

Yet, to point to the dangers of appeals to globalisation as a causal process is not to insist that globalisation is a figment of the imagination, though as argued in the preceding section it may not be a very accurate or useful description. It is merely to suggest the need for considerable caution in the use of the term if we are not further to mystify phenomena which might genuinely be regarded as evidence of globalisation. The challenge, then, for critical political analysts (not, it should be noted, an entirely novel one) is to build upon the foundations laid by the critique of earlier, more cavalier, appeals to the notion of globalisation, to further unpack and demystify this 'process without a subject'. This in turn suggests that we should view globalisation not so much as a process or end-state, but, at best, as a *tendency* to which *counter-tendencies* may be mobilised. Once viewed in such terms, the challenge is to reveal the dynamic and contingent articulation of processes in certain spatial contexts at certain moments in time to yield effects which might be understood as evidence of globalisation. Such scrutiny invariably reveals the causal significance of processes operating at spatial scales below the global and for which strategic political actors might be held accountable.

If we are to do this, it is imperative that we reverse the conventional direction of causality appealed to in the academic literature as, indeed, in the popular discourse of globalisation. *We must ask not what globalisation might explain, but how we might account for the phenomena widely identified as evidence of globalisation.* If we are to resist and reject the deterministic appeal to a process without a subject we must excise all reference to globalisation as an explanatory (or independent) variable. Within such a schema, the term globalisation becomes little more than a convenient short-hand for a confluence of processes which might together be seen as constitutive of any observed globalisation tendency. The existing literature has, to date, given far too limited attention to such genuine (causal) processes, like financial liberalisation, to which actors might be linked directly (though see, for instance, Helleiner 1994, 1996).

Financial liberalisation is a particularly good example. For many accounts of globalisation's seeming 'logic of no alternative' or of neoliberal convergence, in the end, rely on claims not of globalisation *per se* but of financial liberalisation and the resulting increase in the mobility of capital. In such cases, appeal to the term globalisation is quite simply an obfuscation – if the causal agent is the (quite conscious political) decision to engage in a process of financial liberalisation, why not call it as it is?

Recast in this way, there is no need to make deterministic assumptions about the effects, consequences, or even the very existence, of globalisation. For, in so far as globalisation can be identified, it is understood as a tendency – the contingent outcome of a confluence of specific processes to which actors might be linked. Globalised outcomes and effects might then be the product of very different, indeed entirely independent, mechanisms and processes of causation (financial liberalisation, regional economic integration and policy transfer, to identify merely three) that can only be obscured by appeal to a generic logic of globalisation. While problematising and interrogating the processes which underpin globalising tendencies, then, it is important to resist the temptation to appeal to globalisation itself as a causal factor or process working, apparently independently of the actions, intentions and motivations of real subjects. It is precisely this appeal to causal processes *without subjects* that summons the logic of necessity and inevitability so often associated with the notion of globalisation.

If we are then to demystify globalisation (Hay and Marsh 2000), we must ensure that in making what we think are causal arguments, we can identify the actors involved, thus giving due attention to the 'structuration' of globalising tendencies while rejecting structuralist or functionalist 'logics' operating over the heads or independently of social subjects.

It is only by paying careful attention to the problem of structure and agency in this way, dismissing accounts which privilege either structure or (far less frequently in analyses of globalisation) agency in the determination of outcomes, that the notion of globalisation might be used to open up and not merely to obscure the analysis of social, political and economic change.

An inclusive and post-disciplinary conception of political analysis

In Chapters 1 and 2 the case was made for a conception of politics and the political that was inclusive and which did not restrict political analysis to a narrow and exclusive focus upon the interplay of governmental variables. Instead, a 'process' (as distinct from an 'arena') definition of the political was advanced. By such a definition political analysis is synonymous with the analysis of the distribution, exercise and consequences of power. The implications of this were further outlined in Chapter 5 in which the concept of power was explored in more detail.

In making the case for a more inclusive conception of the political I also pointed to the dangers of a rigid policing of the disciplinary faultlines between, say, political and economic analysis and, indeed, political science and international relations. Though arguably it was ever thus, in an era of acknowledged interdependence, there are clear domestic conditions of international dynamics and international conditions of domestic dynamics. An internal division of labour within political analysis will simply not longer suffice, if ever it did.

Yet arguably more important still, particularly in the context of discussions about globalisation, are the external boundaries which political analysts tend to erect around their jealously guarded disciplinary core. What is required – and, again, one can argue that there is nothing new about this – is the development or, indeed, return to modes of political analysis which refuse to confine themselves to political variables and which refuse to leave the analysis of extra-political variables to their appropriate disciplinary 'homes'. In short, what is required is a *post-disciplinary* political analysis. This is, again, nowhere more clear that with respect to the literature on globalisation.

The argument is simply stated though its implications, if taken seriously, are considerable. As political analysts we should be extremely careful not to confine ourselves only to holding opinions on matters in which we might present narrowly political actors as significant agents. There is, understandably, a certain tendency to restrict our analytical enterprise to the description of processes and the elucidation of causal mechanisms in which our self-identified principal agents – traditionally, governmental actors or, within international relations, states – perform as such. The danger is that, in so doing, we effectively silence ourselves on the question of the key exogenous factors, processes and mechanisms held (by others) to circumscribe the realm of feasible political agency for the actors we are principally concerned with. In an era of putative globalisation in which the logic of non-negotiable external economic constraint is frequently invoked, self-declared political analysts cannot but afford to have an opinion on the empirical content of such claims. If that entails a temporary suspension of our analyses until such time as we are better informed as to the nature, extent and uneven geography of processes of economic integration, then so be it.

Here it is important to remind ourselves that the distinction between political and economic variables – and hence, for many, between political science and economics as disciplines – was always arbitrary, the boundary between the two necessarily characterised by interdependencies which have remained poorly understood as a consequence. These are important points in their own right. The key point for now, however, is that if we accept that we live in an interdependent world which does not respect such conventional divisions of analytical labour (if ever it did), such disciplinary parochialism will no longer suffice.

The causal and constitutive role of ideas

If we are prepared to concede that what differentiates social and political systems from their counterparts in the natural sciences is the presence of reflexive actors capable of shaping the environment in which they find themselves, then it is no large step to acknowledge that the ideas actors hold – both normative and descriptive – about that environment must be accorded an independent role in political analysis. Though many political analysts have been reluctant to make this move it is, frankly, implausible to suppose either than actors have complete information of the context in which they find themselves or that their behaviour is rendered entirely predictable by the (presumably transparent) material interests they hold in any given context. Yet qualify either of these assumptions and an independent role for ideas is immediately opened within political analysis.

This, too, has important implications for the analysis of globalisation as a (perceived) constraint upon political autonomy in contemporary societies. Indeed, the self-fulfilling nature of ideas about globalisation has been a consistent theme of previous chapters.

To establish the significance of ideational factors in the generation of the outcomes invariably attributed to globalisation, it is useful to return to those, like Hirst and Thompson, sceptical of the hyperglobalisation thesis.

The implicit supposition which seems to underlie much of the sceptical literature with which such authors are associated and which seeks to expose the 'myth' or 'delusion' of globalisation, is that a rigorous empirical exercise in demystification will be sufficient to reverse the tide of ill-informed public policy made in the name of globalisation. Sadly, this has not proved to be the case. For however convinced we might be by the empirical armoury mustered against the hyperglobalisation thesis by the sceptics, their rigorous appeal to empirical evidence leads them to fail adequately to consider the ways in which globalisation comes to inform public policy-making. As argued above, while the empirical evidence is crucial it is not in itself sufficient.

It is here that the discourse of globalisation – and the discursive construction of the imperatives it is seen to conjure – must enter the analysis. For, as discussed at greater length in Chapter 6, it is the ideas actors hold about the context in which they find themselves rather than the context itself which ultimately informs the way in which they behave. This is no less true of policy-makers and governments than it is of you or I. Whether the globalisation thesis is 'true' or not may matter far less than whether it is *deemed* to be true – or, quite possibly, just useful – by those employing it. Consequently, if the aim of the sceptics is to discredit the political appeal to dubious economic imperatives associated with globalisation, then they might well benefit from asking themselves why and under what conditions politicians and public officials invoke external economic constraints in the first place.

Space prevents a detailed commentary. However, two distinctive causal chains might be identified. In the first, elected officials simply internalise, unwittingly, assumptions about globalisation which just happen to be false. Consequently, where genuine options exist they perceive of no alternative. In the second scenario, by contrast, our elected officials and advisors are rather better informed of the nature of the economic constraints they face. Here the appeal to globalisation is rather more duplicitous. For globalisation may provide a most convenient alibi, allowing politicians to escape the responsibility they would otherwise bear for reforms which might be rather difficult to legitimate.

With a rapidly aging population, declining birth rates and higher rates of unemployment than in the early post-war period – in short a high and rising ratio of net welfare recipients to net welfare contributors – to say nothing of the escalating costs of health care, the spectre which today haunts Europe is that of welfare retrenchment (I. Gough 1996; Hay 2001c). Yet welfare retrenchment is, for social democratic administrations, particularly unpalatable. What could be better, then, than in countries in which globalisation is widely seen to be both desirable and inevitable, to present welfare retrenchment as a necessary consequence of globalisation?

It is important, then, that we differentiate between the internalisation of a discourse of globalisation seen by those who deploy it as an accurate representation of genuine economic constraints (scenario 1) and the more intentional, reflexive and strategic *choice* of such a discourse as a convenient justification for policies pursued for altogether different reasons (scenario 2). In the first scenario ideas about globalisation might be held to be constitutive (at least in part) of the perceived interests of elite political actors; in the latter, they are more of an instrumental device deployed in the promotion of a set of strategic goals. There is plenty of evidence of actors invoking globalisation as a non-negotiable external economic constraint in the attempt to justify often unpalatable social and economic reform (Hay and Rosamond 2002). Whether this should be interpreted as evidence for an unreflexive internalisation of a discourse of external economic constraint or as a strategic exercise in responsibility-displacement is an interesting question which cannot be resolved here. Yet, either way, it suggests a crucial role for ideas about globalisation in the generation of the effects invariably attributed to it. Given the prevalence in contemporary political discourse of the non-negotiable character of external economic constraints that is a very significant observation indeed.

The contingency of political processes

Our journey is now complete. For the above reflections bring us directly to perhaps the central theme of the present volume – the inherently contingent, indeterminant and ultimately unpredictable nature of social and political processes. As the above paragraphs certainly begin to suggest, even globalisation, seemingly the most inevitable and inexorable of processes is, in the end, revealed to be complex, contested and contingent. For those who still cling doggedly to the notion of a predictive science of the political, that is likely to prove a very depressing thought indeed. At best, it suggests that the predictions such a science is capable of generating are likely to have a very limited shelf-life. At worst it suggests they may well prove obsolete at precisely the moment they are made. Yet for critical political analysts in particular, this is a wonderfully liberating thought. Things, in the end, can be different.

Notes

1 Analytical perspectives, analytical controversies

1   Rational actors will only take account of the consequences of their action for others in so far as those consequence are anticipated to have knock-on implications for their ability to maximise their personal utility in the future. In most cases, however, such complex feedback effects are discounted in rationalist models which tend to assume that actors are motivated solely by short-term personal gain, with longer-term consequences essentially discounted.

2   It is important to emphasise that the figures here are schematic representations designed to capture the development of political science and international relations respectively. They are not based on empirical indicators.

3   The term 'rationalism' is here used to denote those analytical traditions within political science and international relations premised upon assumptions as to the rational conduct of political actors (whether individual or collective)

4   Quite what it would have to say about the rise of Thatcherism in an equally bipartisan electoral system in the late 1970s is another matter altogether. By strict Popperian/Lakatosian standards, this would surely count as a refutation of the conjecture.

5   Of course, until we have established a plausible mechanism linking prior and future success at the polls, this is merely a correlation and not, in itself, a causal explanation. I am indebted to Keith Dowding for pointing this out to me. Many potential mechanisms might be posited.

6   This, as we shall see presently, is largely because they accept no separation of appearance and reality. For them, the world presents itself to us as really it is; knowledge of the world is directly amenable to us through our senses.

7   Very similar sentiments are expressed by Nobel Prize-winning economist and prominent rational choice institutionalist, Douglass North, in the following terms. 'Very few economist really believe that the behavioural assumptions of economics [and hence rational choice theory] accurately reflect human behaviour' (North 1990: 17). Milton Friedman goes further still, suggesting that 'truly important and significant hypotheses will be found to have "assumptions" that are wildly inaccurate as descriptive representations of reality, and, in general, the more significant the theory, the more unrealistic the assumptions' (1953: 14–15).

8   Among those unwilling to accept that they do, James C. Charlesworth was particularly vociferous, commenting, 'no matter how often and how emphatically it is stated that mathematics has no substance – that it is only language – and that you cannot get out of a computer something you have not put in, the

261

zealots-of-glyph [algebraic notation] become more and more influential, and political analysis increasingly tends to become mere enumeration' (1967: 6).

9   Of course, rather than treating rationality as an invariant and unquestionable characteristic of all human behaviour, this more conditional mode of analysis relies on treating rationalities as variable and context-dependent.

10   Interestingly, though perhaps unremarkably, the empirical evidence on the effects of central bank independence fails to lend much support to the 'rational expectations' thesis, there being no statically significant correlation between the granting of independence and improved anti-inflationary performance (Posen 1993). When it is considered that central bank independence tends to be seen as an institutional fix for administrations anxious to enhance their anti-inflationary credibility, this is all the more troubling for proponents of this, the latest, economic orthodoxy. For an excellent discussion of these issues, see Watson (2002). Similar observations might be made about capital mobility and corporate taxation regimes. For despite the prediction that the optimal rate of taxation on mobile capital in an open economy is zero, foreign direct investment (FDI) continues to be associated positively with high rates of corporate taxation and the market access this tends to secure (see, for instance, Cooke and Noble 1998; Swank 2001).

11   While rational choice institutionalists clearly embrace rationalism to a significant extent, some (though by no means all) historical institutionalists and constructivists have sought to define their perspectives principally in opposition to rationalism (see, for instance, Thelen and Steinmo 1992: 7–11; Christiansen, Jørgensen and Wiener 2001: 4–6).

12   The rallying call to resist the rationalist and behaviouralist orthodoxy of the day was most clearly expressed by James G. March and Johan P. Olsen in a seminal article in the *American Political Science Review* (1984, see also 1989).

13   Whether rational choice institutionalism is best regarded as a qualified variant of rational choice theory or as a distinctive neo-institutionalist perspective in its own right is an interesting and, again, controversial issue. What is clear, however, is that if it is to be seen as one of a number of new institutionalisms, this makes it far more difficult to posit a range of analytical features by and with respect to which these analytical perspective might be held to constitute a common perspective (on the degree of compatibility between the 'calculus' and 'cultural' logics of rational choice institutionalism and sociological institutionalism respectively, see Hall and Taylor 1996, 1998; Hay and Wincott 1998).

14   Indeed, one might go one step further and argue that it problematises any notion of a unity of method between the natural and social sciences.

15   In so doing, he is not the only one. I, too, was taken in by the ostensibly agent-centred form of rational choice theory (1995: 196). By 1998, however, with the help of Dan Wincott and a wonderfully disarming passage in George Tsebelis' *Nested Games* (1990: 40), I saw the extent to which I had allowed superficial impressions to mask rationalism's profound structuralism and its inability to deal with agency (see Hay and Wincott 1998: 952).

2 What's political about political science?

1 Since I am concerned in this chapter with the extent to which political analysis might be labelled a 'science', I shall use the term political science in its broadest sense to include the professedly scientific study of international relations.

2 North American political scientists, at the conservative estimate of the editors of the *British Journal of Politics and International Relations*, constitutes some 85 per cent of 'the profession' (Marsh *et al.* 1999: 2).

3 At the risk of complicating things further, it is perhaps important to note at this stage that the notion of a 'science' of being represents a potentially dangerous conflation of epistemological concerns (relating to the foundations of knowledge) and ontological concerns (relating to the nature of being). As we shall see, philosophical realists (and many other besides) hold that ontology precedes epistemology in the sense that we cannot even begin to think about acquiring knowledge of the world in which we find ourselves until we have decided what is out there to know about in the first place. To speak of a science of being would, then, seem to prejudge the issue by assuming, at minimum, that there is no separation of appearance and reality such that we can acquire direct knowledge of being itself in an unmediated way.

4 For, clearly, what counts as evidence in the first place depends on one's view of the relationship between that which is observed and experienced, on the one hand, and that which is real, on the other. Accordingly, here as elsewhere, the empirical cannot be used to adjudicate ontological claims unless one takes as a starting point the (ontological) unity of appearance and reality.

5 If the notion of the 'science of being' is a rather paradoxical construct, then that of the 'science of knowledge' is hardly any less so. It is, at best, a glaring tautology, since science might be defined as the acquisition of knowledge itself. Acknowledging this as a tautology also serves to raise the perhaps troubling question of *how* we acquire knowledge of the limits of our capacity to know. Thankfully, it is not our task to resolve that issue here.

6 To suggest that our ideas influence our conduct and that our conduct has, in turn, the capacity to reshape our environment is not, of course, to insist that it necessarily does so in any given setting over any particular time-horizon. It is to suggest, however, that insofar as conduct serves to shape and reshape a given political landscape, the ideas held by actors about that context are crucial to any understanding of such a process of political change. These issues are explored in much greater depth in Chapter 6.

7 Given the diversity of authors in this list and the considerable time-frame it encompasses, it might be tempting to conclude that political analysts have indeed given adequate attention to the question of the boundaries of their discipline. My argument, however, is that these frequently classic texts remain the exception rather than the rule. More significantly, perhaps, whilst one can point to debates in which the subject matter of political analysis is contested, these tend to have had little influence upon the ability of most practising political analysts to render explicit the boundaries of the terrain upon which they focus

their analytical attentions – far less to offer a consistent theoretical justification for such a delineation of the boundaries of the political.

8   For impressive recent additions to this voluminous literature see Benton and Craib (2001); Couvalis (1997); Delanty (1997); Fay (1996); Kincaid (1996); Kukla (2000); McCarthy (1996); May and Williams (1998); Natter, Schatzki and Jones (1995); Payne (1997); M. Williams (2000).

9   Principally, the threat of nuclear annihilation and environmental catastrophe. Among a vast literature see, for instance, Beck (1991, 1996); Giddens (1990, 1994); Irwin (1995); O'Connor (1998); Ratzan (1998).

10 As Alan Chalmers notes, 'Science [for which read, the practice of the natural sciences] is commonly seen as dehumanizing, as involving the inappropriate treatment of people and societies, as well as nature, as objects. The alleged neutrality and value-freedom of science is perceived by many as a sham, a perception encouraged by the increasingly common phenomenon of disagreements between experts on opposite sides of a politically sensitive dispute over matters of scientific fact. The destruction and threat of elimination of our environment resulting from technological advances are widely regarded as implicating science.' Bemoaning such a sorry state of affairs, Chalmers lowers his guard somewhat in the next sentence, pointing to 'those who find the Arts Faculty insufficiently far removed from the oppressive, masculine world of science and turn [instead] to mysticism or drugs or contemporary French philosophy' (1990: 1). Notwithstanding such palpable irritation at this challenge to the reverence to which science had become accustomed, the contrast with the comments with which Chalmers opened his previous book could scarcely be starker. They were these: 'in modern times science is highly esteemed' (1982: 1). The comparison is surely telling.

11 For a similar interpretation see Stoker (1995: 3–7).

12 So as not to prejudge many of the principal concerns of this chapter at the outset, I prefer the more generic and inclusive term 'political analysis' to that of 'political science'. To avoid confusion, then, from here on I shall use the latter term more cautiously and selectively to refer only to the contribution of those espousing a unity of method between the natural and social sciences.

13 Again, it might be noted that those most intransigent in their commitment to an implacably political focus for political science tend to be those most committed to a restrictive definition of the sphere of the political.

14 Though the conceptual difficulties of defining the state in isolation from society should perhaps not be underemphasised. See for instance Mitchell (1991).

15 A random sample of articles from the *American Political Science Review* or *International Studies Quarterly* would surely serve to confirm the point but, from the former source, see, for instance, Erickson and Palfry (2000); Lau and Redlawsk (1997).

16 See Hirschmann and Di Stefano (1996b: 7).

17 Given the historical ascendancy of such a parochial conception of the political within Anglophone political science it is perhaps unsurprising that there are many more feminist scholars in departments of sociology than there are in politics, government and political science.

18 On the ultimately Weberian conception of politics as violence see P. P. Nicolson (1984); on 'symbolic violence' see Bourdieu (1991).

19 The similarities become ever more apparent if we follow Richard Foley in noting Descartes' own confidence that 'God would not allow us to be decieved about what is epistemologically rational for us. For Descartes, this means that God would not allow us to be deceived about what is clear and distinct for us. *A fortiori*, God would not allow most of what is clear and distinct for us to be false' (1987: 162).

20 It is perhaps important to emphasise at this point that the particular reading of Popper that has come to dominate the philosophy of the social sciences – and with which we are concerned here – bears only a partial resemblance to the work of Popper himself. Arguably it is rather more Lakatosian than Popperian in character. In the pages that follow I seek to present what has tended to pass for 'Popperian falsificationism' in the social sciences, leaving the textual analysis of Popper to others. I am greatly indebted to Keith Dowding for pointing this out to me.

21 Thus, for orthodox Marxists, whether the revolution occurred at 5.05 pm on Saturday 22 October or not was less a test of the Marxist theory of history but of the maturity of the mode of production and of the extent of the bourgeois indoctrination the state was able to muster in its defence at this particular moment in time. The thesis that the revolution *will* come at some unspecified point in the future is clearly irrefutable and, as a consequence, not very risky.

22 On Lakatos' modifications to Popper's falsificationism, see the various essays collected in Lakatos (1978). For critical commentary, see Chalmers (1990: 14–23); Couvalis (1997: 69–77).

23 In fact, we are only verifying one of the statement's potential negations and not, it should be noted, the statement 'all swans are not black' – a statement which cannot be verified.

24 This, indeed, is Lakatos' point of departure from what he sees as Popper's 'naïve falsificationism' (1978).

25 Of course to some extent Heisenberg's 'Uncertainty Principle' changes all this at least for the physics of small particles, suggesting that the velocity and position of an object (a sub-atomic particle, say) cannot both be known simultaneously. For to measure one accurately is to impose limits on the accuracy with which the other can be measured. Yet even Heisenberg's principle it should be noted takes the form of a 'law' which is assumed to be immutable, infinitely generalisable and trans-historical.

26 This is not to suggest, of course, that the strength of gravitational fields does not vary (both over time and from system to system), but that the laws governing the gravitational field between two objects can safely be assumed to be immutable. It is this (useful) assumption that ultimately makes trans-Atlantic flight (and hence the means by which sceptics get to international conferences to discuss such issues) possible.

27 Clearly some ideas prove far more influential than others. Ironically, as Director of the London School of Economics and as intellectual guru of the 'Third

Way', Giddens has now had considerably first-hand experience of the double hermeneutic he first identified as a humble social and political theorist.

28 Of course, that the parameters of political and economic possibility are different after Keynes may owe as much, if not more, to the distortion and misrepresentation of his ideas than to the ideas themselves.

3 Beyond structure versus agency, context versus conduct

1 Indeed, this penchant for posing the structure–agency question has even spread to areas, like European integration (see, for instance, Jordan 1999; Peterson and Bomberg 1999) and the study of the British core executive (see, for instance, M. J. Smith 1998, 1999; Theakston 1997), previously not characterised by their theoretical reflexiveness.

2 There are, of course, exceptions even in the natural sciences. Thus, in (sub-atomic) particle physics, the behaviour of a specific particle is not always regarded as entirely predictable in the sense that identical particles are observed to behave differently under the same conditions (for instance photons passing through a diffraction grating). Nonetheless, even here, universal and trans-historical laws are held to govern the distribution of particle behaviour in a wholly predictable and determinant fashion. Given a set of initial conditions and the appropriate theories, we can predict with unerring accuracy if not the behaviour of a singular photon, then the diffraction pattern produced by a stream of photons. Here, paradoxically, the particle's unpredictability is itself structured and, hence, predictable.

3 Inevitably, however, there are exceptions. Thus, for instance, Althusser's structural Marxism gets perilously close, at times, to a theory of absolute determination – as, for example, when he argues that the notion of agency is itself a bourgeois delusion (1971: 160 ff.). As an ontological statement this is, quite simply, irrefutable. The palpable irritation this clearly causes those who refuse to entertain such a notion is well reflected in E. P. Thompson's denunciation of Althusser's offending essay as 'unhistorical shit' (1978).

4 It is perhaps superficially tempting to regard the seemingly less-than-entirely-determined behaviour of a particular photon as evidence of its agency. Yet a moment's reflection reveals this to be a particularly poor analogy. For, notwithstanding the dangers in ascribing human attributes such as free will to an inanimate particle, it is not at all clear that the particle's behaviour does exhibit any trace of 'choice'. The suggestion that the photon chooses its particular path through a diffraction grating, for instance, is rendered extremely dubious when it is considered that the collective outcome of such individual 'choices' is entirely predictable in advance. Perhaps, like Althusser's notion of human agency, the notion of a photon's agency is a purely 'physical delusion'.

5 The distinction between situations in which actors behaving deliberately, consciously weighing up their options, and those in which actors behave intuitively, such that their intentions, motivations and strategies remain unconscious or,

better, pre-conscious, is an important one. Nonetheless, in so far as such forms of 'practical consciousness' might be brought to the surface and thereby rendered conscious, the latter should be regarded as exhibiting agency (on practical consciousness see Giddens 1984: 41–5, 327–34, 375). A classic example is the act of crossing a busy road. Such a seemingly simple task involves a series of quite complex calculations and choices which, though seldom rendered explicit, might well be brought rapidly to the surface – as, for instance, when an angry motorist gesticulates that your actions have caused her to swerve in avoidance.

6   The phrase was first coined by Tony Blair when he was still Shadow Home Secretary and was subsequently taken up by the African National Congress (ANC) during the 1997 South African election campaign.

7   The sole exception is, perhaps, whole animal biology. Yet even here, the general aim would seem to be the elucidation of law-like behavioural propositions. These belie any recognition of agency.

8   Naturalism, let us recall, is a confidence in the unity of method between the natural and social sciences.

9   Rational choice institutionalism is, of course, something of an exception here in its retention of rational choice theory's 'logic of calculus' approach.

10 It is important to note that although structuralism has been exposed to a barrage of critiques, many of the positions which I have here associated with structuralism are not conventionally viewed as such.

11 'The view that social and political processes, particularly processes of change, can be accounted for in terms of an historical end-state to which they are believed to evolve inexorably' (Hay 1995b: 194).

12 The sole exception, perhaps, is ethnomethodology which focuses upon the skilled accomplishment involved in the negotiation of everyday social interactions (see, for instance, Douglas 1970; Garfinkel 1967; Molotch 1974).

13 It should immediately be noted that, for intentionalists, such 'particularisation' is not in any sense 'false', since there are no lessons which can be drawn from own political scenario to another.

14 The term 'structural super-determinism' was, in fact, not directed explicitly at Althusser, but at the early work of Nicos Poulantzas (itself influenced significantly by the target of Thompson's critique). It comes from Miliband's initial rejoinder to Poulantzas in the infamous Miliband–Poulantzas debate – a further bout of structuralist versus intentionalist contention in Marxist theory (on which see Barrow 1993; Hay 1999c: 164–7; Jessop 1985).

15 While each of these authors does seek to transcend the dualism of structure and agency – and is, consequently, committed to a critique of both structuralism and intentionalism – their views on the respective poverties of each vary considerably. Thus, for instance, Giddens seems largely to absolve intentionalist sociologies (such as symbolic interactionism and ethnomethodology) of culpability for their disavowal of structure while unleashing a blistering attack on those (such as Althusser and Poulantzas) who commit the cardinal sin of structuralism (compare Giddens 1986: 73–9, 1995: 214–20 with Giddens 1984: 41–92). Archer, Bourdieu and Bhaskar, on the other hand, begin their move

towards a transcendence of the dualism of structure and agency from a more obviously structuralist starting point.

16   Interestingly, the term is also used by Bhaskar (1989: 92)

17   Bhaskar, of course, supplements Giddens' use of the term 'duality of structure', with his own 'duality of praxis' (1989: 92–3).

18   For a series of more sustained critiques see Hay, O'Brien and Penna (1994); O'Brien, Penna and Hay (1999).

19   While, as Wendt has noted, Giddens' position displays clear affinities with philosophical realism (1987: 336, 355), this part of the structurationalist ontology remains largely implicit and unexplicated. Moreover, the redefinition of structure as the rules and resources operationalised in action does not seem to imply the 'depth ontology' characteristic of such a philosophical realism. Whether the theory of structuration entails a ('scientific') realist ontology, as Wendt implies, is then at best debatable (for an alternative view see, for instance, Archer 1995: 60–1, 70).

20   At this point it is important to remind ourselves that not all critical realists would necessarily accept Archer's reading either of Giddens or, indeed, of Bhaskar. Consequently, it is only if we take Archer's morphogenetic approach as synonymous with the critical realist view of the structure–agency relationship that we need reject the idea that critical realism transcends the dualism of structure and agency. Whether Archer's morphogenetic approach is, in the end, compatible with Bhaskar's critical realism is an interesting point, but one which cannot concern us here. Suffice it to note for now that Archer does seem to round upon all 'those now endorsing the "duality of structure"' (1995: 60), accusing them of the cardinal sin of 'elisionism' or 'central conflation'. This must surely include Bhaskar himself. It should be noted that this is the closest she gets to targeting explicitly Bhaskar's critical realism. Nonetheless, it might well lend credence to the view that the latter ultimately shares rather more with Giddens than with Archer when it comes to the relationship between structure and agency.

21   Whether Bhaskar can, indeed, be interpreted in such terms is a point to which we return.

22   Given the significance of critical realism, and Bhaskar's canonical work in particular, to the claims of both Archer and Jessop it is tempting to adjudicate between the morphogenetic and the strategic–relational approaches on the basis of the accuracy of their reading of Bhaskar. This is a temptation, however, that we must resist. As I have suggested, the issues at stake here are altogether more important than the contested interpretation of the latter's almost indulgently inpenetrable prose. Moreover, in Jessop's central statement of the strategic–relational approach, Bhaskar receives only two cursory citations, one in a footnote (1990a: 17, 295).

23   Where there was once a conceptual dualism there is now, in Jessop's terminology, a 'doubled dualism' (1996).

4 Continuity and discontinuity in the analysis of political change

1 Here it is important to point to the work of those rational choice theorists who have sought to develop and adapt evolutionary game theoretical models to their work as significant exceptions to this general tendency (see, for instance, Axelrod 1984; Binmore 1990; Elster 1979; M. J. Taylor 1987; Witt 1986). Yet even here, the assumption is neither that the rules of the game change with time, nor that rationality is temporally dependent, merely that the rules that pertain at any given time (and hence the concept of rationality itself) have a temporal dimension.

2 Where the mechanism of evolution is, for Comte, Spencer, Tönnies and Durkheim, essentially one of organic differentiation, that for Marx and Engels (drawing on Darwin) is one of natural selection. The famously unsuccessful attempt by Marx to dedicate *Das Capital* to Darwin himself is here telling (Feuer 1977; Mackenzie 1979: 50–2; Tiger 1980; for an interesting discussion of the relationship between historical materialism and Darwinian evolution see Masters 1989: 303–8).

3 There is at least one obvious retort to this. Thus, in a self-consciously mischievous critique of the use of counterfactuals in historical analysis, the distinguished historian Eric Hobsbawm argues that the fact that things turned out the way they did indicates that, in some sense, they couldn't have turned out any other way. 'What actually happened in the past was the only thing that happened, and because it was the only thing that happened it was the only thing that could happen' (1993: 29). Let us be clear, however. Hobsbawm is certainly not seeking to restore an agentless and predestined conception of history. He is merely reminding us that however contingent an event may seem prior to its occurrence, once it is consigned to the historical record that contingency evaporates to be replaced by a rigid necessity. While things *could* have been different, at some point the die is cast and the once contingent becomes a structural necessity.

4 Regulation theory seeks to account for the empirical regularity of capitalism's persistence as a mode of production in the face of its internal contradictions. This it attributes to its ability to respond to periodic crises (invariably associated with problems of underconsumption or overproduction) through the development of a succession of new techno-economic paradigms for reordering productive relations. Each stable phase of economic growth (such as Fordism or post-Fordism), it is argued, is characterised by a virtuous and symbiotic relationship between a regime of accumulation (the techno-economic paradigm and its attendant productive relations) and a mode of regulation (which embeds this socially and politically). (See, in particular, Aglietta 1979; for commentaries and critical evaluation, see Boyer 1990; Hay 2001a; Jessop 1990b.)

5 The notion of the 'survival of the fittest' (Spencer 1865, Part III, Ch. 12), though invariably attributed in popular accounts to Darwin was, in fact, coined by Spencer some sixteen years prior to his reading Darwin (Noble 2000: 51).

6   For representative samples of classical evolutionary thought see, in addition to
    the works of Spencer cited above, Comte (1853); Durkheim (1964[1893]);
    Tönnies (1955[1887]). For representative samples of neo-evolutionary thought
    see Parsons (1966); Rostow (1960); Sahlins and Service (1960); Smelser (1964).

5   Divided by a common language? Conceptualising power

1   In making this claim, Bachrach and Baratz distort somewhat the complexity of
    Dahl's work on community power in New Haven. For Dahl did indeed provide
    an, albeit rough, index of the significance of specific issues – the extent to which
    they were reported in the news media.
2   Of course, this does not exhaust the difficulties of Connolly's definition and the
    use to which it is put by Lukes. For both authors would seem to assume that
    if blessed with complete information two actors in identical situations will share
    a common 'objective' interest. The assumption, though clearly untestable, is at
    best debatable. Suffice it to note that there would be nothing left of the concept
    of objective interests were one to concede that subjects might perceive their
    interests differently even where they share the same material circumstances and
    where those material circumstances are entirely transparent to them.
3   It is in this respect, in particular, that Lukes' otherwise behaviouralist con-
    ception of power (expressed in the inter-personal or behavioural relationship
    between A and B) most closely resembles the more social–structural conception
    of power of Marx, Marcuse or Habermas (see Hindess 1996: Ch. 4).
4   On the affinities between Lukes' three-dimensional conception of power and
    that of the critical theorists, see Hindess (1996: 84–95); Isaac (1987: 35 n. 60).
5   On the evolution of Foucault's conception of power see, in particular, Dallmayr
    (1984: Ch. 3); Hindess (1996); Honneth (1991: Chs 3 and 4); McNay (1994).
6   That Damiens should have exacted the highest price for his crimes is hardly sur-
    prising. For, as Foucault notes, 'the regicide . . . was neither more nor less than
    the total, absolute criminal since, instead of attacking, like any offender, a par-
    ticular decision or wish of the sovereign power, he attacked the very principle
    and physical person of the prince'. Consequently, 'the ideal punishment of the
    regicide had to constitute the *summum* of all possible tortures' (1977a: 54).

6   The discursive and the ideational in contemporary political analysis: beyond materialism and idealism

1   In seeking to challenge the significance of this line of reasoning, Andrew Sayer
    usefully reminds us that, for the most part, political practice proceeds quite
    independently of the political analyst. As he rightly suggests, in the vast major-
    ity of cases, 'the political discourse exists as it is regardless of whether I study

it and whatever I think of it' (2000: 34). However chastening, it is important that we acknowledge this. Yet, Sayer's characteristically disarming candour should not blind us to the still dynamic relationship between social subjects, the social context in which they find themselves and the understandings they develop of that context. If participants in social interaction cannot be regarded as neutral and dispassionate observers of an objective process whose dynamic is external to them, then neither can social or political analysts. Consequently, while it may be rare for political analysts to play a decisive role in shifting the parameters of political practice and political possibility, it is the very *possibility* not the *likelihood* of their ideas having such effects which must lead us to question the appropriateness of an analogy with the natural sciences.

2   Wendt himself, doyen of the constructivist turn in contemporary international relations theory, points to earlier idealist international relations theorists, such as Bull, Deutsch and Haas, as constructivists (1999: 3–4; see also Bull 1977; Deutsch 1954, 1963; Haas 1964, 1983, 1990).

3   Indeed, it might well be argued that it is fundamentally anathema to, and incommensurate with, all but the 'thinnest' of constructivisms. For any more resolutely constructivist author would surely wish to interrogate such a suspiciously essentialist 'construction' – asking, at minimum, how it comes to be that the state is constituted or constitutes itself as the principal actor in the arena of international relations.

4   The optimal rate of taxation on income from capital in small open economies, in such models, tends to zero.

5   Such as complete information and instantaneous exit at no cost to capital. For a full discussion see Hay (2001c).

6   For a useful discussion of the distinction between causal and constitutive logics see Wendt (1999: 26–8, 78–88, 165–78).

7   In one sense the logic was impeccable. 100 per cent taxation would yield zero revenue since there was no incentive to engage in economic activity which might generate taxation receipts; similarly, zero per cent taxation would yield zero revenue since no funds were being diverted to the exchequer. Somewhere between these extremes, then, there must be a point of maximum tax yield. If the US economy were positioned above that point then a decrease in the rate of taxation would indeed result in an increase in revenue.

8   An alternative, and perhaps equally plausible, explanation was that the US economy in 1981, like just about every other economy in the world at the time, was on the portion of the curve where a cut in the rate of taxation would result in a net reduction in revenue to the exchequer.

9   This is, of course, to assume that Reagan's advisors were not entirely disingenuous in seeking to legitimate extremely popular tax cuts in terms of the Laffer curve – a strategy of gain without pain.

7   The Challenge of Postmodernism

1   Here, again, Goodin and Klingemann's introduction to the *New Handbook of Political Science* is usefully indicative of contemporary developments. In strug-

gling to explain why postmodernism – a term making its debut in the *Handbook* in their introductory essay – has made such 'modest inroads' into the discipline, they point to the high plane of theoretical abstraction of most of its central precepts (1996: 21). This is an extremely telling remark and, in effect, an admission that the discipline is extremely wary of the inherently abstract normative, ontological and epistemological issues which define both postmodernism and the challenge of postmodernism. Moreover, it suggests a reluctance to acknowledge, far less to debate, the implicit normative, ontological and epistemological assumptions which inform more conventional approaches. Postmodernism, whatever one thinks of its answers, poses questions which the mainstream would simply prefer to remain unasked. Yet this is not the only respect in which Goodin and Klingemann's essay is noteworthy. For, like much of the political science mainstream which the *Handbook* reviews, they display a rather limited appreciation of postmodernism, taking the post-structuralism with which it is often associated rather too literally. Thus, they suggest, 'wherever once there were clearly defined structures and now there are none (or many disconnected ones), the post-structural theoretical arsenal may well offer insight into how that happened and why' (22). Very few postmodernists, and even fewer post-structuralists, would recognise themselves in what is here described.

2   For an attempt, from a similar position to that advanced here, to take postmodernism seriously, see Sayer (2000); see also Bohman (1991); Daly (1999); Fay (1996); Stones (1996). For rather more intemperate, if nonetheless important and frequently perceptive, accounts, see Best and Kellner (1991); Eagleton (1996); Geertz (1988); Geras (1987, 1988, 1990); Soper (1993).

3   So as to avoid any potential for confusion or misinterpretation, I am not suggesting that Howarth would support such a view. He does, nonetheless, provide a very useful statement of the prevailing orthodoxy within political science and, if to a lesser extent, international relations.

Bibliography

Ackelsberg, M. A. and Shanley, M. L. (1996) 'Privacy, Publicity and Power: A Feminist Rethinking of the Public–Private Distinction', in N. J. Hirschmann and C. Di Stefano (eds), *Revisioning the Political*. Boulder, CO: Westview Press.

Adam, B. (1994) 'Running Out of Time: Global Crisis and Human Engagement', in M. Redclift and T. Benton (eds), *Social Theory and the Global Environment*. London: Routledge.

Adler, E. (1997) 'Seizing the Middle Ground: Constructivism in World Politics', *European Journal of International Relations*, 3(3), 319–63.

Adler, E. and Barnett, M. (eds), (1998) *Security Communities*. Cambridge: Cambridge University Press.

Adorno, T. and Horkheimer, M. (1944/72) *The Dialectic of Enlightenment*. London: Verso.

Aglietta, M. (1979) *A Theory of Capitalist Regulation*. London: New Left Books.

Albrow, M. (1996) *The Global Age: State and Society Beyond Modernity*. Cambridge: Polity.

Alesina, A. (1987) 'Macroeconomic Policy in a Two-Party System as a Repeated Game', *Quarterly Journal of Economics*, 103, 651–78.

————(1989) 'Inflation, Unemployment and Politics in Industrialised Democracies', *Economic Journal*, 81, 1170–88.

Alexander, J. C. (1988) *Action and its Environments: Towards a New Synthesis*. New York: Columbia University.

————(1989) *Structure and Meaning: Relinking Classical Sociology*. New York: Columbia University.

————(1995) *Fin de Siècle Social Theory. Relativism, Reduction and the Problem of Reason*. London: Verso.

Alker, H. (2000) 'On Learning from Wendt', *Review of International Studies*, 26(1), 141–50.

Allan, P. (1992) 'The End of the Cold War: The End of International Relations Theory?', in P. Allan and K. Goldmann (eds), *The End of the Cold War*. Dordrecht: Martinus Nijhoff.

Allen, W. (1990) 'Does Feminism Need a Theory of the State?', in S. Watson (ed.), *Playing the State: Australian Feminist Interventions*. London: Verso.

Almond, G. A. (1990) *A Discipline Divided*. Newbury Park, CA: Sage.

————(1996) 'Political Science: The History of the Discipline', in R. E. Goodin and H.-D. Klingemann (eds), *A New Handbook of Political Science*. Oxford: Oxford University Press.

Alt, J. E. and Alesina, A. (1996) 'Political Economy: An Overview', in R. E. Goodin and H.-D. Klingemann (eds), *A New Handbook of Political Science*. Oxford: Oxford University Press.

Alt, J. E. and Crystal, K. A. (1983) *Political Economics*. Brighton: Harvester Wheatsheaf.

Althusser, L. (1969) *For Marx*. London: New Left Books.

———(1971) 'Ideology and Ideological State Apparatuses', in L. Althusser, *Lenin and Philosophy and Other Essays*. London: New Left Books.

Althusser, L. and Balibar, E. (1970) *Reading Capital*. London: New Left Books.

Anderson, P. (1964) 'Origins of the Present Crisis', *New Left Review*, 23, 26–53.

———(1980) *Arguments Within English Marxism*. London: Verso.

Archer, M. (1989) *Culture and Agency*. Cambridge: Cambridge University Press.

———(1995) *Realist Social Theory: The Morphogenetic Approach*. Cambridge: Cambridge University Press.

———(1998) 'Social Theory and the Analysis of Society', in T. May and M. Williams (eds), *Knowing the Social World*. Buckingham: Open University Press.

Archer, M., Bhaskar, R., Collier, A., Lawson, T. and Norrie, A. (eds), (1998) *Critical Realism: Essential Writings*. London: Routledge.

Arendt, H. (1958) *The Human Condition*. Chicago: University of Chicago Press.

Asad, T. (1979) 'Anthropology and the Colonial Encounter', in G. Huizer and B. Mannheim (eds), *The Politics of Anthropology: From Colonialism and Sexism Towards a View from Below*. The Hague: Mouton Publishers.

———(1991) 'Afterword: From the History of Colonial Anthropology to the Anthropology of Western Hegemony', in G. Stocking (ed.), *Colonial Situations: Essays on the Contextualisation of Ethnographic Knowledge*. Madison, WI: University of Wisconsin Press.

Ashenden, S. and Owen, D. (1999) 'Introduction: Foucault, Habermas and the Politics of Critique', in S. Ashenden and D. Owen (eds), *Foucault Contra Habermas*. London: Sage.

Ashley, R. (1984) 'The Poverty of Neorealism', *International Organisation*, 38(2), 225–86.

———(1987) 'The Geopolitics of Geopolitical Space: Toward a Critical Social Theory of International Politics', *Alternatives*, 12, 213–31.

———(1988) 'Untying the Sovereign State: A Double Reading of the Anarchy Problematique', *Millennium*, 17(2), 227–62.

Ashley, R. and Walker, R. B. J. (1990) 'Reading Dissidence/Writing the Discipline: Crisis and the Question of Sovereignty in International Studies', *International Studies Quarterly*, 34, 367–416.

Axelrod, R. (1984) *The Evolution of Cooperation*. New York: Basic Books.

Ayer, A. J. (1971) *Language, Truth and Logic*, 2nd edition. Harmondsworth: Penguin.

Bachrach, P. and Baratz, M. S. (1962) 'Two Faces of Power', *American Political Science Review*, 56, 947–52.

———(1963) 'Decisions and Non-Decisions', *American Political Science Review*, 57, 632–42.

———(1970) *Power and Poverty: Theory and Practice*. New York: Oxford University Press.

Badie, B. and Birnbaum, N. (1983) *The Sociology of the State*. Chicago, IL: University of Chicago Press.

Bairoch, P. (1996) 'Globalisation Myths and Realities: One Century of External Trade and Foreign Investment', in R. Boyer and D. Drache (eds), *States Against Markets: The Limits of Globalisation*. London: Macmillan.

Baldwin, D. (ed.), (1993) *Neo-Realism and Neo-Liberalism: The Contemporary Debate*. New York: Columbia University Press.

Ball, T. (1992) 'New Faces of Power', in T. E. Wartenberg (ed.), *Rethinking Power*. Albany, NY: State University of New York Press.

Barnes, B. and Bloor, D. (1982) 'Relativism, Rationalism and the Sociology of Knowledge', in M. Hollis and S. Lukes (eds), *Rationality and Relativism*. Oxford: Oxford University Press.

Barnes, T. J. (1996) *Logics of Dislocation: Models, Metaphors and Meanings of Economic Space*. New York: Guilford.

Barnet, R. J. and Cavanagh, J. (1994) *Global Dreams: Imperial Corporations and the New World Order*. New York: Simon & Schuster.

Barrow, C. W. (1993) *Critical Theories of the State: Marxist, Neo-Marxist, Post-Marxist*. Madison, WI: University of Wisconsin Press.

Barthes, R. (1977) 'The Death of the Author', in *Image–Music–Text*. London: Fontana.

Bates, R. H. (1988) 'Contra Contractarianism: Some Reflections on the New Institutionalism', *Politics and Society*, 18(4), 387–401.

Baudrillard, J. (1983) *In the Shadow of the Silent Majorities or, The End of the Social and Other Essays*. New York: Semiotext(e).

———(1984) 'Games With Vestiges', *On the Beach*, 5, 19–24.

———(1994a) *Simulacra and Simulation*. Ann Arbor, MI: University of Michigan Press.

———(1994b) *The Ilusion of the End*. Cambridge: Polity.

———(1996) *The Perfect Crime*. London: Verso.

———(2000) 'The Murder of the Real', in *The Vital Illusion*. New York: Columbia University Press.

Bauman, Z. (1987) *Legislators and Interpreters*. Cambridge: Polity.

———(1992) *Intimations of Postmodernity*. London: Routledge.

———(1993) *Postmodern Ethics*. Oxford: Blackwell.

Baumgartner, F. R. and Jones, B. D. (1993) *Agendas and Instability in American Politics*. Chicago, IL: University of Chicago Press.

Baylis, J. and Smith, S. (2001) (eds) *The Globalisation of World Politics*, 2nd edition. Oxford: Oxford University Press.

Beardsworth, R. (1996) *Derrida and the Political*. London: Routledge.

Beck, U. (1991) *Risk Society: Towards a New Modernity*. London: Sage.

———(1996) *The Reinvention of Politics*. Cambridge: Polity.

Benhabib, S. (ed.), (1996) *Democracy and Difference: Contesting the Boundaries of the Political*. Princeton, NJ: Princeton University Press.

Bennington, G. (1988) *Lyotard: Writing the Event*. New York: Columbia University Press.

———(1994) *Legislations: The Politics of Deconstruction*. London: Verso.

———(1999) *Jacques Derrida*. 2nd edition. Chicago, IL: University of Chicago Press.

———(2000) *Interrupting Derrida*. London: Routledge.

Benthall, J. (1995) 'Foreward: From Self-Applause Through Self-Criticism to Self-Confidence', in A. S. Ahmed and C. N. Shore (eds), *The Future of Anthropology: Its Relevance to the Contemporary World*. London: Athlone.

Benton, T. (1981) '"Objective" Interests and the Sociology of Power', *Sociology*, 15(2), 161–84.

Benton, T. and Craib, I. (2001) *Philosophy of Social Science: The Philosophical Foundations of Social Thought*. Basingstoke: Palgrave.

Berger, P. L. and Luckmann, T. (1966) *The Social Construction of Reality: A Treatise in the Sociology of Knowledge*. Garden City, NY: Doubleday.

Berger, S. and Dore, R. (1996) (eds), *National Diversity and Global Capitalism*. Ithaca, NY: Cornell University Press.

Berggren, W. A. and Van Couvering, J. A. (eds), (1984) *Catastrophes and Earth History*. New Haven, CT: Yale University Press.

Berman, S. (1998) *The Social Democratic Moment: Ideas and Politics in the Making of Interwar Europe*. Cambridge, MA: Harvard University Press.

Bernstein, R. J. (1991) *The New Constellation: The Ethical–Political Horizons of Modernity/Postmodernity*. Cambridge: Polity.

Bernstein, S., Ledow, R. N., Stein, J. G. and Weber, S. (2000) 'God Gave Physics the Easy Problems: Adapting Social Science to an Unpredictable World', *European Journal of International Relations*, 6(1), 43–76.

Berry, B. J. L. (1991) *Long-Wave Rhythms in Economic Development and Political Behaviour*. Baltimore, MD: Johns Hopkins University Press.

Best, S. and Kellner, D. (1991) *Postmodern Theory*. New York: Guilford.

Bhaskar, R. (1975) *A Realist Theory of Science*. Brighton: Harvester Wheatsheaf.

———(1979) *The Limits of Naturalism*. Brighton: Harvester Wheatsheaf.

———(1986) *Scientific Realism and Human Emancipation*. London: Verso.

———(1989) *Reclaiming Reality*. London: Verso.

———(1994) *Plato, Etc. The Problems of Philosophy and their Resolution*. London: Verso.

———(1998) 'General Introduction', in M. Archer *et al.* (eds), *Critical Realism: Essential Readings*. London: Routledge.

Binmore, K. (1990) 'Evolution and Contractarianism', *Constitutional Political Economy*, 1(1), 1–26.

Birn, R. B. (1997) 'Revising the Holocaust', *The Historical Journal*, 40(1), 195–215.

Black, D. (1958) *The Theory of Committees and Elections*. Cambridge: Cambridge University Press.

Blaikie, N. (1993) *Approaches to Social Enquiry*. Cambridge: Polity.

Blair, T. and Schröder, G. (1999) 'The Third Way/Die Neue Mitte', reprinted in O. Hombach, *The Politics of the New Centre*. Cambridge: Polity.

Block. F. (1987) *Revising State Theory: Essays in Politics and Postindustrialism*. Philadelphia, PA: Temple University Press.

Blyth, M. M. (1997a) '"Any More Bright Ideas?" The Ideational Turn of Comparative Political Economy', *Comparative Politics*, 29(1), 229–50.

———(1997b) 'Moving the Political Middle: Redefining the Boundaries of State Action', *Political Quarterly*, 68(3), 231–40.

———(2000) *The Great Transformations: The Rise and Decline of Embedded Liberalism*. Unpublished PhD. Thesis, Columbia University.

Bohman, J. (1991) *New Philosophy of Social Science*. Cambridge, MA: MIT Press.

Booth, K. and Smith, S. (eds), (1995) *International Relations Theory Today*. Cambridge: Polity.

Bourdieu, P. (1977) *Outline of a Theory of Practice*. Cambridge: Cambridge University Press.

————(1984) *Distinction: A Social Critique of the Judgement of Taste*. Cambridge, MA: Harvard University Press.

————(1991) *Language and Symbolic Power*. Cambridge: Polity.

Bowker, M. and Brown, R. (eds), (1993) *From Cold War to Collapse*. Cambridge: Cambridge University Press.

Boyer, R. (1990) *The Regulation School: A Critical Introduction*. Chicago: University of Chicago Press.

Boyer, R. and Drache, R. (1996) (eds) *States Against Markets: The Limits of Globalisation*. London: Routledge.

Brinton, C. (1965 [1938]) *The Anatomy of Revolution*. New York: Harper å Row.

Brinton, M. C. and Nee, V. (eds), (1998) *The New Institutionalism in Sociology*. New York: Russell Sage Foundation.

Brown, C. (1992) *International Relations Theory: New Normative Approaches*. Hemel Hempstead: Harvester Wheatsheaf.

Brown, W. (1992) 'Finding the Man in the State', *Feminist Studies*, 18(1), 7–34.

Bryson, V. (1992) *Feminist Political Theory: An Introduction*. London: Macmillan.

Buchanen, J. M. (1977) 'Why Does Government Grow?', in T. E. Borcherding (ed.), *Budgets and Bureaucrats: The Sources of Government Growth*. Durham, NC: Duke University Press.

Buchanen, J. M. and Tullock, G. (1962) *The Calculus of Consent*. Ann Arbor, MI: University of Michigan Press.

Bull, H. (1977) *The Anarchical Society*. New York: Columbia University Press.

Bulpitt, J. (1986) 'The Discipline of the New Democracy: Mrs Thatcher's Domestic Statecraft', *Political Studies*, 34(1), 19–39.

Burawoy, M. (1989) 'Two Methods in Search of Science: Skocpol Versus Trotsky', *Theory and Society*, 18, 759–805.

Burke, E. [1968] (1790) *Reflections on the Revolution in France*, edited by C. C. O'Brien. London: Penguin.

Burke, P. (1992) *History and Social Theory*. Ithaca, NY: Cornell University Press.

Busch, A. (2000) 'Unpacking the Globalisation Debate: Approaches, Evidence and Data', in C. Hay and D. Marsh (eds), *Demystifying Globalisation*. Basingstoke: Palgrave.

Buzan, B., Jones, C. and Little, R. (1993) *The Logic of Anarchy: Neorealism to Structural Realism*. New York: Columbia University Press.

Callinicos, A. (1989) *Against Postmodernism: A Marxist Critique*. Cambridge: Polity.

Campbell, D. (1992) *Writing Security: United States Foreign Policy and the Politics of Identity*. Minneapolis, MN: University of Minnesota Press.

————(1998) *National Deconstruction: Violence, Identity and Justice in Bosnia*. Minneapolis, MN: University of Minnesota Press.

Campbell, J. L. (1998) 'Institutional Analysis and the Role of Ideas in Political Economy', *Theory and Society*, 27, 377–409.

Campbell, J. L. and Pedersen, O. K. (eds), (2001a) *The Second Movement in Institutional Analysis*. Princeton, NJ: Princeton University Press.

————(2001b) 'Introduction: The Rise of Neoliberalism and Institutional Analysis', in J. L. Campbell and O. K. Pedersen (eds), *The Rise of Neoliberalism and Institutional Analysis*. Princeton, NJ: Princeton University Press.

————(2001c) 'The Second Movement in Institutional Analysis', in J. L. Campbell and O. K. Pedersen (eds), *The Rise of Neoliberalism and Institutional Analysis*. Princeton, NJ: Princeton University Press.

Carlsnaes, W. (1992) 'The Agent-Structure Problem in Foreign Policy Analysis', *International Studies Quarterly*, 6(3), 245–70.

Carmines, E. G. and Huckfeldt, R. (1996) 'Political Behaviour: An Overview', in R. E. Goodin and H.-D. Klingemann (eds), *A New Handbook of Political Science*. Oxford: Oxford University Press.

Carr, E. H. (1939) *The Twenty Years' Crisis*. New York: Harper & Row.

Carrier, J. G. and Miller, D. (eds), (1998) *Virtualism: A New Political Economy*. Oxford: Berg.

Cerny, P. G. (1990) *The Changing Architecture of Politics: Structure, Agency and the Future of the State*. London: Sage.

————(1997) 'Paradoxes of the Competition State: The Dynamics of Political Globalisation', *Government and Opposition*, 32, 251–74.

Chalmers, A. (1982) *What is This Thing Called Science?* Buckingham: Open University Press.

————(1986) 'The Galileo that Fayerabend Missed: An Improved Case Against Method', in J. A. Schuster and R. A. Yeo (eds), *The Politics and Rhetoric of Scientific Method*. Dordrecht: Reidel.

————(1990) *Science and Its Fabrication*. Buckingham: Open University Press.

Charlesworth, J. C. (1967) 'Identifiable Approaches to the Study of Politics and Government', in J. C. Charlesworth (ed.), *Contemporary Political Analysis*. New York: Free Press.

Checkel, J. T. (1997) *Ideas and International Political Change: Soviet/Russian Behaviour and the End of the Cold War*. New Haven, CT: Yale University Press.

————(2001) 'A Constructivist Research Program in European Union Studies?', *European Union Politics*, 2(2), 219–49.

Christiansen, T., Jørgensen, K. E. and Wiener, A. (2001) 'Introduction', in T. Christiansen *et al.* (eds), *The Social Construction of Europe*. London: Sage.

Classen, C., Howes, D. and Synnott, A. (1994) *Aroma: The Cultural History of Smell*. London: Routledge.

Clegg, S. R. (1989) *Frameworks of Power*. London: Sage.

Clifford, J. (1988) *The Predicament of Culture: Twentieth-Century Ethnography, Literature and Art*. Cambridge, MA: Harvard University Press.

Clifford, J. and Marcus, G. E. (eds), (1986) *Writing Culture: The Poetics and Politics of Ethnography*. Berkeley, CA: University of California Press.

Coates, D. and Hay, C. (2001) 'The Internal and External Face of New Labour's Political Economy', *Government and Opposition*, 36(4), 447–72.

Cohen, J. and Rogers, J. (1995) 'Secondary Associations and Democratic Governance', in E. O. Wright (ed.), *Associations and Democracy*. London: Verso.

Collier, A. (1994) *Critical Realism: An Introduction to Roy Bhaskar's Philosophy*. London: Verso.

Collier, R. B. and Collier, D. (1991) *Shaping the Political Arena: Critical Junctures, the Labour Movement and Regime Dynamics in Latin America*. Princeton, NJ: Princeton University Press.

Collins, R. (1988) *Theoretical Sociology*. San Diego: Harcourt Brace Jovanovich.

Comte, A. (1853) *The Positive Philosophy of Auguste Comte*, trans. Harriet Martineau. London: Chapman.

Connolly, W. E. (1972) 'On "Interests" in Politics', *Politics and Society*, 2(3), 459–77.

————(1993) *The Terms of Political Discourse*. 3rd edition. Oxford: Blackwell.

Connor, S. (1997) *Postmodernist Culture: An Introduction to Theories of the Contemporary*. Oxford: Blackwell.

Converse, P. (1964) 'The Nature of Belief Systems', in D. Apter (ed.), *Ideology and Discontent*. New York: Free Press.

Cooke, W. N. and Noble, D. S. (1998) 'Industrial Relations Systems and US Foreign Direct Investment Abroad', *British Journal of Industrial Relations*, 36(4), 581–609.

Corvi, R. (1997) *An Introduction to the Thought of Karl Popper*. London: Routledge.

Couvalis, G. (1988) 'Feyerabend and Laymon on Brownian Motion', *Philosophy of Science*, 55, 415–20.

————(1989) *Feyerabend's Critique of Foundationalism*. Aldershot: Gower.

————(1997) *The Philosophy of Science: Science and Objectivity*. London: Sage.

Culler, J. (1983) *On Deconstruction: Theory and Criticism After Structuralism*. London: Routledge.

Crick, B. (1959) *The American Science of Politics, Its Origins and Conditions*. London: Routledge.

————(1962) *In Defence of Politics*. London: Weidenfeld & Nicolson.

Crook, S, Pakulski, J. and Waters, M. (1992) *Postmodernisation: Change in Advanced Society*. London: Sage.

Dahl, R. A. (1956) *A Preface to Democratic Theory*. Chicago, IL: University of Chicago Press.

————(1957) 'The Concept of Power', *Behavioural Science*, 2(3), 201–15.

————(1958) 'A Critique of the Ruling Elite Model', *American Political Science Review*, 52(2), 463–9.

————(1961a) 'The Behavioural Approach', *American Political Science Review*, 55, 763–72.

————(1961b) *Who Governs? Democracy and Power in an American City*. New Haven, CT: Yale University Press.

————(1963) *Modern Political Analysis*. 3rd edition. Englewood Cliffs, NJ: Prentice-Hall.

Dahl, R. A. and Lindblom, C. (1953) *Politics, Economics and Welfare*. New York: Harper & Brothers.

Dahlhaus, C. (1989) *Schoenberg and the New Music*. Cambridge: Cambridge University Press.

Dallmayr, F. R. (1984) *Polis and Praxis: Exercises in Contemporary Political Theory*. Cambridge, MA: MIT Press.

Daly, G. (1999) 'Marxism and Postmodernity', in A. Gamble, D. Marsh and T. Tant (eds), *Marxism and Social Science*. Basingstoke: Palgrave.

Daly, M. (1978) *Gyn/Ecology*. London: Fontana.

Davies, J. C. (1962) 'Towards a Theory of Revolution', *American Sociological Review*, 6(1), 5–19.

————(1969) "The J-Curve of Rising and Declining Satisfaction as a Cause of Some Great Revolutions and a Contained Rebellion', in H. Graham and T. Gurr (eds), *Violence in America*. New York: Signet Books.

————(1971) *Why Men Revolt and Why*. New York: Free Press.

Debray, R. (1973) 'Time and Politics', in *Prison Writings*. London: Allen Lane.

de Bresson, C. (1987) 'The Evolutionary Paradigm and the Economics of Technical Change', *Journal of Economic Issues*, 21(2), 751–62.

de Certeau, M (1984) *The Practice of Everyday Life*. Berkeley, CA: University of California Press.

de Fontenelle, B. (1686/1929) *The Plurality of Worlds*. London: Nonsuch Press (trans. 1688).

Delanty, G. (1997) *Social Science: Beyond Constructivism and Realism*. Buckingham: Open University Press.

Der Derian, J. (ed.) (1995) *International Theory: Critical Investigations*. New York: New York University Press.

Derrida, J. (1973) *Writing and Difference*. Chicago, IL: University of Chicago Press.

————(1976) *Of Grammatology*. Baltimore, MD: Johns Hopkins University Press.

————(1978) *Writing and Difference*. London: Routledge.

————(1981) *Positions*. Chicago, IL: University of Chicago Press.

————(1982) *Dissemination*. Chicago, IL: University of Chicago Press.

————(1991) *The Derrida Reader: Between the Blinds*. Hemel Hempstead: Harvester Wheatsheaf.

Dessler, D. (1989) 'What's at Stake in the Agent–Structure Debate?', *International Organization*, 43, 441–73.

Deutsch, K. W. (1953) *Nationalism and Social Communication*. Cambridge, MA: MIT Press.

————(1954) *Political Community at the International Level*. New York: Free Press.

————(1963) *The Nerves of Government: Models of Political Communication and Control*. New York: Free Press.

De Vaus, D. (1991) *Surveys in Social Research*. London: UCL Press.

Devetek, R. (2001) 'Postmodernism', in S. Burchill *et al.*, *Theories of International Relations*. 2nd edition. Basingstoke: Palgrave.

DiMaggio, P. J. and Powell, W. W. (eds), (1991) *The New Institutionalism in Organizational Analysis*. Chicago, IL: University of Chicago Press.

Docker, J. (1995) *Postmodernism and Popular Culture: A Cultural History*. Cambridge: Cambridge University Press.

Doty, R. L. (1997) 'Aporia: A Critical Exploration of the Agent–Structure Problematique in International Relations Theory', *European Journal of International Relations*, 3(3), 365–92.

Douglas, J. (1970) (ed.) *Understanding Everyday Life*. Chicago: Aldine.

Douzinas, C., Warrington, R. and McVeigh, S. (1991) *Postmodern Jurisprudence*. London: Routledge.

Dowding, K. (1991) *Rational Choice Theory and Political Power*. Aldershot: Edward Elgar.

————(2001) 'There Must Be an End to Confusion: Policy Networks, Intellectual Fatigue and the Need for Political Science Methods Courses in British Universities', *Political Studies*, 49(1), 89–105.

Downs, A. (1957) *An Economic Theory of Democracy*. London: HarperCollins.

Dryzek, J. S. (1990) *Discursive Democracy: Policy, Politics and Political Science*. Cambridge: Cambridge University Press.

Dubin, S. C. (1992) *Arresting Images: Impolitic Art and Uncivil Actions*. London: Routledge.

Dunleavy, P. (1996) 'Political Behaviour: Institutional and Experiential Approaches', in R. E. Goodin and H.-D. Klingemann (eds), *A New Handbook of Political Science*. Oxford: Oxford University Press.

Dunleavy, P. and O'Leary, B. (1987) *Theories of the State: The Politics of Liberal Democracy*. Basingstoke: Macmillan.

Durkheim, E. (1964 [1893]) *The Division of Labour in Society*. New York: Free Press.

Duverger, M. (1964/66) *The Idea of Politics: The Uses of Power in Society*. London: Methuen.

Dyson, K. and Featherstone, K. (1999) *The Road to Maastricht: Negotiating Economic and Monetary Union*. Oxford: Oxford University Press.

Eagleton, T. (1991) *Ideology: An Introduction*. London: Verso.

————(1996) *The Illusion of Postmodernism*. London: Verso.

Easton, D. (1967) 'The Current Meaning of "Behavouralism"', in J. C. Charlesworth (ed.), *Contemporary Political Analysis*. New York: Free Press.

————(1979) *A Framework for Political Analysis*. Chicago, IL: University of Chicago Press.

————(1997) 'The Future of the Postbehavioural Phase in Political Science', in K. R. Monroe (ed.), *Contemporary Empirical Political Theory*. Berkeley, CA: California University Press.

Edwards, L. P. (1927) *The Natural History of Revolution*. Chicago: University of Chicago Press.

Eldredge, N. and Gould, S. J. (1972) 'Punctuated Equilibria: An Alternative to Phyletic Gradualism', in T. J. M. Schopf (ed.), *Models in Paleobiology*. San Francisco: Freeman, Cooper.

Ellis, B. E. (1991) *American Psycho*. New York: Random House.

Elshtain, J. B. (1981) *Public Man, Private Woman: Women in Social and Political Thought*. Princeton, NJ: Princeton University Press.

Elster, J. (1979) *Ulysses and the Sirens*. Cambridge: Cambridge University Press.

Erickson, R. S. and Palfry, T. R. (2000) 'Equilibria in Campaign Spending Games: Theory and Data', *American Political Science Review*, 94(3), 595–610.

Esping-Andersen, J. (1999) *Social Foundations of Postindustrial Economies*. Cambridge: Cambridge University Press.

Evans, P. B., Rueschemeyer, D. and Skocpol, T. (1985) *Bringing the State Back In*. Cambridge: Cambridge University Press.

Evans-Pritchard, E. E. (1951) *Social Anthropology*. London: Cohen and West.

Fabian, J. (1983) *Time and the Other: How Anthropology Makes its Object*. New York: Columbia University Press.

Fanon, F. (1963) *Wretched of the Earth*. New York: Grove Books.

Fay, B. (1996) *Contemporary Philosophy of Social Science: A Multicultural Approach*. Oxford: Blackwell.

Feuer, L. (1977) 'Marx and Engels as Sociobiologists', *Survey*, 23, 109–39.

Feyerabend, P. K. (1975) *Against Method*. London: New Left Books.

———(1987) *Farewell to Reason*. London: Verso.

Finegold, K. and Skocpol, T. (1995) *State and Party in America's New Deal*. Madison, WI: University of Madison Press.

Finkelstein, N. G. (1997) 'Daniel Jonah Goldhagen's "Crazy" Thesis: A Critique of Hitler's Willing Executioners', *New Left Review*, 224, 39–87.

Finlayson, G. (1970) *Decade of Reform: England in the 1830s*. New York: Norton.

Foley, R. (1987) *The Theory of Epistemic Rationality*. Cambridge, MA: Harvard University Press.

Foster, H. (1996) *The Return of the Real: The Avant-Garde at the End of the Century*. Cambridge, MA: MIT Press.

Foucault, M. (1977a) *Discipline and Punish*. Harmondsworth: Penguin.

———(1977b) 'Nietzsche, Genealogy, History', in D. F. Bouchard (ed.), *Language, Counter-Memory, Practice: Selected Essays and Interviews by Michel Foucault*. Ithaca, NY: Cornell University Press.

———(1979) *The History of Sexuality. Volume 1. An Introduction*. Harmondsworth: Penguin.

———(1981) *Power/Knowledge*. New York: Pantheon.

———(1982) 'The Subject and Power', in H. L. Dreyfus and P. Rabinow (eds), *Michel Foucault: Beyond Structuralism and Hermeneutics*. Chicago: University of Chicago Press.

———(1988a) 'The Ethic of Care for the Self as a Practice of Freedom', in J. Bernauer and D. Rasmussen (eds), *The Final Foucault*. Cambridge, MA: MIT Press.

———(1998b) *The Care of the Self*. New York: Vintage Books.

Friedman, M. (1953) 'The Methodology of Positive Economics', in M. Friedman, *Essays in Positive Economics*. Chicago, IL: University of Chicago Press.

Fukuyama, (1992) *The End of History and the Last Man*. Harmondsworth: Penguin.

Fuller, S. (1998) 'From Content to Context: A Social Epistemology of the Structure-Agency Craze', in A. Sica (ed.), *What is Social Theory? The Philosophical Debates*. Oxford: Blackwell.

Gaddis, J. L. (1992) 'International Relations Theory and the End of the Cold War', *International Security*, 17, 5–58.

Gallie, W. B. (1956) 'Essentially Contested Concepts', *Proceedings of the Aristotelian Society*. 56, 167–98.

Gambetta, D. (1993) *The Sicilian Mafia: The Business of Protection*. Cambridge, MA: Harvard University Press.

————(1994) 'Godfather's Gossip', *Archives Européenes de Sociologie*, 32(2), 199–223.

Garfinkel, H. (1967) *Studies in Ethnomethodology*. Englewood Cliffs, NJ: Prentice-Hall.

Garrett, G. (1998) *Partisan Politics in the Global Economy*. Cambridge: Cambridge University Press.

Geertz, C. (1973) 'Deep Play: Notes on the Balinese Cockfight', in C. Geertz, *The Interpretation of Cultures*. New York: Basic Books.

————(1983) *Local Knowledge: Further Essays in Interpretative Anthropology*. New York: Basic Books.

————(1988) 'Being Here: Whose Life is it Anyway?', in C. Geertz, *Works and Lives: The Anthropologist as Author*. Stanford, CA: Stanford University Press.

————(2000) *Available Light: Anthropological Reflections on Philosophical Topics*. Princeton, NJ: Princeton University Press.

George, J. (1994) *Discourses of Global Politics: A Critical (Re)Introduction to International Relations*. Boulder, CO: Lynne Rienner.

Geras, N. (1987) 'Post-Marxism?', *New Left Review*, 163, 40–82.

————(1988) 'Ex-Marxism Without Substance', *New Left Review*, 169, 34–61.

————(1990) *Discourses of Extremity: Radical Ethics and Post-Marxist Extravagances*. London: Verso.

Giddens, A. (1976) *New Rules of Sociological Method*. London: Hutchinson.

————(1979) *Central Problems in Social Theory*. London: Macmillan.

————(1981) *A Contemporary Critique of Historical Materialism*. London: Macmillan.

————(1984) *The Constitution of Society*. Cambridge: Polity.

————(1986) *Sociology: A Brief But Critical Introduction*. Basingstoke: Macmillan.

————(1990) *The Consequences of Modernity*. Cambridge: Polity.

————(1991) *Modernity and Self-Identity: Self and Society in the Late Modern Age*. Cambridge: Polity.

————(1992) *The Transformation of Intimacy*. Cambridge: Polity.

————(1994) *Beyond Left and Right: The Future of Radical Politics*. Cambridge: Polity.

————(1995) 'Epilogue: Notes on the Future of Anthropology', in A. S. Ahmed and C. N. Shore (eds), *The Future of Anthropology: Its Relevance to the Contemporary World*. London: Athlone.

————(1998) *The Third Way: The Renewal of Social Democracy*. Cambridge: Polity.

————(1999) *The Runaway World*. London: Profile Books.

Gilpin, R. (1981) *War and Change in World Politics*. Cambridge: Cambridge University Press.

Goffman, E. (1959) *The Presentation of Self in Everyday Life*. New York: Doubleday.

————(1963) *Behaviour in Public Places*. New York: Free Press.

————(1972) *Interaction Ritual*. London: Allen Lane.

Golan, D. (1994) *Inventing Shaka: Using History in the Construction of Zulu Nationalism*. Boulder, CO: Lynne Rienner.

Goldhagen, D. J. (1996) *Hitler's Willing Executioners: Ordinary Germans and the Holocaust*. New York: Random House.

————(1997) 'Germany vs. the Critics', *Foreign Affairs*, 76(1), 1997, 163–6.

————(1998) 'The Failure of the Critics', reprinted in R. R. Shandley (ed.), *Unwilling Germans? The Goldhagen Debate*. Minneapolis, MN: University of Minnesota Press (originally published in *Die Zeit*, 2 August, 1995).

Goldmann, K. (1996) 'International Relations: An Overview', in R. E. Goodin and H.-D. Klingemann (eds), *A New Handbook of Political Science*. Oxford: Oxford University Press.

Goldstein, J. and Keohane, R. O. (1993) (eds) *Ideas and Foreign Policy: Beliefs, Institutions and Political Change*. Ithaca, NY: Cornell University Press.

Goldstone, J. A. (1982) 'The Comparative and Historical Study of Revolution', *Annual Review of Sociology*, 8, 187–207.

Goodin, R. E. and Klingemann, H.-D. (1996) 'Political Science: The Discipline', in R. E. Goodin and H.-D. Klingemann (eds), *A New Handbook of Political Science*. Oxford: Oxford University Press.

Gough, I. (1996) 'Social Welfare and Competitiveness', *New Political Economy*, 1(2), 209–32.

Gough, K. (1968) 'New Proposals for Anthropologists', *Current Anthropology*, 9(5), 403–7.

Gould, S. J. (1989) 'Punctuated Equilibrium in Fact and Theory', in A. Somit and S. A. Peterson (eds), *The Dynamics of Evolution: The Punctuated Equilibrium Debate in the Natural and Social Sciences*. Ithaca, NY: Cornell University Press.

Gould, S. J. and Eldredge, N. (1977) 'Punctuated Equilibria: The Tempo and Mode of Evolution Reconsidered', *Paleobiology*, 3, 115–51.

Gourevitch, P. (1986) *Politics in Hard Times: Comparative Responses to International Economic Crisis*. Ithaca, NY: Cornell University Press.

Gramsci, A. (1971) *Selections from Prison Notebooks*. London: Lawrence & Wishart.

Gray, J. (1997) 'After Social Democracy: Politics, Capitalism and the Common Life', in *Endgames*. Cambridge: Polity.

Green, D. P. and Shapiro, I. (1994) *Pathologies of Rational Choice Theory: A Critique of Applications in Political Science*. New Haven, CT: Yale University Press.

Grofman, B. (1997) 'Seven Durable Axes of Cleavage in Political Science', in K. R. Monroe (ed.), *Contemporary Empirical Political Theory*. Berkeley, CA: University of California Press.

Guestzkow, H. (1950) 'Long Range Research in International Relations', *American Perspective*, 4, 421–40.

Gurr, T. R. (1968) 'A Causal Model of Civil Strife', *American Political Science Review*, 62, 1104–24.

————(1970a) 'Sources of Rebellion in Western Societies: Some Quantitative Evidence', *Annals of the American Academy of Political and Social Science*, 391.

————(1970b) *Why Men Rebel*. Princeton, NJ' Princeton University Press.

Haas, E. (1964) *Beyond the Nation-State*. Stanford, CA: Stanford University Press.

————(1983) 'Words Can Hurt You: Or, Who Said What to Whom About Regimes?', in S. Krasner (ed.), *International Regimes*. Ithaca, NY: Cornell University Press.

————(1990) *When Knowledge is Power*. Berkeley, CA: University of California Press.

Habermas, J. (1968) *Knowledge and Human Interests*. Boston, MA: Beacon.

————(1981) 'Modernity Versus Postm-Modernity', *New German Critique*, 22, 2–14.

————(1987) *The Philosophical Discourse of Modernity*. Cambridge, MA: MIT Press.

————(1989) *The New Conservatism*. Cambridge, MA: MIT Press.

————(1993) *Justification and Application: Remarks on Discourse Ethics*. Cambridge, MA: MIT Press.

————(1996) *Between Facts and Norms: Contributions Towards a Discourse Theory of Law and Democracy*. Cambridge, MA: MIT Press.

Hacking, I. (1999) *The Social Construction of What?* Cambridge, MA: Harvard University Press.

Hall, P. A. (1986) *Governing the Economy: The Politics of State Intervention in Britain and France*. Cambridge: Polity.

————(1989) (ed.) *The Political Power of Economic Ideas: Keynesianism Across Nations*. Princeton, NJ: Princeton University Press.

————(1993) 'Policy Paradigms, Social Learning and the State: The Case of Economic Policy-Making in Britain', *Comparative Politics*, 25(3), 185–96.

————(1997) 'The Role of Interests, Institutions and Ideas in the Comparative Political Economy of the Industrialised Nations', in M. I. Lichbach and A. S. Zuckerman (eds), *Comparative Politics*. Cambridge, MA: Cambridge University Press.

Hall, P. A. and Taylor, R. C. R. (1996) 'Political Science and the Three New Institutionalisms', *Political Studies*, 44(4), 936–57.

————(1998) 'The Potential of Historical Institutionalism: A Response to Hay and Wincott', *Political Studies*, 46(5), 958–62.

Hallpike, C. R. (1986) *The Principles of Social Evolution*. Oxford: Oxford University Press.

Hardin, G. (1968) 'The Tragedy of the Commons', *Science*, 162, 1243–8.

Harré, R. (1970) *The Principles of Scientific Thinking*. London: Macmillan.

————(1986) *The Social Construction of Emotions*. Oxford: Blackwell.

Harré, R. and Krausz, M. (1996) *Varieties of Relativism*. Oxford: Blackwell.

Harré, R. and Madden, E. H. (1975) *Causal Powers*. Oxford: Oxford University Press.

Harvey, D. (1989) *The Condition of Postmodernity*. Oxford: Blackwell.

————(1994) 'Class Relations, Social Justice and the Politics of Difference', in J. Squires (eds), *Principled Positions*. London; Lawrence & Wishart.

Hassan, I. (1971) *The Dismemberment of Orpheus: Towards a Postmodern Literature*. Madison, WI: University of Wisconsin Press.

————(1982) *The Dismemberment of Orpheus: Towards a Postmodern Literature*, revised edition. Oxford: Oxford University Press.

Hay, C. (1994/95) 'Postmodern Tension: The Dialectic of Post-Enlightenment Thought', *Arena Journal*, 4, 127–36.

————(1995a) 'Mobilisation Through Interpellation: James Bulger, Juvenile

Crime and the Construction of a Moral Panic', *Social and Legal Studies*, 4(2), 197–224.

———(1995b) 'Structure and Agency', in D. Marsh and G. Stoker (eds), *Theory and Methods in Political Science*. London: Macmillan.

———(1996) *Re-Stating Social and Political Change*. Buckingham: Open University Press.

———(1997) 'Divided by a Common Language: Political Theory and the Concept of Power', *Politics*, 17(1), 45–52.

———(1999a) 'Continuity and Discontinuity in British Political Development', in D. Marsh *et al.*, *Postwar British Politics in Perspective*. Cambridge: Polity.

———(1999b) 'What Place for Ideas in the Agent-Structure Debate? Globalisation as a Process Without a Subject', paper presented at the annual conference of the British International Studies Association, 20–22 December, University of Manchester.

———(1999c) 'Marxism and the State', in A. Gamble, D. Marsh and T. Tant (eds), *Marxism and Social Science*. London: Macmillan.

———(1999d) 'Crisis and the Structural Transformation of the State: Interrogating the Process of Change', *British Journal of Politics and International Relations*, 1(3), 317–44.

———(1999e) *The Political Economy of New Labour: Labouring Under False Pretences?* Manchester: Manchester University Press.

———(2000a) 'Contemporary Capitalism, Globalisation, Regionalisation and the Persistence of National Variation', *Review of International Studies*, 26(4) 509–32.

———(2000b) 'Willing Executors of Hitler's Will? The Goldhagen Controversy, Political Analysis and the Holocaust', *Politics*, 20(3), 119–28.

———(2001a) 'Regulation Theory' in R. J. Barry Jones (ed.), *Routledge Encyclopedia of International Political Economy*. London: Routledge.

———(2001b) 'The "Crisis" of Keynesianism and the Rise of Neo-Liberalism in Britain: An Ideational Institutionalist Approach', in J. L. Campbell and O. K. Pedersen (eds), *The Second Movement in Institutional Analysis*. Princeton, NJ: Princeton University Press.

———(2001c) 'Globalisation, Economic Change and the Welfare State: The Vexatious Inquisition of Taxation', in R. Sykes, B. Pallier and P. Prior (eds), *Globalisation and the European Welfare States: Challenges and Change*. London: Macmillan.

———(2001d) 'Globalisation, Competitiveness and the Future of the Welfare State in Europe', paper presented at the European Community Studies Association's International Conference, Madison, Wisconsin, May–June.

———(2002) 'Globalisation, EU-isation and the Space for Social Democratic Alternatives: Pessimism of the Intellect . . .', *British Journal of Politics and International Relations*, 4(1).

Hay, C. and Jessop, B. (1995) 'The Governance of Local Economic Development and the Development of Local Economic Governance', paper presented to the annual meeting of the *American Political Science Association*, Chicago, September.

Hay, C. and Marsh, D. (1999a) 'Towards a New International Political Economy?', *New Political Economy*, 4(1), 5–22.

———(1999b) 'Conclusion: Analysing the Explaining Postwar British Political Development', in D. Marsh *et al.*, *Postwar British Politics in Perspective*. Cambridge: Polity.

———(2000) 'Introduction: Demystifying Globalisation', in C. Hay and D. Marsh (eds), *Demystifying Globalisation*. London: Macmillan.

Hay, C., O'Brien, M. and Penna, S. (1994) 'Giddens, Modernity and Self-Identity: The Hollowing-Out of Social Theory', *Arena Journal*, 2, 45–76.

Hay, C. and Rosamond, B. (2002) 'Globalisation, European Integration and the Discursive Construction of Economic Imperatives', *Journal of European Public Policy*, 9(2).

Hay, C. and Watson, M. (1998) *Rendering the Contingent Necessary: New Labour's Neo-Liberal Conversion and the Discourse of Globalisation*. Center for European Studies, Programme for the Study of Germany and Europe, Working Paper, #8.4, Harvard University.

Hay, C., Watson, M. and Wincott, D. (1999) *Globalisation, European Integration and the Persistence of European Social Models*. ESRC One Europe or Several Research Programme, Working Paper 3/99.

Hay, C. and Wincott, D. (1998) 'Structure, Agency and Historical Institutionalism', *Political Studies*, 46(5), 951–7.

Hayward, J. (1999) 'British Approaches to Politics: The Dawn of a Self-Deprecating Discipline', in J. Hayward, B. Barry and A. Brown (eds), *The British Study of Politics in the Twentieth Century*. Oxford: British Academy/Oxford University Press.

Heclo, H. (1974) *Modern Social Politics in Britain and Sweden*. New Haven, CT: Yale University Press.

Held, D. and Leftwich, A. (1984) 'A Discipline of Politics?', in A. Leftwich (ed.), *What is Politics?* Oxford: Blackwell.

Held, D., McGrew, A., Goldblatt, D. and Perraton, J. (1999) *Global Transformations: Politics, Economics and Culture*. Cambridge: Polity.

Helleiner, E. (1994) *States and the Reemergence of Global Finance: From Bretton Woods to the 1990s*. Ithaca, NY: Cornell University Press.

———(1996) 'Post-Globalisation and Financial Markets: Is the Financial Liberalisation Trend Likely to be Reversed?', in R. Boyer and D. Drache (eds), *States Against Markets: The Limits of Globalisation*. London: Routledge.

Hempel, C. G. (1965) *Aspects of Scientific Explanation and Other Essays in the Philosophy of Science*. New York: Free Press.

———(1966) *Philosophy of Natural Science*. Englewood Cliffs, NJ: Prentice Hall.

———(1994) 'The Function of General Laws in History', in M. Martin and L. McIntyre (eds), *Readings in the Philosophy of Social Science*. Cambridge, MA: MIT Press.

Henderson, D. (1981) 'Limitations of the Laffer Curve as a Justification for Tax Cuts', *The Cato Journal*, 1, 45–52.

Herzfeld, M. (1987) *Anthropology Through the Looking-Glass: Critical Ethnography in the Margins of Europe*. Cambridge: Cambridge University Press.

————(2001) *Anthropology: Theoretical Practice in Culture and Society*. Oxford: Blackwell.

Heywood, A. (1994) *Political Ideas and Concepts: An Introduction*. London: Macmillan.

Hindess, B. (1996) *Discourses of Power: From Hobbes to Foucault*. Oxford: Blackwell.

Hinich, M. J. and Munger, M. C. (1997) *Analytical Politics*. Cambridge: Cambridge University Press.

Hirschmann, N. J. and Di Stefano, C. (eds) (1996a) *Revisioning the Political: Feminist Reconstructions of Traditional Concepts in Western Political Theory*. Boulder, CO: Westview Press.

————(1996b) 'Revision, Reconstruction and the Challenge of the New', in N. J. Hirschmann and C. Di Stefano (eds), *Revisioning the Political*. Boulder, CO: Westview Press.

Hirst, P. (1976) *Social Evolutionism and Sociological Categories*. London: George Allen & Unwin.

————(1979) 'The Necessity of Theory', *Economy and Society*, 8, 417–45.

Hirst, P. and Thompson, G. (1999) *Globalisation in Question*, 2nd edition. Cambridge: Polity.

Hobden, S. (1999) 'Theorising the International System: Perspectives from Historical Sociology', *Review of International Studies*, 25(2), 257–71.

Hobsbawm, E. (1993) 'Britain: A Comparative View', in B. Brivati and H. Jones (eds), *What Difference Did the War Make?* Leicester: Leicester University Press.

Hodgson, G. M. (1988) *Economics and Institutions: A Manifesto for a Modern Institutional Economics*. Cambridge: Polity.

————(1991) 'Economic Evolution: Intervention Contra Pangloss', *Journal of Economic Issues*, 25(2), 519–33.

————(1993) *Economics and Evolution: Bringing Life Back into Economics*. Cambridge: Polity.

Hoffman, S. (1977) 'An American Social Science: International Relations', *Daedalus*, 106, 41–61.

Hollis, M. (1994) *The Philosophy of Social Science: An Introduction*. Cambridge: Cambridge University Press.

————(1998) *Trust Within Reason*. Cambridge: Cambridge University Press.

Hollis, M. and Lukes, S. (1982) 'Introduction', in M. Hollis and S. Lukes (eds), *Rationality and Relativism*. Oxford: Blackwell.

Hollis, M. and Smith, S. (1990a) 'Beware of Gurus: Structure and Action in International Relations', *Review of International Studies*, 17(4), 393–410.

————(1990b) *Explaining and Understanding International Relations*. Oxford: Clarendon Press.

Honneth, A. (1991) *The Critique of Power: Reflective Stages in a Critical Social Theory*. Cambridge, MA: MIT Press.

Hopkins, D. (2000) *After Modern Art, 1945–2000*. Oxford: Oxford University Press.

Hopkins, T. and Wallerstein, I. (1980) (eds) *Processes of the World-System*. London: Sage.

————(1983) (eds) *World-Systems Analysis*. London: Sage.

Hotelling, H. (1929) 'Stability in Competition', *Economic Journal*, 39, 41–57.

Howarth, D. (1995) 'Discourse Theory', in D. Marsh and G. Stoker (eds), *Theory and Methods in Political Science*. Basingstoke: Macmillan.

———(2000) *Discourse*. Buckingham: Open University Press.

Huizer, G. (1979) 'Anthropology and Politics: From Naiveté Towards Liberation?', in G. Huizer and B. Mannheim (eds), *The Politics of Anthropology: From Colonialism and Sexism Towards a View from Below*. The Hague: Mouton Publishers.

Hunter, F. (1953) *Community Power Structure*. Chapel Hill, NC: University of North Carolina Press.

Huntingdon, S. (1968) *Political Order in Changing Societies*. New Haven, CT: Yale University Press.

Hyland, J. L. (1995) *Democratic Theory: The Philosophical Foundations*. Manchester: Manchester University Press.

Inglis, F. (2000) *Clifford Geertz: Culture, Custom and Ethics*. Cambridge: Polity.

Irwin, A. (1995) *Citizen Science: A Study of People, Expertise and Sustainable Development*. London: Routledge.

Isaac, J. C. (1987) *Power and Marxist Theory: A Realist View*. Ithaca, NY: Cornell University Press.

Jackson, R. and Sørensen, G. (1999) *Introduction to International Relations*. Oxford: Oxford University Press.

Jacobsen, K. (1995) 'Much Ado About Ideas: The Cognitive Factor in Economic Policy', *World Politics*, 47(1), 283–310.

Jameson, F. (1981) *The Political Unconscious*. London: Routledge.

———(1984) 'Postmodernism, or The Cultural Logic of Late Capitalism', *New Left Review*, 146, 53–92.

———(1991) *Postmodernism, Or, The Cultural Logic of Late Capitalism*. London: Verso.

Jay, M. (1993) *Downcast Eyes: The Denigration of Vision in Contemporary French Thought*. Berkeley, CA: University of California Press.

———(1991) *Postmodernism, or, The Cultural Logic of Late Capitalism*. London: Verso.

Jeffreys, H. (1961) *Theory of Probability*. Oxford: Oxford University Press.

Jencks, C. (1977) *The Language of Post-Modern Architecture*. New York: Pantheon.

———(1986) *What is Postmodernism?* London: Academy Editions.

Jennings, J. and Kemp-Welch, T. (1997) 'The Century of the Intellectuals: From the Dreyfus Affair to Salman Rushdie', in J. Jennings and T. Kemp-Welch (eds), *Intellectuals in Politics: From the Dreyfus Affair to Salman Rushdie*. London: Routledge.

Jenson, J. (1989) 'Paradigms and Political Discourse: Protective Legislation in France and United States Before 1914', *Canadian Journal of Political Science*, 22(2), 235–58.

———(1995) 'What's in a Name? Nationalist Movements and Public Discourse', in H. Johnston and B. Klandermans (eds), *Social Movements and Culture*. Minneapolis, MN: University of Minnesota Press.

Jenson, J., Hagen, E. and Reddy, C. (eds) (1988) *Feminisation of the Labour Force: Paradoxes and Promises*. Cambridge: Polity.

Jessop, B. (1985) *Nicos Poulantzas: Marxist Theory and Political Strategy*. London: Macmillan.

————(1990a) *State Theory: Putting Capitalist States in Their Place*. Cambridge: Polity.

————(1990b) 'Regulation Theories in Prospect and Retrospect', *Economy and Society*, 19(2), 153–216.

————(1992) 'From Social Democracy to Thatcherism: Twenty-Five Years of British Politics', in N. Abercrombie and A. Warde (eds), *Social Change in Contemporary Britain*. Cambridge: Polity.

————(1994) 'The Transition to Post-Fordism and the Schumpeterian Workfare State', in R. Burrows and B. Loader (eds), *Towards a Post-Fordist Welfare State?* London: Routledge.

————(1996) 'Interpretative Sociology and the Dialectic of Structure and Agency', *Theory, Culture and Society*, 13(1), 119–28.

Johnston, J. (1999) *The Impact of the British Political Tradition on Labour's Response to Relative Economic Decline*. Unpublished PhD thesis, University of Birmingham.

Jordan, A. G. (1990) 'Policy Community Realism versus "New" Institutionalist Ambiguity', *Political Studies*, 38, 470–84.

————(1999) 'European Community Water Policy Standards: Locked in or Watered Down?', *Journal of Common Market Studies*, 37(1), 13–37.

Kaplan, M. A. (1957) *System and Process in International Politics*. New York: John Wiley.

Katzenstein, P. J. (ed.) (1978) *Between Power and Plenty*. Madison, WI: University of Wisconsin Press.

Kavanagh, D. and Morris, P. (1994) *Consensus Politics: From Attlee to Major*, 2nd edition. Oxford: Blackwell.

Keat, R. and Urry, J. (1982) *Social Theory as Science*, 2nd edition. London: Routledge.

Kegley, C. (ed.) (1995) *Controversies in International Relations: Realism and the Neoliberal Challenge*. New York: St Martin's Press.

Kelly, M. (1994) 'Introduction', in M. Kelly (ed.), *Critique and Power: Recasting the Foucault/Habermas Debate*. Cambridge, MA: MIT Press.

Kenny, M. and Smith, M. J. (1997) '(Mis)Understanding Blair', *Political Quarterly*, 68(2), 220–30.

Keohane, R. O. (1986) 'Theory of World Politics: Structual Realism and Beyond', in R. O. Keohane (ed.), *Neo-Realism and Its Critics*. New York: Columbia University Press.

————(1989) 'International Institutions: Two Approaches', *International Studies Quarterly*, 32(4), 379–96.

————(1996) 'International Relations: Old and New', in R. E. Goodin and H.-D. Klingemann (eds), *A New Handbook of Political Science*. Oxford: Oxford University Press.

————(2000) 'Ideas Part Way Down', *Review of International Studies*, 26(1), 125–30.

Keohane, R. O. and Nye, J. S. (1977) *Power and Interdependence: World Politics in Transition*. Boston, MA: Little, Brown.

Kerr, P. (2001) *From Conflict to Consensus: The Evolution of Post-War British Politics, 1945–1997*. London: Routledge.

Kerr, P. and Marsh, D. (1999) 'Explaining Thatcherism: Towards a Multi-Dimensional Approach', in D. Marsh *et al.*, *Postwar British Politics in Perspective*. Cambridge: Polity.

Kimmel, M. S. (1990) *Revolution: A Sociological Interpretation*. Cambridge: Polity.

Kincaid, H. (1996) *Philosophical Foundations of the Social Sciences: Analysing Controversies in Social Research*. Cambridge: Cambridge University Press.

Kindelberger, C. (1973) *The World in Depression, 1929–1939*. Berkeley, CA: University of California Press.

King, A. (1988) 'Margaret Thatcher as a Political Leader', in R. Skidelsky (ed.), *Thatcherism*. London: Chatto & Windus.

——(1999) 'Against Structure: A Critique of Morphogenetic Social Theory', *Sociological Review*, 47(2), 199–227.

King, D. S. (1987) *The New Right: Politics, Markets and Citizenship*. London: Macmillan.

King, G., Keohane, R. O. and Verba, S. (1994) *Designing Social Inquiry: Scientific Inference in Qualitative Research*. Princeton, NJ: Princeton University Press.

Kirk, R. (1999) *Relativism and Reality: A Contemporary Introduction*. London: Routledge.

Kiser, E. and Hechter, M. (1991) 'The Role of General Theory in Comparative Historical Sociology', *American Journal of Sociology*, 97(1), 1–30.

Kitschelt, H. (1994) *The Transformation of European Social Democracy*. Cambridge, MA: Cambridge University Press.

Klausen, J. (1999) 'The Declining Significance of Male Workers: Trade-Union Responses to Changing Labour Markets', in H. Kitschelt *et al.* (eds), *Continuity and Change in Contemporary Capitalism*. Cambridge, MA: Cambridge University Press.

Kleinknecht, A. and ter Wengel, J. (1998) 'The Myth of Economic Globalisation', *Cambridge Journal of Economics*, 22, 637–47.

Knight, J. (1992) *Institutions and Social Conflict*. Cambridge, MA: Cambridge University Press.

——(2001) 'Explaining the Rise of Neoliberalism: The Mechanisms of Institutional Change', in J. L. Campbell and O. K. Pedersen (eds), *The Rise of Neoliberalism and Institutional Analysis*. Princeton, NJ: Princeton University Press.

Kondratiev, N. D. (1925) 'Long Business Cycles', *Problems of Economic Fluctuations*, 1, 28–79.

——(1935) 'The Long Waves in Economic Life', *Review of Economic Statistics*, 17, 105–15.

——(1984 [1928]) *The Long Wave Cycle*. New York: Richardson & Snyder.

Krasner, S. (1984) Approaches to the State: Alternative Conceptions and Historical Dynamics', *Comparative Politics*, 16, 223–46.

——(2000) 'Wars, Hotel Fires and Plane Crashes', *Review of International Studies*, 26(1), 131–6.

Kratochwil, F. (1989) *Rules, Norms and Decisions*. Cambridge: Cambridge University Press.

————(2000) 'Constructing a New Orthodoxy? Wendt's *Social Theory of International Politics* and the Constructivist Challenge', *Millennium*, 29(1), 73–104.

Kuhn, T. S. (1970/96) *The Structure of Scientific Revolutions*, 3rd edition. Chicago, IL: University of Chicago Press.

Kukla, A. (2000) *Social Constructivism and the Philosophy of Science*. London: Routledge.

Kuper, A. (1994) *The Chosen Primate: Human Nature and Cultural Diversity*. Cambridge, MA: Harvard University Press.

Kurzer, P. (1993) *Business and Banking*. Ithaca, NY: Cornell University Press.

Kuznets, S. (1953) *Economic Change*. New York: W. W. Norton.

Kydland, F. E. and Prescott, E. C. (1977) 'Rules Rather than Discretion: The Inconsistency of Optimal Plans', *Journal of Political Economy*, 85(3), 473–92.

Laclau, E. and Mouffe, C. (1985) *Hegemony and Socialist Strategy*. London: Verso.

Laffer, A. B. (1981) 'Government Exactions and Revenue Deficiencies', *The Cato Journal*, 1, 1–21.

Lakatos, I. (1978) *The Methodology of Scientific Research Programmes. Philosophical Papers, Volume 1*. Cambridge: Cambridge University Press.

Lamy, S. L. (2001) 'Contemporary Mainstream Approaches: Neo-Realism and Neo-Liberalism', in J. Baylis and S. Smith (eds), *The Globalisation of World Politics*. Oxford: Oxford University Press.

Lapid, Y. and Kratochwil, F. (eds) (1995) *The Return of Culture and Identity in International Relations*. Boulder, CO: Lynne Rienner.

Larrain, J. (1994) *Ideology and Cultural Identity: Modernity and the Third World Presence*. Cambridge: Polity.

Lash, S. (1990) *Sociology of Postmodernism*. London: Routledge.

Lasswell, H. (1936/50) *Politics: Who Gets What, When, How?* New York: P. Smith.

Lau, R. R. and Redlawsk, D. P. (1997) 'Voting Correctly', *American Political Science Review*, 91(3), 585–98.

Lawson, H. (1985) *On Reflexivity: The Post-Modern Predicament*. London: Hutchinson.

Layder, D. (1994) *Understanding Social Theory*. London: Sage.

————(1998) 'The Reality of Social Domains: Implications for Theory and Method', in T. May and M. Williams (eds), *Knowing the Social World*. Buckingham: Open University Press.

Leftwich, A. (ed.) (1984a) *What is Politics?* Oxford: Blackwell.

————(1984b) 'On the Politics of Politics', in A. Leftwich (ed.), *What is Politics?* Oxford: Blackwell.

————(1984c) 'Redefining Politics: People, Resources and Power', in A. Leftwich (ed.), *What is Politics?* Oxford: Blackwell.

Lemert, C. (1995) *Sociology After the Crisis*. Boulder, CO: Westview Press.

————(1997) *Postmodernism is Not What You Think*. Oxford: Blackwell.

Levi, P. (1965) *The Reawakening*. New York: Collier Books.

Lévi-Strauss, C. (1966) *The Savage Mind*. London: Weidenfeld & Nicolson.

Levins, R. and Lewontin, R. (1985) *The Dialectical Biologist*. Cambridge, MA: Harvard University Press.

Lipsey, R. (1963) *Introduction to Positive Economics*. London: Weidenfeld & Nicolson.

Lovibond, S. (1991) 'Feminism and Postmodernism', *New Left Review*, 178, 5–28.

Lucas, R. E. (1973) 'Some International Evidence on Output–Inflation Trade-Offs', *American Economic Review*, 63, 326–34.

Lukes, S. (1974) *Power: A Radical View*. Basingstoke: Macmillan.

————(1978) 'Power and Authority', in T. Bottomore and R. Nisbet (eds), *A History of Sociological Analysis*. New York: Basic Books.

————(1979) 'On the Relativity of Power', in S. C. Brown (ed.), *Philosophical Disputes in the Social Sciences*. Atlantic Highlands, NJ: Humanities.

Lunn, E. (1985) *Marxism and Modernism: An Historical Study of Lukács, Brecht, Benjamin and Adorno*. London: Verso.

Lynd, R. and Lynd, M. (1937/64) *Middletown in Transition*. London: Constable.

Lyon, D. (1999) *Postmodernity*, 2nd edition. Buckingham: Open University Press.

Lyotard, J.-F. (1984) *The Postmodern Condition: A Report on Knowledge*. Minneapolis, MN: University of Minnesota Press.

————(1988) *The Differend*. Minneapolis, MN: University of Minnesota Press.

————(1989) *The Lyotard Reader*. Oxford: Blackwell.

————(1992) *The Postmodern Explained to Children*. London: Turnaround.

Lyotard, J.-F. and Thébaud, J.-L. (1985) *Just Gaming*. Minneapolis, MN: University of Minnestoa Press.

Mackenzie, W. J. M. (1979) *Biological Ideas in Politics*. New York: St Martin's Press.

MacKinnon, C. (1985) *Toward a Feminist Theory of the State*. Cambridge, MA: Harvard University Press.

Mäki, U. (2001) 'Economic Ontology: What? Why? How?', in U. Mäki (ed.), *The Economic Worldview: Studies in the Ontology of Economics*. Cambridge: Cambridge University Press.

Mann, M. (1985) *The Sources of Social Power, Volume 1*. Cambridge: Cambridge University Press.

————(1988) *States, War and Capitalism*. Oxford: Blackwell.

March, J. G. and Olsen, J. P. (1984) 'The New Institutionalism: Organisation Factors in Political Life', *American Political Science Review*, 78, 734–49.

————(1989) *Rediscovering Institutions: The Organisation Basis of Politics*. New York: Free Press.

Marsh, C. (1982) *The Survey Method*. London: Allen & Unwin.

Marsh, D. (1995) 'Explaining Thatcherite Policies: Beyond Uni-Dimensional Explanation', *Political Studies*, 43(4), 595–613.

————(1999a) 'Resurrecting Marxism', in A. Gamble, D. Marsh and T. Tant (eds), *Marxism and Social Science*. London: Macmillan.

————(1999b) 'Introduction: Explaining Change in Postwar Britain', in D. Marsh *et al.*, *Postwar British Politics in Perspective*. Cambridge, Polity.

Marsh, D. and Stoker, G. (eds) (1995) *Theory and Methods in Political Science*. Basingstoke: Macmillan.

Marsh, D., Buller, J., Croft, S., Jennings, J. and Wincott, D. (1999) 'Editorial: Studying British Politics', *British Journal of Politics and International Studies*, 1(1), 1–11.

Marsh, D., Buller, J., Hay, C., Kerr, P., Johnston, J., McAnulla, S. and Watson, M. (1999) *Postwar British Politics in Perspective*. Cambridge: Polity.

Marx, K. (1845 [1975]) *Concerning Feuerbach*. Reprinted in L. Colletti (ed.), *Karl Marx: Early Writings*. London: Pelican.

————(1852 [1960]) *The Eighteenth Brumaire of Louis Bonaparte*. Reprinted in K. Marx and F. Engels, *Werke*, Vol. 8. Berlin: Dietz Verlag.

Masters, R. D. (1989) 'Gradualism and Discontinuous Change in Evolutionary Biology and Political Philosophy', in A. Somit and S. A. Peterson (eds), *The Dynamics of Evolution: The Punctuated Equilibrium Debate in the Natural and Social Sciences*. Ithaca, NY: Cornell University Press.

May, T. (1997) *Social Research: Issues, Methods and Process*. Buckingham: Open University Press.

May, T. and Williams, M. (eds) (1998) *Knowing the Social World*. Buckingham: Open University Press.

McAnulla, S. (1999) *Explaining Political Change Under Thatcherism*. Unpublished PhD thesis, University of Birmingham.

McCarthy, E. D. (1996) *Knowledge as Culture: The New Sociology of Knowledge*. London: Routledge.

McGuigan, J. (1999) *Modernity and Postmodern Culture*. Buckingham: Open University Press.

McNamara, K. (1998) *The Currency of Ideas: Monetary Politics in the European Union*. Ithaca, NY: Cornell University Press.

McNay, L. (1994) *Foucault: A Critical Introduction*. New York: Continuum.

Merelman, R. M. (1968) 'On the Neo-Elitist Critique of Community Power', *American Political Science Review*, 62.

Miliband, R. (1970) 'The Capitalist State: A Reply to Nicos Poulantzas', *New Left Review*, 82, 83–92.

Miller, W. E. (1995) 'Quantitative Methods', in D. Marsh and G. Stoker (eds), *Theory and Methods in Political Science*. Basingstoke: Macmillan.

Mills, C. W. (1956) *The Power Elite*. Oxford: Oxford University Press.

Mitchell, T. (1991) 'The Limits of the State', *American Political Science Review*, 85(1), 77–96.

Moe, T. M. (1984) 'The New Economics of Organisation', *American Political Science Review*, 28, 739–77.

Molotch, H. (1974) 'News as Purposive Behaviour', *American Sociological Review*, 39, 101–12.

Montaigne, M. de. (1978) *Les Essais de Michel de Montaigne*. Paris: Universitaires de France.

Moodie, G. (1984) 'Politics is about Government', in A. Leftwich (ed.), *What is Politics?* Oxford: Blackwell.

Mooers, C. (1991) *The Making of Bourgeois Europe*. London: Verso.

Moravcsik, A. (1997) 'Taking Preferences Seriously: A Liberal Theory of International Politics', *International Organisation*, 51(4), 538–41.

————(1998) *The Choice for Europe: Social Purpose and State Power from Messina to Maastricht*. Ithaca, NY: Cornell University Press.

————(2001) 'Constructivism and European Integration: A Critique', in T. Christiansen *et al.* (eds), *The Social Construction of Europe*. London: Sage.

Morgenthau, H. J. (1948) *Politics Among Nations*. New York: Alfred O. Knopf.

Nagel, E. (1961) *The Structure of Science*. Indianapolis: Hackett.

Nairn, T. (1976) 'The Twilight of the British State', *New Left Review*, 101/2, 3–61.

Natter, W., Schatzki, T. R. and Jones, J. P. (eds) (1995) *Objectivity and its Other*. New York: Guilford.

Nelson, A. (1994) 'How *Could* Facts be Socially Constructed?', *Studies in the History and Philosophy of Science*, 25, 535–47.

Nelson, R. R. (1995) 'Recent Evolutionary Theorising about Economic Change', *Journal of Economic Literature*, 33(1), 48–81.

Nelson, R. R. and Winter, S. G. (1982) *An Evolutionary Theory of Economic Change*. Cambridge, MA: Harvard University Press.

Nicholson, M. (1998) *International Relations: A Concise Introduction*. Basingstoke: Palgrave.

Nicolson, P. P. (1984) 'Politics and Force', in A. Leftwich (ed.), *What is Politics?* Oxford: Blackwell.

Nield, K. and Seed, J. (1979) 'Theoretical Poverty or the Poverty of Theory', *Economy and Society*, 8, 383–416.

Niethammer, L. (1992) *Posthistoire: Has History Come to an End?* London: Verso.

Niskanen, W. A. (1971) *Bureaucracy and Representative Government*. Chicago, IL: Aldine-Atherton.

———(1975) 'Bureaucrats and Politicians', *Journal of Law and Economics*, 18(4), 617–43.

Noble, T. (2000) *Social Theory and Social Change*. London: Macmillan.

Norris, C. (1983) *The Deconstructive Turn*. London: Methuen.

———(1987) *Derrida*. London: Fontana.

———(1990) 'Lost in the Funhouse: Baudrillard and the Politics of Postmodernism', in *What's Wrong With Postmodernism?* Hemel Hempstead: Harvester Wheatsheaf.

———(1991) *Deconstruction: Theory and Practice*, 2nd edition. London: Routledge.

———(1992) *Uncritical Theory: Postmodernism, Intellectuals and the Gulf War*. London: Lawrence & Wishart.

North, D. C. (1990) *Institutions, Institutional Change and Economic Performance*. Cambridge: Cambridge University Press.

North, D. C. and Thomas, R. P. (1973) *The Rise of the Western World: A New Economic History*. Cambridge, MA: Cambridge University Press.

Nye, J. S. (1993) *Understanding International Conflicts*. New York: HarperCollins.

O'Brien, M., Penna, S. and Hay, C. (eds) (1999) *Theorising Modernity: Reflexivity, Environment and Identity in Giddens' Social Theory*. London: Longman.

O'Brien, R. (1992) *Global Financial Integration: The End of Geography*. New York: Council on Foreign Relations.

O'Connor, J. (1998) 'Technology and Ecology', in J. O'Connor, *Natural Causes: Essays in Ecological Marxism*. New York: Guilford.

Offe, C. (1984) *Contradictions of the Welfare State*. London: Hutchinson.

Ohmae, K. (1990) *The Borderless World: Power and Strategy in the Interlinked Economy*. London: Collins.

———(1995) *The End of the Nation State: The Rise of Regional Economies*. New York: Free Press.

Olson, M. (1978) *The Logic of Collective Action: Public Goods and the Theory of Groups*. Cambridge, MA: Harvard University Press.

Onuf, N. (1989) *World of Our Making: Rules and Rule in Social Theory and International Relations*. Columbia, SC: University of South Carolina Press.

Osborne, P. (1995) *The Politics of Time: Modernity and Avant-Garde*. London: Verso.

Outhwaite, W. (1987) *New Philosophies of Social Science*. London: Macmillan.

Pareto, V. (1935) *The Mind and Society*. London: Jonathan Cape.

———(1966) *Sociological Writings*. London: Pall Mall.

Parsons, T. (1966) *Societies: Evolutionary and Comparative Perspectives*. London: Prentice-Hall.

Pateman, C. (1989) 'Feminist Critiques of the Public/Private Dichotomy', in C. Pateman, *The Disorder of Women*. Cambridge: Polity.

Payne, M. (1997) *Reading Knowledge: An Introduction to Barthes, Foucault and Althusser*. Oxford: Blackwell.

Pepper, D. (1996) *Modern Environmentalism: An Introduction*. London: Routledge.

Peters, B. G. (1999) *Institutional Theory in Political Science: The 'New Institutionalism'*. London: Pinter.

Peterson, J. and Bomberg, E. (1999) *Decision-Making in the European Union*. London: Macmillan.

Peterson, V. Spike (ed.) (1992) *Gendered States*. Boulder, CO: Lynne Rienner.

Pettee, G. S. (1938) *The Process of Revolution*. New York: Harper & Bros.

Pierson, C. (2001) *Hard Choices: Social Democracy in the 21st Century*. Cambridge: Polity.

Pierson, P. (1994) *Dismantling the Welfare State? Reagan, Thatcher and the Politics of Retrenchment*. Cambridge: Cambridge University Press.

———(1996a) 'The New Politics of the Welfare State', *World Politics*, 48(2), 143–79.

———(1996b) 'The Path to European Integration: A Historical Institutionalist Perspective', *Comparative Political Studies*, 29, 123–63.

———(2000) 'Increasing Returns, Path Dependence and the Study of Politics', *American Political Science Review*, 94(2), 251–69.

———(ed.) (2001) *The New Politics of the Welfare State*. Oxford: Oxford University Press.

Polsby, N. (1961) *Community Power and Political Theory: Problems of Evidence and Inference*. New Haven, CT: Yale University Press.

———(1980) *Community Power and Political Theory: Problems of Evidence and Inference*, 2nd edition. New Haven, CT: Yale University Press.

Popper, K. (1969) 'Science, Conjecture and Refutation', in K. Popper, *Conjectures and Refutations*. London: Routledge & Kegan Paul.

———(1985) *Postscript to the Logic of Scientific Discovery, Vol. 1: Realism and the Aim of Science*. London: Routledge.

Posen, A. (1993) 'Why Central Bank Independence Does Not Cause Low Inflation: There is No Institutional Fix for Politics', in R. O'Brien (ed.), *Finance and the International Economy 7*. Oxford: Oxford University Press.

Powell, J. (1998) *Postmodernism for Beginners*. New York: Writers & Readers Publishing.

Przeworski, A. and Wallerstein, M. (1988) 'Structural Dependence of the State on Capital', *American Political Science Review*, 82(1), 11–30.

Quine, W. V. O. (1953) 'Two Dogmas of Empiricism', in W. V. O. Quine, *From a Logical Point of View*. Cambridge, MA: Harvard University Press.

Ragin, C. C. (1994) *Constructing Social Research: The Unity and Diversity of Method*. Newbury Park, CA: Pine Forge Press.

Ragin, C. C., Berg-Schlosser, D. and de Meur, G. (1996) 'Political Methodology: Qualitative Methods', in R. E. Goodin and H.-D. Klingemann (eds), *A New Handbook of Political Science*. Oxford: Oxford University Press.

Ratzan, S. C. (ed.) (1998) *The Mad Cow Crisis: Health and the Public Good*. New York: New York University Press.

Razin, A. and Sadka, E. (1991a) 'Efficient Investment Incentives in the Presence of Capital Flight', *Journal of International Economics*, 31(1/2), 171–81.

————(1991b) 'International Tax Competition and Gains from Tax Harmonisation', *Economic Letters*, 37(1), 69–76.

Readings, B. (1991) *Introducing Lyotard: Art and Politics*. London: Routledge.

Rhodes, R. A. W. (1995) 'The Institutional Approach', in D. Marsh and G. Stoker (eds), *Theory and Methods in Political Science*. Basingstoke: Macmillan.

Ringmar, E. (1997) 'Alexander Wendt: A Social Theorist Struggling with History', in I. B. Neumann and O. Wæver (eds), *The Future of International Relations: Masters in the Making*. London: Routledge.

Rorty, R. (1982) *Consequences of Pragmatism*. Minneapolis, MN: University of Minnesota Press.

Rose, M. A. (1991) *The Post-Modern and the Post-Industrial*. Cambridge: Cambridge University Press.

Rose, R. (1991) 'Comparing Forms of Comparative Analysis', *Political Studies*, 39(3), 442–62.

Rosen, M. (1996) *On Voluntary Servitude: False Consciousness and the Theory of Ideology*. Cambridge, MA: Harvard University Press.

Rosenau, J. N. (1990) *Turbulence in World Politics: A Theory of Change and Continuity*. Princeton, NJ: Princeton University Press.

Rostow, W. W. (1960) *The Stages of Economic Growth*. Cambridge: Cambridge University Press.

Rothstein, B. (1996) 'Political Institutions: An Overview', in R. E. Goodin and H.-D. Klingemann (eds), *A New Handbook of Political Science*. Oxford: Oxford University Press.

Ruggie, J. (1983a) 'Continuity and Transformation in the World Polity', *World Politics*, 35, 261–85.

————(1983b) 'International Regimes, Transactions and Change: Embedded Liberalism in the Postwar Economic Order', in S. Krasner (ed.), *International Regimes*. Ithaca, NY: Cornell University Press.

————(1998) *Constructing the World Polity: Essays on International Institutionalisation*. London: Routledge.

Rule, J. B. (1997) *Theory and Progress in Social Science*. Cambridge: Cambridge University Press.

Rutherford, M. (1996) *Institutions in Economics: The Old and New Institutionalism*. Cambridge: Cambridge University Press.

Sahlins, M. and Service, E. (eds) (1960) *Evolution and Culture*. Ann Arbor, MI: University of Michigan Press.

Sanders, D. (1995) 'Behaviouralism', in D. Marsh and G. Stoker (eds), *Theory and Methods in Political Science*. London: Macmillan.

Sargent, T. J. (1986) *Rational Expectations and Inflation*. New York: Harper & Row.

Sargent, T. J. and Wallace, N. (1975) 'Rational Expectations, the Optimal Monetary Instrument and the Optimal Money Supply Rule', *Journal of Political Economy*, 83(2), 241–54.

Sartre, J.-P. (1968) *Search for a Method*. New York: Vintage.

Saxonhouse, A. (1993) 'Texts and Canons: The Status of the Great Books in Political Science', in A. Finifter (ed.), *Political Science: The State of the Discipline II*. Washington, DC: APSA.

Sayer, A. (1992) *Method in Social Science: A Realist Approach*. London: Routledge.

———(2000) *Realism and Social Science*. London: Sage.

Scharpf, F. (1991) *Crisis and Choice in European Social Democracy*. Ithaca, NT: Cornell University Press.

Schattschneider, E. E. (1960) *The Semi-Sovereign People: A Realist View of Democracy in America*. New York: Rinehart & Winston.

Schröder, P. (1994) 'Historical Reality vs. Neo-Realist Theory', *International Security*, 19, 108–48.

Schwanhold, E. and Pfender, R. (1998) 'German and European Responses to Globalisation', in D. Dettke (ed.), *The Challenge of Globalisation for Germany's Social Democracy*. Oxford: Berghahn.

Schwichtenberg, C. (1993) 'Madonna's Postmodern Feminism', in C. Schwichtenberg (ed.), *The Madonna Connection*. Boulder, CO: Westview Press.

Scott, D. (1992) 'Theory and Post-colonial Claims on Anthropological Disciplinarity', *Critique in Anthropology*, 12, 371–94.

———(1994) *Formations of Ritual: Colonial and Anthropological Discourses on the Sinhala Yaktovil*. Minneapolis, MN: University of Minnesota Press.

Scott, W. R. (1995) *Institutions and Organisations*. Thousand Oaks, CA: Sage.

Seidman, S. (1992) 'Postmodern Social Theory as Narrative with a Moral Intent', in S. Seidman and D. G. Wagner (eds), *Postmodernism and Social Theory: The Debate Over General Theory*. Oxford: Blackwell.

Shandley, R. R. (ed.) (1998) *Unwilling Germans? The Goldhagen Debate*. Minneapolis, MN: University of Minnesota Press.

Shapiro, I. and Wendt, A. (1992) 'The Difference that Realism Makes: Social Science and the Politics of Consent', *Politics and Society*, 20(2), 197–223.

Shaw, M. (ed.) (1984) *War, State and Society*. London: Macmillan.

Sibley, M. Q. (1967) 'The Limitations of Behaviouralism', in J. C. Charlesworth (ed.), *Contemporary Political Analysis*. New York: Free Press.

Sikkink, K. (1991) *Ideas and Institutions: Developmentalism in Argentina and Brazil*. Ithaca, NY: Cornell University Press.

Simon, H. (1986) 'Rationality in Psychology and Economics', *Journal of Business*, 59, 210–21.

Singer, J. D. (ed.) (1968) *Quantitative International Politics*. New York: Free Press.

Skocpol, T. (1979) *States and Social Revolutions*. Cambridge: Cambridge University Press.

————(1994) *Social Revolutions in the Modern World*. Cambridge: Cambridge University Press.

Skocpol, T. and Ikenberry, J. (1983) 'The Political Formation of the American Welfare State in Historical and Comparative Perspective', *Comparative Social Research*, 6, 87–148.

Skowronek, S. (1982) *Building A New American State: The Expansion of National Administrative Capacities, 1877–1920*. Cambridge: Cambridge University Press.

————(1993) *The Politics Presidents Make: Leadership from John Adams to George Bush*. Cambridge, MA: Harvard University Press.

————(1995) 'Order and Change', *Polity*, 28(1), 91–6.

Smelser, N. (1964) 'Toward a Theory of Modernisation', in A. Etzioni and E. Etzioni (eds), *Social Change*. New York: Basic Books.

Smith, M. J. (1998) 'Reconceptualising the British State: Theoretical and Empirical Challenges to Central Government', *Public Administration*, 76(1), 45–72.

————(1999) *The Core Executive in Britain*. London: Macmillan.

Smith, S. (1995) 'The Self-Image of a Discipline: A Genealogy of International Relation Theory', in K. Booth and S. Smith (eds), *International Relations Theory Today*. Cambridge: Polity.

————(1996) 'Positivism and Beyond', in S. Smith, K. Booth and M. Zalewski (eds), *International Theory: Positivism and Beyond*. Cambridge: Cambridge University Press.

————(2000) 'Wendt's World', *Review of International Studies*, 26(1), 151–64.

————(2001) 'Reflectivist and Constructivist Approaches to International Theory', in J. Baylis and S. Smith (eds), *The Globalisation of World Politics*. Oxford: Oxford University Press.

Smith, S., Booth, K. and Zalewski, M. (eds) (1996) *International Theory: Positivism and Beyond*. Cambridge: Cambridge University Press.

Sober, E. (1988) *Reconstructing the Past: Parsimony, Evolution and Inference*. Cambridge, MA: MIT Press.

Sombart, W. (1924) *Die Moderne Kapitalismus*. Volume I. Munich: Von Duncker & Humblot.

Somit, A. and Peterson, S. A. (eds) (1989a) 'Punctuated Equilibrium: The View from the Elephant', in A. Somit and S. A. Peterson (eds), *The Dynamics of Evolution: The Punctuated Equilibrium Debate in the Natural and Social Sciences*. Ithaca, NY: Cornell University Press.

————(1989b) *The Dynamics of Evolution: The Punctuated Equilibrium Debate in the Natural and Social Sciences*. Ithaca, NY: Cornell University Press.

Sontag, S. (1966) *Against Interpretation*. New York: Deli.

Soper, K. (1993) 'Postmodernism, Subjectivity and the Question of Value', in J. Squires (ed.), *Principled Positions: Postmodernism and the Rediscovery of Value*. London: Lawrence & Wishart.

Spencer, H. (1865) *Principles of Biology*. London: Williams & Norgate.

————(1891) *Essays: Scientific, Political and Speculative*. London: Williams & Norgate.

————(1972) *On Social Evolution*. Chicago, IL: University of Chicago Press.

Steans, J. and Pettiford, L. (2001) *International Relations: Perspectives and Themes*. London: Longman.

Steinmo, S., Thelen, K. and Longstreth, F. (eds) (1992) *Structuring Politics: Historical Institutionalism in a Comparative Perspective*. Cambridge: Cambridge University Press.

Stern, F. (1996) 'The Goldhagen Controversy', *Foreign Affairs*, 75(6).

Stocking, G. W. (1995) *After Tylor: British Social Anthropology 1888–1951*. Madison, WI: University of Wisconsin Press.

Stoker, G. (1995) 'Introduction', in D. Marsh and G. Stoker (eds), *Theory and Methods in Political Science*. London: Macmillan.

Stones, R. (1991) 'Strategic Conduct Analysis: A New Research Strategy for Structuration Theory', *Sociology*, 25(4), 673–95.

————(1996) *Sociological Reasoning: Towards a Post-Modern Sociology*. London: Macmillan.

Suganami, H. (1999) 'Agents, Structures, Narratives', *European Journal of International Relations*, 5(3), 365–86.

Swank, D. S. (1998) 'Funding the Welfare State: Globalisation and the Taxation of Business in Advanced Market Economies', *Political Studies*, 46(4), 671–92.

————(2001) 'Political Institutions and Welfare State Restructuring: The Impact of Institutions on Social Policy Change in Developed Democracies', in P. Pierson (ed.), *The New Politics of the Welfare State*. Oxford: Oxford University Press.

Sztompka, P. (1991) *Society in Action: The Theory of Social Becoming*. Cambridge: Polity.

————(1993) *The Sociology of Social Change*. Oxford: Blackwell.

Tanzi, V. and Schuknecht, L. (1997) 'Reconsidering the Fiscal Role of Government: The International Perspective', *American Economic Review*, 87(2), 164–68.

Tanzi, V. and Zee, H. H. (1997) 'Fiscal Policy and Long-Run Growth', *International Monetary Fund Staff Papers*, 44(2), 179–209.

Taylor, M. J. (1987) *The Possibility of Cooperation*. Cambridge: Cambridge University Press.

Taylor, P. J. (2000) '-Isations of the World: Globalisation, Modernisation, Americanisation', in C. Hay and D. Marsh (eds), *Demystifying Globalisation*. London: Macmillan.

Teeple, G. (1995) *Globalisation and the Decline of Social Reform*. Toronto: Garamond Press.

Theakston, K. (1997) 'Comparative Biography and Leadership in Whitehall', *Public Administration*, 75(4), 651–67.

Thelen, K. (1999) 'Historical Institutionalism in Comparative Politics', *Annual Review of Political Science*, 2, 369–404.

Thelen, K. and Steinmo, S. (1992) 'Historical Institutionalism in Comparative Politics', in S. Steinmo, K. Thelen and F. Longstreth (eds), *Structuring Politics: Historical Institutionalism in Comparative Analysis*. Cambridge: Cambridge University Press.

Thomas, M. I. and Holt, P. (1977) *Threats of Revolution in Britain, 1789–1848*. London: Macmillan.

Thompson, E. P. (1978) 'The Poverty of Theory' in *The Poverty of Theory and Other Essays*. London: Merlin.

Thompson, J. B. (1990) *Ideology and Modern Culture*. Cambridge: Polity.

Thrift, N. (1985) 'Bear and Mouse or Tree and Bear? Giddens' Reconstruction of Social Theory'. *Sociology*, 19.

Tickner, A. (1993) *Gender in International Relations*. New York: Columbia University Press.

———(1996) 'International Relations: Post-Positivist and Feminist Perspectives', in R. E. Goodwin and H.-D. Klingemann (eds), *A New Handbook of Political Science*. Oxford: Oxford University Press.

Tiger, L. (1980) 'Sociobiology and Politics', *Hastings Center Report*, 10, 35–7.

Tilly, C. (1973) *The Formation of the National States in Western Europe*. Princeton, NJ: Princeton University Press.

———(1978) *From Mobilisation to Revolution*. Reading, MA: Addison-Wesley.

———(1991) 'How (and What) Are Historians Doing?', in D. Easton and C. S. Schelling (eds), *Divided Knowledge: Across Disciplines, Across Cultures*. London: Sage.

———(1993) *European Revolutions, 1492–1992*. Oxford: Blackwell.

———(1995) *Popular Contention in Britain, 1758–1834*. Cambridge, MA: Harvard University Press.

Tilly, C., Tilly, L. and Tilly, R. (1975) *The Rebellious Century, 1830–1930*. Cambridge, MA: Harvard University Press.

Tobin, J. (1982) 'The Reagan Economic Plan: Supply-Side, Budget and Inflation', in R. H. Fink (ed.), *Supply-Side Economics: A Critical Appraisal*. Frederick, MD: University Publications of America.

Tocqueville, A. de. (1955 [1856]) *The Old Regime and the French Revolution*. New York: Doubleday Anchor.

Tolbert, P. and Zucker, L. (1983) 'Institutional Sources of Change in the Formal Struture of Organisations: The Diffusion of Civil Service Reform', *Administrative Science Quarterly*, 28(1), 22–39.

Tönnies, F. (1955 [1887]) *Community and Association [Gemeinschaft and Gesselschaft]*. London: Routledge & Kegan Paul.

Trouillot, M.-R. (1991) 'Anthropology and the Savage Slot: The Poetics and Politics of Otherness', in R. G. Fox (ed.), *Recapturing Anthropology: Working in the Present*. Sante Fe, NM: School of American Research Press.

Truman, D. (1951) *The Process of Government*. New York: Knopf Press.

Tsebelis, G. (1990) *Nested Games: Rational Choice in Comparative Politics*. Berkeley, CA: University of California Press.

Tullock, G. (1965) *The Politics of Bureaucracy*. Washington, DC: Public Affairs Press.

———(1976) *The Vote Motive*. London: Institute for Economic Affairs.

Tuma, N. B. and Hannan, M. T. (1984) *Social Dynamics: Models and Methods*. New York: Academic Press.

Tyler, S. A. (1987) *The Unspeakable: Discourse, Dialogue and Rhetoric in the Postmodern World*. Madison, WI: University of Wisconsin Press.

Vasquez, J. A. (1996) 'The Post-Positivist Debate: Restructuring Scientific Enquiry and International Relations Theory After Enlightenment's Fall', in K.

Booth and S. Smith (eds), *International Relations Theory Today*. Cambridge: Polity.

———(1998) *The Power of Power Politics: From Classical Realism to Neotraditionalism*. Cambridge: Cambridge University Press.

Venturi, R., Scott Brown, D. and Izenour, S. (1977) *Learning from Las Vegas*, revised edition. Cambridge, MA: MIT Press.

von Beyme, K. (1996) 'Political Theory: Empirical Political Theory', in R. E. Goodin and H.-D. Klingemann (eds), *A New Handbook of Political Science*. Oxford: Oxford University Press.

Wæver, O. (1996) 'The Rise and Fall of the Inter-Paradigm Debate', in S. Smith, K. Booth and M. Zalewski (eds), *International Theory: Positivism and Beyond*. Cambridge: Cambridge University Press.

Walker, R. B. J. (1987) 'Realism, Change and International Political Theory', *International Studies Quarterly*, 31(1), 65–86.

———(1993) *Inside/Outside: International Relations as Political Theory*. Cambridge: Cambridge University Press.

Wallerstein, I. (1974) *The Modern World-System I*. San Diego, CA: Academic Press.

———(1980) *The Modern World-System II*. San Diego, CA: Academic Press.

———(1989) *The Modern World-System III*. San Diego, CA: Academic Press.

Waltz, K. (1979) *Theory of International Politics*. Boston: Addison-Wesley.

Wanniski, J. (1978) 'Taxes, Revenues and the "Laffer Curve"', *Public Interest*, 50, 3–16.

Ward, H. (1997) 'The Possibility of an Evolutionary Explanation of the State's Role in Modes of Regulation', in J. Stanyer and G. Stoker (eds), *Contemporary Political Studies 1997. Volume 2*. Oxford: Blackwell/PSA.

Watson, M. (2000) *The Political Discourse of Globalisation: Globalising Tendencies as Self-Induced External Enforcement Mechanisms*. Unpublished PhD thesis, University of Birmingham.

———(2001) 'International Capital Mobility in an Era of Globalisation: Adding a Political Dimension to the "Feldstein–Horioka Puzzle"', *Politics*, 21(2), 81–92.

———(2002) 'The Institutional Paradoxes of Orthodox Economic Theory: Reflections on the Political Economy of Central Bank Independence', *Review of International Political Economy*, 9(1), forthcoming.

Weber, C. (1995) *Simulating Sovereignty: Intervention, the State and Symbolic Exchange*. Cambridge: Cambridge University Press.

Weber, M. (1919/46) 'Politics as a Vocation', in H. Gerth and C. W. Mills (eds), *From Max Weber: Essays in Sociology*. Oxford: Oxford University Press.

Weingast, B. R. (1996) 'Political Institutions: Rational Choice Perspectives', in R. E. Goodin and H.-D. Klingemann (eds), *A New Handbook of Political Science*. Oxford: Oxford University Press.

Weiss, L. (1998) *The Myth of the Powerless State*. Cambridge: Polity.

Wendt, A. (1987) 'The Agent–Structure Problem in International Relations', *International Organization*, 41(3), 335–70.

————(1992) 'Anarchy is What States Make of It: The Social Construction of Power Politics', *International Organization*, 46, 391–425.

————(1994) 'Collective Identity Formation and the International State', *American Political Science Review*, 88, 384–96.

————(1995) 'Constructing International Politics', *International Security*, 20(1), 71–81.

————(1999) *Social Theory of International Politics*. Cambridge: Cambridge University Press.

————(2000) 'On the Via Media: A Response to the Critics', *Review of International Studies*, 26(1), 165–80.

Wendt, A. and Shapiro, I. (1997) 'The Misunderstood Promise of Realist Social Theory', in K. Monroe (ed.), *Contemporary Empirical Political Theory*. Berkeley, CA: University of California Press.

Wickham-Jones, M. (1995) 'Anticipating Social Democracy, Preempting Anticipations: Economic Policy-Making in the British Labour Party, 1987–1992', *Politics and Society*, 23(4), 465–94.

————(2000) 'New Labour and the Global Economy: Partisan Politics and the Social Democratic Model', *British Journal of Politics and International Relations*, 2(1), 1–25.

Wight, C. (1999) 'They Shoot Dead Horses Don't They? Locating Agency in the Agent-Structure Problematique', *European Journal of International Relations*, 5(1), 109–42.

Williams, J. (2000) *Lyotard: Towards a Postmodern Philosophy*. Cambridge: Polity.

Williams, M. (2000) *Science and Social Science: An Introduction*. London: Routeldge.

Wilmott, R. (1999) 'Structure, Agency and the Sociology of Education: Rescuing Analytical Dualism', *British Journal of Sociology of Education*, 20(1), 5–21.

Wincott, D. (2000) 'Globalisation and European Integration', in C. Hay and D. Marsh (eds), *Demystifying Globalisation*. London: Macmillan.

Witt, U. (1986) 'Evolution and Stability of Cooperation Without Enforceable Contracts', *Kyklos*, 39, 245–66.

Wolfe, A. B. (1924) 'Functional Economics', in R. G. Tingwell (ed.), *The Trend of Economics*. New York: Knopf.

Wolfinger, R. E. (1971) 'Nondecisions and the Study of Local Politics', *American Political Science Review*, 65.

Woodmansee, M. and Jaszi, P. (eds) (1994) *The Construction of Authorship: Textual Appropriation in Law and Literature*. Durham, NC: Duke University Press.

Woods, N. (1995) 'Economic Ideas and International Relations: Beyond Rational Neglect', *International Studies Quarterly*, 39, 161–80.

Young, I. M. (1987) 'Impartiality and the Civic Public', in S. Benhabib and D. Cornell (eds), *Feminism as Critique*. Cambridge: Polity.

————(1990) *Justice and the Politics of Difference*. Princeton, NJ: Princeton University Press.

Zellner, A. (1984) *Basic Issues in Econometrics*. Chicago, IL: University of Chicago Press.

Zevin, R. (1992) 'Are World Financial Markets More Open? If So, Why and With What Effects?', in T. Banuri and J. B. Schor (eds), *Financial Openness and National Autonomy: Opportunities and Constraints*. Oxford: Oxford University Press.

Zysman, J. (1996) 'The Myth of a Global Economy: Enduring National and Emerging Regional Realities', *New Political Economy*, 1(2), 157–84.

Index